AF505829

The Post 'Great Recession' US Economy

The Post 'Great Recession' US Economy

Implications for Financial Markets and the Economy

Philip Arestis

and

Elias Karakitsos

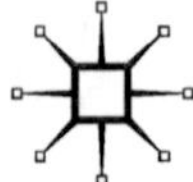

First published 2010 by
PALGRAVE MACMILLAN

Palgrave Macmillan in the UK is an imprint of Macmillan Publishers Limited, registered in England, company number 785998, of Houndmills, Basingstoke, Hampshire RG21 6XS.

Palgrave Macmillan in the US is a division of St Martin's Press LLC, 175 Fifth Avenue, New York, NY 10010.

Palgrave Macmillan is the global academic imprint of the above companies and has companies and representatives throughout the world.

Palgrave® and Macmillan® are registered trademarks in the United States, the United Kingdom, Europe and other countries.

ISBN 978–0–230–22904–4   hardback

This book is printed on paper suitable for recycling and made from fully managed and sustained forest sources. Logging, pulping and manufacturing processes are expected to conform to the environmental regulations of the country of origin.

A catalogue record for this book is available from the British Library.

A catalog record for this book is available from the Library of Congress.

10   9   8   7   6   5   4   3   2   1
19 18 17 16 15 14 13 12 11 10

Printed and bound in Great Britain by
CPI Antony Rowe, Chippenham and Eastbourne

This book is dedicated to our children:
Stefan, Natalia and her husband Tom; and
especially to my grandson, Alec (Philip Arestis)
Nepheli and Eliza (Elias Karakitsos)

Contents

List of Figures

List of Tables

Prolegomena

The issues covered in the book

In the last ten years or so there has been a series of bubbles, but judged in terms of their impact on the economy three have been particularly notable, namely the internet, the housing and the commodities bubbles. Do these bubbles have common roots or are they independent of one another? What are the consequences of the bursting of each bubble? What are the similarities and differences? What policies should be pursued to avert future bubbles from ballooning and bursting? These are the key questions addressed in this book.

The early 2000s US recession was very mild, in spite of the bursting of the internet bubble, which was one of the worst in monetary history. Equity prices fell precipitously, yet the consumer remained resilient. The bursting of a typical bubble implies retrenchment by the personal and corporate sectors, as falling asset prices create a gap (i.e. an imbalance) between the assets and the liabilities of the private sector. In the euphoria years in which the bubble balloons, both companies and households accumulate disproportionate amounts of debt, induced by rising asset prices. Once the bubble bursts and asset prices collapse, the high level of debt is incompatible with the new low level of asset prices. The moment companies and households accept that the new level of asset prices is permanent rather than temporary, they try to repay their debts and rebuild their wealth by saving more, thereby dragging the economy into a severe recession characterised by asset and debt deflation.

This process of asset and debt deflation is a long and painful one, as it usually infects the balance sheet of the commercial banks, which respond by cutting new credit (credit crunch), thereby accelerating the bankruptcies of companies and households. The experiences of the Great Depression of 1876–90, of the Great Depression of the 1930s and of Japan in the 1990s show that the bursting of every bubble has exactly these characteristics and policymakers have little scope to smooth this process. Yet the US experience of the internet bubble was very different. Asset prices fell as in a typical bubble, yet the economy experienced the mildest recession. The personal sector continued to accumulate debt, while the corporate sector reduced it only slightly. Two factors may account for this experience and emergence of imbalances. The first is that monetary policy may have achieved a soft landing of the economy. The second is that investors regarded the bursting of the bubble as a temporary rather than a permanent phenomenon. The two issues may not be independent, however, as the over-accommodative monetary policy adopted in 2001–04 may have transformed the internet bubble into a housing bubble. These are further issues addressed in the book.

The lower level of geopolitical risks after the end of the Iraq War, coupled with the subsidence of the governance crisis and the perfect timing of yet another fiscal package in 2003, as well as the accommodating stance of monetary policy in the downswing, combined to create a booming economy in the last nine months of 2003, which put the US economy on a sustainable path to recovery during the course of 2004. The strength of the US rebound was such as to pull with it the rest of the world. Confidence was buoyed and signs that deflation in Japan was coming to an end boosted hopes that the worst was over. The previous three years looked like a nightmare that belonged to the past. Yet, three years later a much worse storm hit the US economy and the world at large with its toll on citadels like China that were supposed to remain immune to this tsunami. The US housing market dropped, causing huge losses in financial institutions that sparked a credit crisis, which spread very rapidly to the rest of the world. The recession was mild at the beginning, but as the credit crisis unfolded a negative spiral emerged between the economy and the credit crisis. As the recession deepened, the credit crisis was magnified with a further impact on the economy. It is in this context that the questions raised earlier on are pertinent. Are the two crises of the early and the late 2000s independent of each other? Or, do they have common roots? What were the reasons for this contagion effect? The First Edition of this book warned that the imbalances from the bursting of the internet bubble were not corrected, but remained like skeletons in the cupboard, ready to be unleashed once there was a rise in long-term interest rates. Have these imbalances been corrected as a result of the current deep and protracted recession or have they been put back in the cupboard, ready to haunt us yet again at the next opportunity? This Second Edition warns once more that the policies pursued have simply brushed under the carpet the imbalances of the various sectors and it is again a matter of time before they strike yet again. So, what are the prospects of the US economy in the near term and the long term? These are further key questions addressed by this book.

Equity markets recovered after the spring of 2003 and they went from strength to strength over the following three years. Optimism supplanted pessimism with many people believing that this was the beginning of a new and long-lasting bull market. Yet in real terms equity markets have never matched the highs of 2000. Consequently, the rapid advance in stock prices between 2003 and 2007 was simply a protracted strong bear market rally. Equity markets peaked in 2007 and fell precipitously in the following two years, hitting a lower bottom than in the early 2000s bear market. At this juncture the expected recovery has triggered a stupendous rally since March 2009. The shares of zombie financial institutions have produced the most stunning returns in the last six months and optimism is again running high that the worst is over and that the expected recovery heralds the beginning of a new and long-lasting bull market. But is such optimism justified? What are the prospects for the US and global stock markets? What are the prospects for bonds? Are bond yields likely to rise in the next few years causing equity prices to tumble, and thereby triggering a future recession? What are the risks that investors should consider when working their investment strategy over the next few years? Should they overweigh equities and dump bonds in their portfolios? What about the dollar? In the six years to 2008 the dollar fell a great deal, but disproportionately with respect to some currencies, like, for example, the euro and the pound sterling. In the midst of the recent credit crisis the dollar strengthened, but it fell again as hopes of a recovery emerged. Is this temporary or is it, rather, the beginning of a new long-lasting downtrend? The prospects and risks to financial markets is yet another issue addressed in this book. As a precursor of what is to follow, this book again warns that the recent advance of stocks is most likely to be another bear market rally that may last for a number of years before it fizzles out yet again. The premise of this book is that unless the various sector imbalances are corrected the world at large will remain in a protracted bear market with bear market rallies that may be strong and lasting for a few years. However, these rallies will fizzle out ultimately with each bottom being lower than the previous one. The reason why these imbalances have not been corrected in every recession is that the excessive liquidity that has financed these successive bubbles has never been drained from the system. In fact, every time a recession occurs the policymakers pump in increasing amounts of liquidity to deflect the asset and debt deflation process. The verdict on the dollar is that unless the imbalances are corrected it will remain on a long downtrend. A weak dollar provides the mechanism through this excessive liquidity is channelled abroad generating world bubbles.

The policy debate on how to deal with bubbles concentrates on two polar views. The first is that central banks should leave financial markets to function freely on their own and asset price inflation should not be the concern of a central bank. However, a central bank should deal with the consequences of the bursting of a bubble. The opposite view is that asset price inflation is as bad as inflation in goods and services and as the latter is in the realm of a central bank so should the control of asset price inflation be. Thus, the policy debate can be summarised as dealing proactively and pre-emptively with bubbles, or reactively with their consequences. The Fed has clearly played with the proactive approach in the early days of the bubble with the familiar 'irrational exuberance' remarks. But in the event, it opted for the reactive approach of dealing with the consequences, as it cut the Fed funds rate aggressively in the early 2000s recession in a way that was not justified by the depth of the recession. The pursuit of such a policy seems to have paid off and it has done a great deal to restore the tarnished reputation of the Fed in the aftermath of the bursting of the internet bubble. But the bursting of the housing bubble has cast doubt on the Fed's approach of dealing with the consequences of the bursting of the bubble and has put back on the agenda the proactive role of monetary policy in dealing with asset price inflation. Moreover, it has sparked criticism that the housing bubble has its roots to this very accommodative monetary policy that was meant to deflect the asset and debt deflation process.

The difficulty with a proactive and pre-emptive approach stems from what should be the target for monetary policy, as it would be inappropriate for a central bank to have a target for one of its stock market indices or house prices. The book addresses this issue and makes appropriate recommendations, crucially net wealth targeting, which deals with the consequences of the bubble on the spending decisions of households. This can provide the basis for proactive monetary policy on asset price inflation.

How this book should be read and its potential readership

The book is particularly relevant to investors in world financial markets, as it addresses the prospects and risks to financial markets emanating from the post-housing bubble US economy. Although it is confined to the US economy it has implications for global markets, given the leading global role played by the US. The book is not just a narration of events and prospects as well as risks to the economy and financial markets, but also offers an in-depth analysis of the thinking process that underlines the sophisticated formation of the investment strategy of major financial institutions. The methodology of the book, therefore, is that it begins with the realities of the US economy, where the factual analysis makes good use of available data, fully cited and explained, before the analysis builds upon them to articulate the theoretical background involved in each case. The more empirical aspects of the book then follow.

This thinking process is based on a top-down approach, which formalises the view that asset prices, at any point in time, reflect market discounting of how the central bank should respond to the state of the economy, as judged by the latest available information. This thinking process is encapsulated in the macro-financial model, which is an integrated system for analysing systematically macro and financial data that leads to an informed investment decision-making process. The book effectively describes that process by analysing in every chapter one constituent component of the macro-financial model, to which we have just referred, that leads to a synthesis in the last two chapters that deal with the dollar, bonds and equities. The structure of the book follows the rationale of this top-down approach of the macro-financial model.

The book, therefore, may be particularly relevant to Chief Investment Officers, portfolio managers, traders and individual investors, who may be interested in the state-of-the-art methodology for the analysis of financial markets and the process of investment strategy. From this point of view, the emphasis in this book is not on the conclusions of the current investment strategy, which, by definition, would be obsolete by the time the book is published. The emphasis is, rather, on the methodology underlying the analysis of financial markets and investment strategy. However, the book is not solely for the benefit of the sophisticated investor. Indeed, it has been written with the economist also in mind, especially the academics, along with those non-economists who are interested in understanding the causes and consequences for the economy and financial markets of the series of bubbles that have emerged over the course of the past ten years. Policymakers may also be interested in the issue, since there are serious policy implications involved.

The book has been structured in such a way as to embrace such diverse readership. The reader can get a quick first impression of all the issues covered in the book by reading the summary and conclusions at the end of each chapter. All of the chapters have a similar structure so that an approach to reading the book can be formulated. Every chapter begins with the issues that are explored subsequently. It then offers an analysis of the relevant statistics that form the basis of the analysis. This does not require any prior knowledge and provides easy reading. Yet the analysis is deep enough so that the alert reader can guess the model behind the thinking process. Next follows a lengthy explanation of the relevant parts of the model that are relevant to the issue in hand. The purpose of this section is to provide not a textbook treatment of, say, investment or consumption, but rather a formal description of the variables that should be monitored in order to form an opinion of how, say, companies or households reach their decisions on spending and investment and the risks in the current economic climate. A flow chart explains the inter-relationship of the key variables in each chapter, which the interested reader can study independently of the rest of that section.

Reference to the work of others is given so that the reader can put the model in perspective, without burdening the book as if it was a review article. We have avoided mathematics, as they are not appropriate for the general readership we have in mind, although the more mathematically inclined economists should not be disappointed by its absence. We have attempted to describe in words formal mathematical relation-ships and simply summarise the functional forms that hold in the long-run equilibrium, so that the interested reader can form an opinion of the depth of the analysis. Even that simple functional form should not frighten the general reader, who can skip it without missing anything from the relevant sections. For the mathematically inclined reader, though, it might summarise, in a succinct way, the verbal arguments and avoid the confusion that usually arises by verbal explanation. Only our readers can judge whether we have succeeded in this difficult task. Finally, every chapter provides an analysis of the prospects and risks for the relevant section of the economy or financial market. The prospects are evaluated through a projection of the macro-financial model. In this context it is worth mentioning the change of emphasis between the two editions of this book. In the First Edition risk analysis was based on detailed simulation analysis as this was meant for methodological reasons. However, in the Second Edition the scope of the book has been expanded to cover the similarities and differences between the two bub-bles and also how asset-led business cycles differ from those in the past. Space limitation has its casualties and the detailed simulation analysis is one of them.

One final comment is pertinent. Although in every chapter we describe the appropriate part of the macro-financial model utilised, we do not offer the numerical values of the relevant equations. Instead, we provide a graph that depicts how closely the model can explain the relevant variable and offer the forecast error. We believe that a detailed analysis of the numerical values of the model and its statistical proper-ties would not be satisfactory in view of space limitations. In any case, such an attempt would have detracted from the main analysis, purpose and focus of the project, without adding significantly to the book.

Data series

The data used throughout this book cover the period 1947–2009 and they are either quarterly or monthly as indicated. The data are the official figures as made available by Thomson – Reuters – EcoWin Pro, a live databank (see www.thomsonreuters.com). The book has been written using the data available at the time of writing each chapter and no attempt has been made to update each chapter as new data has come in, as otherwise the process would have been never ending. Thus, quarterly data have been used up to the second quarter of 2009 and monthly data up to August 2009.

Acknowledgements

We would very much like to thank Taiba Batool and Gemma Papageorgiou of Palgrave Macmillan, and their staff, for the encouragement and efficiency throughout the duration of this project. We would also wish to thank colleagues at the Cambridge Centre for Economic and Public Policy, University of Cambridge, and at the Departamento de Economia Aplicada V, Universidad del País Vasco, Spain, for comments on a number of occasions on chapters of this book. Also for the comments by the participants to the joint conferences of the two institutions at which chapters included in the book have been presented over a number of years. We are also grateful to a few more individuals. These include, in particular, Epaminondas Embiricos, Jonathan Edwards, John Mather and Lambros Varnavides, who have read the entire manuscript and have made useful comments. We are very grateful to all we have mentioned for their continuous support throughout the period of writing this book. Without their support this project would not have been completed.

Preface to the Second Edition

The asset and debt deflation process (or the economics of depression as they are labelled by Krugman, 2008) is little understood and even less appreciated, in both theory and policy. However, it is precisely this process that has been relevant since the early 1990s, first with balance sheet problems in the corporate sector (the 1991 cycle), then with balance sheet problems in the personal sector (the 2001 cycle) and now (the 2008 cycle) with balance sheet problems in the banking and personal sectors. Alan Greenspan, the ex-governor of the Federal Reserve System (the Fed), was the first to recognise that the 1990s were different than what had gone before when he characterised the rally in equities in 1996 as 'irrational exuberance'. Economic theory and business cycle analysis treats the last three cycles (including the current one) as not different from previous ones. Furthermore in dealing with the past three cycles policymakers have also applied the same medicine as in other cycles.

The failure of theory and policy to appreciate that asset-led cycles are different from the demand cycles of the 1950s and 1960s and the supply cycles of the 1970s and 1980s has made each of the last three cycles worse than the previous one. This is clearly an unstable situation which give rise to successive bubbles, each one being bigger than the previous one and each recession being worse than the one before. In a nutshell it is excessive liquidity that creates these bubbles and it is policy responses that add further liquidity every time a bubble bursts, which sows the seeds for the next bubble. The return to normality requires that policymakers drain the excess liquidity and allow debt deleveraging, while accepting that the current level of asset prices is not far from equilibrium. In other words, policymakers should stop trying to restore previous levels of asset prices. But this has not happened yet! Hence, more trouble is brewing for the future.

In the First Edition of the book, *The Post-Bubble US Economy: Implications for Financial Markets and the Economy* (Arestis and Kararkitsos, 2004), we described the asset and debt deflation process and assessed its impact on the economy through the K-Model. We claimed that an appreciation of this process requires an explanation of the role of the savings ratio in consumer decisions, which contradicts the principles of the widely accepted Life-Cycle and Permanent Income Hypothesis.

In this traditional approach the savings ratio moves pro-cyclically – it rises in a boom and falls in a recession – on the premise that consumers smooth out their consumption in the face of volatile income both in the course of the business cycle and throughout their lifetime. However, we have shown that in leveraged economies this does not characterise the behaviour of households in the real world. In fact, we argued in the First Edition that the opposite is happening; the savings ratio moves counter-cyclically, it falls in the upswing of the cycle, accentuating the boom, and rises in the downswing of the cycle, worsening the recession. This counter-cyclical pattern is built into the K-Model, where the savings ratio depends on the net wealth of the personal sector, job security, income growth prospects and the debt service burden. But rejection of the traditional Life-Cycle and Permanent Income Hypothesis in leveraged economies is only the first step towards the economics of depression. What is also required is an explanation of the net wealth of households and the net worth of the corporate sector. Both of these variables are omitted in any synthesis of current macroeconomics, like the New Consensus Macroeconomics.

Including a net wealth effect in consumption and the net worth of the corporate sector in investment is not sufficient. What is required is models for explaining the constituent components of the asset and liability sides of the net wealth of households and the net worth of the corporate sector. In the First Edition an entire chapter was devoted to housing, while its influence on the savings ratio was analysed in the chapter on consumption. Leamer (2007) claims that the current woes in the economy are due to the omission of housing in macroeconomic theory and business cycle analysis, as well as in policy. In the First Edition we claimed that the internet bubble will be transformed into a housing bubble and we looked at the conditions under which the housing market will burst and whether the housing market will experience a soft landing in 2004 and 2005. In subsequent work, Arestis and Karakitsos (2007, 2008), we warned that the boom in the housing market has turned into a bubble and argued that it will burst when the 30-year mortgage rate exceeds 7 percent – a condition that has proved sufficient. The third step that is required in the economics of depression is an explanation of the role of financial assets (equities, bonds and the dollar) and their interaction with the real side of the economy and inflation. Financial markets play a key role in creating bubbles. Chapters 9 and 10 of the First Edition were devoted to this task.

In this framework, which is exemplified in the K-Model, asset-led business cycles can be understood and appreciated. When excess liquidity is allowed to be generated asset prices (equities in the 2001 cycle and houses in the 2008 cycle) soar and debt leverage is increasing. This boosts the net wealth of households, lowers the savings ratio and stimulates investment and consumption, creating euphoria. In the initial phase of this process inflation declines or simply remains subdued. At some point, though, the economic boom creates overheating and inflation creeps up. The central bank hikes rates to check inflation and by doing so it pricks the bubble, a feature that characterised Japan in the 1990s and the US in the last two cycles. Once the bubble bursts, asset prices fall and what is left is an overhang of debt in the personal and corporate sectors. Whereas access to capital markets eases the required balance sheet adjustment of companies, households try to curb debt and restore the value of their net wealth by raising the savings ratio and cutting consumption. The asset and debt deflation is then unfolding deepening and prolonging the recession.

In this framework policymakers should not allow the expansion of credit in the first instance. They are simply mistaken when they look at the low growth in monetary aggregates that makes them feel that everything is alright, as financial innovation is creating the excess liquidity without this being reflected in monetary aggregates. Strict regulation might do the trick, but in a market economy it may be better if the policymakers adopt a net wealth target in addition to the two traditional targets of inflation and the output gap. These were the conclusions of the First Edition and they are still valid now. But whereas future crises can be averted through the adoption of a net wealth target, the way out of the current crisis is an orderly deleverage of the system through the draining of excess liquidity and the acceptance of subpar growth for the next few years. But this is not what is happening.

In the Second Edition we have retained the same structure, as it essentially explains the asset and debt deflation process. However, we have tried to make it relevant to what will happen next, in view of the current financial crisis. Thus, we have changed the title of this edition to 'The Post 'Great Recession' US Economy: Implications for Financial Markets and the Economy'. This is because the First Edition was preoccupied with whether the housing market will have a soft landing in the two-year projection of 2004–05. There is a difference, though, in the emphasis between the two editions. Instead of illustrating how the K-Model can be used to make a quantitative assessment of the impact of policy, in the Second Edition we attempt to compare and contrast asset-led business cycles with demand and supply ones. We have done this in a systematic way when we examine in the various chapters the components of aggregate demand, inflation and asset prices (houses, equities, bonds and the dollar). Since policy still holds the key to what will happen next, we have assessed the risks to the economy over the next few years in every chapter by contrasting what should happen if the policymakers allowed debt deleveraging to take place with what would happen if the policymakers attempted to restore asset high prices.

From this perspective the following differences have emerged in the Second Edition. The Introduction now puts into perspective the current economic situation and offers an assessment of the opposing policies. Chapter 2 is the same as in the First Edition. It deals with the internet bubble. Chapter 3 is entirely new and is devoted to an in-depth analysis of the current crisis. The remainder of the chapters follow the First Edition, but with the aforementioned change of emphasis and, of course, the full updating of all of them, including chapter 2.

11 October 2009.

1
Introduction

1   The purpose of the book

Over the past couple of decades or so the US economy has gone through a very interesting period. There was a period of expansion in the 1990s that lasted for ten years, the longest ever recorded by an industrialised country. So much so that allegedly a 'new economy' emerged with its own ways, which were different from what, traditionally, had been known. The stock market produced enormous gains in the 1990s, especially so in the areas of Technology, Media and Telecommunications. Beginning March 2000 the stock market simply collapsed. The optimism surrounding the 'new economy' vanished with it, followed by pessimism. In fact, beginning March 2001 the US economy entered a period of a short and shallow recession, but with huge job losses and a deep profits recession. This prompted the Fed and the US fiscal authorities to pursue expansionary policies. There were no less than 13 reductions in the Fed funds rate, the Federal Reserve System (Fed) interest rate, between the early parts of 2001 and mid-2003, along with expansionary fiscal measures. The surplus in the government budget, created during the expansion, turned into a deficit in the downswing and soared in 2004 even though the economy was rapidly expanding.

The recovery in the early 2000s cycle was initially anaemic, but became sustainable after a long lag. However, the new cycle was short-lived. After the boom in 2004, growth slowed to below potential and the US economy finally succumbed to recession at the end of 2007. The housing market played a key role throughout this period. It was buoyed by the Fed funds rate cuts in 2001–03, thereby making the consumer resilient in the early 2000s recession. The shallowness of that recession was due to strong consumption, which continued in the recovery.

In fact, this was the first consumer-led recovery, whereas traditionally it has always been investment-led. The removal of the monetary accommodation bias was delayed until mid-2004, although the negative output gap had been eliminated nine months earlier. Moreover, monetary policy was tightened 'at a pace that can be measured', using the well-known Alan Greenspan slogan, meaning just 25 basis points (bps) in every Fed meeting. These errors in the conduct of monetary policy ballooned the housing market, swelled the current account deficit to unprecedented levels and encouraged financial engineering that expanded the liquidity that was needed to fuel the two most notable bubbles, namely housing and commodities. The consumer already burdened with debt became over-indebted in an effort to maintain consumption expenditure by extracting home equity amid falling living standards and growing income inequality. Bernanke, the successor of Alan Greenspan at the helm of the Fed, continued with the same pace of tightening, but for a much longer period, namely until the second half of 2006 when the Fed Funds rate hit 5.25 percent. Moreover, Ben Bernanke kept rates at this level until the credit crisis erupted in the summer of 2007. The high interest rates pricked the housing bubble, causing a financial crisis that unmistakably steered the US economy into recession. As the credit crisis deepened with Bear Stearns the first serious casualty, the economy fell off the cliff in the second half of 2008 with an unprecedented plunge in consumer expenditure and final sales. The deepening recession had a further backslash on the financial crisis triggering the collapse or the bailout of what were considered the pillars of the financial system, such as Fannie Mae and Freddie Mac in the mortgage market, AIG in the insurance sector and Lehman Brothers and Merrill Lynch in investment banking, while the rest in investment banking, namely Goldman Sachs and Morgan Stanley, quitted the industry and ran for cover by becoming commercial banks. The public outcry against the financial institutions that caused this mess and the anti-Wall Street rhetoric of the Obama Administration in its initial stage in office exasperated the financial crisis, bringing to the point of bankruptcy the entire financial system. However, the Obama Administration did not dare to proceed with the required reform of the financial system, opting instead to adopt a 'business-as-usual' model. It abandoned any plans for reform; it stopped the war of words against Wall Street; it banned the tax on bonuses that the House had passed; it conceded to the demands of the banks to accept the 'business-as-usual' model; and finally allowed them to exercise discretion in valuing their distressed assets. This U-turn of policy marked the turning point in the crisis and heralded the beginning of the economic recovery, which is expected to take place from the second half of 2009 onwards. The Obama Administration opted for the hard way of devising strict regulations to make sure that the credit crisis would not be repeated in the future.

The policy response to the credit crisis and the deep and protracted recession was to provide ample liquidity to the markets to revamp credit flows; cut the borrowing costs; accept lower quality collateral paper for Fed lending; expand the group of institutions eligible for discounting their assets at the Fed; bail out the failing financial institutions; and, finally, provide a sizeable fiscal stimulus. The balance sheet of the Fed expanded to $2.2 trillion under the euphemistic term of 'quantitative easing', which in layman terms means 'printing money'. The fiscal and monetary stimuli pose long-term risks to the sustainability of the recovery. These concerns have been expressed as a call to policymakers to articulate credible 'exit strategies' from these extraordinary measures. What is missing in this analysis is that the policy response to the last three asset-led cycles has been the same as in the previous demand and supply cycles. Yet, adding liquidity to solve the problems that have been created by excessive liquidity may be a short-term solution, but cannot be applied in the long run. Such policy measures help to get the economy out of the recession, but sow the seeds for the next bubble later on. This is how successive bubbles have been created over the last decade or so. The only viable long-term solution is debt deleveraging. But this assumes that policymakers accept the current low level of asset prices as being not far from equilibrium. However, this is not what is happening. The extra liquidity will be channelled to assets, thus creating the delusion that the drop in asset prices is temporary and not permanent. Opposition to draining that liquidity will increase when the time comes with the warning that this will undermine the sustainability of the recovery. Thus, more trouble is brewing for the future.

The purpose of this book is to provide substance to the abovementioned claims on the causes of the boom and burst of the recent bubbles and, in particular, that of the internet and housing. In the euphoria years many seemingly valid arguments are developed to justify that the current economic environment is different than before. But the validity of these arguments is falsified in the aftermath of the burst of the bubble. Thus, one task of this book is to put into perspective the rosy scenarios that have been developed to justify the booms. The book compares and contrasts the consequences of the burst of the housing bubble with those of the internet one, and the demand and supply cycles between the 1950s and the 1980s. It also examines closely the recent experience of the US economy and its financial markets along with their prospects and risks from a short- and long-run perspective. We are keen to study closely the prospects of the post-bubble period, but also the risks, which we believe are serious enough to justify undertaking a project on this aspect of current US economic developments. This examination is particularly pertinent once we have reminded ourselves of the sharp contrast between the 2001 US recession, which was unusually mild along with unemployment and inflation both remaining at relatively low levels and the current recession that was deep and protracted with inflation becoming negative (deflation), unemployment soaring, along with unprecedented job losses. The book assesses the short-term risks to the expected recovery and, in particular, whether it will be anaemic in terms of the pace of job creation and slowness in investment pick-up, as was the case with the 2003 recovery. It also considers the long-term risks for the new business cycle.

At a deeper level of analysis the book has yet another purpose. The current cycle, along with the previous two, have been asset-led because of the excessive liquidity that has financed a series of bubbles. In this context the purpose of the book is to present a model that can explain equally well the last three asset-led cycles as well as the demand and supply ones of the 1950s through 1980s. This model embodies typical structures in the demand and supply sides of the real economy, but with an emphasis on the long-term factors that create sector imbalances, which induce retrenchment in the downswing of the cycle. Moreover, this model also includes an explanation of asset prices (houses, bonds, equities and currencies) that have a feedback effect on sector imbalances, thereby enabling the assessment of the impact on the retrenchment of the various sectors of the economy. This structure, which is embodied in the K-Model, the model we employ for the purposes of this book, is sufficient to account for the experience of the US economy in the last sixty years. The book offers a methodical and systematic review of the various components of the demand and supply sides of the real economy, along with the financial sector, and shows how they should be specified to explain all types of business cycles. Since economic policy affects both financial markets and the real economy, the book reviews the conduct of policy and suggests how policy and, in particular, monetary policy should be conducted in the future to prevent bubbles from ballooning and bursting. The book is not a treatise of economic theory and policy, though. It is empirically oriented. It provides an analysis of the current economic environment and compares and contrasts it to other cycles; it evaluates the likely course of the US economy and of asset prices in the near term and assesses the long-term risks.

This introduction gives a flavour of what is to follow in the book, but also what has been achieved in the book. The next three sections provide a brief resume of where we think the US economy stands at this juncture and its medium-term outlook, as well as its long-term risks. This is followed by a brief description, chapter by chapter, of the contents of the book, along with what we have achieved in each chapter. A brief explanation of the macroeconomic model we have utilised through-out the book to back up propositions made and hypotheses postulated.

2   The forces that shape growth

The forces that shape growth with a yearly view are fiscal and monetary policy, confidence and private sector imbalances. Monetary policy was eased rapidly from the onset of the credit crisis in the summer of 2007 to the end of 2008. The Fed funds rate was cut from 5.25 percent to the range of zero and 0.25 percent, the lowest ever. The degree of monetary easing is reminiscent of that under Alan Greenspan in the early 2000s and embodies the same long-term risks, namely that it will fuel another bubble in the future. The rapid speed of rate cutting was the result of the conclusion reached in a Fed study of the lessons to be learned from the deflation experience of Japan in the 1990s. The argument is that a fast rate cut process is preferable to a slow one, as in the latter inflation becomes increasingly negative, thereby negating the positive impact on the real interest rate. Figure 1.1 provides support for this argument. The graph shows the stance of monetary policy, which is a weighted average of domestic and external monetary conditions, with the weights being the importance of domestic demand and exports to GDP. Domestic monetary conditions are measured by the deviation of the real Fed funds rate from its neutral level, while external monetary conditions are measured by the deviation of the real effective exchange rate from its neutral level.[1] Domestic monetary conditions were eased with the real Fed funds rate falling from 0.8 percent at the onset of the credit crisis to –6.2 percent a year later. But rapidly falling inflation has offset this positive impact on the economy, as the real Fed funds rate climbed back to –0.3 percent at the end of August 2009. So, the prospects of domestic monetary conditions depend on inflation. The outlook for inflation is that it will remain subdued for some time, as its main determinant is the spare capacity of the economy (see Figure 1.2). In spite of this nuance picture, the dynamics of inflation point to the end of deflation

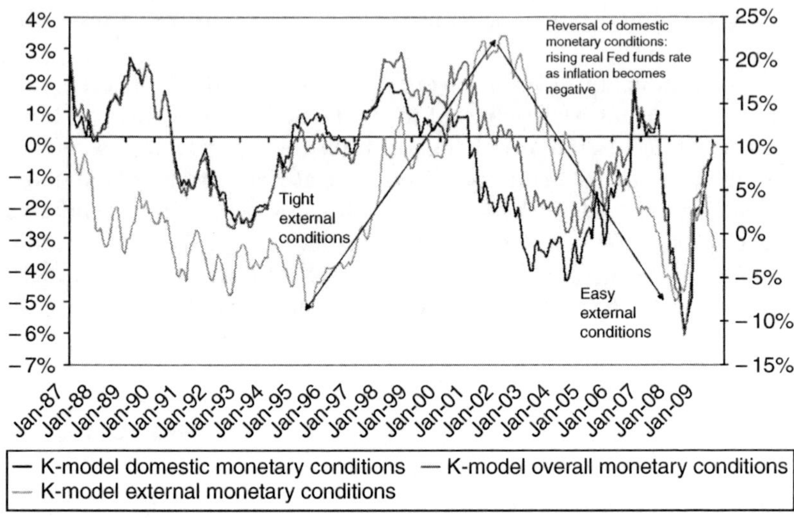

Figure 1.1   The stance of monetary policy

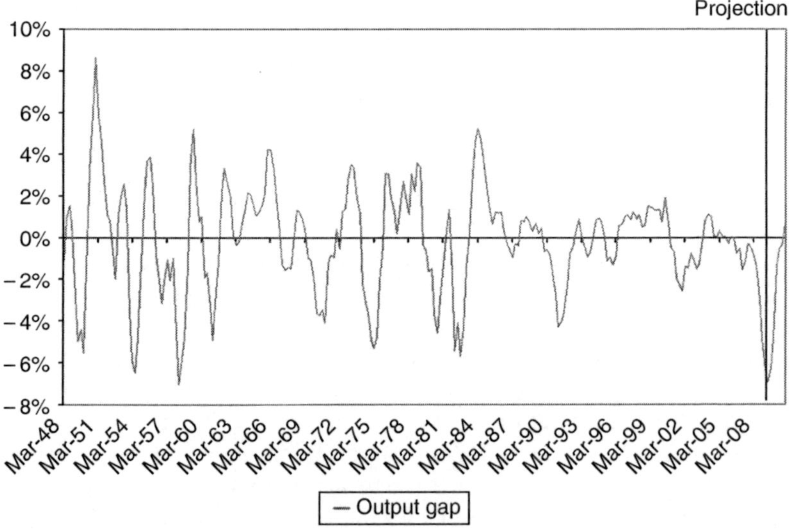

Figure 1.2   The output gap

(see Figure 1.3). This means that domestic monetary conditions will ease in the next 12 months, as the Fed will keep interest rates at the zero range, while inflation rises. The dollar weakness is likely to intensify, thereby re-enforcing the easy stance of overall monetary conditions.

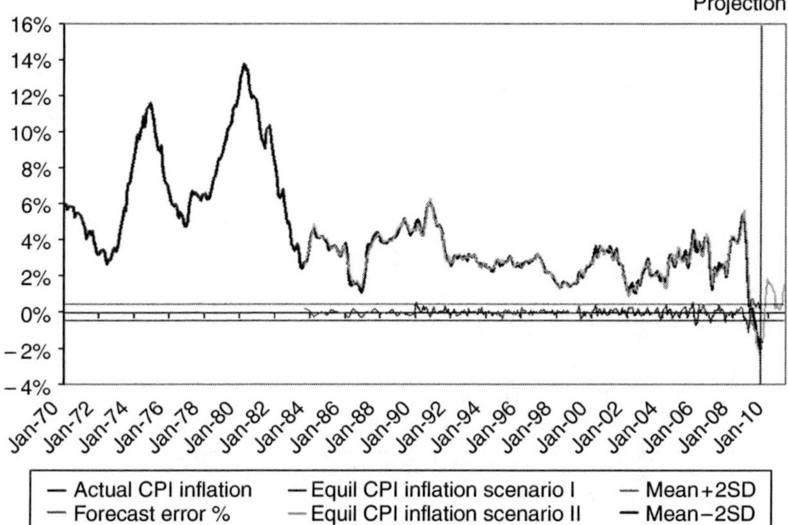

Figure 1.3   Headline CPI-inflation

The elimination of the Federal budget deficit of the Reagan era took an awfully long time, in spite of promises by successive administrations and the Congress that this was a top priority. In the end, it was only eliminated at the end of the 1990s and turned into a surplus just before the burst of the internet bubble (see Figure 1.4). This is indicative of the US approach to the current swelling of the budget deficit that is likely to hit a historical record in the 2009 fiscal year (see Figure 1.4). If previous experience is any guide for the future, it suggests that the current huge budget deficit will remain with us for a very long time. The budget surplus of the early 2000s turned into a deficit in the subsequent recession and swelled with the easy fiscal policy that was pursued to get the economy out of that recession. The budget deficit shrank until the onset of the credit crisis, but then it soared yet again as the bailing out of financial institutions took enormous dimensions and fiscal policy turned easy to alleviate the current recession. The Congressional Budget Office (CBO) estimates this year's fiscal deficit at $1.6 trillion, up from $0.5 in 2008. This amounts to $1.1 trillion net increase in the federal deficit that includes the surpluses in the Social Security Trust as well as the net cash flow of the Postal Service, namely on- and off-balance sheet items. The CBO estimates that the deficit will narrow by $0.2 trillion in

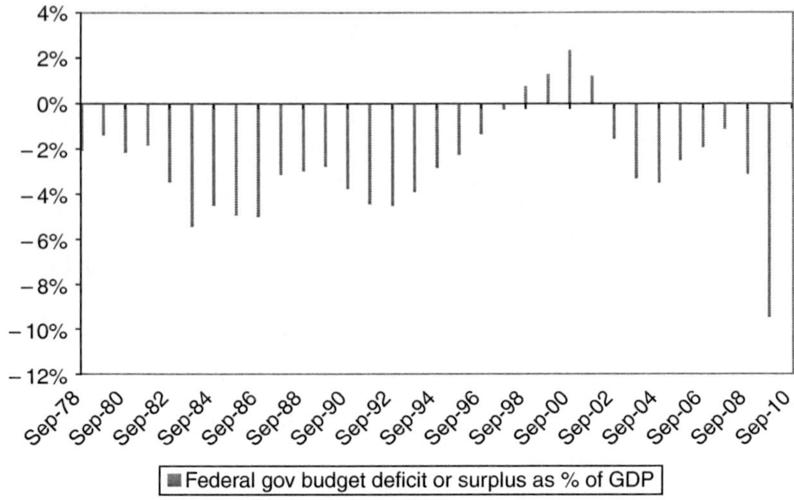

Figure 1.4   Federal government budget deficit or surplus as % of GDP

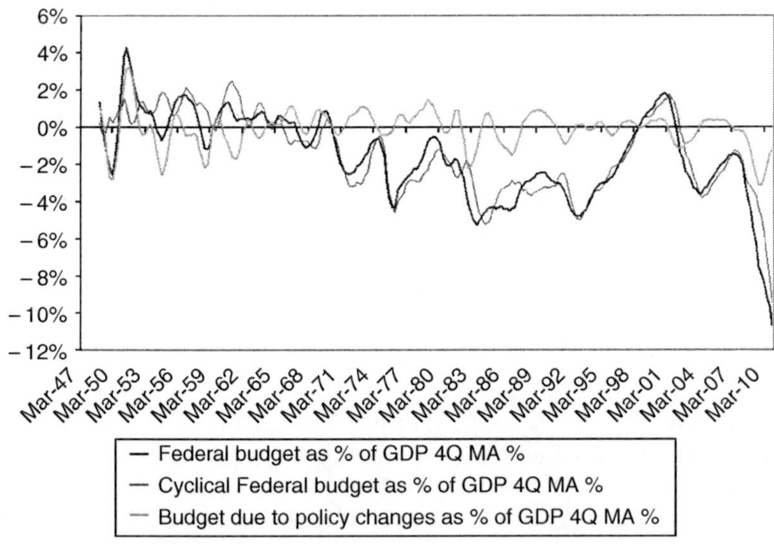

Figure 1.5   Decomposition of Federal budget

the next fiscal year. Figure 1.5 shows the decomposition of the Federal budget deficit, according to the K-Model, into a cyclical component and a portion that is due to fiscal policy. The cyclical component is expected to be corrected in time as the recovery matures. But the part that is due to policy would need corrective action. In the projections reported above the assumption is that the Obama Administration would tighten fiscal policy next year, but this would only turn around the cyclical and overall budget deficit beyond the projection period of 2010. We discuss the risks to this scenario later on in this chapter.

The imbalances of the personal, corporate, banking and federal sectors, along with the external imbalance, will shape the effects of fiscal and monetary policy in the long run (i.e. the fiscal and monetary multipliers in the second year and beyond). These imbalances will affect the speed at which the positive effects of fiscal and monetary policy dissipate, and therefore they are more relevant in 2010 and beyond. The personal sector imbalance reached its maximum in the first quarter of 2009 and narrowed in the second, as equity prices recovered. In the first year of the recovery profit margins soar partly because of productivity gains and partly because the wage bill diminishes, thereby boosting profits. Thus, the equity market rally will continue for some time reducing the personal sector imbalance. The corporate sector balance sheet has not been particularly impaired in the current downturn. Any infection is largely cyclical stemming from the feedback effect from the personal and banking sectors. The latter is problematic, as the profits of the financial institutions are fictitious stemming from the suspension of the mark-to-market fair value method of valuing distressed assets. The banking sector imbalance diminishes the value of both the fiscal and monetary multipliers, thereby weakening the efficacy of economic policy, as bank lending remains subdued. The external imbalance is likely to widen in the forecast period as the US is likely to grow faster than its main trading partners.

Other short-run factors will determine the extent to which fiscal and monetary policy creates growth over the next 12 months. The most important is consumer and business confidence, which is expected to strengthen on evidence that the economy is rebounding. All these forces determine the outlook for the US for the next two years.

3   The case for a weak cyclical upturn and the outlook for the US economy

The combination of easy fiscal policy with easy monetary policy and increased confidence, due to the subsidence of the credit crisis and the rebound in equity prices, should help the US economy to recover from the worst recession in the post-Second World War era. The most likely outcome is growth in 2010 that will match that of potential output.

But this is not what is happening in a typical recovery, in which growth exceeds potential, thereby generating many new jobs and unemployment begins to fall with a lag. The expected recovery in this sense will be anaemic. The case for a recovery, albeit anaemic, besides the boost from the fiscal and monetary stimulus rests on the restocking that is now taking place. The collapse of consumer expenditure in the second half of 2008 was unexpected by the corporate sector. The dramatic fall of consumption especially in the fourth quarter of 2008 led companies to cut production drastically, shed labour at an unprecedented pace and slash investment. In the first quarter of 2009 the consumer took a breather from the retrenchment of the previous six months, while the adjustment of output, labour and investment by the corporate sector took place in that same quarter. As a result, there was an unanticipated fall in inventories that prompted companies to increase production to replenish their stocks. Figure 1.6 shows the gap between new orders and inventories and the consequent changes in production. In February 2009 the new orders–inventories gap reached –9 percent, the second worst record in the entire post-Second World War era (see Figure 1.6). This prompted a rebound of production, which is the common experience of all cycles. The restocking is a powerful engine for growth for a year or so. Hence, the case for a recovery of the economy until the spring of 2010 is well founded. The stimulus from restocking is further boosted by easy fiscal and monetary policy and rising confidence.

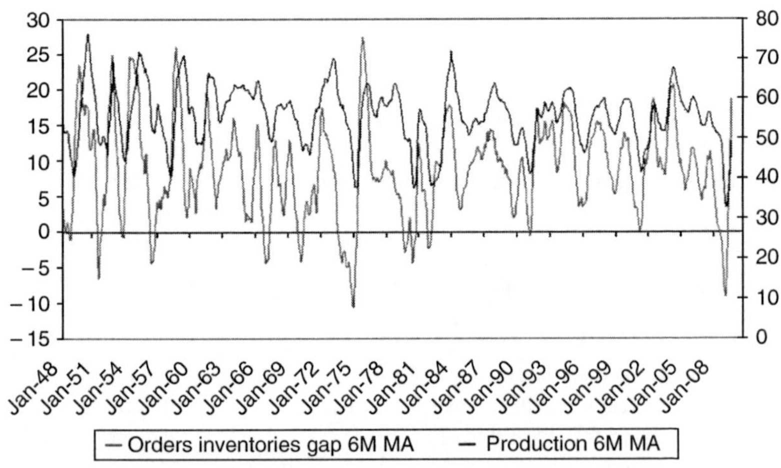

Figure 1.6   Orders–inventories gap and production

Hence growth will accelerate until the end of 2010. This forms the mainline scenario.

In the second half of 2008 the US economy fell off a cliff, with growth plummeting in the second quarter of 2009 to nearly –4 percent relative to the year earlier period (y-o-y). Although this was the worst performance throughout the entire the Second World War era, growth increased to –1 percent relative to the previous quarter (q-o-q) from –6.4 percent (q-o-q) in the first, thereby suggesting that the contraction eased (see Figure 1.7). The K-Model suggests that the second quarter of 2009 marks the bottom of the recession (y-o-y) with a recovery in the second half that will gather steam in 2010. However, the expected recovery will most likely be anaemic and reminiscent of the last two recoveries, with very little job creation and unemployment continuing to rise.

Weak consumption since mid-2008 was the main reason for the deepest recession in the Second World War era (see Figure 1.8). Only twice in the past has consumption slumped to the extent that it did in the current downturn. This is in sharp contrast to the resilience of consumption during the 2001 recession and the leading role it played in the recovery. This is due to the diverse fortunes of the housing market in the two cycles. In the early 2000s recession the housing market was buoyed in view of the Fed

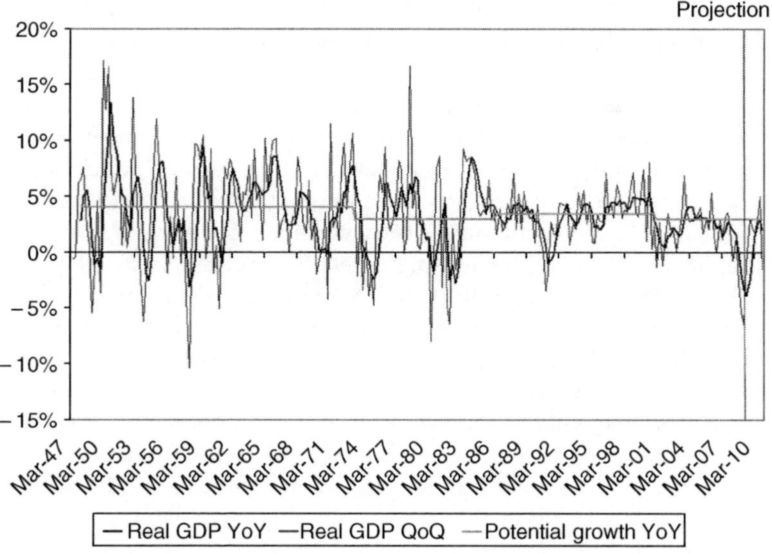

Figure 1.7   Real GDP

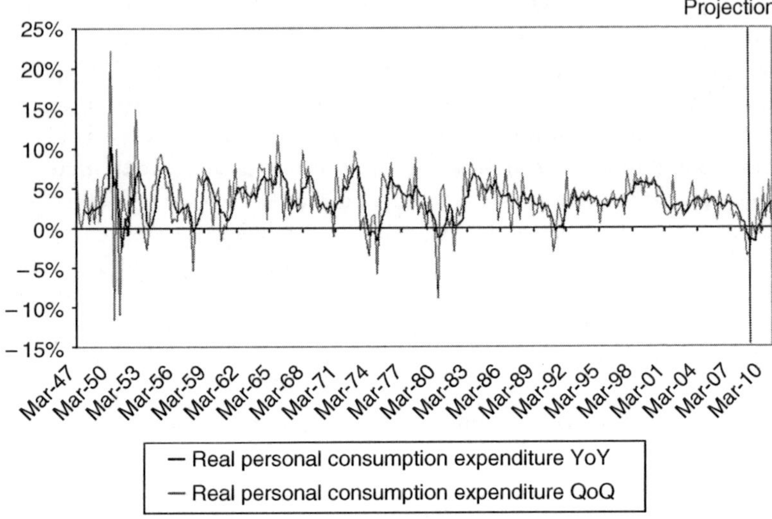

Figure 1.8   Real consumer expenditure

rate cuts and went from strength to strength in the recovery until it became a bubble. In the current recession it is the burst of the housing market that triggered a collapse of equities, too, which is responsible for the weakness of consumption. The fall in asset prices (houses and equities) eroded the net wealth of households, while the credit crisis sapped consumer confidence and consumer credit dropped partly because the demand for credit dried up and partly because banks tightened the supply of credit. This adjustment in asset prices and debt created an imbalance in the personal sector balance sheet and induced households to save a greater proportion of their income (that is, a rise in the savings ratio). Notwithstanding this rise in the savings ratio, the real disposable income of households has been bolstered because of the rapid fall in inflation in the last 12 months and the tax cuts in the spring of 2009. Moreover, consumer confidence has recovered as the credit crisis has subsided, signs of easing of the contraction of the economy have emerged and equity markets have rallied. All these factors suggest that the savings ratio may fall in the near term, thereby underpinning consumption growth. Finally, one-off measures to help the auto-industry are bound to strengthen the demand for consumer durables in the third quarter of 2009. The K-Model suggests that consumption growth will recover in the second half of 2009, but will remain weak in 2010, as the recovery in the economy will be anaemic with hardly any job creation and unemployment

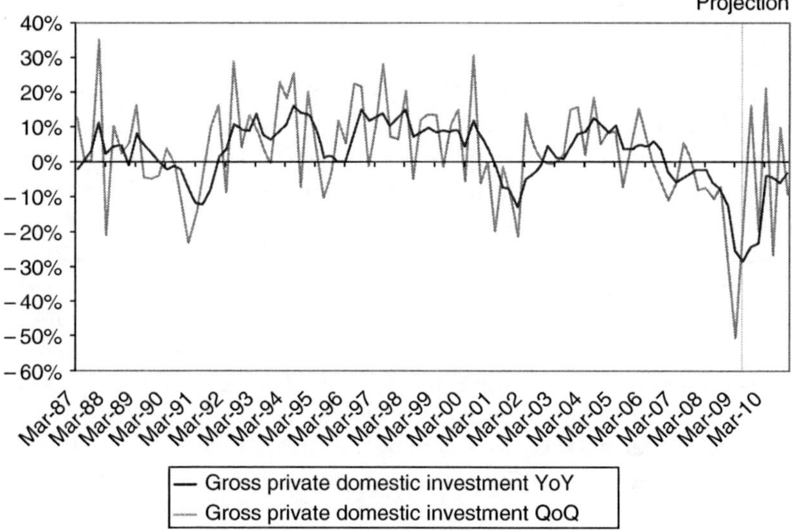

Figure 1.9   Real gross private domestic investment

continuing to rise (as Figure 1.8 implies). Moreover, the personal sector imbalance has not been corrected as debt has remained elevated and this poses risks to the sustainability of the recovery in the long run.

As the fall in consumption in the second half of 2008 was unexpected, companies saw their stock of unsold inventories piling up. This triggered sharp cuts in production, shedding of labour at an unprecedented pace and slashing investment. The slump in fixed investment further contributed to the contraction of GDP in the current downturn. This adjustment in the corporate sector was very swift, thus paving the way for a recovery later on. In spite of improving conditions in final demand, companies are in no rush to increase fixed investment, as they anticipate a weak recovery. This self-fulfilling prophecy lies at the heart of the K-Model assessment for an anaemic recovery. Nonetheless, this unfavourable climate might change for the better if a second fiscal package were introduced at the beginning of 2010 or exports were to strengthen through a sharp rebound in world trade. Although 'animal spirits', in the words of Keynes, might govern the pattern of investment in the near term, there are fundamental reasons for a weak investment recovery (see Figure 1.9). Despite the unfreezing of credit markets, banks have tightened lending standards and the low cost of bank borrowing from the Fed has not filtered through the economy. In fact, quite the opposite has happened; the cost of bank lending has increased. A large proportion of the investment is financed by borrowing and, therefore, there are downside risks to the investment outlook. However, these downside risks are counterbalanced to some extent by the effects of 'quantitative easing'. Although the initial aim of quantitative easing was to unfreeze bank-lending constraints to companies and households, this has so far failed. Banks are hoarding the extra cash mainly in the form of deposits at the Fed and in US Treasuries and Agency Notes. But the quantitative easing has had some favourable indirect effects. The Fed's purchase of asset-backed securities and US Treasuries aims to keep long-term interest rates low and to narrow credit spreads. Low Treasury yields keep the whole spectrum of long-term interest rates from mortgage rates to corporate yields down. Moreover, credit spreads are narrowing as the economy rebounds, while the Fed buying is further intensifying the narrowing process. Thus, companies that have access to capital markets can benefit by the quantitative easing, as the cost of borrowing is reduced. This may be true for large companies, but not for the majority which are small ones. Moreover, it is the small companies that employ the bulk of the labour force. Thus, the quantitative easing even through this indirect channel has a limited impact. Consequently, the balance of risks is on the downside rather than on the upside.

The strength of exports was the only bright spot of the economy and an engine for growth in the initial phase of the mild recession in the nine months to mid-2008 (see Figure 1.10). But the collapse of the commodities

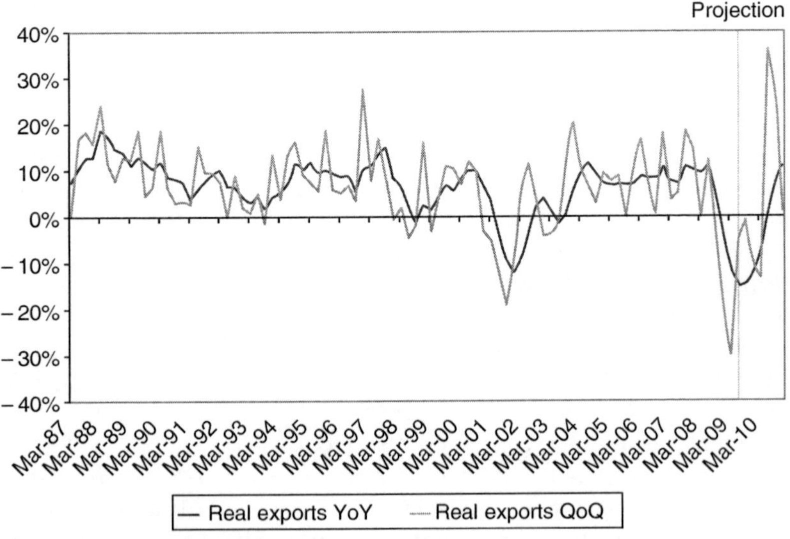

Figure 1.10   Real exports of goods & services

bubble in the second half of 2008, sparked by the tumble of US consumption, pulled the carpet from under the feet of exports, triggering a slump. Exports fell a staggering 30 percent (q-o-q) in the first quarter of 2009, but improved in the second quarter to –5 percent (q-o-q). The K-model suggests that the second quarter of 2009 will mark the bottom of exports growth on a (y-o-y) basis with a recovery in the second half that will gather steam in 2010. Exports growth might hit double-digit figures at the end of 2010. The good prospects of exports stem from the multiplier effects of world trade, which is greater than unity, and the improved competitiveness of the US economy that will enable it to benefit from its own recovery.

4 Long-term risks

There are long-term risks both on the upside and downside around the mainline scenario well beyond the restocking period depending on the policies that will be pursued in the future. Let us consider first the down-side risks, which stem from the 'exit strategies' and the largely unaffected sector imbalances. Consider first the implications of the balance sheet problem of the banking sector. The aim of the quantitative easing was to help banks restore bank lending to normal levels. But bank lending has not recovered either because banks are unwilling to lend or because the demand for credit has dried up. Without a revival of bank lending the recovery of the economy is likely to falter once the restocking period is over. Second, the positive impact from the fiscal stimulus wanes from the second year of its implementation onwards. Accordingly, without any further fiscal stimulus aggregate demand in the economy will weaken from the middle of 2010, thus raising the downside risks in 2011 and beyond. Moreover, if the Obama Administration is faithful to its rhetoric of fiscal rectitude and adopts tight fiscal policy from next year onwards in an attempt to curb the budget deficit and rein in the soaring debt, then tight fiscal policy will reinforce the natural waning of this year's stimulus, thereby weakening aggregate demand in 2011 and beyond. The most serious downside risk arises from the implementation of the exit strategy from quantitative easing. If the Fed proceeded with this exit strategy from the spring of 2010 onwards, then government bond yields on the entire maturity spectrum are bound to rise pushing up mortgage rates and lifting the floor of corporate bond spreads. Rising interest rates will weaken the demand for capital goods and consumer durable goods and will under-mine a fragile housing market. Finally, any narrowing of the personal sec-tor imbalance relies on a continuation of the equity market rally, as it will bolster the belief of households that the fall in asset prices is temporary rather than permanent. But after the first year of the recovery in which equities rebound strongly because profits soar as a result of improving profit margins, the equity market rally fizzles out on the grounds that there is profit fatigue in the second year of the recovery. Hence, if the recovery falters in mid-2010, then equities will fall inducing households to save more, thereby intensifying the downward spiral of the economy.

But there are upside risks to the main scenario outlined above. Experience shows that fiscal rectitude amongst US policymakers is only rhetorical. In practice the US policymakers have always opted for more fiscal stimulus and there is little doubt that they might do the same on this occasion. Thus, there is a non-negligible risk that instead of austerity the Obama Administration might come up with yet another fiscal package in 2010. Easy fiscal policy will strengthen demand in 2010, as the first year multiplier is at its highest level. This will probably bolster growth in the economy to above potential levels, threatening to rekindle inflation, where the dynamics are already pointing to higher levels in 2010, albeit less than the implicit Fed target of 2 percent.

The balance sheet expansion of the Fed, which has euphemistically been termed quantitative easing, implies printing of money of the order of $1.4 trillion. This huge money supply is not circulating in the economy and provided the economy retains some spare capacity it does not pose any risks of reigniting inflation for the time being, as the banks have placed this liquidity in the form of deposits at the Fed and in US Treasuries or Agency Notes. But if growth in the economy were to exceed potential, and this is likely with another fiscal package, then inflation will turn out to be a problem forcing the Fed to tighten aggressively and exit in a panic from the quantitative easing programme.

In theory there is no problem in draining the liquidity that has been injected from the quantitative easing programme. The Fed can employ reverse repo agreements through which it will sell back to the banks the low-quality assets it bought from them in the first place. Secondly, the Fed can raise the interest rate at which it lends money to commercial banks. But in practice this process is likely to be fraught with difficulties. There is bound to be a lot of resistance from the banks in the exercise of these reverse repo agreements, as there has been little progress so far in repairing their impaired balance sheet. More resistance from the banks is likely to arise from the consequences of stricter regulation. Although there is a heated debate on the details of the new regulation of the financial system there is little doubt that all banks would be required to increase their capital, but even more so the so-called 'too-big-to-fail' banks. Financial markets have so far shrugged off the suspension of the mark-to-market fair practice of valuing distressed assets. But this market complacency may come to an abrupt end as in the recovery firms and banks attempt to raise capital from financial markets. Any attempt by the Fed to unload from its balance sheet the distressed assets and put them back to the balance sheet of the banks will make the task of capital-raising for the banks much more difficult than otherwise. Hence, banks are most likely to resist fiercely the exit strategy from quantitative easing. Indeed, the Fed is already leaning on the demands of the banks. In its recent meeting in late September 2009 the Federal Open Market Committee (FOMC) decided to delay the end of the buying programme of asset backed securities and US Treasury and Agency Notes from October 2009 to March 2010 with a commitment to exhaust the originally announced amounts of purchases. Thus, far from preparing for an exit strategy the Fed is intensifying its efforts with quantitative easing.

With easy fiscal and monetary policy in 2010, there is little doubt that growth will accelerate to above potential. Equity markets will rally strongly putting back in the cupboard the skeletons of the various sector imbalances and delaying the inevitable asset and debt deflation process. But as a result of the overheating inflation will be reignited with a lag, most probably at the end of 2011 or in 2012. Strong growth in 2010 and 2011 is likely to keep inflation subdued for some time, as productivity will carry on improving, pushing down unit labour cost. No doubt policymakers will congratulate each other for making the recovery sustainable, as they have done recently at the G20 meeting in Pittsburgh for jump-starting the recovery. But the rekindling of inflation later on will cause panic amongst policymakers and the Fed will embark on a fast track to drain the excessive liquidity and hike interest rates. This will plunge the economy at the end of 2012 or in 2013 to yet another recession.

The overall conclusion from the analysis of the upside and downside risks suggests that the next cycle will be very short. Either the recovery will falter after the restocking period is over or growth will strengthen for two more years because policy continues to be easy, but then the economy will dive into yet another recession. This bleak outlook is the inevitable conclusion of the wrong policies that are pursued in asset-led business cycles, a central issue in this book. Reflating the economy and injecting more liquidity beyond the strict period of recession when excessive liquidity has been the problem in the first instance can only fuel more bubbles in the future. These bubbles will be pricked once the Fed hikes rates. But as the experience has shown the level of interest rates required to prick the new bubble is lower than the one before and the interest rate cuts to avoid the inevitable asset and debt deflation process must be deeper. In the internet bubble the Fed cut rates to

1 percent, but in the housing bubble the Fed had to cut them to the range of zero to 0.25 percent. Is the Fed prepared to introduce negative interest rates in the next recession? The only viable policy in asset-led cycles is the drain of liquidity in the recovery phase of the cycle and acceptance of subpar growth for a number of years until debt deleveraging takes place to the level that is compatible with the lower asset prices. However, this is not what is happening. The policymakers pursue policies that attempt to restore the previous high, but unsustainable, level of asset prices with the aim of averting debt deleveraging.

5   The structure of the book and what we have achieved

Chapters 2 and 3 are devoted to the causes of the internet and the housing bubbles, respectively, and the consequences of their burst for the economy and financial markets. The housing bubble is compared with the internet one and the 'new economy' paradigm is analysed critically. Chapter 3 explains in depth how the excessive liquidity was created. The debate of whether monetary policy should also include asset price inflation targeting is discussed therein and a proposal is put forward on how this can be made possible without interfering with the free function of financial markets.

As was discussed in the previous section there are upside and downside risks to the mainline scenario. To analyse these risks and assess them quantitatively we must first evaluate the conduct of monetary policy. The outlook for inflation will ultimately determine the degree, if any, of monetary tightening in the next two years. This is one of the reasons chapter 4 is devoted to wages and prices. Allegedly the Fed policy actions affect inflation with a long lag of approximately two years. It is this consideration that has led us to choose a two-year horizon in analysing the prospects and risks to the economy and financial markets. Inflationary pressures can be gauged before they surface on CPI-inflation by examining producer prices of finished goods, intermediate supplies and crude material prices. The latter are influenced by commodity prices and the price of oil. Moreover, the labour cost is the most important determinant of producer prices. This, in turn, depends on employment, wages and productivity. Hence, an assessment of future inflationary trends requires an analysis of the whole wage–price nexus. But there are two more reasons why we study inflationary pressures thoroughly in chapter 4. First, wages and prices determine the pricing power of companies, profit margins and overall corporate profitability, which affect investment and equity prices. Second, inflation is also a major determinant of bond yields. The conclusion of this chapter is that inflation will rise gently from its negative levels reached in the middle of the recent recession, but will remain subdued, within the target range of the Fed. However, there are upside risks to inflation if fiscal and monetary policy is easy in 2010.

The inflationary pressures and the likely conduct of monetary policy set the scene for the rest of the developments in the economy and financial markets. Chapter 5 analyses thoroughly corporate profitability by breaking it down into unit profit, volume of sales and profit margin. Corporate profitability depends on the entire wage–price sector and the output gap and consequently on the entire macro-financial model. Profits are a major determinant of investment and equity prices, which have a feedback effect on profits. Therefore, to assess the risk on profits the whole model has to be used. Chapter 5 shows that profits are likely to soar in the first year of the recovery, but to decelerate in the second year. The abovementioned upside and downside risks to this mainline scenario are discussed in the context of profitability.

Chapter 6 is devoted to the analysis of investment. Corporate profits as well as wages and prices are key determinants of investment and hence the analysis of the previous two chapters is pertinent. However, in addition, industrial production, capacity utilisation, interest rates and expectations, what Keynes called 'animal spirits', play a significant role in investment decisions. A full model that incorporates these additional factors is presented and analysed in order to assess the prospects and risks of investment. Therefore, the investment model is simulated simultaneously with all the other blocks to assess quantitatively the prospects and risks of investment. Investment plays a key role in business cycle analysis and any long-term weakness of the economy, and decline in equity prices, is likely to come from investment. The conclusion of this chapter is that the recovery of investment is likely to be weak, thereby contributing to an overall anaemic recovery. But there are long-term risks both on the upside and on downside.

Chapters 7 and 8 focus on the housing market and consumer behaviour. Chapter 7 analyses the US residential investment and the housing market; the latter is of course an important component of personal sector wealth. A thorough analysis is given of the role of the housing market in contributing to consumer resilience in the aftermath of the internet bubble and also its role in the current downturn. A model of the housing market is then presented that enables the quantification of the prospects and long-term risks of the housing market. Chapter 7 shows that long-term interest rates are the single most important determinant of the housing market; thus, the importance of running the housing market model simultaneously with the entire macro-financial model. The conclusion that emerges from this chapter is that easy fiscal and monetary policy may resuscitate the housing market for a while, but at the expense of increasing the risks for another plunge later on. Chapter 8 is devoted to consumption, which is the biggest component of demand in the economy. The fortunes of households depend on the corporate sector and fiscal as well as monetary policy. Consumer decisions on how much to spend depend on wages, employment, inflation, taxes and subsidies, interest rates, the net wealth of the personal sector, unemployment and confidence. Hence, the analysis of all previous chapters is important in analysing consumption. A full model of consumption is presented and is run simultaneously with the entire model to assess the prospects and long-term risks of consumption. The conclusion of this chapter is that consumption is likely to contribute to an anaemic recovery for the overall economy. Moreover, expansionary policies in 2010 pose long-term risks to consumption.

Chapter 9 is devoted to export demand as another determinant of growth in the economy. This involves an analysis of the world economy, which we highlight by considering the role of a US-led world recovery. The chapter investigates the determinants of exports in the euro area and Japan and the feedback to the US. Competitiveness plays an important role in exports and the chapter analyses its gains and losses as well as consequences for G-3 exports. Strong growth in the US in 2010 is likely to boost exports throughout the rest of the world, including the euro area, and despite serious losses in the latter's competitiveness. The chapter concludes that a US-led world recovery would boost US exports and that, in turn, strong US exports diminish the need for yet another fiscal package to boost the economy.

Chapter 10 considers the implications of the economy for the dollar. Both a theoretical and an empirical model are put forward to analyse the dollar trends. The theoretical model is based on earlier work by one of us, Elias Karakitsos, which emphasises the role of the US as a leader in a game-theoretic framework. This framework provides new insights for dollar trends. It asserts that none of the variables of the small open economy model or the two-country model are relevant in the dollar determination. The empirical model is based on the theoretical model and is part of the K-Model that predicted in 2002 the collapse of the dollar with accuracy.

The analysis of all previous chapters culminates in Chapter 11 in an investigation of the prospects and long-term risks of the bond and equity markets. The models for bonds and equities are presented in some detail so that the reader can appreciate how they are expected to perform and why. But the emphasis is again on the risks to financial markets from easy fiscal and monetary policy in 2010. With growth below potential output, bond yields are likely to rise gently in 2010, but sharply beyond the forecast period to the critical levels that threaten to tumble the economy back to recession. The outlook for the equity market is that the current rally is yet another bear market rally. But the length of this bear market rally and its likely gains depend on the policies that will be pursued in 2010. If the policymakers choose to drain the excessive liquidity and impose fiscal austerity, then the equity rally will fizzle out, but will not develop into a bear market. A significant correction, though, is in order. If policymakers choose to bolster the recovery, then the equity market rally will continue for one or two more years, but at the expense of another bear market when the economy falls into recession that will take the S&P 500 to a lower bottom than the 666 hit in 2009, around 450.

Such events are likely to happen beyond the period of analysis of the current study. With fast growth, bond yields will remain lower throughout the two-year period and the housing market may be spared from collapse. This may as appear to be a good excuse for yet another fiscal package. Unfortunately, growth below trend for a number of years is preferable to another cycle of boom and bust.

6 The macroeconomic model employed for the purposes of the book

In pursuing the objectives of the book we make a great deal of use of a macro-econometric model which is utilised throughout the book. This has been developed by one of us (Elias Karakitsos; the model is referred to in the book as the K-Model) and its essentials are summarised in the book as appropriate. The K-Model is a proprietary model that depicts the interaction of the macro economy with financial markets, in particular, money, bonds, equities and foreign currency for the US.

The K-Model was developed and perfected by Elias Karakitsos over the course of the past thirty years or so, and, in its various forms, it has been used to provide advice to HM Treasury, the House of Commons, the European Commission, the Brookings Institution and major financial institutions including Citigroup, Allianz, Oppenheimer, Crédit Agricole, Standard Chartered, Abbey National, Kredit Bank, Nestlé Pension Funds and corporations such as British Airways. Interested readers wishing to obtain more and specific details, in addition to what is explained throughout this book, of the K-Model should contact Elias Karakitsos (e-mail: eliask@guildhall.gg).

The estimated relationships of the K-Model are well specified with satisfactory statistics/diagnostics. The model structure is stable in that it is capable of explaining, with relatively great precision, the behaviour of investment over the span of the last sixty years that includes 11 business cycles and over 700 monthly observations. This is remarkable because five of these cycles are demand-led; three of them are supply-led, while the last three are related to serious imbalances in the corporate, personal, banking, government and external sectors.

2
The Causes and Consequences of the Internet Bubble

1   Introduction

On 26 November 2001 the National Bureau of Economic Research declared that the US economy's recession had begun in March 2001. The expansion had lasted for ten years and was one of the longest ever recorded by any industrialised country. In the fourth quarter of 1999 the US growth rate reached 7 percent, the highest in the 1990s. Unemployment fell to a 30-year low (3.9 percent by April 2000), the rate of inflation was low (averaged 2.5 percent throughout the whole of 1990s), faster growth in productivity was recorded, and faster growth in real wages. All these factors helped to reduce poverty and stabilise wage inequality (Temple, 2002). Subsequent data (see Council of Economic Advisors, 2004, Table A33), though, reveal that this is true only for the years 1998–2001. The stock market also produced massive gains, so that by the late 1990s the price/earnings ratios reached record levels for the whole of the twentieth century. Every year between 1995 and 1999 the US stock exchange Standard and Poor's Composite Index (S&P 500) produced an annualised total return (including dividends) over 20 percent. By the end of that period, the performance of the stock market was concentrated in the stocks of large companies and of growth companies (those that had been delivering strong growth in earnings per share and were expected to continue to do so), especially in the areas of Technology, Media and Telecommunications (TMT). The NASDAQ Composite Index, which was a large proportion of technology shares, reached the level of 2,000 for the first time during 1998 and peaked at 5,048 on 10 March 2000.

The years 1998–2000 experienced internet euphoria. Indeed, by 1998 the internet share bubble had become a mania (Lee, 2004, p. 11; see also

Schiller, 2000, who identifies the internet phenomenon as the main factor behind the US stock market mania). The success of the US was the envy of the rest of the world – politicians across the globe were urging their governments and people to follow the US example. But less than two years after the peak of the business cycle had been reached in 1999, the US economy went into recession and dragged the rest of the world into it. The collapse of the stock market beginning March 2000 caused the optimism that had surrounded the 'new economy' to be followed by pessimism.

The mania to which we have just referred was not confined to the US only. It had spread around the world. By the end of the mania, it was actually more extreme outside the US, and some of the valuations achieved by companies in the stock market were even more far-reaching (Lee, 2004). An interesting characteristic of the 1990s financial bubble is that it incorporated not merely the US stock market, but also the global stock market and later on the bond markets. Its impact on wealth (in the form of financial market capitalization) probably represented the greatest financial mania in monetary history. Its international dimension was far reaching. It was a truly 'global bubble', in as much as it affected all financial markets of the world. The reaction of the monetary authorities to the burst of the bubble, in the US in particular and to a lesser extent in the rest of the world, was unparalleled in world monetary history in that they reacted aggressively and pre-emptively, slashing interest rates to historically low levels.[1]

The purpose of this chapter is to investigate the causes of the bursting of that bubble and its consequences. It is also to examine whether targeting asset prices might avoid bubbles.

2   The 'new economy'

Those developments produced what one might label the 'new economy' with its own rules, different from what had been conventionally known. In this 'new paradigm' opportunities for growth, particularly in the TMT industry, were thought to be limitless. This 'new economy' was based on the premise that its composition comprised services, essentially information which became more important than physical commodities such as steel and copper. Tevlin and Whelan (2002) report that growth in real equipment investment over the period 1992–1998 averaged 11.2 percent a year, due essentially to soaring investment in computers. Indeed, Oliner and Sichel (2000) and Stiroh (2002), amongst others, refer to the business investment in computers and related equipment. The former note that it rose more than fourfold between 1995 and 1999, while the latter suggests that US firms invested more than $2.4 trillion in information technology-related assets.

A further important characteristic was that of increasing returns to scale, given that in the knowledge- and information-based economy the cost of producing more units of a given output is very small after the initial investment is undertaken. But above all it was the unexpected acceleration of productivity growth in the mid-1990s that can be construed as the most important characteristic of the 'new economy' (see also Temple, 2002). Using growth accounting the contribution of Information and Communication (ICT) capital (it includes computer hardware, software and telecommunications equipment) to productivity growth can be assessed. Temple (2002) provides a summary of studies that have undertaken this exercise. The overall conclusion of this study is that a substantial increase in the contribution of ICT investment to aggregate growth took place, and that 'the production and adoption of ICT can account for most of the acceleration in labour productivity growth between the first and second halves of the 1990s' (p. 248).

Low inflation and falling unemployment are two further characteristics of considerable significance over the period. This, however, appears to be an interesting puzzle about the 'new economy'. How can low and stable inflation be associated with unemployment rates that would normally make rising inflation inevitable? By the beginning of 2000 inflation was at 3.3 percent and unemployment at 4 percent. The latter was, in fact, below the 'consensus' estimate of the Non Accelerating Inflation Rate of Unemployment (NAIRU) by about 2 percentage points. Inflation should have been accelerating and monetary policy should have been aggressively tightening. By contrast, the Federal Reserve System (Fed) held interest rates steady. US monetary policy authorities resorted to the 1990s productivity growth to justify a 'loose' rather than a 'tight' policy. Greenspan (2004a) is very explicit on the matter:

> As a consequence of the improving trend in structural productivity growth that was apparent from 1995 forward, we at the Fed were able to be much more accommodative to the rise in economic growth than our past experiences would have deemed prudent. We were motivated, in part, by the view that the evident structural economic changes rendered suspect, at best, the prevailing notion in the early 1990s of an elevated and reasonably stable NAIRU. Those views were reinforced as inflation continued to fall in the context of a declining unemployment rate that by 2000 had dipped below 4 per cent in the United States for the first time in three decades. (p. 3)

However important that recognition was for the policy stance of the Fed, productivity growth in itself cannot explain the behaviour of inflation and unemployment at the time. A challenge for the adherents of NAIRU thereby emerged, as Greenspan (2004a) makes clear in the quote just cited. A number of explanations were inevitably put forward. Favourable supply shocks, a decline in the NAIRU, unexpected productivity growth, or a combination of all these factors have been proposed (see, for example, Temple, 2002, for a brief summary, p. 251).

The 'globalised' world economy was another important dimension of the 'new economy'. National economies became interdependent with companies being able to sell into a competitive world economy. In such an economy, the growth potential could be said to be limitless and the 'perfect' nature of competition should not allow inflation to materialise given that 'pricing power' weakened substantially. With inflation being conquered, the possibility of recessions disappeared because no longer would inflation tend to get out of control once economic growth was sustained for some time. The rise in productivity that the TMT supposedly made possible, should have resulted in profit share rising. This, however, could not possibly have materialised in view of the substantially weakened 'price power'. If anything it was higher labour productivity that emerged, which increased real wages rather than the profit share.

In terms of the policy contribution to the 'new economy', Greenspan (2000) distinguishes between the effects of monetary and fiscal policy. In terms of monetary policy he suggests that although it 'did not produce the intellectual insights behind the technological advances that have been responsible for the recent phenomenal reshaping of our economic landscape', it has, nonetheless, 'been instrumental ... in establishing a stable financial and economic environment with low inflation that is conducive to the investments that have exploited these innovative technologies' (p. 3). Fiscal policy also played a crucial role:

> The emergence of surpluses in the unified budget and of the associated increase in government saving over the past few years has been exceptionally important to the balance of the expansion, because the surpluses have been absorbing a portion of the potential excess of demand over sustainable supply associated partly with the wealth effect.[2] Moreover, because the surpluses are augmenting the pool of domestic saving, they have held interest rates below the levels that otherwise would have been needed to achieve financial and economic balance during this period of exceptional economic growth. They have, in effect, helped to finance and sustain the productive

private investment that has been key to capturing the benefits of the
newer technologies that, in turn, have boosted the long-term growth
potential of the U.S. economy. (p. 3)

It is implicit in Greenspan's argument that if the surpluses had not
reduced demand, the Fed might have raised interest rates to cool the
economy down. Indeed, and more recently, Greenspan (2004a) claimed
victory in the Fed's battle to limit the damage from the burst of the
stock market bubble. The claim focuses on the observation that 'There
appears to be enough evidence, at least tentatively, to conclude that
our strategy of addressing the bubble's consequences rather than the
bubble itself has been successful. Despite the stock market plunge, ter-
rorist attacks, corporate scandals, and wars in Afghanistan and Iraq, we
experienced an exceptionally mild recession – even milder than that of
a decade earlier ... much of the ability of the U.S. economy to absorb
these consequences of shocks resulted from notably improved structural
flexibility. But highly aggressive monetary policy ease was doubtless
also a significant contributor to stability' (p. 4).

There are strong doubts, however, about the 'new economy' paradigm.
Critics claim that there has been no big increase in trend economic
growth; this has certainly not been the case globally and perhaps not
even in the US. What actually happened was that the financial asset
mania suppressed inflation in the US, thereby enabling the business cycle
expansion, and the accompanying cyclical upswing in productivity, to be
sustained for a longer time period, making what in effect was a cyclical
phenomenon look like a secular shift (Lee, 2004). Gordon (2000) expresses
similar doubts in his observation that the productivity gains of the 1990s
may be temporary. Furthermore, there is no guarantee that inflation will
remain low either. Given that there was no productivity acceleration outside the manufacturing sector (although non-manufacturing sector companies were often intensive users of ICT), a great deal of doubt is, in fact,
cast on the 'new economy' model. A further blow to the 'new economy'
model was the stock market mania, which actually received a great deal
of media attention. By 2002, however, the stock market fell substantially
so that the 'new economy' optimism disappeared. Indeed, the supporters
of the 'new economy' model have been proved wrong!

While it is true that there is some support for the argument that there
was no productivity miracle and no increase in potential output growth
in the 1990s, in reality the truth may be somewhere in between. TMT
produced some productivity gains, especially in the non-manufacturing
sector (mainly services), and probably raised potential output growth

from 2.2 percent in the 1980s business cycle to 3–3.5 percent in the 1990s cycle. With hindsight potential output growth was 3.1 percent measured from peak to peak of the cycle (i.e. between 1989 and 2000). The advocates of the new economy paradigm have argued that improved productivity raised potential output growth to 4 or even 6 percent.

In fact, equity prices fell continuously between March 2000 and the beginning of 2003. In magnitude that bear market resembles the mid-1970s plunge in equity prices. But it differs in terms of the causes, and consequently with respect to the factors that should be monitored to test its progress. In the 1970s, soaring inflation due to the surge in the price of oil was the reason for the bear market. It eroded households' real disposable income and corporate profits. That was a supply-led business cycle. Now, the bear market is caused by asset and debt deflation triggered by the burst of the 'new economy' bubble.

The 2001 recession was very mild, as it was caused by the inventory correction associated with the burst of the 'new economy' bubble. Although with current economic fundamentals based on quarterly data up to the fourth quarter of 2003 the Standard and Poor (S&P) index may be fairly valued the fair value may fall if the economy moves into a situation which triggers a property market crash. This may very well happen if there is a rise in interest rates. Then poor prospects in the corporate sector may materialise that might affect the real disposable income of the personal sector. The forces that may drive the economy into that situation are related to imbalances in the corporate and personal sectors that they begin to infect the balance sheet of the commercial banks. The final stage of this process involves a spiral between banks and the non-bank private sector (personal and corporate). Banks cut lending to the non-bank private sector (credit crunch) that worsens the economic health of the latter, which is reflected subsequently as a further deterioration of the balance sheet of the banks. As the income of the personal sector falls households find it increasingly difficult to service their debt. House repossessions soar as the recession deepens. Similarly, companies cannot service their debt as profits plunge. Banks respond to this adverse development by cutting on new lending (credit crunch) and the liquidity that the central bank injects into the economy fails to reach the ultimate borrowers (what Keynes called the liquidity trap).

3   The bubble and its aftermath

In the course of 1999 fears of a recession following the SE Asian and the Russian crisis in 1997–98 were quickly dispelled and the US economy grew stronger than during the whole of the 1990s. The corporate sector was in a spending spree on IT, in the hope of huge productivity gains that would allow profits to grow even more strongly. The personal sector was engaged in an even stronger spending spree, buying houses, cars and other durable goods, as well as services as if there was no tomorrow. The Fed started tightening monetary policy in the middle of 1999 for fear that this huge growth might rekindle inflation. But the Fed move was mainly pre-emptive, as inflation remained tamed, and a soft landing in 2001 had been predicted, meaning a cooling down of the economy to more sustainable rates of growth that would prolong the business cycle and allow prosperity to continue without the threat of inflation. But the economy refused to slow down and the Fed continued to tighten with the Fed Funds rate rising from 4.75 percent to 6.5 percent. However, once the economy started responding to the high level of interest rates it decelerated sharply and the pace gathered steam. In the first quarter of 2001 the economy fell into recession. Not only interest rates but also the price of oil contributed to the recession. The price of oil soared from less than $10 per barrel at the end of 1998 to more than $35 in August 2000. The rise in oil price eroded both the income of households and the profits of the corporate sector and accelerated the downswing.

The first signs of strain appeared in manufacturing with a build up of inventories of unsold goods, in particular durables. The manufacturing sector responded in the second half of 2000 by cutting production, shedding labour and slashing investment expenditure. Services continued to be buoyant and consumer spending remained resilient, giving rise to hopes that the soft landing was on target. However, in spite of the huge efforts of the corporate sector to reduce their unwanted stocks the inventories-to-sales ratio continued to rise as sales fell faster than inventories. In the first quarter of 2001 the weakness in manufacturing, instead of having been contained, it spread to other sectors of the economy and the NBER officially declared in November the beginning of the recession in March 2001.

What is puzzling in this story is that the economy fell into recession because of excess inventories. This had not been the cause of any recession in the previous fifty years. But the overhang of inventories was only the symptom of the recession, not the cause. The true cause was the bursting of the NASDAQ (technology) bubble in March 2000. The technology miracle that promised so many hopes and gave so much prosperity between 1994 and 2000 simply collapsed. The budget surplus of the period 1997–2001 may have caused relevant problems, of course. To the extent that it reduced non-government savings, it may have caused severe problems to the credit structure of the system, thereby promoting the bursting of the bubble.

The problem with the NASDAQ bubble was the ever-increasing gap between what is technologically feasible that captures the imagination of the stock market and the harsh reality of the slow adjustment of change in consumer habits. IT companies invested and created the capacity as if all people were to shop from the internet, talk on mobiles with all people around the world all day long and do things that people could not even dream about in less than a decade ago. All of a sudden everything that one could imagine was technologically feasible and companies offered it as if everyone was ready to change their way of lives. Before one generation of telecom was utilised, another was ready to take its place.

This does not mean that the technology would never be used. With time, the economy, the consumer and the society's habits would adapt and the technology would be fully utilised. The dream of the new society where technology would play centre role would become a reality, but it will take a long time. The daydreamers thought that all this change would take place overnight. Dot companies mushroomed and their stock market value soared. Investors adopted the dream and priced such companies as if the dream had become a reality. Unfortunately, most dot companies were making losses, but they held the promise of making profits in the future. For as long as the corporate spending growth on equipment and software carried on increasing the promise of future profitability of internet companies was kept alive. But in March 2000 (after the 2000 computer debug was over) the corporate sector cut drastically its expenditure on equipment and software and with it was lost the dream that the dot companies would ever become profitable. The NASDAQ bubble had been pricked!

The harsh reality is that every bubble follows the same pattern. The bubble is always created by an event that brings about a permanent change in future profitability. Every discovery that changed permanently future profitability resulted in a bubble. The bubble was always fuelled by credit that allowed the financing of the dream. But in every case the bubble burst because the discovery is not made in a vacuum. For the discovery to be fully exploited the overall economy needs time to adapt and the society's habits need time to change. From this point of view the technology bubble is not different from the railway or canal bubble.

The effects of the bursting of a bubble are also qualitatively the same. As asset prices (stock prices, property and land prices) fall the corporate and/or the personal sectors are left with huge debts that must be serviced and ultimately repaid. These debts are accumulated when optimism is running high and asset prices are soaring, as in the NASDAQ case, and reflect the perception of the permanent improvement in corporate profitability. Companies are not worried in accumulating debt and banks and investors are not worried in granting the loans or investing in the companies when the corporate expenditure is thought profitable. But because it takes time for the economy and the society habits to adapt to the new environment the expenditure is never profitable in the short run; and if the government budget is in surplus it deteriorates the whole process. The tragic economic consequences of the burst of a bubble are always positively related to the debt level that was accumulated in the rosy years of the expansion. The picture was very different in 1987 when the fiscal deficit helped to prevent similar consequences. The 1987 crash was different in that there was sufficient spending to keep the real economy afloat; indeed, there was enough financial equity to support the credit structure.

There have been three episodes of an asset and debt deflation causing recession in the nineteenth and twentieth centuries.[3] The Great Depression of 1876–90 (associated with the railway bubble), the Depression of 1929–40 (associated with the electricity and automobile bubble) and the deflation of Japan that started in 1989 and has not yet finished (associated with electronics). The current asset and debt deflation is associated with the telecommunications and internet bubble. In all these cases the process of eliminating the serious imbalances associated with the burst of the bubble took a long time, over a decade. As the recent experience of Japan shows, in a secular bear market there are sharp, but short-lived, rallies that give rise to false hopes of an end of the bear market. In an asset and debt deflation environment the non-bank private sector retrenches, as its huge debt, acquired in the rosy years of rising asset prices, is inconsistent with falling asset prices. The process of reducing debt through saving and curtailing spending is long causing a secular bear equity market. This is exactly what happened in the US recently.

The pre-bubble stock market mania produced a huge increase in investment, and a sharp decline in private savings (helped by the government surplus). Historically, the personal and non-financial business sectors in the US (the bulk of the private sector) had not run a deficit until the 1990s (US governments, not all of them, had run deficits; see Arestis, Cipollini and Fattouh, 2004); subsequently their financial balance plunged into huge deficit. By 2001, the financial balance of the corporate sector had reached its lowest level over the entire previous fifty years. Thereafter, the corporate sector financial balance turned into a surplus, as a result of corporate restructuring. One important implication of this imbalance was the creation of an enormous build-up of debt within the economy. By 2003, total private debt reached a level equivalent to one-and-a-half times GDP, compared to roughly equal to GDP in the early 1980s (see *Flow of Funds Accounts of the United States*, Federal Reserve System, October 2003). Another significant imbalance is the US current account deficit, which has recently reached over 5 per cent of GDP on an annual basis (and by now it is showing little sign of improvement). This has been financed by the huge inflow of capital from overseas, emanating from the desire to save in dollar denominated assets by non-US residents – which resulted in a flood of cheap imports. A staggering $47bn inflow is needed per month to finance this deficit (although one might suggest that this is how much the overseas sector has to export to meet its savings desire). The relevant monthly average figure for the first eight months in 2003 was $59bn, actually up from $47.9bn in 2002. But it slumped in September and October, 2003, to $4.3bn and $27.8bn, respectively, thereby falling significantly below the threshold of $47bn. However, the November and December 2003 figures jumped to $87.5bn and $75.7bn, respectively (data from the monthly report of the US Treasury, as reported in *Financial Times*, 18 February, 2004).

The behaviour of the US bond market is relevant to our discussion. The bond markets of the US, and also of other governments, suffered in 1999 as the internet boom entered its most frenzied phase and the Fed began to raise interest rates. When the equity bubble burst took place, bonds appreciated as investors switched out of equities into bonds. So much so that the argument has been put forward that a complete collapse of the equity market is unlikely so long as the bond market performs strongly (Warburton, 1999). This is possible when central banks keep interest rates low, so that large investors and hedge funds can borrow short term to fund positions in long-term debt.

It may be fruitful to look at the standard income identity as a way of summarising the argument so far:

$$(S-I) + (T-G) = (X-Q)$$

where S is savings, I is investment, T is taxes, G is government expenditure, X is exports, and Q is imports. It suggests that the surplus of the private sector, that is the personal sector and the corporate sector combined, $(S-I)$, plus the surplus of the government sector $(T-G)$, should always be equal to the foreign sector surplus $(X-Q)$. The equity bear market was accompanied by a sharp fall in investment, so that the corporate sector's deficit was thereby corrected to a significant degree, although it is doubt-ful whether this correction is yet sufficient. The personal sector deficit has also improved slightly, but it remains a long way from its historic large sur-pluses. So $(S-I)$ is still in deficit. The government sector $(T-G)$ has turned from surplus to a deeper, so that $(X-Q)$ has also moved into deficit; this, of course, shows the deficiency of savings for the economy as a whole.[4]

In principle, five possible solutions to the problem suggest themselves: (i) a decline in the stock market of sufficient magnitude; (ii) a severe recession in the economy; (iii) a major fall in the dollar exchange rate (in excess of 30 percent); (iv) a proactively large government deficit; and (v) a combination of the four factors to which we have just alluded. The first two along with the fourth is the result of insufficient aggregate demand due to a small government deficit that fails to accommodate the savings desires of the domestic and foreign sectors. The third possibility happens when the foreign sector tries to spend rather than save its dollar holdings, which would also tend to increase US aggregate demand.

The inevitable conclusion then is that the US financial bubble exac-erbated imbalances in the economy: namely, excessive debt, deficient savings and a growing external imbalance. The financial bubble encour-ages stronger domestic demand, but it does not necessarily encourage stronger overseas demand. In the ballooning of the bubble the currency may be strengthened by capital inflow attracted by the bubble-boosted returns on domestic assets, but the deterioration in the balance-of-payments trade and current accounts is not sustainable indefinitely, unless, of course, the foreign sector wishes to accumulate US dollar-denominated assets indefinitely. Ultimately, though, it is conceivable that the foreign sector may not wish to carry on accumulating US dollar-denominated assets. Indeed, 'given the already-substantial accumulation of dollar-denominated debt, foreign investors, both private and official, may become less willing to absorb ever-growing claims on U.S. resi-dents' (Greenspan, 2004b, p. 6). In a general sense, the currency would then fall. Just as the financial bubble was the cause of the (real) dollar exchange rate appreciation, due to investment being higher relative to savings which drew capital into the US, its bursting should be expected to lead to (real) dollar depreciation. But still, there is the question of why the dollar has not depreciated even more than hitherto, as the bubble has been unwinding.[5] Three explanations suggest themselves:

- the global nature of the asset bubble and foreign central bank reaction to its unwinding. The asset bubble was, of course, global in nature. Central banks outside the US also accommodated the financial bubble. However, in the US the monetary authority response was a great deal more aggressive than elsewhere. In the short run, this supports the dollar because of the impression that the European economies are faring no better than the US. In the long run it means that the 'day of reckoning' is simply postponed.

- foreign government and central bank support of the dollar. The bank of Japan has been intervening in the foreign exchange market in an attempt to prevent the yen from appreciating; the other Asian central banks have been accumulating foreign reserves, mostly dollars (the Chinese central bank in particular) and US Treasuries in an attempt to manage their exchange rates against the dollar.
- the exceptionally aggressive easing in US fiscal policy. The federal budget turned from a surplus equivalent to 2.3 percent of GDP in 2000(1Q), when we had the stock market peak, to a deficit of 4.2 percent of the GDP by 2003(2Q), a massive swing of 6.5 percent of GDP. Higher government deficit has been adding to private savings, domestic and overseas; but still government deficit is not enough to meet savings desires. It would appear that the US desired saving rate is short relative to desired investment, and this may be a factor that mitigates the fall in the dollar exchange rate.

The issues raised in this section are dealt with in what follows in the book. More precisely, though, in terms of the three 'reasons' to which we have just alluded a whole chapter is devoted to it, where a different theoretical explanation is put forward (chapter 10).

4   Should asset prices be controlled?[6]

Central banks have an aversion to bailing out speculators when asset bubbles burst, but, ultimately, as custodians of the financial system, they have to do exactly that. Their actions are justified by the goal of protecting the economy from the bursting of bubbles. While their intention may be different, the result is the same: speculators, careless investors, and banks are bailed out. A far better approach is for central banks to widen their scope and target the net wealth of the personal sector. Using interest rates in both the upswing and the downswing of a (business) cycle would avoid moral hazard.

A net wealth target would not impede the free functioning of the financial system, as it deals with the economic consequences of the rise and fall of asset prices rather than asset prices (equities or houses) per se. Thus, it is not a target, say, on the S&P 500 or on house prices or their rates of growth. Although a boost in house or equity prices will increase gross wealth, this is not a one-to-one relationship. First, the volume of houses may increase proportionately less or the capitalisation of the stock market may change. Second, if an increase in gross wealth is matched by a corresponding increase in debt or in disposable income net wealth will not increase. In the last two years of the house bubble gross wealth increased but net wealth decreased. A wealth target would also help to control liquidity and thus avoid future crises. The woes of the current crisis have their roots in the excessive liquidity that has financed a number of bubbles over the past ten years. This liquidity is the outcome of 'bad' financial engineering that spilled over to other banks and the personal sector through securitisation; and an over-accommodating monetary policy in the last ten years in view of the type of monetary policy pursued over the period (Arestis, 2007; Arestis and Karakitsos, 2009b). Hence, targeting net wealth will also help control liquidity, without interfering with the financial engineering of banks.

4.1   Targeting net wealth

One can sympathise with those who argue that central banks should not rescue speculators, careless investors, or banks when bubbles burst because they encouraged the sale (purchase) of assets in the upswing of the economic cycle. A rescue encourages one-way bets on future bubbles, as investors expect central banks to bail them out in an economic downswing. Many commentators during the current crisis have advocated policies that avoid moral hazard. As custodians of the financial system, central bankers share this concern, but they must act when markets are dysfunctional. In the current crisis they have injected temporary liquidity and provided direct loans to banks in trouble. In the beginning (of the crisis) they refrained from lowering interest rates that would make their temporary liquidity injections permanent, thereby avoiding moral hazard issues. As the crisis deepened, however, the Federal Reserve (Fed), the Bank of England (BoE), and the European Central Bank (ECB), although very reluctantly, made temporary liquidity permanent by cutting interest rates. This action raises the issue of whether the central banks are too monolithic by merely concentrating on inflation (an argument propounded in Arestis and Karakitsos 2004 and 2009b). Leamer (2007) makes the point well when he argues that the Fed's focus on issues other than housing led to an overheated housing market whose unravelling threatens to plunge the US economy into recession (which has come to pass). The experience of many countries as well as the United States shows that successful control of CPI-inflation does not guarantee control of asset price inflation. The thrust of the argument is succinctly summarised by Claudio Borio (2008), who labels it a 'paradox of credibility', implying that the more a central bank succeeds in keeping prices stable, the more likely that asset bubbles will be the first signal of an overheating economy.[7]

The standard argument in terms of asset price control is that asset price inflation (the percentage yearly change in equity prices, house prices or land prices) is out of the realm of central banks, as it reflects market forces and any control is widely regarded as infringing with the principles of the free market economy, or, indeed, it is the result of 'irrational exuberance' (Greenspan, 1996, 2005a). Bernanke and Getler (2000) argue that trying to stabilise asset prices is problematic, essentially because it is uncertain whether a given change in asset values results from fundamental or non-fundamental factors or both. In this thesis, proactive monetary policy would require the authorities to outperform market participants. Inflation targeting in this view is what is important, where policy should not respond to changes in asset prices. Clews (2002) argues along similar lines, and concludes that asset price movements 'rarely give simple unequivocal messages for policy on their own' so that they are 'unlikely to be suitable as intermediate targets for a policy whose main aim is to control inflation' (p. 185). Greenspan (2002a) argues that the size of the change in the rate of interest to prick a bubble may be substantial and harmful to the real economy.[8]

Yet the experience of many countries, including of course the US during the period under investigation, shows that the successful control of CPI-inflation does not guarantee low asset price inflation. When asset price inflation gets out of control bubbles are built and while they grow they generate a lot of euphoria. But bubbles ultimately burst with devastating consequences not only for the investors in the stock markets, but also for the economy as a whole. The experience of the last twenty years shows that the adverse consequences of the burst of a bubble hit not only weak economies, but also strong economies such as the US and Japan. Goodhart's (2001) suggestion, based on Alchian and Klein (1973), that central banks should consider housing prices and, to a lesser extent, stock market prices in their policy decisions, is very pertinent.

The way to avoid these problems is to monitor and target the implications of asset prices for consumer spending patterns. A primary candidate for this purpose is the net wealth of the private sector. Net wealth is defined as (financial and tangible) assets less personal sector liabilities, including mortgage debt and consumer credit. The ratio of net wealth to disposable income fluctuates widely in the short term but there is no trend in the long term because to imply otherwise would mean intergenerational changes in savings habits. Net wealth is an ideal variable for monitoring (and controlling) bubbles because it is at the heart of the transmission mechanism between asset prices and debt, and consumption.

Since the end of the Second World War, average net wealth in the United States has been approximately five times the level of annual disposable income. The peak of the recent equity bubble became transparent when net wealth hit a high of 6.2 times annual disposable income. The peak ratio subsided when equity prices fell, but it revived with the emergence of a new (housing) bubble. Thus, the Fed should maintain a target ratio of net wealth to disposable income in the range of, say, 4.3 to 5.3, similar to its implicit target of 1 to 2 percent for core PCE (personal consumption expenditure) inflation. The target range could be revised to account for demographics or to anchor expectations of asset price inflation. Furthermore, monetary policy should be tightened or relaxed to maintain this particular threshold. This action would not only allow asset price booms but it would also prevent bubbles, and their huge adverse economic consequences.

This approach would also help to regulate financial engineering. Securitisation implies a transfer of risk from banks to the personal sector, making banks more willing to promote both lending and the sale of asset-backed securities to the personal sector. Financial engineering enabled the US housing market bubble, and its complexity means that central banks would find it difficult to measure, monitor, and control total liquidity in the economy. A wealth target, however, would mitigate the consequences of liquidity and not impede the financial engineering of banks.

4.2 The merits and perils of wealth targeting

If monetary policy is guided solely by inflation, then a central bank is unlikely to deal adequately with a credit crisis because the volatility of the output gap is greater than the volatility of inflation in an asset-led business cycle. When credit expands and asset prices soar in a cycle upswing, inflation remains subdued for two reasons. First, potential output increases, thus dampening the positive output gap and containing inflationary pressures. Second, cyclical productivity improvements (which appeared to be structural in the United States in the late 1990s) reduce unit labour cost and also put a lid on inflation. But the expansion of credit and soaring asset prices increase output disproportionately compared to the default demand-led business cycle. Therefore, a central bank is well advised to have two targets in an asset-led business cycle – inflation and the output gap – in order to successfully deal with a credit crisis and the consequences of a bursting asset bubble (and despite the fact that its only instrument is interest rates).

In a highly leveraged economy like the United States, however, even these two targets would be inadequate to deal with an economic crisis; increasing leverage means that monetary policy would likely lead to a prolonged crisis and possibly to instability, because the economy responds to changes in interest rates and profitability at different rates (see Karakitsos, 2009). The rationale is as follows. Net wealth depends on interest rates, which affect house prices and equities, and on profitability, which influences aggregate demand and equities. Both of these items of net wealth are related to the degree of leverage, and the higher the leverage, the higher the items' sensitivity to interest rate changes. As an example, consider the implications of structured investment vehicles (SIV). SIV created a shadow banking system outside the control and regulation of authorities, who significantly expanded liquidity (Arestis and Karakitsos, 2009c). SIV activities were financed through the London money market, and their profitability depended on the yield curve (the relationship between short- and long-term interest rates). They were very sensitive to interest rates, and collapsed when the yield curve became slightly inverted by a small rise in money market rates above mortgage rates. Since the asset-backed securities issued by SIVs were held by the personal sector, household net wealth also became very sensitive to changes in interest rates.

Thus, central banks face a much more difficult problem in stabilising a leveraged economy. The credit crisis is prolonged by the heightened response of net wealth to interest rates and profitability, as central banks are forced to move interest rates up and down within target ranges. This response makes the system unstable, and an economy never converges to its initial steady state following a (temporary) credit crisis (see Karakitsos, 2009). Oscillating interest rates from the central bank ultimately cause instability because the economy responds to profitability faster than to interest rates, which are a stylised fact of the real world. Given that the real profit rate plays an important and more immediate role than interest rates in stabilising an economy, and given that the interest rate influences the real profit rate (which is responding to economic developments), it is not unreasonable that the actions of the central bank may destabilise a highly leveraged economy. Karakitsos (2009) has shown that this is indeed the case. Therefore, the response of monetary policy to inflation and the output gap in a highly leveraged economy will likely be inadequate in dealing with a credit crisis. Mild wealth targeting would prove beneficial in this environment.

A wealth target would reduce the impact of widening credit spreads on net wealth, so there would be a milder recession in light of smaller falls in profits and in interest rate cuts by central banks, leading to lower costs in terms of lost output and enabling the economy to weather the bursting of a bubble. A mild wealth targeting agenda at central banks is therefore beneficial in stabilising an economy around potential output during an asset-led business cycle.

We caution that overly zealous enthusiasm for wealth targeting might cause instability and lead to a deeper recession than that associated with mild wealth targeting, despite initially arresting the fall in net wealth. Large swings in interest rates, combined with lags in the effects of monetary policy and the quick response of demand and wealth to profitability, would create volatility that destabilises an economy, leading to prolonged recession (see Karakitsos, 2009). Mild wealth targeting, therefore, is preferable to either no or excessive wealth targeting. In the real world, profitability adjusts faster than interest rates, and economies respond faster to changes in profitability than in interest rates.

We may conclude this section by suggesting that the sole reliance of monetary policy on inflation is highly unlikely to deal with the current global credit crisis in an asset-led business cycle because the volatility of the output gap is greater than the volatility of inflation. Adding the output gap to a central bank's target list would enhance its ability to stabilise an economy around potential output. In a highly leveraged economy, however, these two targets would do little to free up credit, because the economy responds faster to profitability than to interest rates. Mild, but not excessive, wealth targeting would reduce the lost output in a credit crisis as well as the amplitude of the business cycle.

5   Summary and conclusions

Many countries suffered in the last ten years or so from the boom and bust of bubbles and, in some of them, popular demands for action by the authorities have not abated. In this chapter we have dealt with the US experience. We have examined the 2000 US bubble, the related issue of the 'new economy' paradigm, the aftermath of the bubble, concentrating on its consequences, before dealing with the issue of how we might tackle it. We have suggested that asset price inflation targeting may be both desirable and feasible and in no way conflicts with other policy objectives of the central bank, as for example in the case of inflation targeting.[9]

The process of asset price inflation targeting involves monitoring and targeting the implications of asset prices on the spending patterns of consumers and companies, rather than asset prices themselves. It would simply be unacceptable for a central bank to have a target for one of the main stock market indices. The variable that lends itself as a primary candidate for monitoring and control of asset price inflation is the net wealth of the personal sector as a percentage of disposable income, as it is at the heart of the transmission mechanism from asset prices and debt to consumption. This variable is trendless (i.e. it is stationary) and reverts back to its mean, which is five times annual disposable income for the US. Monetary policy can be tightened when the ratio of net wealth to disposable income rises above a particular threshold, say 550 percent for the US.

Critics of asset price inflation targeting claim that monetary tightening kills good growth that generates prosperity. Such arguments are based on the premise that the lack of CPI-inflation when the economy is overheated is evidence of productivity improvement that has raised the growth of potential output. But this is an erroneous conclusion. Simply, the overheating is channelled to asset price inflation rather than CPI-inflation. Clearly, the Fed never contemplated a rate hike to control the bubble, although its chairman tried to influence it with his by now familiar remarks about 'irrational exuberance'. In fact, and more recently, the ex-chairman of the Fed argued that there is tentative evidence to suggest that dealing with the consequences of the bubble is preferable to dealing with the bubble itself (Greenspan, 2004a, 2004b). The case for asset price inflation targeting would become weak if the economy were to remain firmly on a sustained path to recovery. However, and as this book shows, in spite of hopes of a recovery in the second half of 2009 and beyond, there are still substantial risks to the economy, emanating from the fact that the imbalances that were created by the boom and bust of the bubble have not been corrected. If the economy were to stumble, and these imbalances were reawakened, thereby driving the economy down once again, then the case for asset price inflation targeting would become more pertinent.

3
The Current Financial Crisis and the Origins of Excessive Liquidity[1]

1 Introduction

The prevalent view is that the current credit crisis has its origin in the bursting of the housing bubble. But what is missing from this view is that the financing of a bubble is only possible through a corresponding increase in credit – no credit, no bubble (see Karakitsos, 2008). Thus at the heart of the current woes lies the excessive liquidity that had been put in place in the last ten years or so.[2] This liquidity financed in the first instance the internet bubble, but because there was no deleverage following the bursting of this bubble the liquidity went on to finance other bubbles, including housing, private equity and commodities. Thus, the housing bubble is a transformation of the previous internet bubble.

The excessive liquidity in the 2000s was the result of three forces: financial liberalisation, financial innovation and easy monetary policy in the US and Japan. In the US, Alan Greenspan injected liquidity and cut interest rates following the Asian-Russian crisis of 1997–98, which was only partially drained later on. Afraid of deflation in the aftermath of the burst of the internet bubble, Alan Greenspan cut interest rates from 6.5 percent to 1 percent and injected huge liquidity. More important, he was late and slow in draining that liquidity and reversing the rate cuts from the middle of 2004. Ben Bernanke has imitated Alan Greenspan and injected further liquidity following the credit crisis that erupted in the summer of 2007. This liquidity financed the last and most pronounced phase of the commodity bubble in the first half of 2008 – for example, pushing the price of oil to \$147 per barrel. The commodity bubble was the last one in the current cycle, as it affected CPI-inflation. Whereas central banks are loath in hiking rates to curb asset price inflation, a surge in CPI-inflation falls squarely into their realm. The surge in commodity prices forced some central banks, like the ECB, to tighten monetary policy, whereas it delayed others, like the Fed and the Bank of England, from the urgently needed rate cuts, thus contributing to the downturn in the second half of 2008. The acceleration of the economic downturn in the third quarter of 2008 burst the commodity bubble and demolished the myth of decoupling between developing and developed countries.

The Bank of Japan has also contributed to this huge liquidity by printing money aggressively over the period 2001 to 2006 through buying back government bonds from financial institutions. The monetary base increased at nearly 20 percent per annum in the three years to 2004, in what is called the era of 'quantitative easing'. But even before that the monetary base was increasing at 7 percent per annum in 1993–99. This huge liquidity bolstered the yen 'carry-trade', which acquired its own momentum by leading into yen depreciation that further bolstered yen carry-trade.

It is also true that financial liberalisation, which had been going on since the 1970s, along with the financial innovations that emanated from that era, played an equally, if not more important role than easy monetary policy in creating the huge liquidity of the 2000s. The financial liberalisation era allowed financial institutions to initiate a new financial activity, which was based on the discretion of the banks to dispose of their loan portfolio in accordance with risk management. That financial innovation relied heavily on interlinked securities and derivatives, all related to asset-backed securities and subprime mortgages in particular. Subprime mortgages are a financial innovation designed to offer home ownership to risky borrowers. It is therefore the contention of this chapter that the origins of the current financial crisis can be explained by three interrelated features that have been going on since the 1970s. The first feature is the financial liberalisation policies initiated by governments in both the developed and developing world since that time.[3] The second feature is an important financial innovation that emerged following the experience of financial liberalisation. The financial innovation in question is based on the issue of financial structured products, such as Collateralised Debt Obligations (CDOs), that played a key role in the swelling of the subprime market. Other forms of asset-backed securities were also issued related to commercial real estate, auto loans and student loans, whereas credit default swaps (CDSs) were issued to insure investors against the risk of default of the issuer.

The third feature springs from the type of new economic policies pursued by a significant number of central banks around the world, which aspire to the New Consensus in Macroeconomics (see, for example,

Arestis, 2007). This new policy is focused entirely on monetary policy at the expense of the nearly total demise of fiscal policy, and, more importantly from the point of view of this chapter, its emphasis on frequent interest rate changes as a vehicle for controlling inflation. The impact of these three types of development has been the creation of enormous liquidity and household debt in the major economies, but in the US and UK in particular, which has reached unsustainable magnitudes and produced the current crisis. This chapter relies on these three features for a possible explanation of the origins of the current crisis. But the root of the current financial crisis is the creation and subsequent developments in the subprime mortgage market, the focus of this chapter.

We begin with a brief discussion of financial liberalisation in section 2. This is followed in section 3 by an extensive discussion of the financial innovation, the subprime mortgage market, which helped to promote the climate for the financial crisis of August 2007. Section 4 is devoted to the current economic policies as an additional potential source of the current financial crisis. Section 5 attempts to derive lessons from the current financial crisis. Section 6 summarises and concludes.

2   Financial liberalisation

Ever since 1975 there has been a period, which we may label as neoliberalism, or Washington Consensus or globalisation consensus. The main characteristic of this period has been financial deregulation and free capital mobility, or, more succinctly, financial liberalisation. This is justified by the 'efficient markets hypothesis', which assumes that all unfettered markets clear continuously thereby making disequilibria, such as bubbles, highly unlikely. Economic policy designed to eliminate bubbles would lead to 'financial repression', a very bad outcome in this view. The principle of financial liberalisation is based on the premise that the financial sector of an economy provides real services, whereby financial instruments, markets and institutions arise to ameliorate market frictions: they can mitigate the effects of incomplete information and transaction costs. The early experience of countries, which went through financial liberalisation, leads to the conclusion that what happened in the relevant economies was that financial liberalisation typically unleashed a massive demand for credit by households and firms that was not offset by a comparable increase in the saving rate. Loan rates rose as households demanded more credit to finance their purchases of consumer durables, and banks were very happy to oblige. In terms of bank behaviour, banks increased deposit and lending rates to compensate for losses attributable to loan defaults. High real interest rates completely failed to increase savings or boost investment – they actually fell as a proportion of GNP over the period. The only type of savings that *did* increase was foreign savings, i.e. external debt. This, however, made the 'liberalised' economies more vulnerable to oscillations in the international economy, increasing the debt/asset ratio and thus service obligations and promoting the debt crises experienced in the 1980s and 1990s. Financial liberalisation thus managed to displace domestic for international markets. Long-term productive investment never materialised either. Instead, short-term speculative activities flourished whereby firms adopted risky financial strategies, thereby causing banking crises and economic collapse.

Despite, however, the early troublesome attempts at financial liberalisation, and the increasing problems and scepticism surrounding the financial liberalisation thesis over the years since its inauguration, it nevertheless had a relatively early impact on development policy through the work of the IMF and the World Bank. The latter two institutions, perhaps in their traditional role as promoters of what were claimed to be free market conditions, were keen to encourage financial liberalisation policies in developing countries as part of more general reforms or stabilisation programmes. But the near unanimity of the international agencies on the benefits of financial liberalisation has never found widespread support among other commentators. It would appear actually to be the case that financial liberalisation is a very controversial issue. Be that as it may, when events following the implementation of financial liberalisation prescriptions did not confirm their theoretical premises, there occurred a revision of the main tenets of the thesis. In practice, gradual financial liberalisation is to be preferred. In this gradual process a 'sequencing of financial liberalisation' is recommended. A further response by the proponents of the financial liberalisation thesis has been to argue that where liberalisation failed it was because of the existence of implicit or explicit deposit insurance coupled with inadequate banking supervision and macroeconomic instability. These conditions were conducive to excessive risk-taking by the banks, a form of moral hazard, which can lead to 'too high' real interest rates, the bankruptcies of firms and bank failures. This experience led to recommendations, which included 'adequate banking supervision', aiming to ensure that banks have a well-diversified loan portfolio, 'macroeconomic stability', which refers to low and stable inflation and a sustainable fiscal deficit, and sequencing of financial reforms.

These *post hoc* theoretical revisions were thought sufficient to defend the original thesis of a disappointing empirical record. Despite all these modifications, however, there is no doubt that the proponents of the financial liberalisation thesis do not even contemplate abandoning it. No amount of revision has changed the objective of the thesis, which is to pursue the *optimal* path to financial liberalisation, free from any political – that is, state – intervention. We suggest that it was essentially the financial liberalisation era which promoted the financial innovation that caused the current financial crisis along with the new monetary policy as argued below.

3   Financial innovations

A new financial development emerged following the financial liberalisation era, which has played an equally, if not more important role than easy monetary policy in creating the huge liquidity and debt of the 2000s. In terms of financial liberalisation in the US, the repeal of the US 1933 Glass–Steagall Act in 1999 was an important event. The repeal of that act allowed for the merging of commercial and investment banking and thereby enabled financial institutions to separate loan origination from loan portfolio.[4] Banks were no longer obliged to keep their own loan portfolio. It was at the discretion of the banks to dispose of their loan portfolio in accordance with risk management. The repeal of the 1933 Act promoted an important financial innovation, which encouraged banks to provide *risky* loans without applying the three C's to each borrower – Collateral, Credit history and Character. This was the case because banks could easily sell these mortgages or other loans to an underwriter, or act as an underwriter to sell to the public exotic mortgages backed by low-quality securities. This led to the unprecedented growth of the subprime market (loans to borrowers with poor credit history or with questionable ability to service their loans in adverse economic conditions) especially in the last three years to 2007.[5] Banks set up Structured Investment Vehicles (SIV) with a simple legal structure (trust or just a limited liability company) that required a very small capital base. This created a 'shadow-banking' working in parallel to banking, but outside the regulatory umbrella and sowed the seeds for the current credit crisis.

That innovation was heralded as

> a movement that seems to reconcile socioeconomic equity with the imperatives of profitability in a competitive and turbulent industry ... mortgage lending has emerged as the key to revitalizing the inner city, opening access to suburban housing markets, and promoting household wealth accumulation. Prodded by policy makers, the housing

> finance industry is now racing to tap new markets for homeownership by reaching traditionally undeserved populations of racial and ethnic minorities, recent immigrants, Native Americans, and low- to moderate-income (LMI) households. (Listokin et al., 2000, p. 19)

The new financial innovation was based on the idea that the borrower and the lender can benefit from house price appreciation over short horizons, whereby the mortgage was rolled into another mortgage. The appreciation of housing becomes the basis for refinancing over short periods of time. Borrowers thereby were able to finance and refinance their homes in view of the capital gains as a result of house price appreciation. The appreciation enabled borrowers to turn it into collateral for new mortgages or to extract the equity for consumption. Lenders are also willing to lend to riskier borrowers. When the prices of houses rise, and the borrowers 'extract equity' through refinancing, lenders incorporate high fee prepayments to secure themselves.

The main characteristic of a subprime mortgage market is that it is designed to force refinancing over a period of two to three years. Subprime mortgages are, thus, short term, thereby making refinancing important. But there is a prepayment penalty, meaning that too early refinancing is undesirable. Most subprime mortgages are adjustable-rate mortgages, in that the interest rate is adjusted at a 'reset' date and rate, where the latter is significantly higher than the initial mortgage rate, but affordable (Gorton, 2008, p. 13). There is, thus, the incentive for the borrowers to refinance their mortgage before the 'reset' date. But the prepayment penalty makes too early refinancing undesirable.[6] In fact, 'no other consumer loan has the design feature that the borrower's ability to repay is so sensitively linked to appreciation of an underlying asset' (Gorton, 2008, p. 19). The subprime mortgage market worked well, precisely as it was supposed to work, over the period 1998 to 2007. And as Gorton (2008, p. 18) reports, the fraction of subprime refinancing, which involved equity extraction, is calculated to have been anything between 51.3 percent and 58.6 percent over that period.

The next question is how the subprime mortgages were financed. The short answer is securitisation, and as mentioned in footnote 1 between 2005 and 2006 the subprime mortgage origination was about $1.2 trillion, 80 percent of which was securitised (see table on p. 20 of Gorton, 2008). Banks set up trusts or just limited liability companies, what is known as Structured Investment Vehicles (SIV), which required a very small capital base.[7] This created parallel banking outside the regulatory umbrella and sowed the seeds for the current credit crisis.

The SIV operations were financed by borrowing from the short end of the capital markets, the rate which is linked to the interbank rate of interest, the LIBOR rate. This short-term capital was then used to buy the risky segment of the loan portfolio of the mother company. The loan portfolio was then re-packaged in the form of Collateralised Debt Obligations (CDO), which was sold to other banks and to the personal sector. In the process and so long as the interbank LIBOR rate remained below the rates of CDOs, SIV made profits.

CDOs are financial securities that bundle different kinds of debt. They range from corporate bonds to securities underpinned by mortgages to debt backed by money owed on credit cards, and thereby cut debt into slices. These slices are then sold to investors in the form of bonds. While the slices contain the same debt, they differ in terms of which pay the most interest and which are at the lowest risk of losing money. Slices that pay lower amounts of interest are the last to get wiped out by losses if there are defaults in the debt pooled in the CDO. Slices that pay more will feel any pain more quickly. This is the way that some high-risk debts can be packaged to receive investment-graded credit ratings. It is a result of the CDO structure and the diversification gained by bundling different debts. At the same time, CDOs use borrowed money to amplify returns. The popularity of CDOs grew as low interest rates caused investors to embrace products that offered the promise of higher yields. Advocates argue that CDOs allow investors to buy into higher-yielding securities while taking on the same risk as they would with safe, lower-yielding securities. They also insist that CDOs are another tool that allow financial markets to further spread risk so it is not concentrated in financial institutions but shared with the personal sector, thereby reducing systemic risk. However, opponents think CDOs are an example of financial engineering gone haywire. CDOs are 'more sleight of hand' than a sound way to generate diversified returns. They are a method for Wall Street to repackage securities as a way to make more money. Indeed, in recent years Wall Street has made millions of dollars in fees through the creation of CDOs, selling them, servicing them and helping investors to trade them. They are vehicles that are generally used by institutional investors, such as pension funds or hedge funds, rather than individual investors.

As a result, these days banks hold few traditional liquid assets, such as government bonds; they are loaned up with claims of varying quality on the private sector, largely based on residential or commercial property. The housing bubble burst when the yield curve became inverted with long-term interest rates lower than the interbank LIBOR rate of interest.

This confirms the myopic attitude of financial institutions in making profits and raises the issue of whether management acts in the best interest of shareholders in the long run. The cynics would say that as the remunerations of management are linked to current profits they have an incentive to make risky investments that would, in the long run, hurt the interests of shareholders. If and when these investments turn sour a new management would be called in to clear the mess. The old management will walk away with huge profits.

The complex structure and highly illiquid nature of the CDO market has complicated the task of credit rating institutions, which erroneously assigned AAA-status to many worthless papers. The overstated credit rating has contributed to the growth of the CDO market in the upswing of the cycle, but also to its downfall in the downswing. This aggravated the losses of financial institutions during the credit crisis. The CDO market, which hit $10 trillion at its peak, injected huge liquidity into the system. This was not reflected in monetary aggregates and, therefore, not monitored by central banks with respect to its implications for financial markets and the economy. The sale of CDOs to international investors made the US housing bubble a global problem and provided the transmission mechanism for the contagion to the world economy and Europe, in particular. The complex interlinking of securities, structures and derivatives resulted in asymmetric information and loss of information, especially so in terms of the risks involved, which unknown to anyone (Gorton, 2008, p. 45). The chain of interlinked securities does not allow the location of the risk involved to be determined in that its resting place cannot be ascertained. Ultimately, loss of confidence emerged since establishing the underlying mortgages was not possible.[8] Interestingly enough, while this interlinking implied spreading the risk around, it resulted in a loss of transparency as to where the risks in question would eventually emerge. The banks were so greedy in providing risky loans that in the upswing of the cycle the pace of accumulation was faster than the pace of unloading them from their books. Thus, when the credit crisis started many banks found a higher than desired stock of CDOs in their balance sheets. The losses from CDOs exacerbated the losses of financial institutions. For reasons of reputation, many banks were forced to incorporate the balance sheets of the SIVs into their books.

In normal times financial innovations reduce risk and convince central bankers that there is a minimal systemic risk of contagion. This is indeed what happened in the first year of the subprime crisis. Prior to the eruption of the credit crisis in August 2007, central bankers on both sides of the Atlantic had underestimated the systemic risk from the collapse of the subprime market. They claimed in the spring of 2007 that only a few individuals and institutions would be hurt with minimum damage to the economy as a whole. This led the Fed chairman to keep interest rates high as late as August 2007. But there was a drastic reversal of that policy following the plunge of equity prices and the widening of credit spreads in August 2007. The Fed injected liquidity and cut interest rates aggressively from 5.25 percent to 0.25 percent over the period August 2007 to December 2008. The Fed also took extraordinary steps over this period to extend liquidity to brokers and investment banks in addition to commercial banks. In the US, when all programmes are put together, the total liquidity injected into the system amounts to $7.4 trillion or 50 percent of nominal GDP. This huge liquidity poses problems for an orderly deleverage of the financial system in the future unless it is drained after the ending of the panic phase of the bubble.

All major central banks have an aversion to bailing out speculators when asset bubbles burst, but ultimately, as custodians of the financial system, they have to do exactly that. They justify their actions as stemming from the goal of preventing the bursting of the bubble from taking its toll on the economy. The intention may be different, but the result is the same: speculators, careless investors and banks are bailed out. Thus instead of encouraging deleverage and taking steps to drain the excess liquidity that has been at the root of all problems in the current decade, central banks rushed to act as lender of last resort and prevent the risk from becoming systemic, thereby posing a threat to the whole financial system in the long run. The Fed adopted a risk management approach to the current crisis with the epitome the bailout of Bear Stearns in March 2008, which set a precedent for the bailouts of Fannie Mae, Freddie Mac and AIG in September 2008, but the bankruptcy of Lehman Brothers, which fuelled the losses of financial institutions and aggravated the financial crisis. After the collapse of Lehman the US policymakers have not allowed anyone to fail, with the latest example being the Citigroup bank.

The Fed, for reasons of moral hazard, suggested a low price for the takeover of Bear Stearns by JP Morgan, which, however, penalised shareholders and not the management that was responsible for the bad investments. While there is no doubt that the Fed response is right in the short run, it is wrong from a long-term perspective. The prodigious liquidity injected since the outbreak of the crisis came back to haunt us through the last phase of the commodities bubble in the first half of 2008, as it fanned CPI-inflation and called for central banks to act.

Some central banks, such as the ECB, hiked rates, while others were prevented from cutting rates at a time when growth was weakening, thus precipitating the downturn in the global economy since the third quarter of 2008. The commodity bubble burst in the summer of 2008, as expectations of decoupling between the growth rate of Brazil, Russia, India and China (the BRIC Countries) and the mature economies were dashed, in view of the international contagion of the credit crisis.

More recently, middle of September 2008, what began in August 2007 with market turmoil surrounding US subprime mortgages became a financial storm of historic proportions. The US government announced sweeping actions to head off wider market disruptions, including plans to purchase distressed mortgage-related securities on a massive scale, as well as a one-year guarantee of money market mutual funds. Consequently, one may restate the problem by suggesting that financial innovations and closer links between banks transformed what started in August 2007 as a liquidity crisis into a solvency issue for the financial sector.[9]

The credit crisis can be seen as unfolding in three stages. In the first stage credit spreads are widening as banks become unwilling to lend to each other for fear of contagion from potential losses on the assets of the borrowing banks. In the second stage the losses of the financial institutions are unravelling, while in the third stage the ramifications to the economy are felt. Credit spreads widened from the summer of 2007, reaching their pinnacle in October 2008. So far the losses of financial institutions have reached nearly \$1.6 trillion, as asset-backed securities have lost around 80 percent of their value. In this process the systemic risk to the entire financial system heightened to the point of collapse, as Fannie Mae and Freddie Mac that hold or guarantee nearly half of mortgage-backed securities (\$5.4 trillion) came to a bankruptcy point and had to be bailed out by the US Treasury. In spite of the bailout of the two giants in the US mortgage market and the near collapse and eventual bailout of AIG, the systemic risk remained high with the bankruptcy of Lehman. The crisis has brought the demise of the investment-bank model and the remaining institutions (Morgan Stanley and Goldman Sachs) ran for cover behind the façade of commercial banks. As noted above, the Citigroup bank was the latest victim in this process.

The ramifications to the economy are likely to stem from the response of the banks to these losses – the tightening of lending standards, the higher cost of lending, the lower availability of credit, and the hoarding of money balances. The only certain way that banks will get out of this mess in the long run is through a very steep yield curve in government bonds. The Fed adopted a zero interest rate policy, while the 10-year yield is hovering around 3.5 percent, offering a 3.5 percent gain in the banking system. The financial crisis will impair growth and reduce the rate of growth of potential output, as even companies with good ideas and profitable new products will be denied credit. But the financial crisis will enable households and companies to curb their debt through time, thus rebuilding their impaired balance sheets. But as asset prices (houses and equities) fall, the net wealth of the personal sector will be further eroded, thus forcing the savings ratio up and consumer expenditure down. With consumption falling companies will respond by shedding their labour force, cutting production and curtailing investment expenditure, thus further harming the incomes of households. This is the asset and debt deflation process.

4 Current economic policies

The major policy implication is that monetary policy has been upgraded in the form of interest rate policy, while fiscal policy has been downgraded. One major objective of policy is 'maintaining price stability' (King, 2005, p. 2). King (2005) also argues that 'Far from being ineffective, a monetary policy aimed at price stability has proved to be the key to successful management of aggregate demand' (p. 2). However, the experience since the credit crisis of August 2007 does not seem to validate this claim. Be that as it may, this policy is undertaken through Inflation Targeting (IT). Fiscal policy, by contrast, over the last ten years has been concerned with broadly balancing government expenditure and taxation. Its importance has been effectively downgraded as an active instrument of economic policy. The downgrade of fiscal policy is based on the usual arguments of crowding out government deficits and thus the ineffectiveness of fiscal policy has relied on an assumption (see, however, Arestis and Sawyer, 2003, for a critique and a different view).

One important assumption that permits monetary policy to have the effect as described above and within the NCM theoretical framework is the existence of temporary nominal rigidities in the form of sticky wages, prices and information, or some combination of these frictions. This means that the central bank, by manipulating the nominal rate of interest, is able to influence real interest rates and hence real spending in the short run. In the long run, changes in interest rates affect inflation but have no impact on real spending or the level of economic activity, or indeed the level of unemployment; all of which can only be affected by the supply side of the economy.

The financial liberalisation policies pursued since the 1970s and the financial innovation, both discussed above, have produced excessive liquidity in the system, thereby substantially increasing household debt. The excessive liquidity, which became apparent by the early 2000s, was not merely the result of financial innovation, itself promoted by the financial liberalisation experience as discussed above. It has also come about from the type of monetary policy following the introduction of the new monetary policy framework, the focus of which, as shown above, is the frequent manipulation of interest rates. In the US at the time, the Fed chairman, Alan Greenspan, injected liquidity and cut interest rates following the Asian-Russian crises of 1997 and 1998, which was only partially drained later on. In view of the deflation dangers in the aftermath of the bursting of the internet bubble in March 2000, Alan Greenspan cut interest rates in a sequence of steps from 6.5 percent to 1.0 percent and injected huge liquidity into the US economy. Moreover, he was late and slow in draining that liquidity and reversing the rate cuts. Ben Bernanke, Greenspan's successor, pursued a similar policy, injecting further liquidity following the ongoing credit crisis that erupted in the summer of 2007.

This experience has resulted in a serious build-up of household debt and asset holdings. Looking at debt statistics, we find that between 1998 and 2002 outstanding household debt, including mortgage debt, in the UK was 72.0 percent of GDP; between 2003 and 2007 it shot up to 94.3 percent of GDP. In the same periods as above, outstanding household debt jumped from 76.7 percent to GDP to 97.6 percent of GDP in the case of the US. And in the euro area it rose from 48.5 percent to 56.6 percent (see BIS, 2008, p. 29). Clearly, this has made household expenditure more sensitive to short-term changes in interest rate. Consequently, the dangers with the current conduct of monetary policy are clear: frequent changes in interest rates can have serious effects: low interest rates cause bubbles; high interest rates work through applying economic pressures on vulnerable social groups. Monetary policy, therefore, that depends on manipulating the rate of interest to control inflation cannot prevent the ramifications of the credit crisis. It surely is the case that regulatory and prudential controls have become extremely necessary.

During the crisis many commentators have advocated policies that avoid moral hazard. Central bankers share these concerns, but as custodians of the financial system they have to take action when markets are dysfunctional. In the current crisis they have injected temporary liquidity and provided direct loans to banks in trouble, albeit at a penal rate. At the beginning of the crisis central banks refrained from lowering rates that would turn the temporary injection of liquidity into a permanent one, thereby avoiding issues of moral hazard. But as the crisis deepened the Fed, but not the ECB, cut interest rates and turned temporary liquidity into permanent. This raises the issue of whether in concentrating merely on inflation a central bank is rather too monolithic in its approach. The Fed's focus on issues other than housing has given us the overheated housing market this decade, the unravelling of which is threatening to plunge the US into the worst recession in the post-Second World War era. The experience of many countries, including of course the US, shows that successful control of CPI-inflation does not guarantee control of asset price inflation. The thrust of the argument is the 'paradox of credibility', implying that the more a central bank succeeds in keeping prices stable, the more likely that signs of an overheating economy will show up first in asset bubbles.

5   Lessons from the current financial crisis

The US housing market was the primary cause of the credit crisis. That was helped by the huge liquidity that was put in place by 'bad' financial engineering and some mistakes in the conduct of monetary policy, especially in the US. As a result of both forces the global economy is now in the midst of a very serious downturn. The liquidity to which we have just referred to has financed a number of bubbles in the last ten years with a major impact on the economy (internet, housing, and commodities) and a few more (shipping and private equity) with a minor impact on the economy. From a European perspective micro-economic fundamentals and country-specific factors have differentiated the countries in the euro-zone area with housing bubbles emerging in some countries, like Spain, but not in others, like Germany. Thus, what is needed is both a macro- and micro-perspective to understand the full story.

From a macro-perspective liquidity is the real culprit. Without this excessive liquidity there would have been no bubbles – no credit, no bubble. Although one might point to some errors on the part of the Fed in removing the accommodation bias on a number of occasions over the past ten years, 'bad' financial engineering has played a far more important role in creating this prodigious liquidity. 'Bad' financial engineering purports to find loopholes in the law and the regulatory environment to make money. 'Bad' financial engineering has resulted in a 'shadow-banking' that developed and worked in parallel with regulated banking. The 'shadow-banking' operated outside the regulation and control of the authorities. So whatever was not allowed in regulated banking was developed in the 'shadow-banking'.

The backlash of the greed of financial institutions is likely to be increasing calls for strict regulation of the industry. As the taxpayer is called to clean up the mess of the banks tougher regulation of the industry is very likely to ensue. But from a policy perspective it should be recognised that regulation is backward- rather than forward-looking. Smart people will always take advantage of any given legislation by finding loopholes. Regulators will always react with a long lag to close the loopholes and in some occasions, like the current crisis, too late to prevent a calamity. A better approach than overregulation is for the central bank to have a target on asset prices in a way that does not impede the functioning of free markets and does not prevent 'good' financial innovation. Since securitisation implies the transfer of assets and the risk to the personal sector the ideal target variable for a central bank is the net wealth of the personal sector as a percentage of disposable income, which is a stationary variable and therefore a target range can be set. In the US, for example, this can be a range around five times the net wealth of the personal sector. In this way the central bank will monitor the implications of financial innovations as they impact on net wealth, even if it is ignorant of these innovations as in the case of SIV. With a wealth target the central bank will act pre-emptively to curb an asset upswing cycle from becoming a bubble. Information on the constituent components of net wealth is available in the US with a one-quarter lag, a month after the release of the NIPA accounts, thus making it useful for policy analysis and targeting. In the euro-zone there are huge efforts to compile such data, a prerequisite for any such targeting.

Asset-led business cycles, like the current one, or those that affected Japan in the 1990s and the US in the 1930s, produce a larger variability in output than in inflation. In the upswing of the cycle output growth surpasses historical norms, giving the impression that potential output growth has increased, and creating a general feeling of euphoria and prosperity, as it did in the US in the second half of the 1990s. But in the downswing the recession is deeper than normal, and even more importantly, it lasts for a long time with many false dawns, as in the case of Japan. As asset prices fall the past accumulation of debt becomes unsustainable and households and businesses engage in a debt reduction process by retrenching. This depresses demand, putting a new downward pressure on asset prices and thereby creating a vicious circle. The policy implication is that in asset-led business cycles guiding monetary policy by developments in inflation alone will not prevent the bubble from becoming bigger than otherwise. Monetary policy should be formulated with at least two targets: inflation and the output gap. In addition, there are merits for a mild, but not excessive, wealth targeting. The problem with excessive wealth targeting is that there are three targets and just one instrument – interest rates. Although a rate hike might reduce the output gap, diminish inflation and curb the net wealth of the personal sector, the impact on each target would be felt with a variable lag. This differential speed of adjustment of each target to monetary policy poses perils to the central bank task of stabilising the economy along the potential output growth path. Thus, strict adherence to the fulfilment of each target by the central bank may cause instability rather than stability.

But these are long-term policies, and as such they are not helpful in getting out of the current crisis. On many occasions over the past five hundred years the bursting of a bubble has entailed asset and debt deflation that has triggered retrenchment on the part of households and firms – with severe consequences for profits, the incomes of households and jobs. The deflation process is usually long and painful and the evidence of the last three episodes (1870s, 1930s and Japan in the 1990s) is that it usually lasts for ten years. The policymakers' efforts so far have concentrated on unfreezing the credit markets and restoring confidence in banks by pumping liquidity and guaranteeing bank loans so that the interbank market can start to function again. They have also assigned public funds to recapitalise banks by buying mostly preferred shares and increased the guarantee limit on deposits to deflect runs on depository institutions. In the US the Fed has, in addition, extended credit facilities to non-depository institutions and has lowered the quality of assets that it accepts as collateral for lending. Although these measures may be adequate to ease the panic phase of the bursting of a bubble, they are inadequate to deal with the crisis in the long run, as they deal with the supply side of credit, but not with the demand for it.

The challenge for the policymakers is to break the vicious circle between falls in house prices and bank losses if they are to shorten the asset and debt deflation process to less than ten years. This requires preventing households from falling into negative equity; otherwise, delinquencies rise and bank losses mount; mortgage lenders repossess the properties and dump them onto the market which causes still lower house prices and even higher bank losses. Spending public money to cover the losses of the banks without supporting households to keep their homes and encourage others to obtain new mortgages is like throwing money into a black hole. Hence, the policies that should be pursued are on both sides of the credit market: demand and supply. Unless demand for credit and demand for the general products of the banks are boosted, no amount of money can salvage the financial system. Dealing only with the supply side of credit by ignoring its dependence on demand will be a waste of resources. The hoarding of cash by banks, mutual funds, hedge funds, businesses and individuals is a terrible blow to demand for credit that triggers new losses for the financial institutions, thus creating a vicious circle. This is what Keynes called a 'liquidity trap'. Monetary policy does not work in this environment and neither does fiscal policy in the form of tax cuts; people hoard the extra money – they do not spend it. What is needed is public works. A new Fannie Mae should be created, along the lines of the original model of the 'New Deal', as the current one does not inspire confidence. The new Fannie should take from the banks the loans of all those who are threatened with foreclosure or business bankruptcy and offer them affordable loans to boost demand.

Although the measures adopted so far are dealing with the panic, the policymakers are inconsistent in their long-term objectives in that they want to achieve both deleverage and high asset prices. They should either engineer an orderly deleverage, while at the same time accepting that in the new long-run equilibrium asset prices would be substantially lower; or they should flood the system with liquidity to prevent the erosion of asset prices, but knowing that this would not produce deleverage. In other words the policymakers are not clear as to whether their long-run target is deflation or inflation. It is a hard fact of life, however, that from a long-term perspective the first target is what makes sense; otherwise, the excess liquidity that financed so many bubbles in the last ten years will not be drained and will carry on financing new bubbles. Irrespective of whether the policymakers target deflation or inflation, the forces of deflation are more powerful than those of inflation. So, even if the policymakers wished to reflate asset prices, they might find it extremely hard to achieve their objectives.

6   Summary and conclusions

We need to regulate financial engineering. Securitisation implies a transfer of risk from banks to the personal sector and makes banks more willing to promote both lending and the sale of asset-backed securities to the personal sector. We should avoid the problem of fraud in the subprime arena; the problem has never been with the subprime model per se. It is the financial engineering that allowed US housing to become a bubble. Financial engineering is so complex that central banks would have a tough time if they wanted to measure, monitor and control the levels of total liquidity in the economy. New policies are needed urgently, and targeting the net wealth of the personal sector is one such policy suggested in this chapter. Above all, we should not lose sight of the fact that this crisis is the result of regulatory failure to guard against excessive risk taking in the financial sector. Policymakers must ensure that it does not happen again. Work has actually started to rebuild the architecture and the leading industrialised countries have already put forward recommendations for better prudential regulation, accounting rules and transparency. The role of credit agencies will also need to be rethought, with a greater role being given to public scrutiny. In a globalised world, these efforts will have to be broad-based if they are to be effective. With regard to the real sector it ought to be emphasised yet again that under current circumstances public spending is the most effective means of getting the economy out of the current financial and economic trouble.

4
Wages and Prices and the Proper Conduct of Monetary Policy

1 Introduction

Inflation plays a vital role in macroeconomics and financial markets. First, it is the only variable that is targeted by *all* main central banks. Accordingly, it determines the policy interest rates and hence short-term money market rates, which, in turn, influence the entire maturity spectrum of interest rates that potentially affect all components of aggregate demand as well as the demand for assets. Second, the level of prices deflates all macro and financial variables, such as the disposable income of households, financial and tangible wealth that determine consumption, profits that determine investment, as well as equity prices, to name only but a few. The demand for assets (money, bonds, equities and property) as well as the demand for goods and services is proportional to the price level. Thus, positive inflation pushes up the level of prices and raises the nominal demand for assets and goods and services changing the desired level of inventories of goods that firms wish to keep and hence production and employment. Third, inflation is a key variable in shaping the risk premia in financial markets, which play a vital role in the demand for the various assets (money, bonds and equities). It is through the widening of these risk premia that the current credit crisis has been reflected. Accordingly, the outlook for the entire economy crucially depends on the trajectory of future prices and inflation.

Although we usually refer to inflation as if it is a single variable, there is a whole nexus of prices, such as consumer and producer prices, which crucially depend on the costs of factors of production – labour, intermediate supplies and raw materials. Notwithstanding this perplexity there is a time-dependence amongst these key prices and costs that justifies referring to inflation as if it was a single variable. Moreover, all prices share a common structure – a mark-up on average variable cost in which demand–supply conditions (the output gap) plays an important role.

It is the goal of this chapter to throw light on the interrelationship of costs and prices and to explore whether inflation targeting to the exclusion of other targets, such as the output gap and asset prices can be relied upon to steer the economy on its potential path under all conceivable shocks – demand, supply and financial. In the next section we examine the stylised facts of inflation in the post-WWII era; we also illustrate the interdependence of the various price indices. In section 3 we examine whether inflation is purely a monetary phenomenon, as some schools of economic thought claim, or a mark-up on the average variable cost in which the demand–supply balance plays a crucial role. Section 4 explains the wage–price nexus by using the theoretical structure of the K-Model that follows the mark-up approach to inflation, as this is capable of analysing the risks in the current environment. Section 5 analyses the relationship between GDP growth and inflation from a theoretical perspective. Section 6 uses this theoretical structure to explain the stylised facts of inflation as well as its relationship to the growth of the economy. Section 7 analyses the risks of inflation/deflation for the next two years, which might trace future long-term trends, while Section 8 summarises and concludes.

2 Stylised facts and inflation persistence

Inflation has fluctuated widely since the end of the First World War with most of the time being positive and in some periods double-digit, while there were also occasions in which it was negative (deflation) (see Figure 4.1). The volatility of inflation fell after the Second World War and in the first half of the 1960s – 'the golden age' – inflation was steady and less than 2 percent, leading today's central bankers to assert that this should be the ideal inflation target. But from the second half of the 1960s to the beginning of the 1980s inflation crept up in three distinct cycles. At the peak of each cycle inflation was higher than in the previous one, exhibiting a persistent trend despite the cyclicality. The backbone of high inflation was broken in the first half of the 1980s and although it rose gently in the second half of the 1980s, it resumed the downward trend in the 1990s hitting less than 2 percent towards the end of the old millennium. Inflation increased gently as the internet bubble ballooned, but fell again after the burst of the bubble in March 2000. Inflation started to climb again as the economy recovered

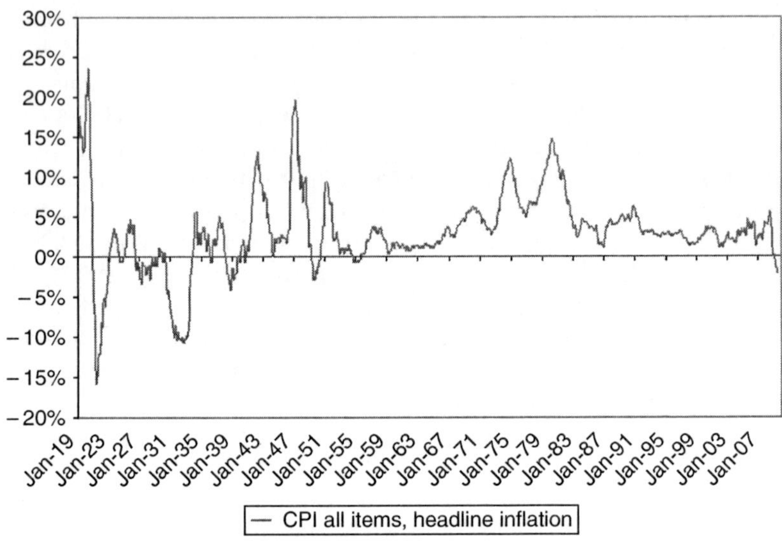

Figure 4.1   CPI all items, headline inflation

and the housing bubble ballooned; it remained elevated even after the property bubble burst and the economy had entered a recession for six months. However, inflation fell rapidly from the second half of 2008 as the economy fell off a cliff, which is now threatening to become deflation.

The stylised facts of inflation refer to the most important price index, the Headline Consumer Price Index (HCPI), as this is the variable that is targeted by many central banks. However, the HCPI includes food and energy prices, which are volatile and some central banks prefer to target the core-CPI (CCPI), which excludes these items on the argument that targeting the HCPI might entail unnecessary swings in interest rates with a potentially harmful impact on the economy. Indeed, the CCPI may be a more accurate reflection than the HCPI of the abating inflationary pressures emanating from the economy. For example, the CCPI fell consistently throughout the 1990s reflecting the trend towards lower inflation, whereas the headline measure oscillated around 3 percent for most of that period. Similarly, core inflation began to increase once the economy recovered from the recession in the early 2000s, whereas the headline measure began to climb even earlier, pushed by rapidly rising commodity prices – in particular, oil – reflecting the increased importance of BRIC countries in world trade.

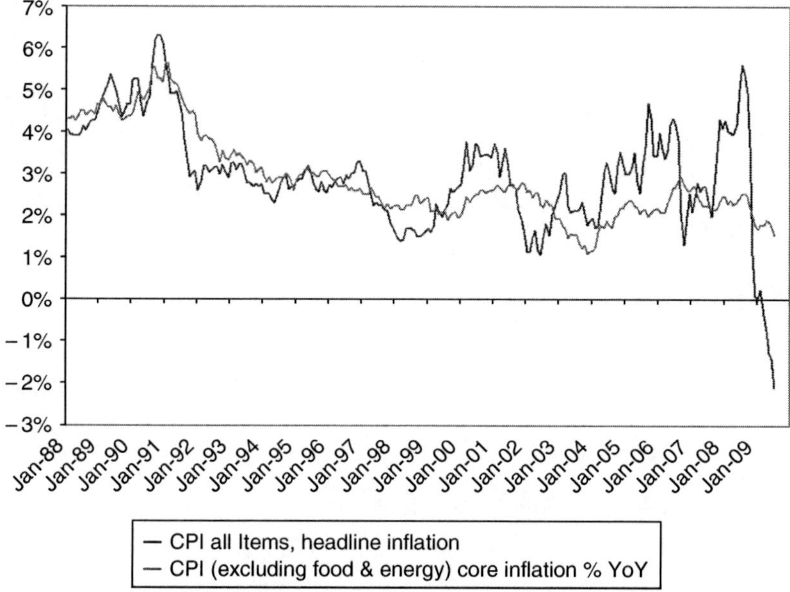

Figure 4.2   CPI, headline & core inflation

But for the representative household it is the HCPI that should be used to calculate its standard of living in terms of purchasing power. As a result of the preference of core inflation over headline by some central banks households might experience long periods of an unwelcome reduction in their real incomes, although on average over a longer period the impact might be zero. A cursory look at Figure 4.2 shows that this was, indeed, the case in the six years to November 2008, in which the headline exceeded core-CPI for most of the time, although the average since 1958 is the same at 4.0 percent for the two inflation figures. It is likely that in the years ahead HCPI will be lower than CCPI, thus reversing the process and the losses in the purchasing power of households.

Some central banks, such as the Fed, prefer to utilise the core personal consumer expenditure (PCE) deflator, which may be more appropriate for a larger proportion of households than the representative household, as the weights in calculating the PCE deflator are constantly changing, whereas for the CPI they are fixed over a long period of time. Nonetheless, the general pattern that holds between headline and core-CPI inflation also holds between the headline and core PCE deflator.

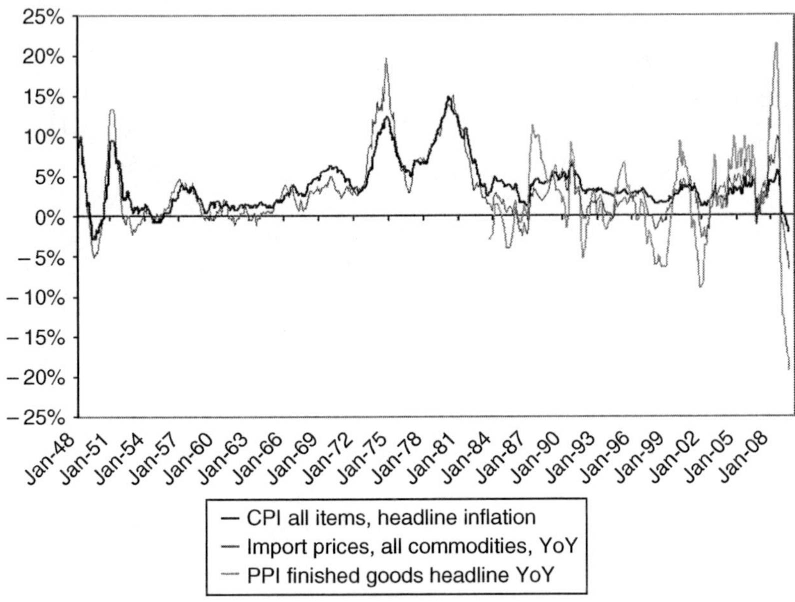

Figure 4.3   CPI, PPI & imported inflation

Figure 4.3 exhibits the relationship between CPI, PPI (the Producers Price Index for final goods) and import prices. Clearly, both the PPI and import prices affect the CPI and fluctuations in the latter, to a large extent, reflect much larger fluctuations in the two determinants. The most volatile index is import prices, as it is affected by the world economy in which many prices are determined in perfectly competitive (auction) markets that are subject to wide fluctuations. PPI is the next volatile inflation index and the smaller volatility in the CPI inflation suggests that retailers absorb in their profit margins some of this excessive volatility either in import prices or the PPI.

Figure 4.4 shows the dependence of PPI finished goods on PPI intermediate supplies and PPI crude materials. Again there are significant lags between the levels of the various PPI indices, albeit not always in inflation rates. These lags reflect the delay in feeding the pressures from one stage of the production US process to the next. But there is a basic principle that is shared by the various PPI prices, namely that as we move from perfectly competitive markets to imperfect ones the volatility is subsumed in the profit margins of the producers in the various stages of the production chain. Thus, an extremely high volatility in

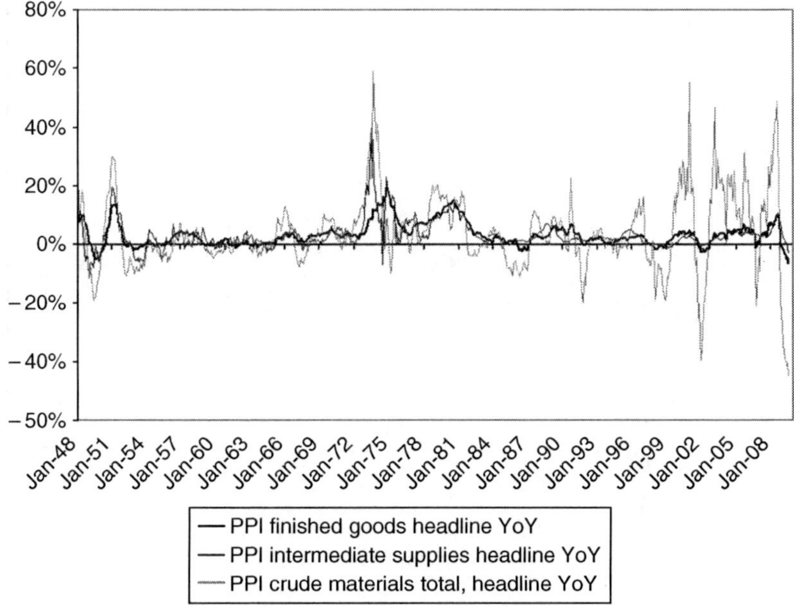

Figure 4.4 The PPI inflation chain

crude material prices is to some extent absorbed by the intermediate supply manufacturers and the remainder is passed on, with a lag, to the producers of final goods.

Figure 4.5 exhibits the strong relationship between PPI for final goods and unit labour cost that suggests that prices are determined on the basis of a mark-up on average variable costs with the labour cost being the most important one.

Figure 4.6 portrays the relationship between unit labour cost, wages and productivity. The unit labour cost is largely a mirror image of productivity, while developments in wages simply accentuate these trends. These stylised facts suggest that the time dependence or the persistence of inflation (in technical terms, the significant autocorrelation of inflation) is the outcome of cost developments in the various stages of the production process from crude raw materials, to intermediate suppliers, to the factory gate prices of final goods and, finally, to the retailers. These costs are affected by unit labour cost, which, in turn, depend on wages and the multi-factor productivity of the employed labour force, as well as the costs of crude material, intermediate supplies and final goods.

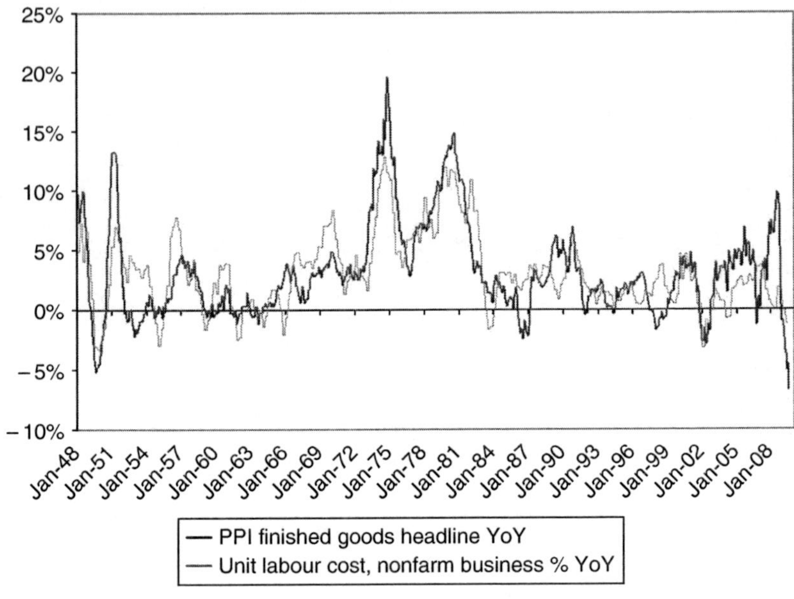

Figure 4.5   Output prices and labour cost

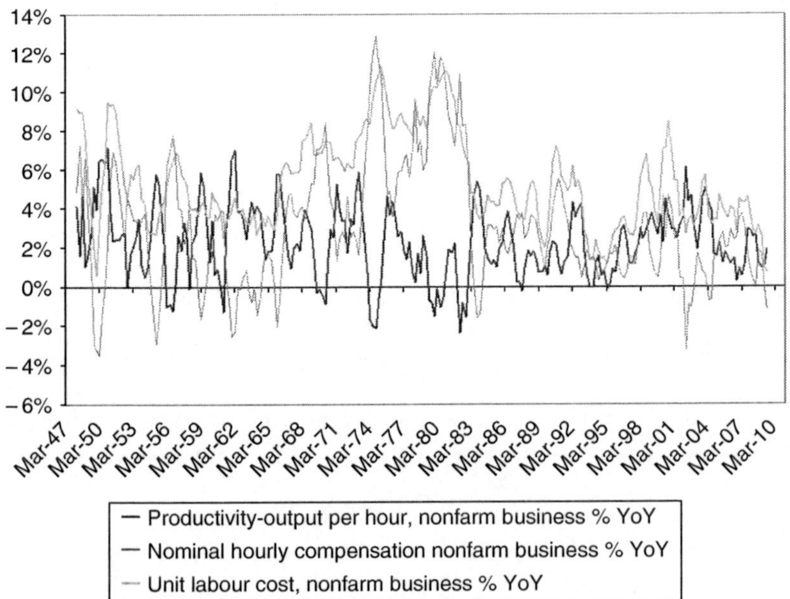

Figure 4.6   Wages, productivity and unit labour cost in nonfarm business

How, then, do policymakers, and in particular central banks, hope to affect inflation by changing interest rates? The simple answer is that all these costs and their impact from one stage of the production process to the next depend on the output gap – the difference between actual output and potential output. If policymakers were unable to affect the output gap, inflation will lie out of their realm of influence. The interdependence of the various inflation indices explains the persistency of inflation, which is reflected in the strong autocorrelation of inflation, namely the dependence of inflation on past values of itself. This interdependence simplifies the picture of inflation and justifies why modern theories of inflation suggest that inflation depends on the output gap. To varying degree the output gap affects the CPI, PPI for final goods, PPI for intermediate supplies, PPI for crude materials and wages, while it makes productivity largely pro-cyclical, thus further enhancing the task of the central banks in controlling inflation through interest rates.

Because of the dependence of inflation on the output gap many central banks would argue that successful inflation targeting has the consequence of stabilising the demand for output around its exogenously given supply, namely it also smoothes business cycles by minimising their amplitude. In some extreme cases, such as the European Central Bank (ECB), successful targeting of inflation makes it unnecessary to target the output gap. However, this is not widely accepted, as shocks into the system, such as oil shocks in the 1970s and positive or negative shocks in the 1980s or shocks in other commodities as in the 2000s, or productivity shocks in the 1990s, might make the control of inflation within a narrow range problematic. From this perspective the additional target of the output gap is usually beneficial and reliance on inflation as the only target of monetary policy may prove in many instances troublesome. Moreover, in the current environment of the burst of the property bubble, targeting inflation alone may be inadequate to minimise the impact on output and the Fed and Bank of England are pursuing other non-conventional methods, such as quantitative easing (i.e. printing of money).

3   Old and new views of inflation

Old theories of inflation emphasise the importance of money – inflation is *always* and *everywhere* a monetary phenomenon. Although in the short run other factors than the money supply, such as oil shocks, may contribute to the surge in inflation, the advocates of this school of economic thought would argue that increases in the money supply are

Table 4.1   A naïve inflation model based on money supply and the price of oil

Dependent variable: D12LCPI
Sample (adjusted): 1962M11 2008M12

Variable	Coefficient	Std. Error	t-Statistic	Prob
C	0.008190	0.002242	3.653695	0.0003
D12LM2(–34)	0.464083	0.029834	15.55530	0.0000
D12LOIL(–1)	0.041363	0.003157	13.10335	0.0000
R-squared	0.477931	Mean dependent var		0.043868
Adjusted R-squared	0.476036	S.D. dependent var		0.028717
S.E. of regression	0.020787	Akaike info criterion		–4.903607
Sum squared resid	0.238080	Schwarz criterion		–4.880229
Log likelihood	1361.299	Hannan-Quinn criter.		–4.894474
F-statistic	252.2083	Durbin-Watson stat		0.055993
Prob(F-statistic)	0.000000			

necessary because they validate the importance of oil shocks – without an increase in the money supply growth the oil shock on its own would be incapable of causing a sustainable increase in inflation.

A crude estimate of the importance of money in the inflation generation process is provided in Table 4.1, which shows that around one-half of the variance of inflation in almost the last fifty years can be attributed to the variability of the growth in the money supply (M2), nearly three years ago, and the price of oil in the previous month, with the former being slightly more important than the latter.

In the table D12LCPI stands for the y-o-y inflation rate, D12LM2 is the growth rate of the money supply and D12LOIL is the growth rate in the price of oil. However, in spite of the seeming success in explaining the inflation variance such naïve models of inflation leave a lot to be desired. The pattern of the residuals, which exhibit significant autocorrelation, suggests that this is not a valid model of the inflation generation process, as inflation was persistent from 1965 to 1980 (see Figure 4.7). This persistency cannot be explained by the money supply and oil alone and it is due, as we have suggested, to the feed of costs from one stage of the production process to the next that created a psychology of inflation. In other words, expected inflation, based on the previous record of inflation, boosted inflation.

The interpretation of inflation as a monetary phenomenon has been challenged more recently, but the dependence on money has been retained as a long-term property. This may be an accurate picture when the economy is at full capacity, which is a feature of the long-run equilibrium. It is also true that the successful targeting of inflation by central banks

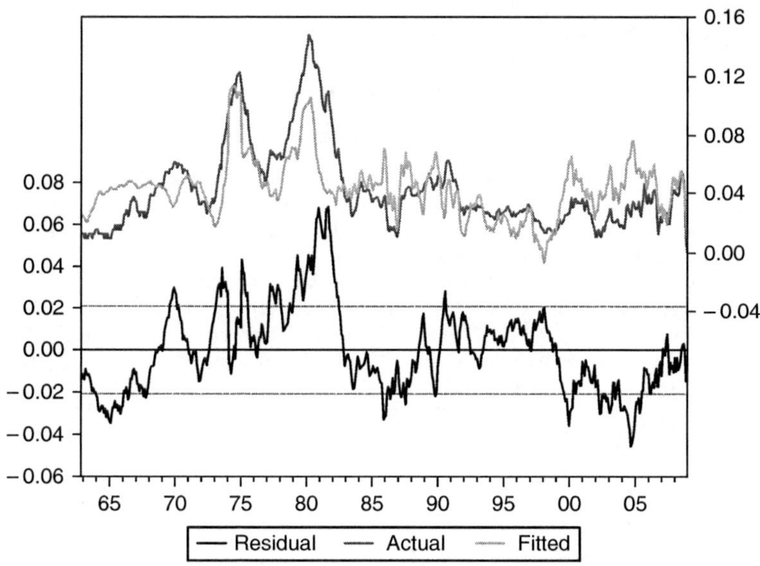

Figure 4.7   A naïve inflation model based on money supply and the price of oil

in the last 25 years or so has diminished the dependence of inflation on money. But, whenever the supply of money has been out of control double-digit inflation or hyperinflation has always emerged – and not just in developing economies. This poses a risk in the current environment where the threat of deflation has made central banks less vigilant or even careless about the control of the supply of money. Such practices might easily make inflation a monetary phenomenon yet again, if the huge liquidity that is injected into the system is not drained rapidly when the economy returns to positive growth.

In modern theories inflation responds to the gap between the demand for and supply of output; it rises when the output gap is positive and falls when the output gap is negative, although in both cases with a one-year lag. In the long-run equilibrium, when the output gap is zero inflation is steady – it neither increases nor decreases; it is a constant which is usually positive. We can show the success of this structure by applying it on the most general index of inflation, the GDP-deflator, which to a large extent is immune to imported inflation. Table 4.2 shows that the output gap along with the persistence of inflation, captured here by the first two lags of inflation itself, are sufficient to explain today's inflation in nearly the last sixty years with a margin of error of only 0.3 percent

Table 4.2   A model of the US GDP-deflator

Variable	Coefficient	Std. Error	t-Statistic	Prob.
C	0.000597	0.000440	1.357388	0.1761
OG(–1)	0.030898	0.010630	2.906673	0.0040
D4LP(–1)	1.441203	0.059853	24.07897	0.0000
D4LP(–2)	–0.456809	0.060007	–7.612593	0.0000
R-squared	0.976775	Mean dependent var		0.035068
Adjusted R-squared	0.976446	S.D. dependent var		0.021837
S.E. of regression	0.003351	Akaike info criterion		–8.540534
Sum squared resid	0.002381	Schwarz criterion		–8.478029
Log likelihood	926.3777	Hannan-Quinn criter.		–8.515282
F-statistic	2972.035	Durbin-Watson stat		2.112637
Prob(F-statistic)	0.000000			

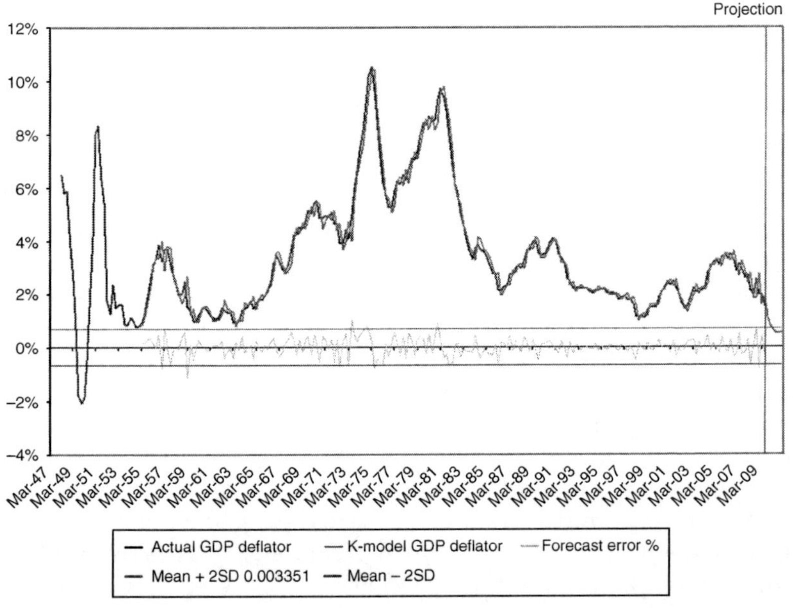

Figure 4.8   GDP deflator

(see Figure 4.8). The pattern of residuals exhibits no autocorrelation, thus confirming the validity of the model as a 'true' inflation generation process.

In Table 4.2 P4LP is the y-o-y inflation in the GDP-deflator and OG is the output gap – the log difference between real GDP and its potential level.

The persistence of inflation is due to an entire nexus of prices and costs that are interacting but with significant lags that feed from one stage of the production process to the next. The next section deals with the structure of the K-Model, which provides an explanation of the persistence of inflation and shows the various channels through which the output gap affects inflation.

4   The K-Model of the wage–price sector

The K-Model of the wage–price sector consists of ten equations – one for each of the headline and core inflation indices.

1. CPI-inflation (CPI)
2. PPI-inflation (output-prices) (PPI)
3. PPI-inflation of intermediate supplies (PPIS)
4. PPI-inflation of crude materials (PPCM)
5. Wage earnings (W) growth
6. Employment creation (E)
7. Employer's labour cost (ELC)
8. Total hours worked in non-farm business (h)
9. Productivity (PRO)
10. Unit labour Cost (ULC)

Companies price their products in the same way, whether they belong to the retail or producer (wholesale) sector. The structure, therefore, of the first four equations dealing with CPI- and the three categories of PPI-inflation is the same. All companies price their products as a mark-up on average variable cost. The differences arise, first, from the degree of competition they face in their product markets and therefore on the ability to charge supernormal profits; and secondly, on what variables should be included in the calculation of the average variable cost. Competition is increasing as we move from consumer (or retail) prices to the various categories of producer prices. Companies in the retail sector are the ones that are best shielded from competition. As we move to producer-finished goods, intermediate supplies and crude materials, competition becomes fiercer.

In the long run, consumer prices increase at the same rate as producer output prices, but augmented by a variable-profit margin that depends on the business cycle. When the economy is growing faster than potential output (i.e. when the economy is overheated), the profit margin increases and when the economy is growing at a smaller pace than potential (i.e. when the economy is operating with excess capacity), the profit margin is squeezed, as companies strive to remain in business and maintain market share. Finally, consumer prices in the long run are affected by oil price inflation, but not oil prices. This implies that steady oil prices have a zero effect on consumer prices in the long run.

In the short run CPI-inflation adjusts to previous disequilibria. If consumer prices were higher than in equilibrium, CPI-inflation would fall; and if consumer prices were lower than in equilibrium CPI-inflation would then increase. It takes almost two years for the market to move back to equilibrium. CPI-inflation also responds to the acceleration in PPI-inflation and the acceleration of oil price inflation. CPI-inflation exhibits strong inertia to past CPI-inflation because of adjustment costs. We may, therefore, have equation (1) as our long-run relationship for CPI:

$$CPI = C(PPI, D12LPOIL, OG) \tag{1}$$

where the symbols are as above, with the exception of OG which stands for the output gap – the difference between the log of real GDP and its log potential level; POIL is the price of oil and D12L is the year-on-year rate of growth.

Producer output prices would increase, in the long run, at the rate of average variable cost, but augmented by a variable-profit margin that depends on the output gap. The average variable cost consists of labour cost, producer prices paid for intermediate supplies and crude materials and oil. In the steady state unit labour cost accounts for 45 percent of variable cost, intermediate supplies for 43 percent, crude materials for 10 percent and oil for just 2 percent. The impact of the profit margin on producer prices is only one-half of that of consumer prices. Producer output prices are exposed to fierce foreign competition that halves super normal profits compared to consumer prices. US retailers are somewhat shielded from foreign competition allowing a higher degree of imperfect competition and thus higher supernormal profits than US manufacturers.

In the short run, PPI-inflation responds to previous disequilibria in a self-correcting manner. It takes more than two years for the market to move back to equilibrium. PPI-inflation responds to current and past unit labour cost growth, PPI-inflation of intermediate supplies, PPI-inflation of crude materials and of oil inflation. PPI-inflation also exhibits strong inertia to past inflation. Moreover, the profit margin is affected by rate of growth of the output gap; an increase in the rate of growth of the output gap augments the profit margin thus putting upward pressure on PPI-inflation. So that we can formally write the long-run relationship for PPI as in equation (2)':

$$PPI = P(ULC, PPIS, PPCM, OG) \qquad (2)'$$

Producer prices of intermediate supplies increase, in the long run, at the rate of average variable cost, augmented again by a variable profit margin that depends on the output gap. The average variable cost consists of labour cost, prices paid for crude materials and other raw materials bought in auction markets, captured by the CRB index. Labour cost accounts for 75 percent of average variable cost, crude materials for 7 percent and the CRB for the remainder. In the short run, PPI-inflation of intermediate supplies adjusts to previous disequilibria in a self-correcting manner. It takes a year for the market to move back to equilibrium, which is twice as fast as in final products. PPI-inflation of intermediate supplies responds to current and past labour cost growth and PPI-inflation of crude materials. PPI-inflation of intermediate supplies exhibits inertia to past inflation. As with producers of finished goods, producers of intermediate supplies can earn supernormal profits in booms and earn less than normal profits in recessions both in the short run and in the long run. We may, therefore, formally depict PPIS as in equation (3):

$$PPIS = S(ULC, PPCM, PWC, OG) \qquad (3)$$

where the new symbol is PWC which stands for prices of world commodities (the CRB futures index is utilised for this purposes; see, for example, any issue of the *Financial Times*, under Commodity Prices).

Producer prices of crude materials increase at the rate of average variable cost, augmented by a variable-profit margin that depends on the output gap, in the long run. The average variable cost consists of labour cost, the price of commodities in world perfectly competitive markets and the price of oil. Labour cost accounts for 50 percent of average variable costs and all commodities, including oil, for the remaining 50 percent. In the short run, PPI-inflation of crude materials adjusts to previous disequilibria in a self-correcting manner. It takes just less than two months for the market to move back to equilibrium. PPI-inflation of crude materials responds to current and past inflation in world commodity prices and oil. Equation (4) represents the functional form for PPCM:

$$PPCM = M(ULC, PWC, POIL, OG) \tag{4}$$

Substituting equations (3) and (4) in (2)' we can arrive at equation (2):

$$PPI = I(ULC, PWC, POIL) \tag{2}$$

In the long run, wage earnings grow at the rate of productivity plus expected CPI-inflation, which is equal to actual, as in the long run expectations are realised. Such an increase in wages is fair because it implies an unchanged distribution of income. However, in the short run wage growth can deviate from its fair value depending on the bargaining power of employees in wage negotiations with employers. In these wage negotiations employees have a target real wage rate and when bargaining they attempt to restore previous deviations from the target real wage rate. The target real wage rate is derived from the worker's perception of the demand for labour (Sargan, 1964; Sawyer, 1982a, 1982b; Arestis, 1986; Rowthorn, 1995). The perceived demand for labour depends negatively on the real wage rate and positively on the demand in the economy for goods and services, CPI-inflation and productivity. In the K-Model the negative slope of the perceived demand for labour implies a trade-off of a drop of 2.7 percent in the real wage rate for a permanent gain in employment of 100,000. The bargaining power of employees is inversely related to unemployment. A rise in unemployment weakens the bargaining power of employees and they are prepared to accept a smaller than fair increase in wages, and vice versa. Wage growth exhibits very strong inertia to past rates of growth. It takes 12 months for the market to move back to equilibrium. We may write formally the long-run wage earnings relationship as in equation (5):

$$W = W[[(W/P)^a - (W/P)^d], U, CPI, PRO] \tag{5}$$

where $(W/P)^a$ is actual real wage and $(W/P)^d$ is desired real wage; U stands for unemployment, and PRO stands for productivity. We may also have that:

$$(W/P)^d = D(IP, PRO, CPI, E) \tag{5a}$$

where the symbols are as above and IP, E stand for industrial production and employment, respectively.

We also specify an E-relationship as follows:

$$E = E(IP, TP, [(W/P)^a - (W/P)^d]) \qquad (6)$$

where TP stands for total profits.

The demand for labour is a positive function of the level of industrial production and profits and a negative function of the deviation of the real wage rate from its target (or desired value). The real wage rate is deflated by producer output prices, rather than consumer prices, because for companies what is essential is the share of labour cost to output price rather than the purchasing power of wages, which is important for employees.[1] In the K-Model a one percent increase in industrial production and corporate profits leads in the long run to an increase of 0.5 percent in the demand for labour, and 0.1 percent respectively, while a one percent increase in the real wage rate leads to a 0.4 percent fall in the demand for labour. In the short run, the rate of growth of employment (job creation) adjusts to previous disequilibria in a self-correcting manner. For example, if actual employment were higher than that implied by the demand for labour, then the current pace of job creation would be lower so as to bring the market back to equilibrium. In the K-Model it would take 12 months for the market to go back to equilibrium. Job creation exhibits strong inertia to past rates of job creation, as there are significant costs of adjustment, such as training and compensation for laid-off employees. It is worth noting that although the real wage rate affects the demand for labour in the long run, it plays no role in the short run dynamics of job creation. These are strongly affected, though, by current and past rates of growth of industrial production and profits. The pace of job creation, therefore, in the short run is affected by the good prospects of the corporate sector.

Unemployment depends positively on the rate of growth of industrial production and negatively on employment and the number of those marginally attached to the labour force, M. Discouraged workers are an important part of those marginally attached to the labour force, which, in turn, depends on the economic prospects of the economy.

$$U = U(E, M, D12LIP) \quad \text{and} \quad M = M(D12LIP, E) \qquad (7)$$

Labour cost to employers depends on wage growth and employers' contributions for employees' benefits, in the long run. In the short run, labour cost inflation responds to past disequilibria and current as well as past wage inflation and inflation of benefits, with strong inertia. It takes almost forty months for the market to move back to equilibrium, the longest lag in the wage-price sector. In the long run, the total number of hours worked by the labour force depends on the number of employed people, the average weekly hours and the average overtime hours per week. In the short run, the growth rate of hours worked responds with strong inertia to the past rates of hours worked because of high costs of adjustment of the labour force. The growth rate of hours worked also responds to current and past rates of growth of employment, weekly hours and overtime. It takes nine months for the market to move back to equilibrium. We may, therefore, have:

$$ELC = L(W, BEN) \tag{8}$$

where BEN stands for employers' benefits; we also specify that hours worked, h, depend on the weekly working hours, WH, and the overtime hours, OH

$$h = h(E, WH, OH) \tag{9}$$

By definition, the rate of growth of productivity is determined by the output growth of non-farm business less the rate of growth of hours worked. The rate of growth of unit labour cost is defined as the rate of growth of wages less the rate of growth of productivity.

The rationale of the K-Model is summarised in Figure 4.9. The wage–price spiral is depicted with the medium grey boxes. The light

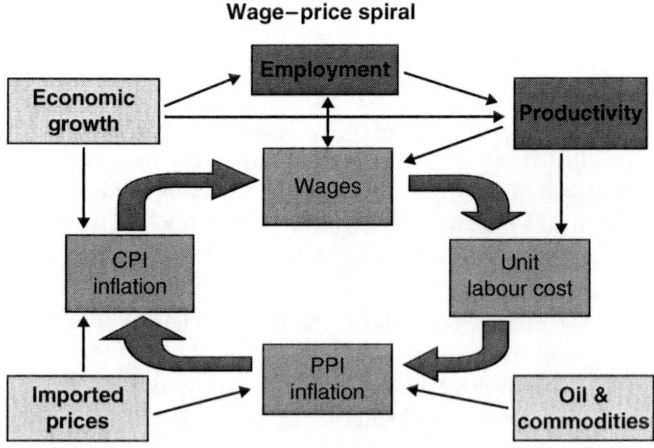

Figure 4.9   The rationale of the K-Model (wage–price spiral)

grey boxes illustrate the exogenous variables that introduce shocks in the wage–price spiral, while the dark grey boxes denote other important variables that provide an extra loop. The rationale of the K-Model is as follows. Consider a shock in fiscal or monetary policy or a shock in world trade that lifts growth. Faster economic growth leads to higher labour productivity in the short run, as employment is fixed. However, over time employment will increase, which, in turn, will lower productivity. The increased demand for labour will raise wages, which will be boosted further by the higher, albeit diminishing, productivity. The higher wages will raise unit labour cost that will be offset in the short run by increases in productivity. However, the increase in unit labour cost will accelerate through time, as the higher level of employment will gradually erode the initial gains in productivity. The higher unit labour cost will feed through into higher producer prices of finished goods (i.e. higher PPI inflation of finished goods) that will then affect consumer paid prices or retail prices (i.e. CPI-inflation). The latter will lead to expectations of higher inflation, which will then affect the new round of wage negotiations setting in motion the wage–price spiral.

The wage–price spiral is usually stable. This means that once a shock sets it in motion it does not become explosive. After a large number of rounds that may take more than three years, in which the marginal increase in wages and prices diminishes in every round, the wage–price spiral converges to a new steady state in which wages, unit labour cost, PPI-inflation and CPI-inflation are all higher than the initial steady state. The stability of the wage–price spiral is ensured by rising unemployment that caps wage growth and falling profitability, through lower profit margins, that curbs the ability of companies to pass on to their prices the higher cost of production. If the wage–price spiral is unstable, it leads to hyperinflation, which has been experienced by many countries. In this case expectations of inflation are rising faster than the curb of inflation through higher unemployment and falling profitability. Since the expectations of inflation are the problem of hyperinflation, what is needed for the system to become stable again is appropriate and credible economic policies.

Imported inflation feeds through to consumer (retail) prices both indirectly and directly. Imported final goods and services and certain commodities, like oil, have a direct effect on consumer prices. Imported crude materials and intermediate supplies affect consumer prices indirectly through the chain link of producer prices. These factors are reflected as the two bottom boxes in Figure 4.9.

5   The relationship between inflation and growth in the business cycle

The essence of the theoretical model in the previous section is that inflation depends on the output gap and the persistence of inflation. Thus, the relationship between inflation and growth is a key for an explanation of the stylised facts of inflation. Figure 4.10 portrays this relationship in the course of the business cycle. At point A the economy is growing at the rate of potential (or capacity) output. This is defined as the maximum rate of growth, which the economy can achieve with inflation remaining stable (i.e. non-accelerating). When the economy is growing faster than potential output there is overheating and when it is growing at a slower rate there is slack in capacity. Hence, point A is something like a golden rule and policymakers aim to keep the economy as close to this rate as possible because in doing so they prolong the cycle and reduce its amplitude.

The cycle is divided into five phases in accordance with the peak and trough of growth and inflation. Point-B represents the peak of the business cycle. This is the maximum rate of growth in the business cycle. Point-D is the trough of the recession, the lowest rate of growth in the cycle. Point-C represents the maximum rate of inflation in the cycle, while point-E is the lowest.

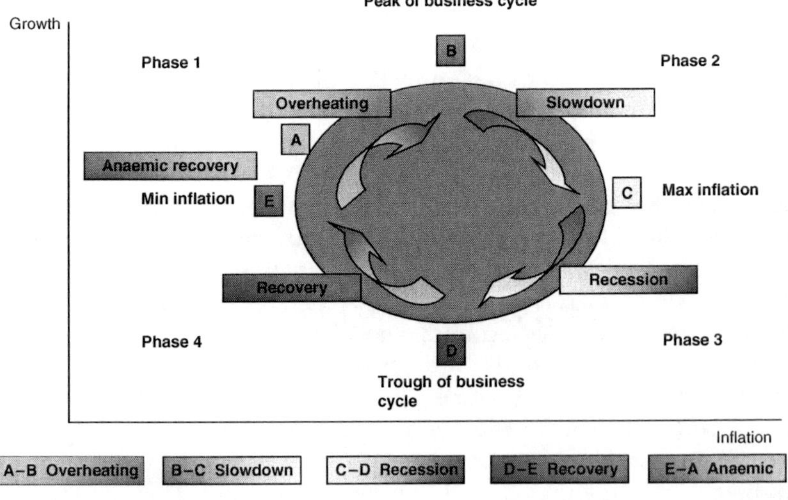

Figure 4.10   Business cycle

The natural course of the economy is a clockwise movement. Phase (I) is between A and B. As the economy moves from A to B growth is rising and inflation increases too. Hence, in phase (I) the correlation between growth and inflation is positive. In phase (I) the economy is overheated and bottlenecks emerge both in the output and input markets. Demand is rising faster than potential output and firms respond by increasing both prices and output. In order to increase production and meet the extra demand firms have to pay higher wages to employ more intensely the existing labour force through overtime (increasing the number of working hours) or to attract the required additional skilled labour force, which however is becoming increasingly scarce as the overall level of demand in the economy is rising. Moreover, as demand is rising fast and firms find it difficult to meet the extra demand they become less worried about losing market share and may raise their profit margins above normal. This is adding to the cost pressures and inflation accelerates. Hence, in phase (I) as growth increases inflation is rising, although with a lag of around one year, thereby resulting in a positive correlation.

Phase (II) is between points B and C. In phase II the economy is decelerating (that is, the rate of growth is decreasing) but inflation continues to rise, causing a negative correlation. This is due to the persistence of inflation or price inertia characteristic of most industrialised countries. This persistence is the result of two main factors. The first is uncertainty. Given the cost of hiring and firing, firms do not lay off workers in response to falling demand, as they are not sure that this is permanent. Hence, in the short run demand is falling while employment lags behind. This results in a reduction in productivity and therefore an increase in unit labour cost. However, in the medium term employment is adjusting to the perceived permanent fall in demand, but this takes time.

The second reason for the persistence of inflation relates to the behaviour of wages, which continue to rise in phase (II). As inflation increases backward-looking expectations boost expected inflation. The more backward-looking is expected inflation, as opposed to forward-looking, the higher is expected inflation inducing workers to demand higher wages to protect the real value of their wages. Wage inflation is not moderating for most of phase (II) and this exacerbates the increase in unit labour cost. Firms respond to the increased labour cost by passing it onto the consumers via raising prices thereby setting in motion a wage–price spiral. In most situations the wage–price spiral is not explosive (i.e. it does not lead to hyperinflation). As unemployment is rising and profits fall the effects of the wage–price spiral taper off.

Phase (III) is between points C and D. In this phase both inflation and growth are falling. Thus, the correlation is again positive. Inflation usually peaks (i.e. in terms of Figure 4.10 point C is reached) when the economy is in the neighbourhood of the recession. In phase II the deceleration of the economy gathers pace. In this process an increasing number of firms are convinced that the reduction in demand is permanent and accordingly fire workers to adjust the labour force to a falling level of demand thereby containing the rise in unit labour cost through increases in labour productivity. Moreover, although the cost of hiring and firing deters firms from adjusting instantaneously the labour force to demand conditions in the goods market, it is only sensible that as the process of falling demand gathers pace they are less deterred in adjusting employment. Thus, unemployment rises throughout phase II, albeit initially at a lower rate. In phase (III) unemployment soars and this forces workers to moderate their wage demands for fear of losing their job and as outside opportunities deteriorate. Hence, the rate of change of unit labour cost is declining as both wage inflation is reduced and productivity rises through the adjustment of employment. It is through this process that inflation peaks at C. Moreover, this process gathers pace throughout phase (III).

In parallel, as demand falls in phase (II) firms find it increasingly difficult to pass on to the consumers the increased unit labour cost because their profits are squeezed. Hence, an increasing number of firms absorb through their profit margins the higher unit labour cost as they strive for survival in trying to maintain their market share. This second force also causes inflation to peak at C. Throughout phase (III) these two forces reinforce each other. Hence, there are falls in both wage inflation and price inflation. In phase (III) the economy is in recession, meaning that there is a positive correlation between inflation and growth.

Phase (IV) is between points D and E. In this phase the economy is recovering from the recession, but inflation continues to fall. Therefore, the correlation between growth and inflation is once again negative – growth increases while inflation subsides. Phase (IV) is symmetric to phase (II), but with the picture reversed. The reasoning for the negative correlation is therefore similar to that in phase (II). As the economy recovers firms are hesitant about increasing employment because they are unsure if the recovery is sustainable. This uncertainty leads firms to increase the working hours or employ temporary staff. Accordingly, productivity rises and unit labour cost falls, thereby reducing inflation. Moreover, profitability is low and the costs of hiring deter firms from increasing employment. However, as the recovery firms and confidence builds up employment is increasing. Thus, as phase (IV) matures the reduction in unit labour cost moderates and the gains on the inflation front are reduced.

Finally, phase (V) is between points E and A. In phase (V) the economy is returning back to normal with both growth and inflation rising. We can thus summarize the relationship (correlation) between inflation and growth in the course of the business cycle as being either positive or negative. In phases (I), (III) and (V) the correlation is positive, while in phases (II) and (IV) it is negative.

Although the natural course of the economy in terms of Figure 4.10 is a clockwise movement, shocks can distort it forcing the economy to move anti-clockwise (or more precisely to loop around) or enter abruptly another phase. The most commonly observed shocks in the real world are a sudden large change in the price of oil and changes in economic policy. In practice, the attempt by policymakers to steer the economy on a target (desired) path, for example to bring the economy back to point A, can be considered as a shock which forces the economy to loop around (move anti-clockwise). Whereas exogenous shocks are unpredictable, the behaviour of the policymakers in the course of the cycle is systematic and therefore predictable.

6   An explanation of the stylised facts

Table 4.3 provides a summary of the US business cycles in the post-Second World War era; Table 4.4 lists the length of each phase in these business cycles, while Figure 4.11 is an empirical version of the theoretical graph Figure 4.10; it identifies the various phases of the business cycles since 1960. There is a difference, though, between the two aforementioned tables. Table 4.3 follows the official definition of measuring cycles by looking at the level of GDP. In this approach the cycle is defined from the maximum level of GDP to the next time the economy returns to this level. The minimum level defines the trough of the recession, which is defined as the period between the peak and the bottom. The recovery is defined as the period of time between trough and the time it gets to return to the previous peak. The expansion phase is defined as the time the economy spends from the recovery point to the next peak. Table 4.4, on the other hand, applies these concepts to the rate of growth rather than the level of GDP. This approach is more informative as it takes into account that the economy exhibits an uneven pattern of growth due to random shocks and equally, if not more important, to the fluctuations of growth around potential because of the fine tuning

Table 4.3 US business cycles in the post-Second World War period

Cycle (peak to recovery)	Cycle length (quarters from peak to recovery)	Characteristics	Recession	Depth of the recession (peak to trough % fall)	Length of the recession (quarters between peak and trough)	Recovery	Recovery length (time between trough and previous peak level)
1948-IV–1950-I	5	Double dip recession	1948-IV–1949-II	–1.7	2	1949-II–1950-I	3
1953-II–1954-IV	6	V-type recovery	1953-II–1954-I	–2.7	3	1954-I–1954-IV	3
1957-III–1958-IV	5	V-type recovery	1957-III–1958-I	–3.7	2	1958-I–1958-IV	3
1960-I–1961-II	5	V-type recovery	1960-I–1960-IV	–1.6	3	1960-IV–1961-II	2
1969-III–1971-I	6	Double dip recession	1969-III–1970-IV	–0.6	5	1970-IV–1971-I	1
1973-IV–1975-IV	8	False recovery 74-II	1973-IV–1975-I	–3.4	5	1975-I–1975-IV	3

1980-I–1981-I	4	First leg of recession	1980-I–1980-III	–2.2	2	1980-III–1981-I	2
1981-1-1983-II	9	Second leg of recession	1981-I–1982-III	–2.4	6	1982-III–1983-II	3
1990-II–1992-I	7	Aneamic recovery	1990-II–1991-I	–1.5	3	1991-I–1992-I	4
2001-I–2001-IV	4	Aneamic recovery	2000-IV–2001-III	–0.6	3	2001-III–2001-IV	1
2007-IV–2009 II		Aneamic recovery?	2007-IV–2009-II?	–3.9	7?		
Average	5.9			–2.2	3.4		2.5
Aver demand cycle	5.4			–2.1	3		2.4
Aver supply cycle	7			–2.7	4.3		2.7

Table 4.4   Cycle characteristics

Cycle trough-to-trough	Phase IV years	Phase I years	Phase II years	Phase III years
1961–70	<2	5½	2	1
1970–75	<2	<1	2	<1
1975–82	<2	2½	2	<3
1982–91	4½	1	3	<1
1991–01	7	2	<1	1
2001–10?	<1	5	<1	3?

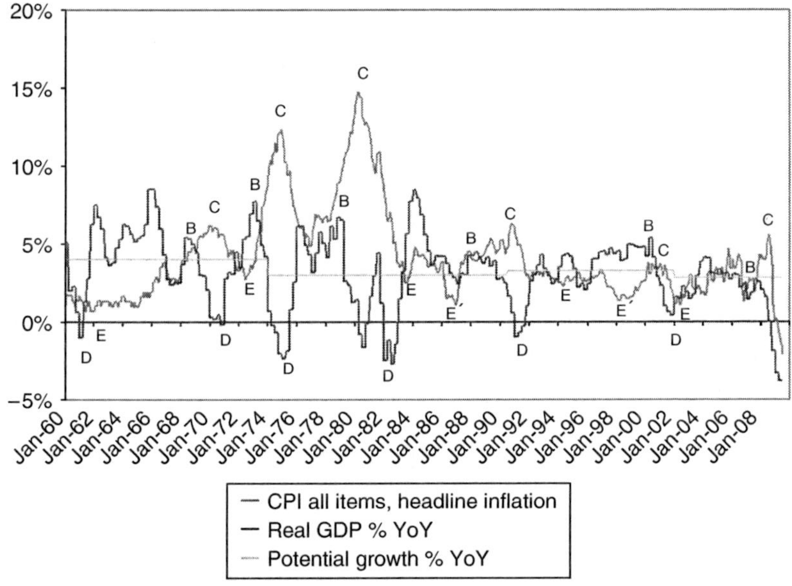

Figure 4.11   US business cycles

of the economy by the policymakers. However, the drawback of this approach is that the peak of the cycle is not easily discernible as it does not coincide with the maximum rate of growth, but with the last peak before the recession.

A cursory look at Table 4.4 and Figure 4.11 shows that each cycle is different and that each phase varies between cycles. The shortest cycle was less than five years, in the first half of the 1970s and the longest was in the 1990s, more than ten years, exceeding by a whisker the 1960s cycle. The length of a cycle depends on its nature and the shocks that might hit the economy. It also depends on which phase the economy happened to be in when it was hit by a shock. We can distinguish three types of business cycles – demand-, supply- and asset-led. The five cycles after the war until the early 1970s and the early 1990s cycle were demand-led. The two cycles in the early 1970s and early 1980s were supply-led. The last two cycles in the early and late 2000s are asset-led.

The default cycle is demand-led, which means that in the absence of shocks the cycle is demand-led. Usually, these cycles are long as demand expands until inflation gets out of control. The policymakers then react by tightening either fiscal and/or monetary policy to rein in inflation, thus causing a recession. The average length of the first five post-war cycles was 16 months; the average recession lasted for nine months and its depth was –2.1 percent of GDP; the recovery was mainly buoyant (V-type) and quick (seven months).

Supply-led business cycles are caused by supply shocks, such as the major oil shocks in the early and late 1970s. Once these shocks occur, the default demand-led cycle is turned into a supply-led one. The average length of the two supply-led cycles in the early 1970s and early 1980s was 31 months, which is double that of the average demand cycle. The average recession was nearly 20 months, which is again more than double the average demand cycle. The average depth of the recession was –2.7 percent, not much deeper than the average demand cycle (–2.1 percent). The recovery, however, was again buoyant (V-type) and quick, albeit a bit longer than the average demand cycle (nine months compared to seven). It should be noted that there are other supply shocks, such as a permanent improvement in productivity caused by the widespread use of computers in manufacturing and services (1990s) or new legislation that supported the introduction and enhanced the adoption of 'flexible labour markets', meaning the ability of firms to fire easily and the weakening of collective wage negotiations (1980–90s). However, the effect of these shocks is gradual and its impact can be observed between cycles than phases. Asset-led business cycles are a relatively new experience with the last two episodes being Japan in the 1990s and the US in the 1930s. Both the early 2000s US downturn and the current one are due to the bursting of a bubble; the internet bubble in the former incident and the property bubble in the current one. The characteristic of asset-led cycles is that the expansion phase is very long and inflation is subdued, but the recession is long and deep.

In the absence of shocks and hence for the default demand cycle, the wild card that decides the length of a cycle is the length of the over-heating stage (phase I). Table 4.4 shows that the length of phase (I) has varied from less than a year to nearly six years; but this is mainly due to shocks. In the absence of shocks, the length of phase (I) depends on the number of soft landings the central bank can engineer in the course of a business cycle. A soft landing is defined as the pre-emptive tightening of monetary policy (and/or fiscal policy) when the economy is overheated, which manages to cool the economy down before inflation had a chance to accelerate and get out of control. Assuming that the central bank is competent, its ability to create soft landings depends on the nature of the cycle. If the cycle is demand-led then it is relatively easy to engineer soft landings. The reason is that if the boom is caused by increased demand, say a reduction in the personal sector saving ratio or a surge in capital spending because of increased confidence in the corporate sector, then monetary policy has a good chance of cooling the economy down because it has a direct bearing on the level of demand. After all, monetary policy is an instrument of demand management. Hence, the likelihood of success is rather high. It involves estimating the degree of overheating a year ahead and raising interest rates sufficiently to choke it off. In a supply-led cycle the chances of a soft landing are negligible because the shock causes stagflation (stagnation and inflation). In such a case the tightening of the central bank aggravates the deceleration of the economy usually turning it into a recession.

The clearest example of a soft landing is the US experience of 1994–96. The Fed tightened monetary policy throughout 1994 by lifting interest rates from 3 percent to 6 percent on the accurate projection that the economy would become overheated that year. The tightening was pre-emptive, as inflation fell in the first half of 1994 and increased in the second half remaining, on average, stable over the entire period. The higher interest rates succeeded in cooling the economy down (growth less than potential) in 1995 (see Figure 4.11). However, a central bank cannot go on forever engineering soft landings even if it is extremely competent. The reason is that the overheating has a ratchet effect on inflation. Every time the economy becomes overheated inflation is creeping up. When the economy cools down inflation subsides but bottoms at a slightly higher level than the last time. Hence, after a number of soft landings, in reality just one, the central bank has to tighten severely as the last overheating unleashes a wage–price spiral. In this case the tightening leads to a hard landing (a recession). The business cycles in the 1950s and 1960s, up until the first oil shock in 1973–74 (OPEC-I), were demand-led for all industrialised countries and soft landings were, at least conceptually, relatively easy. Hence, the cycles tended to be rather long. For example, phase (I) in the 1961–70 cycle was almost six years long. Demand management (either through monetary, but mainly through fiscal policy) until OPEC-I was relatively successful.

The length of phase (I) depends not only on the ability of the central bank to engineer soft landings but also on random shocks. For example, the German reunification occurred when the economy was in phase (I), which prolonged it to four and a half years. If the shock that hits the economy is a supply one and the economy happened to be in the overheating or slowdown phase, then this phase would be cut short with the economy entering quickly into a recession. For example, in the US the shortest phase (I) occurred in the cycle of 1970–75 (see Table 4.4). In this cycle inflation bottomed in mid-1972, point E, and growth peaked in the first quarter of 1973, point B, making phase (I) only nine months long. The slowdown in the economy was turned into a recession in the aftermath of the quadrupling of the price of oil (OPEC-I) following the Arab–Israeli war of 1973. This turned the cycle into supply-led. The increase in the price of oil exacerbated the recession, making it longer and deeper, while at the same time the inflation rate at its peak, point-C, doubled relative to the previous cycle.

The second example of a supply shock toppling demand management occurred in the cycle that lasted for something more than seven years from the beginning of 1975 to the second half of 1982. Phase (IV) was less than two years, up to the end of 1976. Phase (I) was extended until the end of 1978 thanks to the locomotive strategies adopted by the G-3. In this scheme one of the G-3 would act as the locomotive in reflating the world economy and would pass on that role to the other after a while so that the costs of reflation, mainly in the form of current account imbalances, would be shared by all of them. The second oil shock of 1979 (OPEC-II), during which there was a doubling in price, forced the economy into another recession in 1980 and exacerbated the upward trend of inflation. Point C was reached at the end of 1979, meaning that phase (II) was again less than two years. The sharp change in the conduct of monetary policy caused the second leg of the 1980–82 recession (see below), prolonging phase (III) to two and a half years.

The length of the deceleration stage (phase II) depends on the flexibility of the labour market and the extent of overheating in phase (I). In general, the greater the flexibility of the labour market and the smaller the extent of the previous overheating the shorter would be phase (II). The underlying rationale is simple. The length of phase (II) depends on the ferocity of the wage–price spiral. This captures the struggle between workers and firms over income distribution. Inflation is a mechanism for redistributing income. Those with weak industrial muscle or any strong political voice, such as the pensioners, see their real income eroded by higher prices.

For those employees whose jobs are relatively secure the primary concern is the preservation of the real wage rate. For the unemployed the concern is employment. For a number of different reasons those who care about their real wage rate outweigh those who care about employment and unemployment increases throughout the slowdown and recession phases.

If the workers fight to preserve their real wage rate when the economy decelerates and there is an increase in unemployment, then they intensify the wage–price spiral and prolong the slowdown phase (II). This would be the case if demand conditions in the labour market play a relatively small role, while deviations from the target real wage are more important (what is called 'real wage resistance'). Legislation in the labour market, minimum wages, employment protection legislation and trade union power and practices weaken the importance of demand conditions in the labour market and enhance real wage resistance. Moreover, unemployment benefits and social welfare influence the target real wage rate. If large unemployment benefits are paid, then the supply of labour is reduced (the incentive to participate in the labour force declines) and demand conditions in the labour market play a smaller role thereby prolonging the slowdown phase (II). The high natural rate of unemployment in Europe in the 1980s is usually regarded as having being caused, to a large extent, by the high unemployment benefits. On the other hand, the structural changes in the UK labour market in the Thatcher years provide evidence that the impact of the wage–price spiral can be reduced, thus shortening the length of phase (II). In the US downturn in the 1990s firms started laying off workers much earlier than the early 1980s downturn, thereby allowing greater role for demand conditions in the labour market.

The effects of the wage–price spiral depend not only on workers but also on firms. If firms find it difficult to pass on labour cost increases to their consumers, then the wage–price spiral is reduced, thereby shortening phase (II). Both the cost of firing and hiring and the degree of competition are important in this respect. If the market structure of the economy is competitive rather than monopolistic, then firms will find it difficult to pass on the labour cost to the consumers as they will be struggling to maintain market share. Hence, cost increases will tend to be absorbed in profit margins, thereby shortening phase (II).

In the absence of shocks the length of phase (II) tends to be less variable than other phases as it reflects structural characteristics of the economy, e.g. the degree of competition, and the labour market, in particular. For most industrialised countries it is between one and two years (see Table 4.4). In the US the average length of phase (II) is two years. The exception to this rule was the 1980s business cycle in which phase (II) lasted for three years – from the fourth quarter of 1987 (the peak of the cycle coincided with the stock market crash of 1987) to the end of 1990. At the time the Fed was trying to engineer a second soft landing, the first one being in 1984–86. The Fed tightened for a year until February 1989 with the Fed funds rate being lifted from 6.5 percent to 9.75 percent; it then began to lower rates to avoid the slowdown turning into a recession. In all probabilities the Fed would have succeeded in engineering a soft landing as the economy had decelerated to the rate of growth of potential output by mid-1990. However, the surge in the price of oil as a result of the Iraqi invasion in Kuwait in August 1990 and the resultant surge in the price of oil, albeit short lived, exacerbated the inflationary pressures and turned the soft landing into a hard one (the recession of 1990–91).

Phase (III) is the shortest in the cycle, usually one year long. In the absence of shocks it does not vary a great deal as it comes after the wage–price spiral is broken. The only notable exception to this rule was the 1975–82 cycle in which phase (III) lasted for two and a half years. But this was due to a substantial shift in the objective function of the Fed. The then chairman, Paul Volcker, put an end to the commitment to full employment in order to eradicate the inflationary pressures which soared to an all-time high following the second oil shock in 1979–80. The two successive oil shocks in the 1970s, along with the commitment of the policymakers in the Anglo-Saxon world to full employment, which was a legacy of the Great Depression, led to a persistent inflation surge. As the stylised facts suggest inflation peaked at much higher level in every successive cycle despite its cyclicality. In other words, the two oil shocks and the commitment to full employment fuelled inflation expectations in the 1970s and led to explosive inflation. It was in this climate that Paul Volcker decided to break the inflation psychology by creating another recession the moment the last one had finished. The Fed tightened for a second time after inflation had peaked at the beginning of 1980 causing the second leg of the 1980–82. Had the Fed not tightened, phase (III) would have been less than a year as the economy emerged from the first leg of the double dip recession.

Phase (IV), the recovery phase, is long and variable. In the last thirty years it has varied from just over a year to seven years. In the absence of shocks the length of phase (IV) is usually two years. Its length depends on the depth and the length of the preceding recession and the buoyancy of the recovery. The rationale is very simple as phase (IV) is symmetric to phase (II) with the picture reversed. The deeper and longer the preceding recession, the greater the productivity gains and hence the larger the reduction in unit labour cost and therefore the fall in inflation. Moreover, the more anaemic the recovery, the more hesitant firms are in increasing permanent employment and therefore again the larger are the productivity gains and hence the larger the decline in unit labour cost and therefore the fall in inflation. If the recovery is anaemic, as it has been since the early 1990s, and hence firms are doubtful about the sustainability of the recovery they will respond by increasing the working hours of the existing labour force or they will hire more temporary staff and will delay the hiring of permanent staff.

If an adverse supply shock, such as a drastic rise in oil prices, hits the economy while in phase (IV) the inflationary consequences would be relatively subdued while the recessionary effects will be large. The reason is that unemployment is high and profitability is low. Therefore, firms are willing to absorb the higher cost of energy into their profit margins and workers are prepared to accept a real wage cut. For example, the increase in the price of oil in 1980 when the US economy was coming out of the first leg of the recession caused only a slight increase in inflation and only for a short period – less than two quarters. However, the economy fell into a double-dip recession, although that was caused in addition by the Fed's tightening of policy.

But supply shocks need not be adverse. There are instances in which they are fortuitous. For example, the economy came out of the 1981–82 recession in a very buoyant way, thus becoming overheated almost immediately (see Figure 4.11). The then Fed Chairman, Paul Volcker, tightened monetary policy not with a view to engineering a soft landing, as Greenspan did in the mid-1990s, but because he wanted to eradicate the extremely high inflationary expectations, which to a large extent were responsible for the double-digit inflation of the mid-1970s and early 1980s. The Fed tightened monetary policy aggressively from early 1983 until late in the summer of 1984 with the fed funds rate rising from 8.5 percent to 11.5 percent on evidence that the economy was becoming overheated. Such tightening would have been sufficient to throw the economy back into recession. Indeed, the deceleration of the economy was dramatic and went on until the beginning of 1987 (see Figure 4.11). However, the economy managed a soft and not a hard landing because of a fortuitous supply shock – the collapse of the price of oil in 1984–85. The OPEC cartel was in conflict mainly with other non-OPEC oil producers, but there was also war within the cartel. Saudi Arabia increased production to drive non-compliant oil producer countries or cartel cheaters out of the market. The price of oil fell to less than $10 per barrel. This decreased inflation and boosted the incomes of households and the profits of companies thus ameliorating the impact of the slowdown and enabling the Fed to lower interest rates to less than 6 percent by late 1986. The economy not only avoided a recession in 1985–86, but recovered to exceed potential (overheating) in 1987. Had it not been for the fortuitous supply shock the economy would have been in phase (I), as inflation had previously bottomed in mid-1983. However, the collapse of the price of oil prolonged phase (IV) from one year to four and a half years.

Fortuitous shocks can also come from the demand side. For example, in the 1991–2001 cycle inflation had bottomed in mid-1994 and the US economy was in phase (I). However, the Asian-Russian crisis of 1997–98 triggered a collapse in the prices of many commodities and industrial supplies. This lowered US inflation from 3.3 percent at the beginning of 1997 to 1.4 percent by the spring of 1998, producing the lowest inflation in the 1990s. The Fed lowered interest rate pre-emptively from 5.5 to 4.75 percent to bolster confidence and to avert a worldwide recession. The combination of falling inflation and lower interest rates maintained growth intact. However, the economy was already over-heating and remained so, paving the way for a revival of inflation and presaging the end of the business cycle in early 2000. Had it not been for the Asian-Russian crisis, phase (IV) would have been three years long, but the shock prolonged it to seven years.

Phase (V) may not be observed if the recovery is buoyant with the economy becoming overheated straight away. If, however, the recovery is anaemic with growth not exceeding potential for a long time, then phase (V) is detectable. Phase (V) was not observed in all recoveries in the post-war period until the recession in the early 1990s. However, since then all recoveries have been anaemic; in all likelihood the recovery from the current credit crisis, when it comes, will also be anaemic. This new feature of the recent recoveries may be the result of globalisation and the adop-tion of flexible labour markets. Companies take advantage of globalisation and shift production to low-wage countries when the home country is in recession or in recovery, thus causing the recovery at home to become anaemic. Similarly, flexible labour markets have made companies more cautious in hiring during a recovery until they are convinced about the sus-tainability of the recovery. This hesitancy has turned recoveries anaemic.

7   The last two asset-led cycles – the risks of the current crisis

As we noted in the previous section the Fed eased monetary policy during the Asian-Russian crisis to stem the systemic risk from pushing the world economy into recession. Three interest-rate cuts, each by

0.25 percent, which reduced the Fed funds rate to 4.75 percent managed to restore the shattered confidence and, at least, the US growth remained intact. However, these rate cuts came at a time when the US economy was overheated and inflation, which had receded during the Asian-Russian crisis, rekindled in the aftermath of the crisis. This prompted the Fed not only to remove the previous three rate cuts, but also to lift the Fed funds rate to 1 percent higher than the pre-crisis level – 6.5 percent. The Fed kept interest rates at these elevated level throughout 2000, even though the economy had already fallen in recession. Inflation hovered between 3.1 and 3.8 percent throughout 2000 and began to fall in 2001 when the economy was in recession. Hence, tight monetary policy put an end to the ten-year cycle because inflation was getting out of hand, as it has happened in almost all post-war cycles.

However, by historical standards inflation was low at its peak in early 2001. The problem was not so much inflation in goods and services, but in asset prices. The NASDAQ had soared to 5,000 by early 2000 from 1,000 at the beginning of 1996, when the internet bubble started building up. Even the broad market S&P 500 index exceeded 1,500 from just 600 in the same period. The driving engine behind this soaring asset inflation was a rapidly expanding liquidity caused by financial engineering and easy monetary policy. Although Greenspan (1996; see, also, 2005a) warned of an 'irrational exuberance', the Fed did not tighten monetary policy to restrain the ballooning of the asset bubble, but acted to control CPI-inflation. As the internet bubble ballooned to disproportionate levels by early 2000 the lift of interest rates to 6.5 percent, which by historical standards was low, was sufficient to prick the bubble. Although the Fed lacked the statutory rights to stem the bubble, as its two targets are inflation and full-employment, the question that arises is whether the Fed had any room to act, had it wished to do so.

The Fed justified the relatively low interest rates on the grounds that the widespread use of computers had lifted long-term multi-factor productivity, which, in turn, had raised the rate of growth of potential output thus capping inflationary pressures. Moreover, Greenspan claimed that it would have been inappropriate for the Fed to hike rates to stem asset prices because that would have required it to outsmart investors. He further claimed that dealing with the consequences of the crisis was more appropriate – a policy that was later endorsed by other major central banks. The risk of the bursting of a bubble is asset and debt deflation that usually causes a deep and long recession (i.e. depression). To minimise this risk the Fed lowered interest rates to 1 percent by mid-2003 from 6.5 percent when the bubble burst. This prodigious easing shielded the economy from the plague of asset and debt deflation, but did nothing to drain the liquidity that had been responsible for the ballooning of the bubble.

In scrutinising these Fed arguments it is true that multi-factor productivity, which had fallen to 1.5 percent from 1975 to 1996, improved to 2.7 percent in the period 1996–2003, matching that of the 1960s. Productivity, however, has declined since 2003, thus supporting the view that the higher figures in the earlier period masked some cyclical improvement; the increase was not entirely structural. Projections with the K-Model until the end of 2010 assess it at 2.2 percent for the period 2003–10. Notwithstanding the smaller improvement in multifactor productivity, it is the case that the degree of overheating was modest by historical standards, justifying the mild uptrend of inflation until 2001. According to estimates based on the K-Model the economy was 1 percent overheated between mid-1996 and mid-2000 (see Figure 4.12). This suggests that there was room for the Fed to hike rates a bit higher than 6.5 percent, had it wished to restrain asset inflation. Instead, it concentrated on CPI-inflation and became a passive spectator of the ballooning of the internet bubble.

There is no doubt that monetary policy became extremely accommodative in 2003, with rates falling to 1 percent at a time when the economy was recovering and the slack in capacity had been eliminated by mid-2003 (see Figure 4.12). The over-accommodative monetary policy not only was

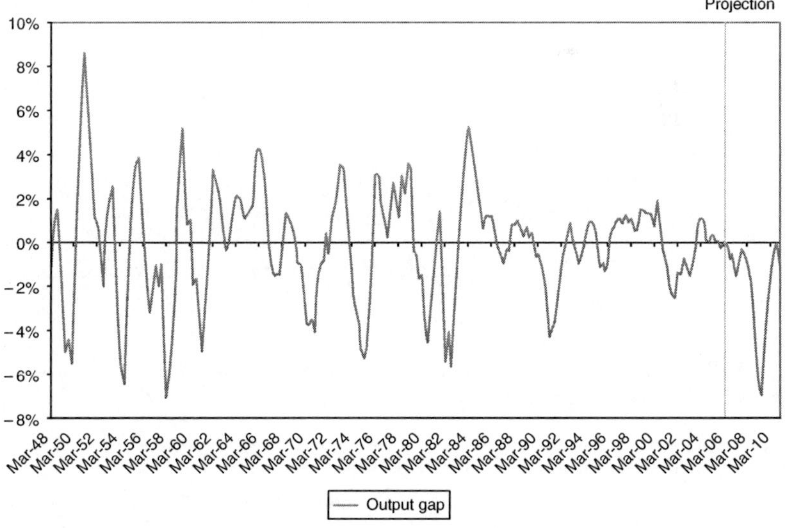

Figure 4.12　The output gap

maintained for one more year, until mid-2004, but it was removed very sluggishly at a 'pace that can be measured', meaning 25 basis points in each FOMC meeting (Greenspan, 2005a). The successor of Greenspan, Bernanke, retained the same sluggish pace in removing the accommodation bias and interest rates hit 5.25 percent by mid-2006, a level that was maintained until mid-2007. Again, on the basis of GDP growth there was no overheating with the exception of 2004 (see Figure 4.12). In fact, a small negative gap of 0.5 percent was maintained for most of the time until the beginning of the recession in the fourth quarter of 2007. Thus, it is fair to say that the Fed did a decent job in avoiding any overheating in the economy throughout the 2000s. This interpretation is justified by the core PCE-inflation that hardly increased from mid-2004 to mid-2008. However, this mild inflation picture was not shared by the headline measure. The latter fell during the recession of 2001 and bottomed in mid-2002 at around 1 percent. However, it began to climb after this time, hitting 5.5 percent by mid-2008 (see Figure 4.13). Hence, the acceleration of inflation was due to non-indigenous factors, namely to the rapidly rising prices of commodities, and in particular oil, and other industrial supplies. A rapidly depreciating dollar between 2002 and mid-2008 accentuated the increase in import prices, thus enhancing the inflation uptrend.

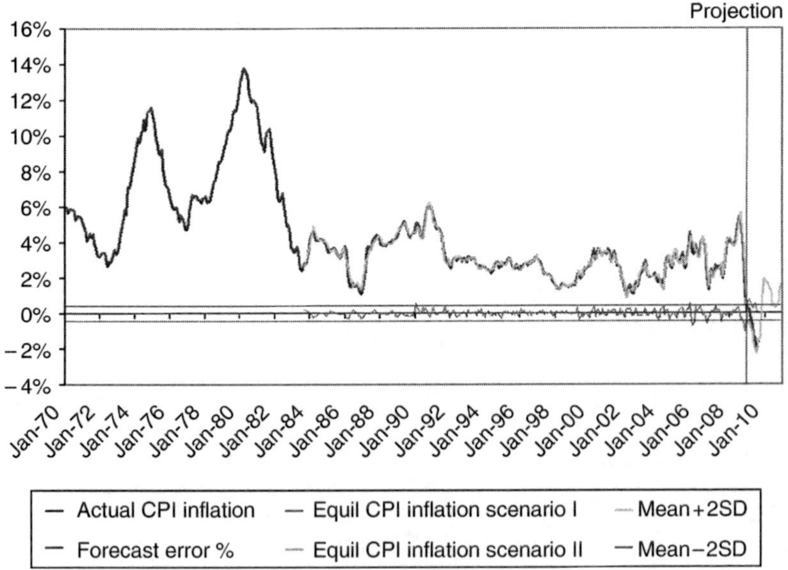

Figure 4.13   Headline CPI-inflation

Thus, for a second time the Fed focused on CPI-inflation and the output gap and adopted a policy of benign neglect to the ballooning of the housing bubble. Although this is not the time to assess the adequacy of those policies as the current crisis necessitates fire-fighting, the experience of the last two asset-led cycles shows that monetary policy cannot be formulated alone by the two targets of inflation and the output gap. As we show later on there are clear benefits in adding a third target to guide monetary policy. This is the net wealth to income ratio, which has on both occasions (the internet and the housing bubble) clearly shown the magnitude of the bubbles.

Although core inflation remained subdued in the 2000s and creeping headline inflation was the result of developments in the world economy, the excessive liquidity that was responsible for the ballooning of the internet bubble not only was not drained but was allowed to expand because of financial engineering and an over-accommodative monetary policy. This liquidity fuelled a second bubble in the 2000s; that was housing. Soon after the recovery began in 2003 asset inflation in houses and equities reached double-digit figures that were maintained until the housing bubble burst in 2007. Since the eruption of the credit crisis in mid-2007, further liquidity has been injected into the system. Unless this liquidity is drained the moment the economy begins to recover there are major risks for the US economy and the world economy. It should be remembered that in extreme circumstances the quantity theory of money and the monetarist views on exchange rates are more likely to accurately reflect the real world than in normal conditions. This means that the huge liquidity, if not drained, has the potential of causing either huge inflation or dollar depreciation. Projections of the K-model suggest that the recession will be one of the deepest and longest in the post-Second World War era without further policy support. A huge negative output gap is expected until the end of 2010 (see Figure 4.12). Thus, in the current environment there is no risk that the excessive liquidity will rekindle inflation. However, the dynamics of inflation are already pointing to higher levels in 2010, albeit less than the implicit Fed target of 2 percent (see Figure 4.13). Nonetheless, the huge liquidity is likely to cause huge dollar depreciation, probably in 2010 and beyond. The US Treasury is expected to issue \$2.5 trillion of Treasuries to cover the bailout of financial institutions and the stimulus package of \$776 billion. In spite of this unprecedented issuance, for the time being, the dollar is likely to remain strong, as the policy mix of easy fiscal and monetary policy creates expectations of a recovery. However, in the long run, which nonetheless may be as early as 2010, the combination of the huge issuance of Treasuries and the excessive liquidity, if not drained, will cause huge dollar depreciation. This may trigger a collapse in the long run of the euro-currency system with many countries, such as Italy, Spain, Portugal, Greece, Ireland and Austria leaving willingly or unwillingly the euro and resurrecting their old national currencies. A weak dollar will cause further loss of competitiveness in the euro-area, thereby threatening to thwart the expecting recovery. The financial crisis in Europe is likely to re-emerge when the US falls into recession in two or three years' time, as bank losses mount from their exposure in Eastern Europe. In this environment even small dollar depreciation may be sufficient to trigger the collapse of the euro system.

8   Summary and conclusions

Inflation is not *always* and *everywhere* a monetary phenomenon, but it may be so under abnormal or extreme conditions, such as exist at present. Under normal conditions inflation is shaped by developments in costs and the demand–supply balance – the output gap. There are four major price indices: CPI, PPI for finished goods, PPI for intermediate supplies and PPI for crude materials. Each price index is feeding, albeit with a lag, into the next one in a logical sequence (crude materials into intermediate supplies and so on until we come to the CPI). This time-dependence of CPI on all previous price indices (called inflation persistence) justifies a reference to inflation as if it was a single variable. Moreover, all price indices share a common structure – each one is formulated as a mark-up on average variable costs, where the mark-up is variable and depends on the output gap. The mark-up increases as economic conditions improve, namely when the economy booms, and vice versa. The cost of labour is the most important component contributing between 45 percent and 75 percent to the average unit variable cost in the various stages of the production chain. Wages, though, are not very sensitive to demand conditions in the short run, thereby further enhancing the persistency of inflation. The unit labour cost is by definition affected by wages and productivity, which, in turn, partly depend on the output gap. This structure, which is reflected in the K-Model, means that CPI-inflation today reflects persistent inflation trends from the past and previous developments in the output gap. Moreover, CPI-inflation is also shaped by developments in the world economy through imports of final goods and services and oil, which directly enters into the CPI. But the dependence on oil and other commodities is also indirect, through their impact on the various PPI-indices, which then feed with a lag in the CPI. All these effects intensify the persistency of inflation.

The inflation structure means that central banks can affect inflation with a significant lag, around two years, through the impact of interest rates on growth and therefore on the output gap. The inflation persistency has one more implication; central banks must be consistent in the direction they are bending; they cannot afford to oscillate by changing their minds. Thus, if they decide that inflation is a problem they must persevere with rate hikes until inflation is broken. The impact of the world economy on inflation means that central banks must target core components of inflation, such as the PCE or CPI, although this may not be palatable to consumers for a long period of time, as was the case in the last six years. The advantage of targeting core-inflation over the headline measure is that it avoids swings in interest rates that may have an adverse effect on the economy.

The inflation persistency and the required consistent pursuit of monetary policy mean that inflation has a predictable relationship with growth. In other words, we can exploit the relationship between inflation and growth in the business cycle in order to discern inflation trends and predict similar trends in policy interest rates over a period of between one and four years. Using this approach we can identify five phases in the course of the business cycle: overheating, slowdown, recession, recovery and anaemic recovery. In the overheating, recession and anaemic recovery phases the correlation between inflation and growth is positive, while in the slowdown and recovery phases the correlation is negative – without that implying stagflation. In the absence of shocks each of the slowdown and recovery phases is two years long, while the recession phase is around one year in length. An anaemic recovery may not be observed, although it has become a permanent feature since the 1990s as a result of globalisation and the adoption of flexible labour markets.

In the absence of shocks the length of the overheating phase depends on the number of soft landings that the central bank might engineer. In effect, every soft landing adds two more years to the length of the business cycle. Although in theory there is nothing to stop a central bank from engineering more than one soft landing, in practice the Fed has never managed more than one.

Nonetheless, unexpected shocks occur very frequently and therefore not only is the length of each cycle different, but so is the length of each particular phase. This makes every cycle unique and requires much more detailed knowledge of the events that shaped each cycle in order to isolate the unique events and identify the common trends. We have endeavoured to throw light on these shocks and their impact on each phase and the overall cycle, so that the reader can be guided on how to use these techniques to understand future business cycles and in particular the relationship between inflation and growth.

The last two business cycles have been asset-led and we have spared no effort in our attempt to throw light on their implications. In doing so, we have identified the risks of the current credit crisis in view of the measures that have been adopted by the policymakers; that is, the injection of more liquidity, when excessive liquidity has been at the root of the current problems. Although inflation is not *always* and *everywhere* a monetary phenomenon, the monetarist views of inflation and exchange rates are particularly pertinent in abnormal or extreme conditions such as exist at present. This liquidity may be siphoned to the exchange rate with huge dollar depreciation being the most likely outcome in the long run, which might nonetheless be as soon as 2010. The legacy of this prodigious liquidity is unlikely to rekindle inflation in the next two years or so. This does not mean that inflation will remain subdued in 2011–13; in fact, if expansionary policies are pursued that create overheating in 2010 and 2011, then inflation will soar any time between 2011 and 2013. However, if this were to happen, then policy would be tightened aggressively with the economy falling back into recession. Deflation then will re-emerge as a major problem.

In terms of policy we have indicated that the Fed policy of being concerned with core inflation and the output gap has proved successful during the last two asset-led cycles. Core inflation has been kept under control and for the majority of the period the output gap has been close to zero. The rise in headline inflation has been the result of developments in the world economy, where there has been soaring demand for commodities and oil from many developing countries, in particular the BRIC countries. Nonetheless, the successful targeting of core inflation and the output gap has not averted the worst crisis since the Great Depression. In this respect we have suggested that the net wealth–income ratio should be added as a third target in guiding monetary policy in the future, if we are to avoid bubbles in the future.

5
Corporate Profits and Relationship to Investment[1]

1 Introduction

Profits play a crucial role in business investment and the equity market. The former has a major impact on long-term GDP growth and in business cycle analysis. The equity market, on the other hand, affects both investment and, via the wealth effect, consumer expenditure. But profits are one of the most volatile variables in the economy. Accordingly, they play a key role in long-term growth trends and in business cycle analysis. Until very recently a prevalent view was that the long-term decline in profitability that took place from the late 1960s to the early 1980s had been reversed. Such a decline was associated with the heyday of trade union power and the interference of Keynesian-type demand management with laissez-faire economics. Defenders of such policies attributed the decline to the two oil shocks that redistributed income and wealth from the oil-consuming to the oil-producing countries. There was a strong belief that neoliberalism invigorated the power of the market mechanism and managed to reverse the long-term decline in profitability. But the burst of the recent house bubble has cast doubt on such an interpretation. The last two bubbles may have masked the downtrend, giving rise to false hopes and erroneous interpretations about the success of neoliberalism. In this chapter we examine the evidence and offer projections of long-term trends in profitability. Moreover, the bursting of the housing bubble has hit profits hard and this raises the issue of whether that will delay the recovery of the economy by affecting investment and consumption. Hence, another objective of this chapter is to assess the risks of the slump of profits on the depth and length of the current recession. This necessitates an analysis of the proximate causes of profit levels, the rate of growth and its volatility. In later chapters we make use of that information to analyse investment behaviour and share prices.

This chapter is organised as follows. The next section examines the stylised facts of profits in terms of long-term trends and cyclical patterns; the major determinants of profits and their relationship to growth in the course of the business cycle. Section 3 analyses the theoretical structure of the K-Model to throw light on the profits determinants and how they behave in the business cycle. Section 4 employs this structure to explain the stylised facts. Section 5 analyses the risks of the current crisis on corporate profits and the economy, while section 6 summarises and concludes.

2   The stylised facts – long-term trends and cyclical patterns

Corporate profits oscillated around 11 percent of GDP for the twenty years up to the late 1960s, before assuming a downtrend that lasted until the trough of the recession in 1982 (see Figure 5.1). However, this long-term downtrend in profitability seems to have been reversed in the last quarter-century. Indeed, profits in the second half of 2006 came within a whisker of the all-time high achieved in 1950. This apparent reversal coincided with the advent of Thatcherism and Reaganism and

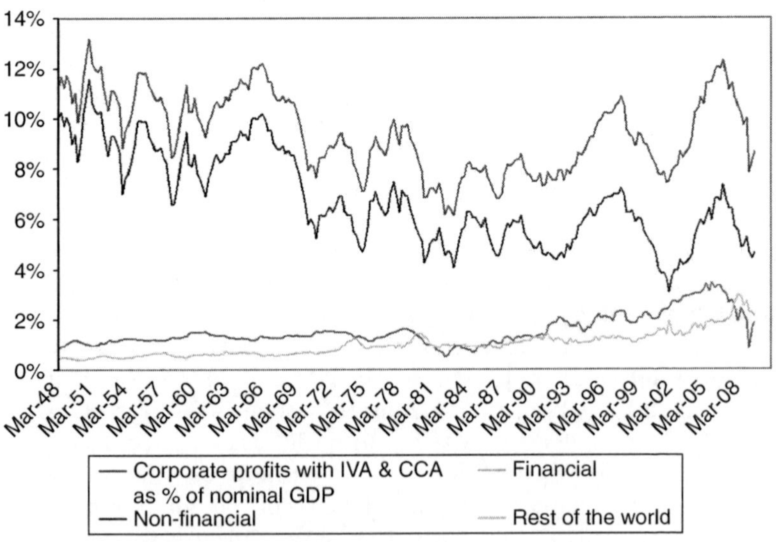

Figure 5.1   Corporate profits with IVA & CCA as % of nominal GDP

their efforts to resuscitate trust in the free market economy (what has been dubbed neoliberalism), but also with the end of the two oil shocks, which may have contributed to the reversal in profitability. Until very recently the verdict between these two competing explanations appeared to be in favour of neoliberalism and the market economy. But the burst of the house bubble has cast doubt on such an interpretation as the last two bubbles may have exaggerated the buoyancy of profitability.

This reversal of the downtrend in profitability was supported by reported earnings in the second half of the 1990s that created euphoria and support for neoliberalism. But reported earnings were greatly exaggerated and offered a more sanguine picture than that emerging from the NIPA accounts. Thus, a cursory look at Figure 5.1 shows that NIPA profits peaked in 1997, three years earlier than the burst of the internet bubble, while reported earnings were showing buoyant growth. The 'governance crisis' that ensued from the Enron scandal confirmed that creative accounting was mainly responsible for the discrepancy between NIPA and reported earnings. Up until the 'governance crisis' equity markets concentrated on reported earnings and the inflated figures may have significantly contributed to the euphoria and the 'irrational exuberance' of the internet bubble. Nonetheless, the discrepancy between reported earnings and NIPA estimates has virtually disappeared since the overhaul of the governance crisis in early 2000s and now both measures give more or less the same picture.

Further doubts have emerged after the bursting of the housing bubble, which question the proposition that there was a reversal in the downtrend of profitability. The two bubbles, in the early and late 2000s, may have masked the continuous downtrend, erroneously supporting the view of a reversal of the trend. Such a view is supported by the fact of no change in the long-term profitability of non-financial companies, as shown in Figure 5.1. If anything, the bottom of profitability at the end of 2001 hit an all-time low. This downtrend may be the result of shifting production abroad, which gathered pace in the era of globalisation, but also to the increasing challenge of the US from other industrialised countries, such as Japan, Europe and, more recently, China. But the bleak picture of non-financial profitability is not shared by other subcategories. Financial companies have seen a sharp uptrend in their profitability since 1982, recording nearly a sixfold increase (see Figure 5.1). The financial deregulation, which commenced at that time, and the repeal of the Glass–Steagall Act in 1999 certainly contributed to the long-term improvement of the profitability of financial companies. But these developments are at the heart of the current woes as they enabled the creation of liquidity that financed two major bubbles – internet and housing – and others of less importance, such as commodities, shipping and private equity. Now that the house bubble has burst and deleverage is taking place, it is very likely that the long-term uptrend in the profitability of financial companies will be reversed, thus undermining the view that there has been a reversal of the downtrend in total profits. The other major category of profits is repatriated profits from overseas operations of US companies. This category also confirms a big improvement in profitability – profits nearly tripled since the mid-1980s (see Figure 5.1). This trend highlights the globalisation process that gathered steam since the mid-1990s. This trend is unlikely to be reversed, as after every recession more companies have shifted production to low-wage countries, such as China, in order to survive. The combined profits of non-financial companies and those from abroad still confirm a downtrend, albeit milder than that of non-financial companies. This suggests that globalisation is only part of the reason and fierce competition from Europe, Japan and China has also played a role.

Therefore, the long-term outlook for profits, from the point of view of a 'sector bottom up' approach, is not sanguine. The profitability trend of non-financial companies is downward and this is simply a continuation of a trend that began in the early 1970s, due to globalisation and the challenge from other industrialised countries. The reversal of the trend for financial companies since the early 1980s was due to deregulation and 'bad' financial engineering that financed the two bubbles of the 2000s. But after the burst of the house bubble, the new trend is downwards because of deleveraging. Traditional banks are more likely to return to the basic function of intermediation between savers and investors. This function does not require supernormal profits and therefore the new trend is downward. The investment bank model has become bankrupt and the companies that have survived have run for cover and became depository institutions to qualify for assistance from the Fed. The only category that is likely to continue on an uptrend is profits from the rest of the world, as more companies shift production to low-wage countries, such as China and India, although there are doubts stemming from protectionist measures. An upward trend in profitability from overseas operations may not be beneficial to the US economy, as it implies fewer jobs in the US and therefore lower levels of income growth for US employees. The US Congress may enact a law to tax profits from overseas operations at a higher rate than at home, thus encouraging companies to shift production back home. But even if protectionism is kept under control an upward trend in profitability from overseas operations is unlikely to dominate the other sectors of the economy. Hence, the overall conclusion is that the long-term trend of profitability is down.

Let us now turn to the cyclical behaviour of profits and in particular to their behaviour in the course of the business cycle (see Figure 5.2). The level of profits is highly pro-cyclical; profits rise in the upswing of the cycle and fall during the downswing. The rate of growth of profits, however, tends to peak long before the level of GDP, which is the official measure of the peak and bottom of the cycle. It should be noted, however, that the rate of growth of profits provides more timely information about the peak and the bottom of the rate of growth of real GDP than the level of profits. The highest rate of growth of profits occurs during the recovery phase or very early in the overheating phase. After that there is a mid-cycle crisis, in which the growth of profits shows some fatigue. Profits growth recovers before the economy peaks, although nowhere near the earlier peak. Almost invariably the profits growth peaks before that of the economy, acting as a leading indicator of the peak of the business cycle. The profits recession usually begins when GDP growth peaks. Profits growth hits bottom either at the trough of the recession or, sometimes, a little earlier than the trough (see Figure 5.2). In other words, most of the time profitability is a coincident of the trough of the recession.

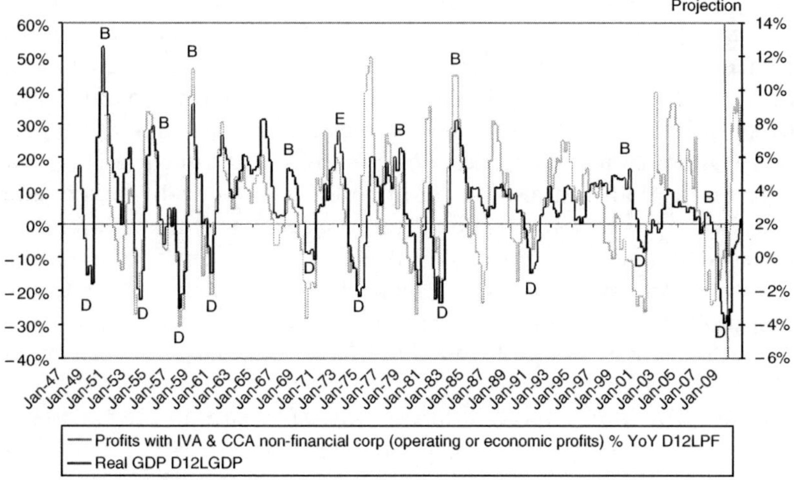

Figure 5.2   GDP and profits

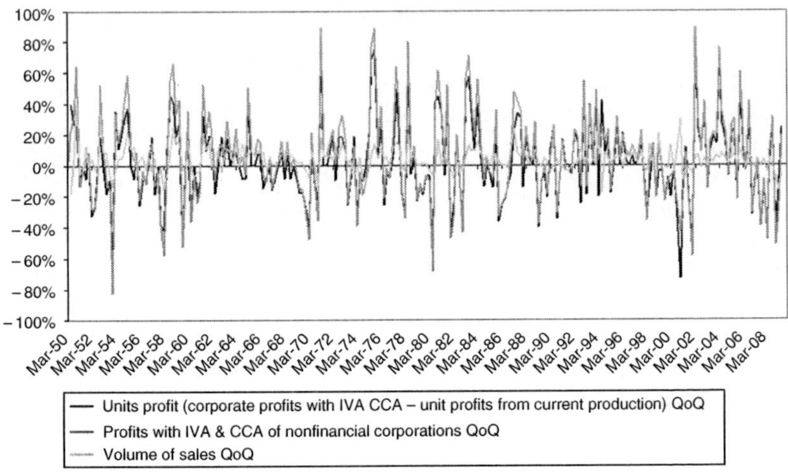

Figure 5.3   Contribution of unit profit and volume of sales to total profits

Total profits can be decomposed into unit profit and the volume of sales. Figure 5.3 shows the contribution of unit profit and the volume of sales to the total profits of non-financial companies. This is the highest level of aggregation for which profits are decomposed into their constituent components. A cursory examination of the data suggests that the variability of unit profit contributes much more than the volume of sales to total profits; this is particularly so in the case during the early phase of the recovery. This shows that the dramatic variation in profits from quarter to quarter is due mainly to a corresponding change in unit profit. Accordingly, a huge improvement in profitability can only occur by an increase in unit profit. The volume of sales is of secondary importance, although its importance increases as the cycle matures.

The unit profit can also be decomposed into the profit margin and the pricing power of companies. Figure 5.4 shows that the unit profit is closely associated with the profit margin. Thus the contribution of the profit margin greatly exceeds the contribution of pricing power in the unit profit. Hence, an improvement in unit profit can only come about by an increase in the profit margin. The pricing power of companies plays a secondary role.

Finally, the most important factor that contributes to the variability of profit margin is the unit labour cost. Figure 5.5 shows the significant negative relationship between profit margin and unit labour cost. This means that an improvement in the profit margin can only take place

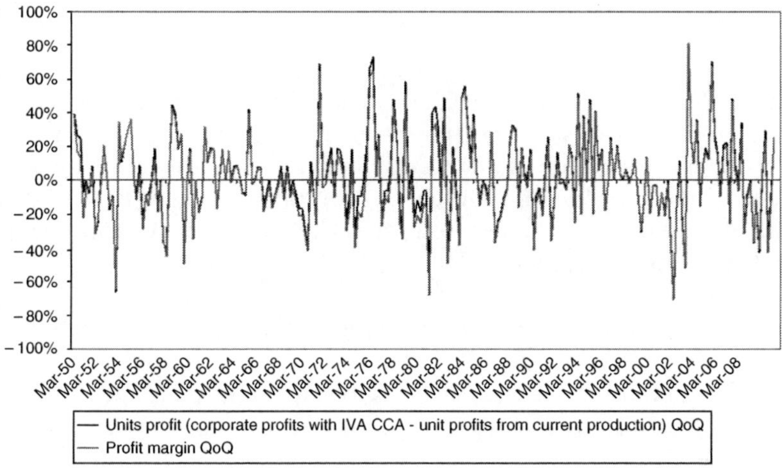

Figure 5.4   Unit profit and profit margin

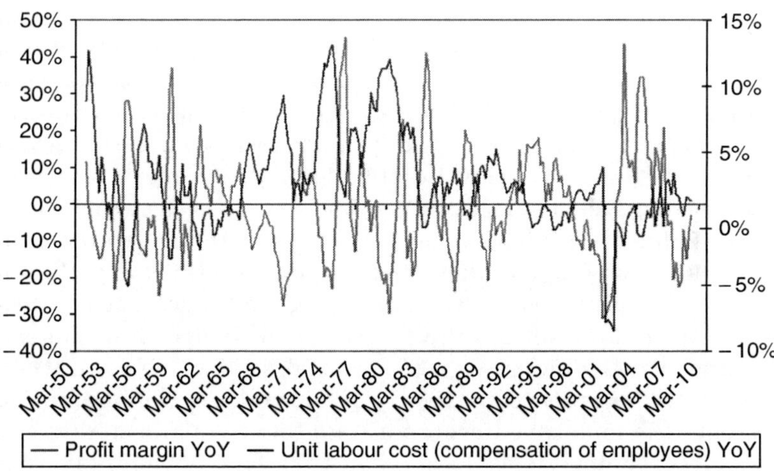

Figure 5.5   Profit margin and unit labour cost

by a decrease in unit labour cost. Thus, a reduction in unit labour cost increases the profit margin, which, in turn, pushes up the unit profit and that contributes to a large improvement in total profits. The volume of sales, the pricing power of companies and the non-labour cost play a secondary role in the variation of total profits.

3   The K-Model of corporate profits

Our approach to profits in this chapter is tightly linked to the chapter that follows on investment. This is crucial to our explanation of corporate profits and their relationship to investment. In fact, the dependence of profits on investment emanates from the theory of income distribution, and from Kaldor's (1955) contribution in particular. More precisely, and in its simplest form, the relationship can be couched as in the following expression:

$$P = (I - s_w Y) / (s_p - s_w)$$

where P is profits, I is investment, Y is the level of income, and s_p, s_w are the marginal propensities to save out of wages and profits respectively (Kalecki, 1971; see also Sawyer, 1985). Profits would be negative unless investment is greater than $s_w Y$. The direction of causation runs from investment to profits, so that a larger volume of investment produces a higher level of profits. However, the drive for higher profits and the search for profitable opportunities, in which to invest, leads to increased production. Clearly, the pursuit of profits and the availability of past profits lead to higher investment. Indeed, if there were no higher investment, there would be no requirement for profits to finance investment. Consequently, a higher level of profits provides the finance for investment in the form of retained profits. Profits are a major source of finance and the ability to raise further finance is affected by the level of profits (Eichner, 1987). This argument, along with the above expression for profits, clearly implies that there is a double-sided relationship in all this: profits finance future investment, but investment (actual) augments capital stock, which helps to create more profits in the future, if of course there is sufficient aggregate demand (see also Robinson, 1964). Minsky (1986) has also emphasised this double-sided relationship: just as profits determine investment so investment determines profits.

A number of other studies focus on the crucial role of profits to investment. These contributions build on ideas of Kalecki (1943), Minsky (1986), and on Keynes's (1936) 'animal spirits'. Kalecki (1943) argues for the importance of financing constraints, and suggests that this may affect decision on net investment (capital accumulation) via profits, which determine the ability of the firm to invest in the future (see also Baddeley, 2003). Stegman (1982) tests for the impact of corporate profitability on investment within an accelerator type of model. The results of this study support the contention that profitability is best viewed as a constraint to investment, rather than as a conventional explanatory variable. It is shown that using 'switching regression' analysis, profitability as a constraint outperforms conventional accelerator-type specification. However, the presence of what Keynes (1936) labelled volatile 'animal spirits' can render these relationships unstable. Our approach in this book builds on the insights of the contributions to which we have just referred.

The K-Model of corporate profits and of investment determination (see next chapter), for non-financial companies (the highest level of aggregation for which data exist), are based on the theoretical propositions just summarised. It consists of the following six equations.

1. The output of non-financial corporations (QNFC)
2. The unit labour cost of non-financial corporations (ULCNFC)
3. The price per unit of output charged by non-financial corporations (PQNFC)
4. The profit margin of non-financial corporations (PMNFC)
5. The unit profit of non-financial corporations UPNFC)
6. Total profits of non-financial corporations (TPNFC)

In the long run, the output of NFC grows at the same rate as real GDP, thereby connecting the outlook for profits to the rest of the real sector of the economy and hence to fiscal and monetary policy. It also connects developments in the rest of the world, which are best reflected in changes in world trade and currency movements. In the short run, output growth adjusts to correct any previous deviation from equilibrium in output. Thus, when output is higher than in equilibrium, there is a slowing of growth; similarly, growth accelerates if output is less than in equilibrium. It takes just over a year for output to come back to equilibrium. Output growth adjusts to current real GDP growth and exhibits strong inertia to past output growth. This enables us to write formally the long-run relationship for QNFC as in equation (1):

$$QNFC = Q(GDP, WT, ER) \tag{1}$$

where GDP is Gross Domestic Product, WT stands for World Trade and ER for the Exchange Rate.

In the long run the unit labour cost of NFC grows at the same rate as the unit labour cost of non-farm business, thus connecting the outlook of profits to the whole wage–price sector of the economy. In the short run the unit labour cost of NFC adjusts to correct any previous disequilibria. Thus, when the unit labour cost is higher than in equilibrium, unit labour cost growth slows down; when unit labour cost growth is lower than in equilibrium, it accelerates. It takes almost twenty months for the labour cost to adjust back to equilibrium. Unit labour cost inflation exhibits strong inertia to past inflation. The unit labour cost inflation of NFC also adjusts to current and past unit labour cost inflation of non-farm business. We may, thus, write:

$$ULCNFC = U(ULCNFB) \tag{2}$$

where ULCNFB stands for the ULC of the Non Farm Business.

In the long run the unit price of NFC grows at the same rate as PPI-inflation of finished goods, thus again linking the outlook for corporate profits to the wage–price sector. In the short run price inflation in NFC adjusts to correct any previous disequilibria. Thus, when the unit price of NFC is lower than in equilibrium, then the price inflation of NFC accelerates; conversely, it decelerates when it is higher than in equilibrium. Price inflation adjusts to current and past PPI-inflation and exhibits strong inertia to the past price inflation of NFC. Equation (3) depicts the long-run relationship for PQNFC:

$$PQNFC = P(PPI) \tag{3}$$

In the long run, the profit margin (the ratio of unit profit to unit price, i.e. UPNFC/PQNFC) depends negatively on unit labour cost and positively on output. In the short run the growth of profit margin adjusts to correct any previous deviation from equilibrium. Thus, if the profit margin is lower than in equilibrium, then its rate of growth will increase in the future, and decrease if it is greater than in equilibrium. It takes about 16 months for the profit margin to come back to equilibrium. The growth of profit margin adjusts to current and past unit labour cost inflation, current and past output growth and exhibits strong inertia to past growth rates of profit margin. Unit profit growth is, by definition, equal to profit margin growth plus unit price inflation. Total profits are the product of unit profit by output. Hence, profits growth is equal to the sum of unit profit growth and output growth. We may now write:

$$PMNFC = M(ULCNFC, QNFC) \tag{4}$$

We may also have for the sake of completeness:

$$UPNFC = PM \times PQ \tag{5}$$

and

$$TPNFC = UPNFC \times QNFC \tag{6}$$

The rationale of the K-profits Model is summarised in Figure 5.6. The medium grey boxes illustrate the variables that belong to the profits loop or spiral. The light grey boxes illustrate the variables that cause a shock to the profit spiral. Shocks to the profit spiral are introduced by fiscal and monetary policy, developments in the rest of the world that affect world trade or the exchange rate. Shocks are also introduced by all of the variables that affect the wage–price spiral. Finally, corporate taxes, depreciation incentives and interest rates affect non-labour cost and set in motion the profit spiral.

Consider, for example, a permanent shock in policy (domestic or foreign) that stimulates the real sector of the economy and leads to higher real GDP growth. This increases the output of NFC, thereby raising productivity, which lowers unit labour cost; this, in turn, boosts the profit margin. The latter is also stimulated directly by the higher output, as the profit margin is pro-cyclical; companies raise profit margins when the economy recovers and lower them when the economy slows or enters a recession. The higher profit margin raises the unit profit,

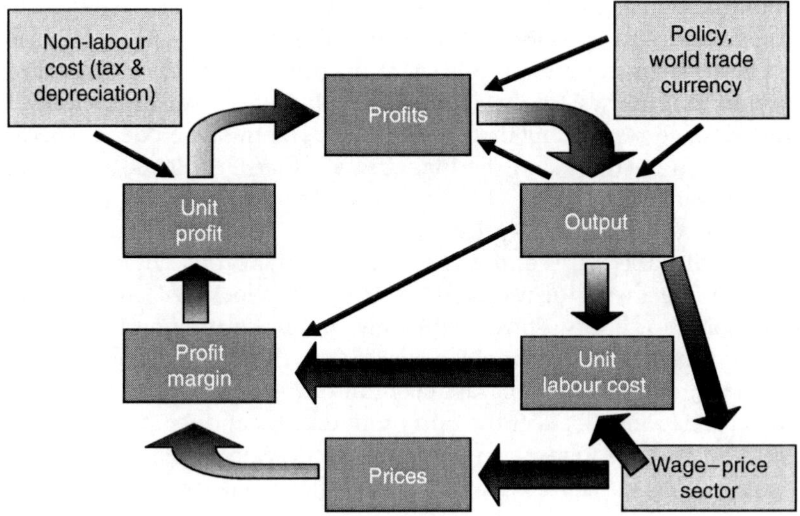

Figure 5.6   The profit model

which pushes up total profits. The latter is also boosted by the increase in output, as by definition total profits is the product of the unit profit times the volume of sales. The increase in profits further boosts output through investment and consumption, setting in motion a positive feedback loop or spiral. This positive loop continues to operate lifting profits in every round.

However, there is a parallel loop in operation that counters the positive feedback. The increase in output sets in motion the wage–price spiral. The combination of higher output and profits encourages firms to hire labour and this gradually erodes the initial and subsequent gains in productivity from the positive loop. This increases the unit labour cost, which counterbalances the initial drop from the positive loop. The unit labour cost is further increased by more rapid wage growth, as unemployment begins to fall and raises the bargaining power of employees. Moreover, the higher unit labour cost increases the price of NFC that reduces the profit margin. Through time this negative loop tends to offset partially the positive loop; but the overall impact is still positive. The interaction of the positive and negative loops will have the overall effect that initially the profit margin, the unit profit and total profits will increase quickly. However, in every round the marginal increase in profits will be smaller than the one before and after approximately 16 months the system would reach a new long-run equilibrium in which the profit margin, unit profit and total profits would be higher than the initial equilibrium. From another angle the interaction of the two loops ensures that the initial output shock does not lead to an explosive profit spiral. In other words, the interaction ensures that the system is stable. The stability of the system is ensured because of corresponding increases in employment that erode the initial gains in productivity and the higher wages that feed directly into the unit labour cost.

Any shock in the wage–price sector, such as commodity prices or oil prices, will raise prices and will set in motion a profit spiral too, that would interact with the wage–price spiral. Such shocks will create a negative spiral in profits. Thus, in the new equilibrium the profit margin, unit profit and total profits will be lower than in the initial equilibrium. Moreover, changes in corporate taxation or interest rates or incentives on depreciation will affect the unit profit directly and set in motion the profit spiral. The increase in profits from any shock is not explosive. This means that the profit spiral is always stable. The stability is ensured because of corresponding increases in employment that erode the initial gains in productivity and increases in unit labour cost.

4   An explanation of the stylised facts

4.1   Leading indicator property of the cycle peak

It has been argued in section 2 that both the level and rate of growth of profits act as a leading indicator of the peak of the business cycle. The rate of growth of profits peaks on average ten quarters earlier than the peak of the business cycle. The level of profits, though, continues to increase, as the rate of growth is slower but not negative; it peaks much later – six quarters earlier than the peak of the cycle. Thus, the signal from the rate of growth is far too early in the business cycle to be of practical use; whereas the level of profits provides more timely information of the peak of the cycle.

It is easy to explain these stylised facts within the context of the K-Model. The surge in the rate of growth of profits early in the cycle is due to the rapid improvement in productivity, which takes place when the economy begins to recover. The faster the rate of growth of the economy, the greater is the improvement in productivity. This is due to the sluggish pace of job creation in the early stages of the recovery. Firms are reluctant to hire new workers, as they are uncertain about the sustainability of the recovery. Moreover, companies would need to boost their profitability before they hire new workers. Finally, there is a lot of spare capacity as the economy emerges from the recession and this means that companies can make more intensive use of the existing labour force before they are required to employ more. The vast improvement in productivity in the early stages of the recovery is a characteristic of all business cycles (see Figure 5.7).

The huge improvement in productivity in the recovery phase leads to a sharp decline in unit labour cost. This is further enhanced by slower wage growth in the recovery phase. Unemployment is a lagging indicator of the business cycle and this implies that it continues to rise during the recovery. As a result of the continuing increase in unemployment the bargaining power of employees is weakening, thus diminishing wage growth. Hence, under the twin pressures of rising productivity and falling wage inflation, unit labour cost falls. In fact, throughout the recovery phase inflation continues to abate driven lower by falling unit labour cost. This is the period of 'good' growth, meaning that the more buoyant the recovery, the greater the reduction in unit labour cost is. As a result of falling unit labour cost the profit margin increases. This is also boosted by the increase in output, as the profit margin is largely pro-cyclical. Companies increase their profit margin in the upswing of the cycle and reduce it in the downswing. The higher profit margin

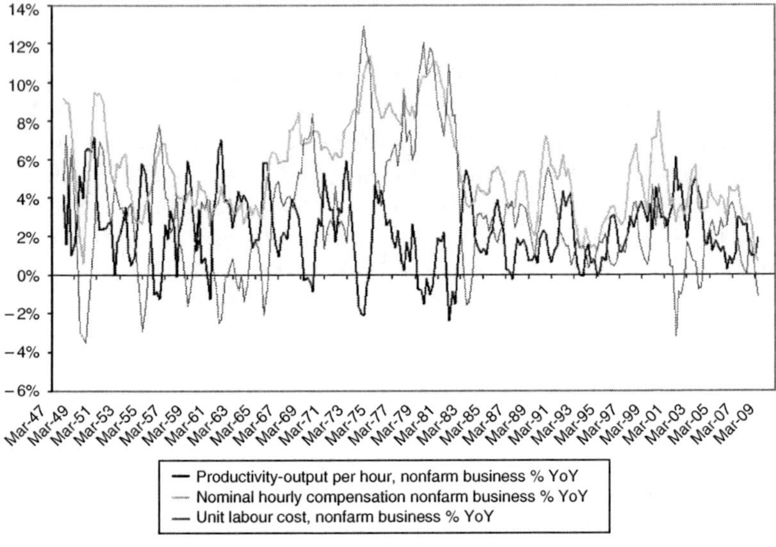

Figure 5.7   Wages, productivity and unit labour cost in nonfarm business

pushes up the unit profit and this boosts profits. Therefore, profits soar in the recovery phase.

As the recovery of the economy matures firms are becoming more confident that it is sustainable and therefore are willing to expand their labour force. Moreover, as the recovery matures spare capacity is diminishing and this necessitates hiring more labour. Finally, unemployment levels off and begins to decline. This increases the bargaining power of employees and wage inflation begins to rise yet again. Hence, the early gains in productivity are eroded through time and the reduction in unit labour cost peters out and in time it is reversed. This pares the gains in profit margins, unit profit and consequently in total profits. This is what happens in the overheating phase of the business cycle. In this phase higher growth is 'bad' growth in the sense that the higher the rate of growth is, the higher the increase in unit labour cost and the greater the erosion in profit margins and total profits. Therefore, the rate of growth of profits peaks at the end of the recovery phase or early in the overheating phase. But although the rate of growth of profits peaks on average ten quarters earlier than the peak of the business cycle, the level of profits continues to increase, as the rate of growth is slower but not negative. Hence, the level of profits peaks much later; it does so six quarters earlier than the peak of the cycle.

However, averages conceal the fact that every cycle is different. The minimum lead of the rate of growth of profits in the cycle is three quarters, while the maximum is 25 quarters. The variation is not as great for the level of profits. The minimum lead is three quarters and the maximum is ten quarters. In the average demand cycle and in the 1990 cycle, the level of profits peaked nearly six quarters before the peak of the business cycle. But in the average supply cycle, profits peaked four quarters ahead of the cycle peak, while in the 2001 cycle they were 13 quarters earlier. The rate of growth of profits, on the other hand, provides an even earlier warning of the peak of the business cycle than the level, which for this reason is of less practical use. In the average demand and supply cycle the rate of growth of profits peaked seven quarters earlier than the peak of the business cycle; in the 1990 cycle the lead was 11 quarters; and in the 2001 cycle the lead was an astonishing 25 quarters. This variability is accounted for by the varying length of the recovery phase in each business cycle. The interested reader should go back to chapter 4 to recall the factors that lengthen or shorten the recovery phase. But the quick answer is fortuitous or adverse shocks and the strength of the recovery – anaemic or buoyant. A fortuitous shock, such as the collapse of OPEC in the mid-1980s or the Asian-Russian crisis in 1997–98, or a long-term improvement in productivity, as in the second half of the 1990s, prolongs the recovery phase, whereas an adverse shock, such as a pronounced and long-lasting increase in the price of oil, shortens the recovery phase. The principle is that the longer the recovery phase, the more delayed is the peak of profitability. The buoyancy of the recovery is also of crucial importance. The more anaemic the recovery, the more delayed is the peak of profitability.

4.2   Coincident indicator property of the cycle trough and mid-cycle profit crisis

Whereas profits are undisputedly a leading indicator of the business cycle, they are mainly a coincident indicator of the trough. Figure 5.8 shows the bottom of the rate of growth of profits for eight quarters before and after the trough of the business cycle. In the average demand cycle and in the 2001 recession, profits bottomed at the same time as the economy – a coincident indicator. In the average supply cycle profits bottomed one quarter earlier, but in the 1991 recession they bottomed five quarters earlier.

The largely coincident property of profits can easily be explained in terms of the K-Model. In a recession profits are falling and the feedback loop in Figure 5.6 is negative. But this negative feedback loop is reversed

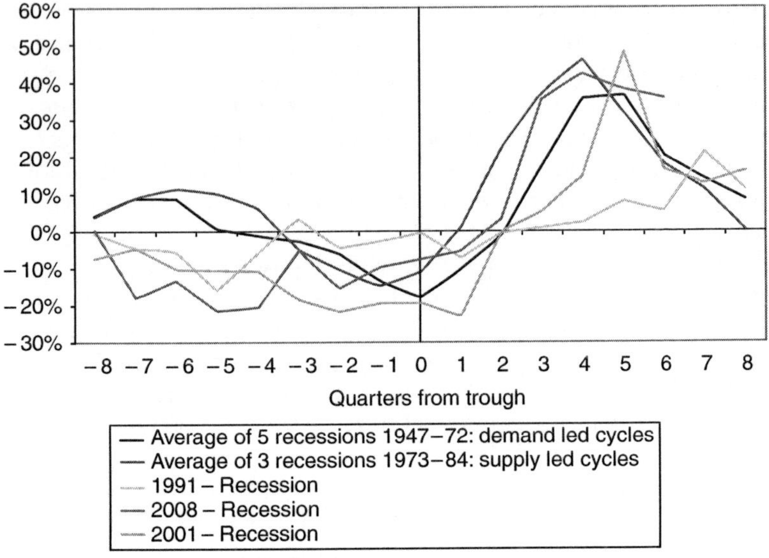

Figure 5.8   Total profits NFC %YoY

at some point in time. The reversal occurs when the pace at which employment falls exceeds that of economic growth. As the recession unravels, output falls faster than employment, but at some point in time firms begin to lay off employees at an even faster pace than the fall in output. At this point the fall in productivity is reversed, which triggers a reversal in unit labour cost and hence in profit margins. Sometimes, this process is delayed or shortened by developments in the pricing power of companies. If companies are unwilling to cut prices, then, *ceteris paribus*, the profit margin falls, and vice versa. Thus, the more companies delay cutting prices, the longer it takes for a reversal of the profit margin. The pricing power may cause a variation of a few months around the point where the profit margin turns around as the catalyst for the reversal is the bottom of the economy. When the economy hits a trough the negative feedback loop is changed into a positive loop. Hence, profits are largely a coincident indicator of the trough of the business cycle.

Figure 5.8 illustrates yet another feature of profitability – a mid-cycle crisis. In the first year of the recovery profits soar between 35 and 50 percent, but in the second year there is profit fatigue. The rate of growth of profits declines between zero and 15 percent. This is due to the reversal of unit labour cost, which bottoms roughly a year after the economy hits the trough. The average increase in unit labour cost is around 3 percent and this coincides with the period of profit fatigue. The increase in unit labour cost lowers the profit margin, thus causing the mid-cycle profit crisis. However, profitability recovers subsequently as the volume of sales keeps increasing and pricing power returns, as the economy becomes overheated. Hence, the volume of sales and pricing power become a significant factor in profitability as the recovery matures and mainly in the overheating phase.

4.3   The odd 1990 cycle – an anaemic recovery

In many ways the 1990 cycle is an exception to the norm. The rate of growth of profits bottomed five quarters before the economy, but it remained mainly negative even after the trough of the cycle (see Figure 5.8). In the following 12 months the recovery of profitability was disappointing compared to the norm; profits growth hit a high of just 10 percent compared with 35–50 percent in other cycles. The untypical pattern of profitability in the 1990 cycle is due to the anaemic recovery of the next three years.

The rate of growth of profits peaked in the fourth quarter of 1987, triggering the stock market crash of October 1987, as the new chairman of the Fed, Alan Greenspan, took the helm in July and started tightening monetary policy as inflation was on the increase and the economy was overheating. The tightening bias was briefly relaxed in the aftermath of the stock market crash, but it was resumed from February 1988 until mid-1989, as the economy remained overheated. The Fed was hoping to engineer a second soft landing in this long cycle, the first one being in 1984–85, and pre-emptively started cutting interest rates from mid-1989. Indeed, the economy began to cool down six months later and the overheating was replaced with some spare capacity in the first half of 1990. Greenspan cautiously lowered interest rates from nearly 10 percent to 8 percent by the time of the Iraqi invasion in Kuwait in August 1990. Corporate profits bottomed at the end of 1989 and began to recover. But the Gulf crisis, with the resulting sharp surge in the price of oil, tipped the balance and the economy fell into recession. Profits dived once more, as unit labour cost soared by nearly fivefold. In the first year of the recovery economic growth was subdued barely exceeding potential, while in 1993 spare capacity had re-emerged once more. In spite of the hesitant recovery in profits in the first three years of the recovery, there was a surge in profitability later on when the economy became overheated in 1994 with the rate of growth peaking at 27 percent in late 1994. Therefore, the 1990 cycle was odd in that the surge in profitability did not occur in the first year of the recovery, but was delayed for three years because the recovery was anaemic. In spite of this delay the rate of growth of profits finally shot up, albeit at a slightly lower peak that usual.

4.4   The last two asset-led business cycles

After the soft landing of 1994–95 and the easing of monetary policy in the second half of 1995, US economic growth exceeded potential once more in the spring of 1996 (see Figure 4.11). As a result of this overheating wage inflation accelerated and unit labour cost soared. It quadrupled to more than 4 percent in the 12 months to the autumn of 1998 (see Figure 5.7). The level of the profit margin peaked the moment the unit labour cost began to accelerate in the autumn of 1997 (see Figure 5.5). The Asian-Russian crisis of 1997–98 put a lid on wage growth for a year (from the autumn of 1998 to the autumn of 1999) and unit labour cost slowed down. However, the easing of monetary policy during the Asian-Russian crisis kept US economic growth intact with the economy remaining overheated. As a result wage growth and unit labour cost soared once more and the profit margin declined (negative rate of growth) from the end of 1999 causing a profits recession. A year later (i.e. at the end of 2000) the economy entered into a recession, which broke the wage–price spiral. Both wage inflation and the rate of growth of unit labour cost peaked in the autumn of 2000, thus paving the way for a revival of the profit margin. In the first half of 2001 employment was falling at a smaller pace than GDP growth thus delaying the revival of the profit margin for six months. But in the second half of 2001 the profit margin began to recover as the rate at which firms shed labour exceeded the pace of decline of economic growth, thus causing an improvement in productivity. The rate of growth of profits bottomed at the same time as the economy confirming the typical pattern of profits as a coincident indicator of the business cycle.

Profits surged in the first year of the recovery from the 2001 recession to more than 50 percent (see Figure 5.2). This was caused by plummeting unit labour costs that were triggered not so much by gains in productivity as in other cycles, as by plunging wage growth (see Figure 5.7). This untypical behaviour is mainly due to the weakening bargaining power of employees since the introduction of flexible labour markets in the 1990s. In the first year of the recovery, growth was anaemic (i.e. less than potential), causing the rally in profits to run out of steam in the second year of the new cycle. But unit labour cost remained extremely low, oscillating around zero, until mid-2004, thus paving the way for a second wave of a surge in profitability. The second wave occurred as growth finally picked up exceeding potential in 2004. In the second wave profits growth surged to 45 percent, slightly less than the peak in the first wave. But as the economy became overheated unit labour cost shot up and this put an end to the second wave of the boom in profitability. In spite of the anaemic recovery in the US, the world economy was booming and the demand for commodities, including oil, soared. This continued to push up unit labour cost that hit more than 4 percent in the first half of 2007, in spite of the economy growing around potential until mid-2006. Since mid-2004 the Fed was in the process of gradually removing the accommodation bias, which cooled the economy down creating some excess capacity from the second half of 2006 onwards. Under the twin pressure of rising unit labour cost and weak growth profits peaked in the autumn of 2006 and from the beginning of 2007 a profits recession began signalling a forthcoming recession for the economy as a whole, which indeed started in the fourth quarter of 2007. The Fed kept interest rates high until the eruption of the credit crisis in August 2007, as in spite of rapidly falling unit labour cost, the commodities bubble kept fanning CPI-inflation that only peaked in mid-2008 at nearly 6 percent. The high interest rates in the US and the rest of the world precipitated the simultaneous downturn of all major economies and resulted in an inverted yield curve in the US that pricked the house bubble causing huge losses for financial institutions in the course of 2007 through the exposure of the 'shadow banking' to the subprime market in the first instance and the overall market later on.

5   The outlook for profits and long-term risks

As the recession deepened a negative feedback loop in profits emerged with falling output forcing down profits. This negative spiral will be reversed when the pace at which firms shed labour exceeds the pace of decline in output. As we know from previous cycles the reversal in productivity will coincide with the bottom of the economy. Productivity bottomed in the first quarter of 2009 and unit labour cost peaked in the same quarter, thereby boosting the profit margin up. This heralds the beginning of a recovery in profitability. The figures in the second quarter of 2009 have endorsed this reversal of trends. Wage inflation is also declining and this will foster the improving trend in profitability. The K-Model suggests that profits will soar by 40 percent in the first year of the recovery, in line with other recoveries (see Figures 5.8 and 5.9). The expected surge in profitability in spite of an anaemic recovery should

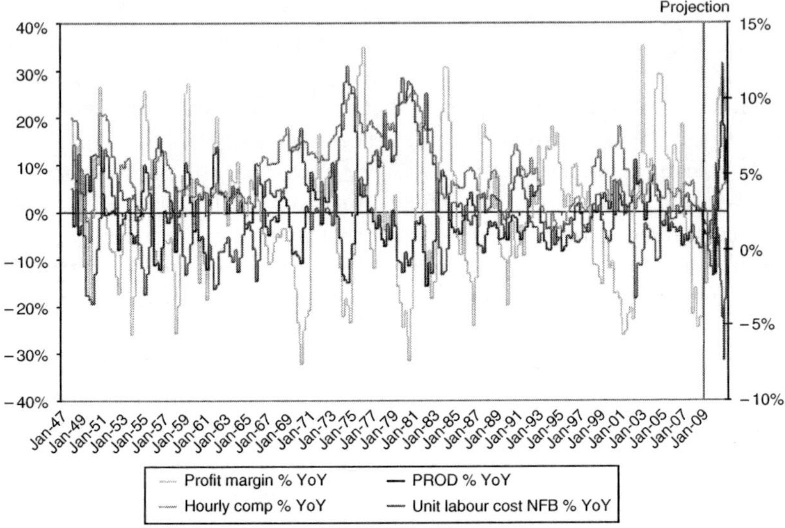

Figure 5.9   Profit margin and wage–price spiral

not be surprising. In fact, it is because of the anaemic recovery that the surge might occur. With an anaemic recovery there would be hardly any job creation and unemployment would continue to rise further weakening the bargaining power of employees. Accordingly, wage inflation would carry on abating, which along with further productivity gains would push down unit labour cost, thereby raising profit margins.

However, there are downside and upside risks to this mainline scenario after the first year of the recovery, namely from the spring of 2010 onwards. The recovery of the economy might falter, as the restocking process comes to an end and the positive impact of the fiscal and monetary stimulus wanes in the second year of its implementation. There are further downside risks if policymakers proceed with the 'exit strategy' and from the little progress that banks have made in repairing their impaired balance sheets, as a result of which bank lending remains subdued. If tight fiscal policy is adopted in 2010 to rein in the unprecedented budget deficit and soaring Federal debt, it will intensify the natural wearing of the fiscal multiplier in the second year onwards. The removal of quantitative easing will push up long term interest rates, thus undermining demand in the economy and the fragile housing market. The natural fatigue of profits in the second year of the recovery will be augmented if any one, or all, of these risks were to materialise.

But there are also upside risks. Fiscal policy might turn easy, in spite of the rhetoric of fiscal rectitude. The exit strategy from quantitative easing might be delayed once more and the Fed might even buy more asset-backed securities and US Treasuries. In this case the natural profit fatigue in the second year might be postponed until 2011. The economy will most probably become overheated with growth exceeding potential, thereby rekindling inflation with a lag. Fiscal and monetary policy would then be tightened, but in all probability that would be too much, too late. A profits recession will emerge first, followed after a year or so by a recession in the economy reigniting the forces of deflation.

6   Summary and conclusions

The long-held belief that the decline in long-term profitability was reversed with the support of Thatcher and Reagan of the free market economy has been refuted with the burst of the housing bubble. The profitability of non-financial companies, which forms the bulk of the total, has been in a long-term decline since the late 1960s. Shifting production abroad as a means of gaining competitiveness, which later gathered steam under the banner of globalisation, but also fierce competition from Europe, Japan and recently from China are the two most important contributors to this downtrend. The delusion of the reversal of this downtrend is due to three factors. First, there was a steep upward trend in the profitability of financial companies – a sixfold increase between 1982 and 2007. This was due to financial deregulation that started at the time and provided the framework for the development of financial engineering. The repeal of the Glass–Steagall Act in 1999 exaggerated this trend by fostering the development of 'bad' financial engineering. Second, repatriated profits from operations abroad also increased rapidly, a threefold increase in the last 25 years. Third, inflated profits in reported earnings, especially in the second half of the 1990s, have also contributed to this mistaken belief.

However, the bursting of the housing bubble not only revealed that this profitability is unsustainable in the long run, but also further undermined the profitability of non-financial companies. Moreover, the overhaul of the governance crisis has removed the upward bias of reported earnings and put them on a par with estimates from the NIPA accounts that were less sanguine. Finally, rising protectionism and 'beggar-thy-neighbour' policies, which are creeping up as of late, will further undermine long-term profitability. The inevitable conclusion is that overall profitability has resumed its downtrend after a 25-year long period of an uptrend.

Profitability is largely pro-cyclical; it rises in the upswing and falls in the downswing of a business cycle. The rate of growth of profits is a leading indicator of the peak of the business cycle, but the warning comes far too early in the cycle to be of any practical use. Profits growth peaks on average ten quarters earlier than the peak of the cycle, at the end of the recovery phase or early in the overheating phase. The level of profits, though, peaks on average six quarters before the peak of the cycle, thus being a timely leading indicator. A profits recession usually begins at the peak of the cycle, thus providing a further signal of a forthcoming recession for the economy as a whole. The rate of growth of profits is mostly a coincident indicator of the trough of the business cycle.

Output, unit labour cost, profit margin, price of output, unit profit and total profits form an upward or downward loop that is set in motion by shifts in policy variables, shocks in the wage–price spiral, world trade and the exchange rate. Once this spiral is set in motion, say, because of a fiscal or monetary stimulus, it produces a big jump in profits, which in time subsides, as in every round the additional stimulus is smaller than before. But in the new long run equilibrium the profit margin, unit profit and total profits are higher.

Unit profit plays a more important role than the volume of sales in boosting profitability, especially in the recovery phase. The volume of sales becomes important much later on – in the overheating phase – when the rate of growth of profits is more subdued. The profit margin also plays a more important role than pricing power in the recovery phase. Pricing power, as the volume of sales, becomes important much later on in the overheating phase. Profit margins are mainly affected by unit labour costs throughout the course of the business cycle, which in turn depend on productivity and wages. This taxonomy implies that for a turnaround of profitability what is required is an improvement in productivity that would lead to a reduction in unit labour cost, an increase in profit margin and unit profit. In fact, the condition that turns around a negative profit spiral is that the pace at which firms shed labour exceeds the pace of decline in output, as this implies a reversal in productivity. Profits register their best performance in the recovery phase, as there is a huge productivity improvement, which leads to a big reduction in unit labour cost causing a big leap in profit margin and unit profit. As the recovery matures the initial big impact in profits is pared as firms hire more labour and wages begin to increase once more. This leads to profit fatigue, which may develop into a mid-cycle profits crisis. At this stage the volume of sales and enhanced pricing power help propel profits further into the cycle. But as the economy becomes increasingly overheated proportionately more labour is required to increase output at even higher wages. This leads to the peak in profitability in the business cycle, which is turned into a profits recession once the rate of growth of output peaks and the economy enters the slowdown phase. This is the rationale of the K-Model, which is capable of explaining the stylised facts of all business cycles in the post-Second World War era.

In the current downturn the profits of financial companies have plunged to levels that are unprecedented in the entire post-Second World War era. On the other hand, the profits of non-financial companies have fared better than in other recessions. According to the K-Model the second quarter of 2009 is likely to mark the reversal of the year-on-year rate of growth of profits. Profitability will soar in the first year of the recovery in line with other cycles. However, there are downside and upside risks to this mainline scenario after the first year of the recovery. The current engine of growth is restocking, which is bolstered by a huge fiscal and monetary stimulus. But the restocking period will not last for more than a year. Moreover, the best impact of fiscal and monetary policy is felt also within the first year. Thus, both forces that underpin the recovery are likely to fade away after the first year of the recovery. The escalation of the Federal debt has caused great concerns and calls for its reversal. The unprecedented monetary stimulus that has brought interest rates to zero and the printing of money also give rise to concerns about inflation once the negative output gap is eliminated. If the policymakers were to reverse these strategies in 2010, then the recovery of profitability is most likely to falter in the second half of 2010 and beyond. The upside risks stem from further stimulus from fiscal and monetary policy in the course of 2010. In this case, there would be no profit fatigue in the second year of the recovery. Although such a stimulus will make the recovery sustainable in the short run, it will sow the seeds for another bubble that will burst later on, probably in 2012 or 2013. In the long run asset and debt deflation is inevitable, although the road would be bumpy with ups and downs. Thus, it is likely that the expected recovery will gather steam before it ends in tears. The forces of deflation are likely to prevail in the end.

6
Long-Term Risks to Investment Recovery

1 Introduction

Real gross private domestic investment, or simply investment, consists of residential and non-residential investment. The latter is usually referred to as business investment and includes office buildings, factory plants, equipment and inventories. Business investment plays a key role in business cycle analysis; it also holds the key to growth as it affects the capital stock in the economy and therefore capacity as well as long-term multi-factor productivity. A higher investment rate increases the capital stock in the economy and lifts (multi-factor) productivity. This increases the rate of growth of potential output and enables the economy to grow faster without producing higher inflation. Countries with fast growth have a high savings ratio and therefore a high investment to GDP ratio; and vice versa. In this chapter we analyse the long-term factors that affect investment.

Investment is the most volatile component of aggregate demand that invariably leads the economy into recession, but is a coincident or lagging indicator in recoveries. It is, in fact, 'the pace and pattern of business investment in fixed capital' that 'are central to our understanding of economic activity' (Chirinko, 1993, p. 1875). Hence, investment plays a key role in business cycle analysis and this chapter aims to explain the factors that cause short-run volatility in investment.

This chapter is organised as follows. Section 2 analyses the stylised facts of investment from a secular and business cycle point of view. Section 3 examines the short-run factors that affect investment, while section 4 the long-run factors that affect the volatility of investment. Section 5 provides an overview of the K-Model that integrates the short and long-run factors into a coherent whole. Section 6 analyses the risks to investment in the current environment. Finally, Section 7 concludes and summarises.

2   The stylised facts

Business investment as percent of GDP is characterised by two distinct trends in the post-war period – a mild upward trend that lasted until 1981 and a mild downtrend thereafter (see Figure 6.1).

Investment climbed in every cycle from a low of just over 2.5 percent of GDP just after the Second World War to a zenith at 13.5 percent of GDP in 1981; but declined since then with increasing volatility. The uptrend is the result of switching from a war machine in the 1940s to a peace economy that produces goods and services for the private sector. The uptrend in investment is associated with a corresponding downtrend in government expenditure (see Figure 6.1). The mild downtrend of the last thirty years, on the other hand, is more problematic to explain. There are two rival hypotheses. According to the first the mild downtrend stems from the tendency of US companies to shift production abroad as a means of cutting costs and remaining competitive against newly industrialised countries with modern capital stock. The shift of production abroad has accelerated in the chimera of the globalisation era in the 1990s. However, this hypothesis is not supported by the data. Although there is a clear upward trend in overseas US Foreign Direct Investment (FDI) since 1994, when the data begin, there is a

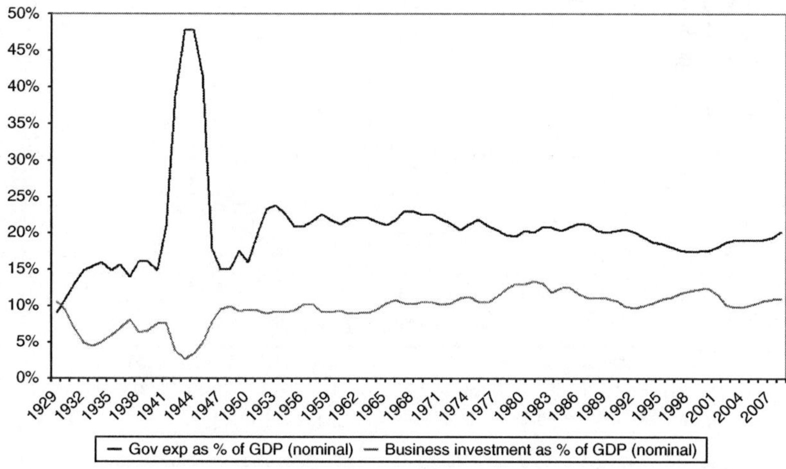

Figure 6.1   Business investment and government expenditure as % of GDP

corresponding foreign direct investment in the US so that net FDI is zero on average. The offsetting FDI in the US is the result of a strategic decision by foreign companies from developed as well as newly industrialised countries to capture market share in the biggest consumer market in the world without suffering from large exchange rate fluctuations or being subject to import restrictions of any sort or, finally, for beating the signal 'buy home products'. According to the second hypothesis the mild downtrend is the result of US facing stifle competition from newly industrialised countries. This seems a more plausible explanation and we shall return to it later on in this chapter when we consider the long-term factors that affect investment.

We now turn to the role of investment in business cycles. Figure 6.2 shows the behaviour of investment for eight quarters before and after the trough of the recession as a percentage of GDP. To simplify comparisons only the following are shown in this figure: the average of the five demand-led recessions in 1947–72, the average of the three supply-led business cycles in 1973–84, the early 1990s, the 2001 and the 2008 recession. For the latter the prediction of the K-Model is that the trough of the business cycle is the second quarter of 2009, which is also the latest point for which data are available. Thus points to the right of the trough on the line labelled '2008 recession' represent the K-Model forecast. In all cyclical downturns investment bottoms either at the trough of the business cycle or with a lag of one quarter. Hence, investment is

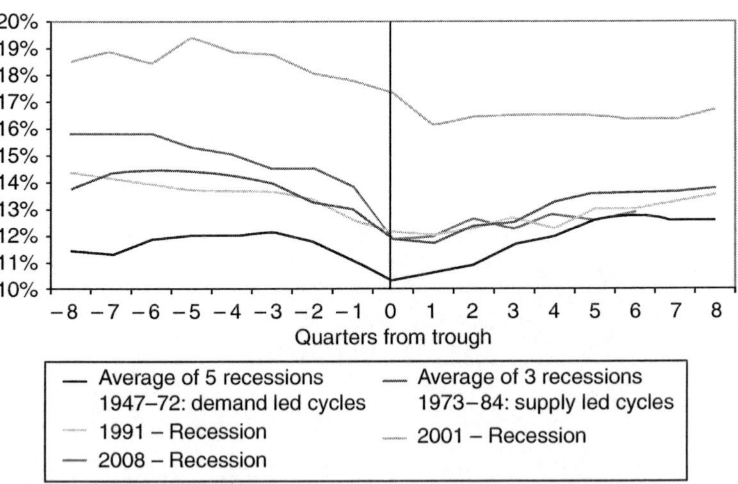

Figure 6.2   Investment as a % of GDP

either a coincident or lagging indicator of the trough of the business cycle. On the other hand, investment downturns invariably drag the economy into recession. The fall in investment in the current downturn, since August 2007, is the steepest of all recessions, 4.0 percent of GDP. In the average demand-led cycle, investment fell by 1.9 percent of GDP, while in the average supply-led cycle it fell by 2.8 percent; in the 1991 downturn it fell by 2.4 percent and in 2001 by 3.3 percent.

Upturns in investment usually lead the economy to recovery and an investment rebound is a sine qua non for the sustainability of the recovery of the overall economy. However, in the recovery of 1991 investment grew at the smallest pace of all nine previous business cycles, leading the recovery to be called anaemic. In the first year of the recovery investment grew by 1.0 percent of GDP, compared with 1.8 percent in the average demand- and supply-led cycle. In the first year of the 2001 recovery, investment was even more anaemic than in 1991, increasing by a meagre 0.3 percent of GDP. In the current downturn, the K-Model suggests that investment will increase by 1 percent of GDP, in line with the 1991 anaemic recovery. We shall examine the causes of the anaemic recovery in section 4, where we examine the long-run factors affecting investment. But in a summary statement the anaemic nature of the 1991 recovery was due to the balance sheet problems (or imbalances) of the business sector; while the even more anaemic nature of the 2001 recovery was due to the added balance sheet problems of the personal sector. In the current downturn the balance sheet problems of the business sector are due to a spillover effect from the personal and banking sector, which are the worst since the Great Depression.

3   Short-run factors affecting investment

Investment must turn around if the recovery is to become sustainable. This, in turn, implies that profitability must begin to recover and capacity utilisation must also bottom and improve. In the average downswing capacity utilisation fell by –12 percent from the peak, but in the current downturn it has declined the more than in any other recession, –18 percent, mostly as a result of the unexpected collapse of consumption in the second half of 2008 which prompted companies to slash production and investment land shed labour at an unprecedented rate (see Figure 6.3). The same figure shows that capacity utilisation is a coincident or lagging indicator of the trough of the business cycle. It bottoms either at the trough or more usually with a one-quarter lag. In the average demand cycle capacity utilisation recovered fully within

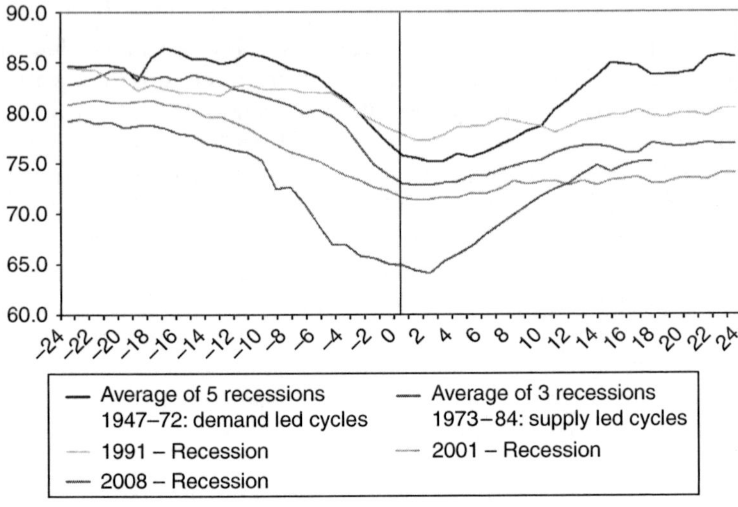

Figure 6.3   Capacity utilisation in manufacturing

two years from the bottom, but in all subsequent cycles it recovered only partly. In the two anaemic recoveries of 1991 and 2001 capacity utilisation did not improve as fast as in the average demand cycle. Two years after the trough, capacity utilisation recovered a meagre 30–40 percent of the ground lost in the downswing because of too much capacity in relation to demand. In the case of the 2001 downturn the excess capacity that was installed in the euphoria years of the internet bubble in the second half of the 1990s was not dented because of the resilience of consumption in the downswing of the cycle. The low capacity utilisation (or excess capacity) shows the extent to which demand was overestimated in the second half of the 1990s that acted as a hindrance to the recovery of investment. In spite of the worst ever decline in capacity utilisation in the current downturn, the K-Model suggests that the worst is over, but the improvement will be at best modest as the recovery is expected to be anaemic because of the balance sheet problems of households and banks.

Figure 6.4 shows the profits of non-financial companies as a growth rate on the period a year earlier. Profits are highly cyclical; they fall in the downswing and rise in the upswing of the cycle. Profitability is largely a coincident indicator of the trough of the cycle; profits usually bottom in the trough of the cycle. In the average demand and supply cycle profits fell in the downswing by something less than

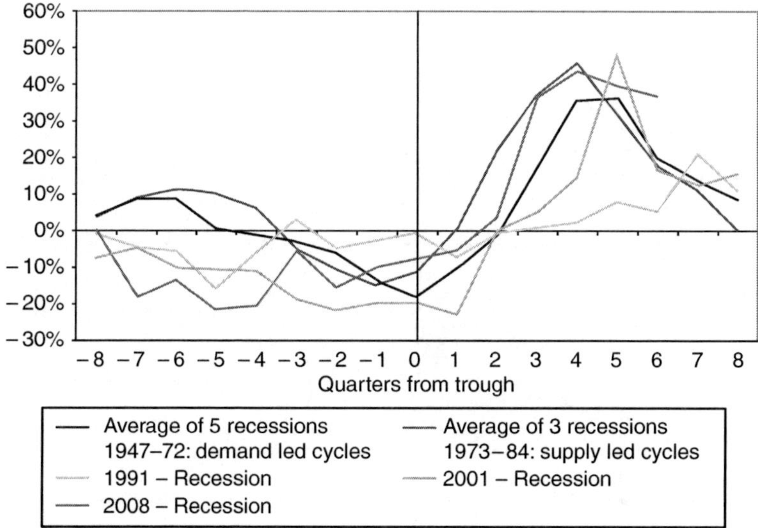

Figure 6.4   Total profits NFC % YoY

20 percent. In the 2001 cycle profits fell much more, nearly 30 percent. But profitability recovers in the upswing, thus enabling investment to rebound and make the recovery sustainable. In the first year of the recovery profits rebound very strongly. In the average demand- and supply-cycle profits skyrocketed by 40 percent (y-o-y). In the 2001 cycle profits rebounded at an even faster pace than in other cycles, more than 50 percent. The exception was the 1991 cycle. Profits fell less in the downswing – by just over 10 percent – but in the upswing the recovery was meagre at best. In the current downturn profits have fallen as much as in the average cycle, less than 20 percent. But this, of course, refers to non-financial companies, whereas the profits of financials have plummeted by 75 percent from peak to bottom. In the first year of the expected recovery profits are likely to soar by 40 percent according to the K-Model (see Figure 6.4). As it is known from chapter 5 profits improve once the unit labour cost peaks; this boosts the profit margin that triggers a rebound in unit profit.

Most of the time the year-on-year rate of growth of unit labour cost is a leading indicator of the trough of the business cycle, but by a variable lead of one to five quarters (see Figure 6.5). In the average demand cycle, although unit labour cost peaked five quarters ahead of the trough, there was no significant improvement until the trough was reached. In the

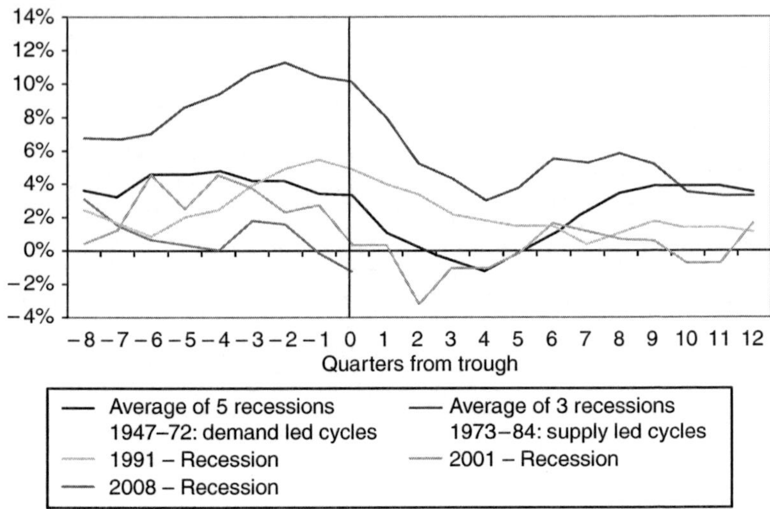

Figure 6.5   Unit labour cost % YoY

first year of the recovery, though, the unit labour cost fell dramatically and this improved profit margins and therefore profits skyrocketed to 35 percent in the first year of the recovery. In the average supply cycle unit labour cost peaked one quarter ahead of the trough and fell even more sharply than the demand cycle. Hence, the rebound in profits was even bigger; in the first year of the recovery profits jumped 45 percent compared to 35 percent in the demand cycle. In the 1991 cycle unit labour cost peaked again one quarter ahead of the trough, but the fall in the next year was small because the recession was shallow and short. The small improvement in unit labour cost is responsible for the partial recovery of profitability. In the 2001 cycle unit labour cost peaked three quarters ahead of the trough and fell in the first year of the recovery. The much longer fall in unit labour cost contributed to a phenomenal rebound in profits that jumped to more than 50 percent in the first year of the recovery, the biggest ever. In the current downturn unit labour cost peaked three quarters ahead of the bottom and is already on a downtrend. The K-Model suggests that unit labour cost will continue to fall within the next four quarters and this will improve profitability. In the first year of the recovery profits will jump by nearly 40 percent, but with some faltering in the second year.

The other factor that restrains earnings and must be corrected in order for the recovery to take place and for investment to pick up is that

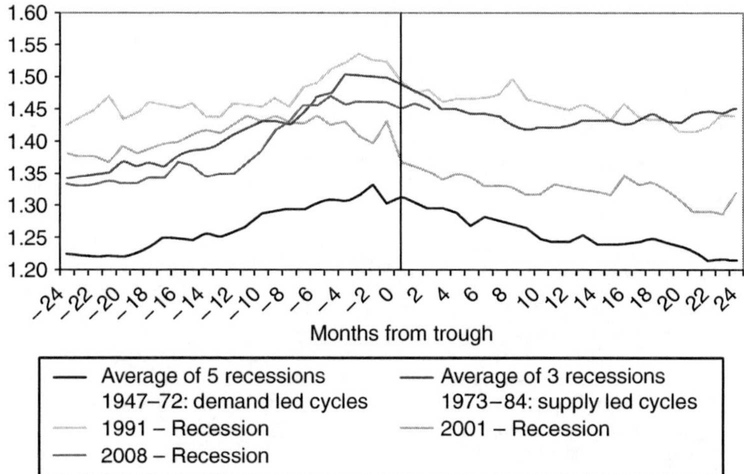

Figure 6.6   Inventory to sales ratio in manufacturing

companies must first liquidate their inventories of unsold goods. Thus, the inventory-to-sales ratio in business and in manufacturing for which the data are longer is a leading indicator of the trough of the business cycle by one or five months (see Figure 6.6). The inventory-to-sales ratio rises in the downswing and falls in the recovery. The correction phase lasts for the first two years of the recovery, as the ratio dwindles since companies are meeting demand by partly running down their inventories. In the current downturn business inventories swell in the second half of 2008 with the ratio jumping from 1.25 to 1.46 in January 2009. However, companies started to liquidate unwanted inventories since the beginning of 2009, a process that is expected to last until the end of 2010, thereby paving the way for a recovery in investment.

In a typical cycle production is resumed after excess inventories are liquidated. Hence, industrial production is a lagging indicator of the trough of the business cycle by one or two months (see Figure 6.7). In the 1991 recession it bottomed with a one-month lag and at a higher rate than the average demand- or supply-led business cycle. However, it grew at a smaller pace during the recovery, thereby underlining the anaemic nature of the recovery. In the 2001 cycle it bottomed with a one-month lag again, but the recovery fizzled out after the first year. During the second round of retrenchment production cuts led to a double-dip recession in manufacturing, but the reduction in unit labour

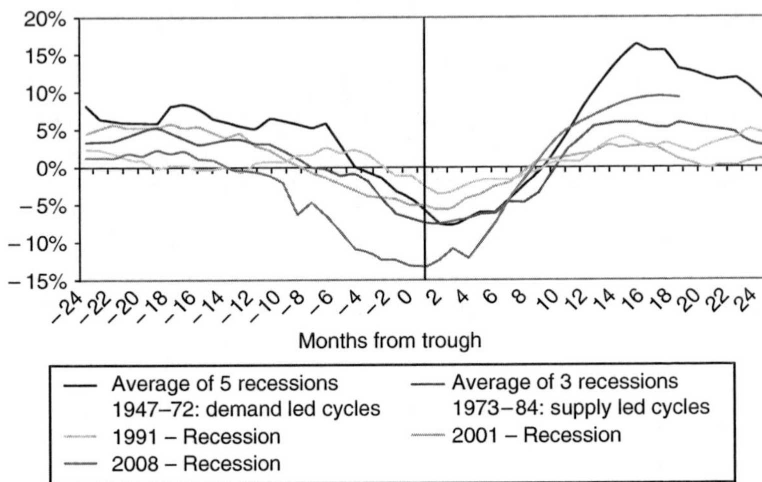

Figure 6.7   Total industrial production % YoY

cost, the restoration of profitability and the lean inventories paved the way for increased production later on. In the current downturn industrial production fell nearly twice as much as during the typical cycle, thus making the current recession the worst in the post-Second World War era. According to the K-Model, industrial production is very near the bottom, but it will not return to positive growth before the beginning of 2010. However, in the course of 2010 industrial production growth will gather steam (see Figure 6.7).

Overall, for investment to turn around and make the recovery sustainable a number of short-run factors must be fulfilled. First and foremost profitability must rebound. This is largely a coincident indicator but occasionally it can be a leading indicator of the trough of the business cycle by just one quarter. Usually, the rebound of profits is very strong in the first year of the recovery. But this necessitates an early peak in the cycle in unit labour cost and a decline later on before it gathers pace in the first year of the recovery. In the 1991 cycle the fall in unit labour cost, although it began two quarters ahead of the trough, was very mild, thereby restraining the recovery of profitability and hence that of investment. This was partly due to the short and shallow recession, in which unemployment did not increase substantially. In the 2001 cycle unit labour cost fell significantly and profitability recovered to a record in the first year of the recovery. However, huge excess capacity that was installed in the second half of the 1990s because of overoptimistic expectations of demand growth restrained investment, thus making the recovery anaemic as in the 1991 cycle. In the current cycle a healthy rebound in profitability is expected in line with other cycles (see Figure 6.4).

Two further considerations suggest themselves. One such consideration that has to be accounted for in investment recovery is that capacity utilisation must bottom and begin to rebound. In the current downturn capacity utilisation fell more than in any other cycle, as consumption plummeted in the second half of 2008. However, the K-Model suggests that capacity utilisation will begin a modest recovery (see Figure 6.3). Another consideration is that businesses must liquidate their unwanted inventories that piled up in the downswing. In the current downturn stocks piled up in the second half of 2008, but companies started since January 2009 to clear them. This, according to the K-Model, paves the way for easing of the production cuts with positive growth expected at the beginning of 2010.

4   Long-run factors affecting investment: corporate sector imbalances

The current business cycle and the previous two are associated with balance sheet adjustments of a sector (corporate, personal or banking), in contrast to the typical cycle in the post-Second World War era, which was free of such problems. These balance sheet adjustments give rise to an anaemic recovery, which is the most likely scenario for the current crisis.

A measure of the poor financial health of the corporate sector is its net worth, measured as assets less liabilities at current prices, as a percentage of nominal GDP. At the trough of the 1991 downturn the net worth of the corporate sector was 84 percent of GDP, lower than in any other cycle (see Figure 6.8). In the 2001 downturn the net worth was 92 percent, while in the 2008 downturn it is 93 percent. The anaemic recovery of corporate profitability in the early 1990s downturn was due to the poor financial health of the corporate sector. The net worth of the corporate sector deteriorated even during the recovery phase of the 1991 downturn. By contrast, it improved around the trough in the demand- and supply-led business cycles and fluctuated within a small range throughout the cyclical downturn (see Figure 6.8). Moreover, throughout the early 1990s downturn (two years before and after the trough) the net worth of the corporate sector was on a downward trend. This is due to the high debt gearing, characteristic of modern corporate finance. In every business cycle debt levels have increased.[1] In the demand-led

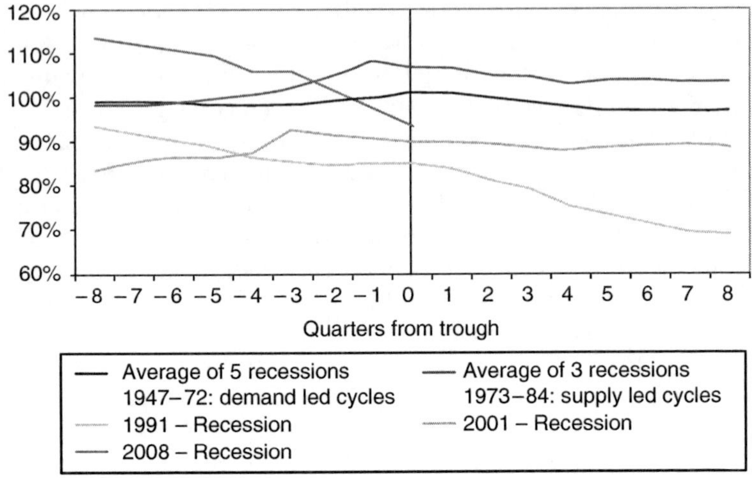

Figure 6.8   Corporate sector net worth as % of GDP

business cycles debt as a percentage of GDP peaked at the trough at 28 percent, while in the supply-led business cycles it increased to 33 percent (see Figure 6.9). But in the last three cycles (1991, 2001 and 2008) it soared to 43 percent, 47 percent and 52 percent, respectively, thus suggesting yet another anaemic recovery from the current crisis.

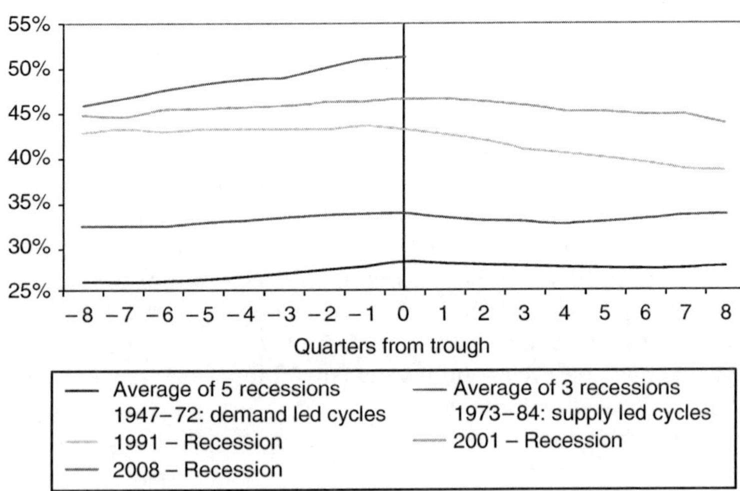

Figure 6.9   Corporate sector debt as % of GDP

The high debt levels require not only more expensive servicing, as interest rates are usually high during the downswing, but also large volumes of new issues to replenish maturing debt. In the downswing access to capital markets and the terms of issuing new debt deteriorate. Companies are, therefore, forced to cut drastically on new credit poised to finance investment and refrain from refinancing existing obligations on worse terms. This makes the recovery anaemic, as companies attempt to pay back debts and curb spending on new investment; and all this on top of low demand for company products. This is exactly what happened in the recovery of the 1991 cycle. Thus, the 1991 cycle differed substantially from the previous recessions of 1947–72 because the corporate sector was involved in the long process of curbing its high debt levels and restoring a healthy balance sheet. By the end of the second year of the 1991 recovery companies had repaid 5 percent of their debt as a percentage of GDP. By contrast, in the average demand- and supply-led cycle companies repaid debt only in the first year of the recovery and only by 1 percent of GDP, while debt was again on the increase in the second year. In the 2001 cycle, although debt levels increased in the downswing, they fell in the upswing returning to the level where they started from. In the current downturn a similar process of paying back debt is expected that is very likely to cause an anaemic recovery.

The rate of growth of corporate debt peaks between one or two years before the trough, as companies cut back on new investment (see Figure 6.10). In the average demand- and supply-led business cycle the

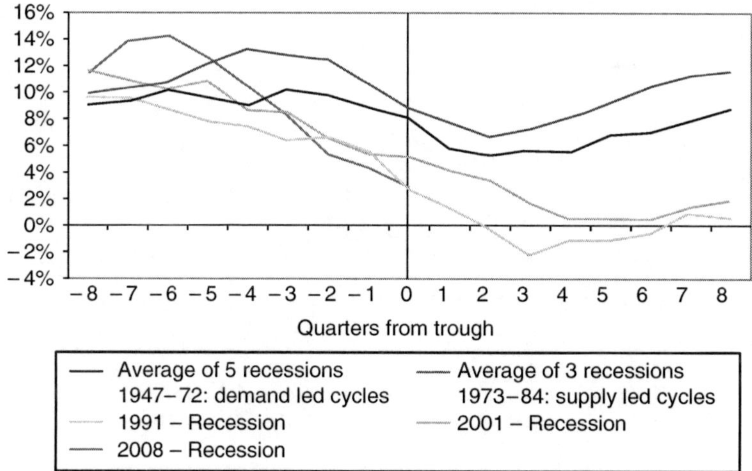

Figure 6.10   Corporate debt % YoY

rate of growth of debt bottomed two quarters after the trough, but at a positive rate. Hence, debt never stopped growing – its rate of growth simply slowed. By contrast, in the early 1990s downturn the growth of debt bottomed in three rather than two quarters, but also at a negative rate. So, for the first time firms reduced debt levels to restore financial health on their balance sheet. Debt began to increase again nearly two years after the trough. In the 2001 downturn, demand for credit was reduced from 11.2 percent at the peak to 1.4 percent five quarters after the trough. Debt increased only slightly throughout the recovery (see Figure 6.10). Hence, companies were very cautious in borrowing despite the buoyant recovery in the second half of 2003. In the current cycle the growth rate of debt peaked six quarters before the trough, but fell even more sharply than the 2001 cycle. The K-Model suggests that firms will continue to curb debt well into the recovery of 2010, thereby making the recovery anaemic.

The ways debt levels affect other company decisions can be judged by an examination of the degree of debt leverage, measured by the stock of debt as a percentage of internal funds. The latter is defined as after-tax corporate profits, less dividends plus depreciation (net cash flow). Figure 6.11 shows this measure of debt leverage. Although companies are usually cutting on debt growth in the downswing of the cycle, internal funds decline even faster and debt leverage is increasing. In the

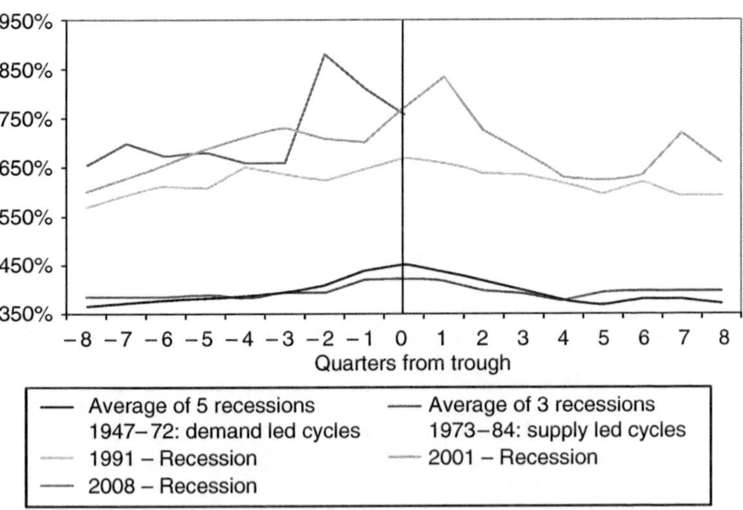

Figure 6.11   Degree of debt leverage: corporate sector debt as % of internal funds

recovery internal funds improve faster and debt leverage is decreasing. In the average demand-led cycle debt leverage increased 87 percent in the downswing, but it fell 80 percent in the recovery. In the average supply-led cycle debt leverage increased 37 percent in the downswing, but fell 26 percent in the recovery. In the 1991 downturn debt leverage increased 90 percent in the downswing, but fell 72 percent in the recovery. In the 2001 downturn debt leverage soared 170 percent in the downswing, but fell 204 percent in the recovery. Hence, in the 2001 cycle companies managed to restructure their balance sheet faster than any other business cycle, although part of this success is due to the one-off measures that boosted profitability; increased government deficit helped, too. In the current downturn debt leverage jumped before the trough, but shows signs of abating. The K-Model suggests that the robust improvement of profitability will curb debt leverage in the upswing, thus paving the way for a recovery of investment later on, as it happened in the 2001 cycle.

The extent of any retrenchment depends on the ease of refinancing the stock of debt and the burden of servicing it on profits and net cash flow. The ability to refinance debt depends on its composition as well as on the Fed funds rate. The more companies rely on long-term debt as opposed to short-term debt, the easier it becomes to sustain a high level of debt in a cyclical downturn, other things being equal. Figure 6.12

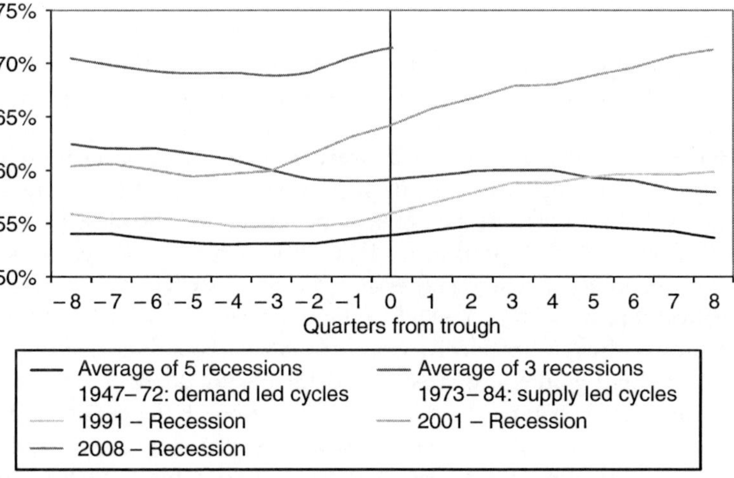

Figure 6.12   Long-term debt (securities & mortgages) to total debt

shows the long-term debt relative to the total. Long-term debt is defined as corporate bonds, municipal securities, which are issued by the local authorities to provide finance to local businesses, and mortgages. Short-term debt is defined as commercial paper, bank loans and other loans and advances, mainly from finance companies. In the average demand- and supply-led business cycle the ability of firms to switch from short- to long-term debt was limited. It only started one or two quarters before the trough and was maintained for one year into the recovery. In the average demand-led cycle the switch to long-term debt was only 1.7 percent of the total. In the average supply-led cycle the switch was only 1 percent of the total. By contrast, in the 1991 downturn companies found it easier to switch into long-term debt by over 5 percent. Thus, despite the fact that the level of debt was much higher in the 1991 downturn than in previous recessions, companies found it easier to switch into long-term debt. In the 2001 downturn companies started switching into long-term debt much earlier than ever before, five quarters compared to one or two; indeed, companies switched almost 12 percent of total debt into long-term debt. But whether such a switch is beneficial to the net cash flow depends on the relative cost of finance between capital markets and banks. In this context it is worth mentioning that the Fed dropped interest rates much faster and more aggressively during the 2001 downturn than the 1991 one and this helped enormously the speed of the balance sheet adjustment, thus paving the way for a rebound in investment later on in the cycle, despite an anaemic recovery in the first two years. In the current downturn companies started to switch into long-term debt two quarters ahead of the trough, but it remains to be seen whether they will continue to do so in view of the higher cost of borrowing in the capital markets compared to banks.

Figure 6.13 shows the spread between Moody's AAA bond yield and the bank prime-lending rate. In the average demand-led cycle this spread was almost zero in the downswing and around 50 basis points in the recovery. So, the switch from short- to long-term debt was not very important. In the average supply-led cycle the switch into long-term debt would have been beneficial to the net cash flow, as it would have been much cheaper to borrow from capital markets than from banks. However, high-grade companies were unable to do so. In the 1991 cycle, high-grade companies switched much more than ever before into long-term debt. In the downswing it was beneficial, as it was cheaper to borrow from the capital markets than the banks, but the benefit was lost in the recovery, as the relative cost of borrowing was reversed. This

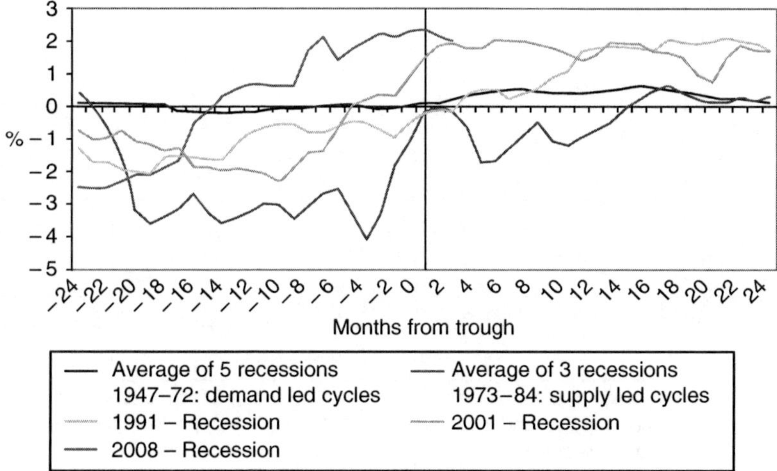

Figure 6.13   Spread between AAA yield and prime lending rate

adversely affected the net cash flow of the high-grade companies in the recovery phase and provides another cause for the anaemic recovery. In the 2001 downturn the switch into long-term debt was even more pronounced and took place much earlier. However, the benefit also disappeared sooner. In the first two years of the recovery it was more expensive for high-grade companies to borrow from the capital markets than the banks. Hence, the switch into long-term debt became a hindrance in the recovery. In the current downturn the benefit of borrowing from the capital markets disappeared sooner than in any other cycle. The K-Model suggests that the cost of borrowing from the capital markets will remain higher relative to the banks well into the recovery, thus proving a hindrance to the recovery of investment.

For low-grade companies the situation was even worse. Figure 6.14 shows the spread between Moody's Baa bond yield and the bank prime-lending rate. Very soon in the 1991 cycle, it became more expensive than ever before to borrow from capital markets than from banks. This was another reason for the anaemic recovery. In the 2001 downturn the situation was much worse in the first two years of the recovery. The large switch into long-term debt was misconceived, as the rate spread increased by nearly 5 percent, making borrowing from capital markets totally unattractive in the first two years of the recovery, thereby explaining the worst ever anaemic recovery. So, in the 2001 downturn companies were more indebted than ever before, but they managed to switch from short- to

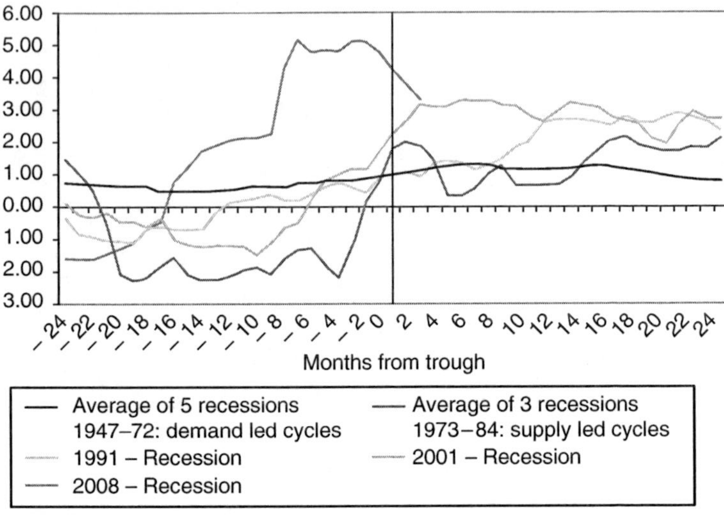

Figure 6.14   Spread between Baa yield and prime lending rate

long-term debt. This represents a reversal of a long-term trend. In the early 1950s the dependence on long-term debt was around 70 percent. In the following thirty years companies reduced their dependence on long-term debt and increased that on short-term debt. Indeed, the ratio of long-term to total debt was reduced to 53 percent by 1985, some 17 percent less than in the early 1950s. From then onwards companies increased their dependence on long-term debt again and reduced that on short-term debt. At the end of the second year of the 2001 recovery the proportion of long-term debt to total stood at 72 percent. Hence, there was a complete reversal. Although the dependence on long-term debt is beneficial in the long run, it can be a drawback in the recovery phase. This is so since, although the cost of borrowing from banks is reduced, that on capital markets is increased, thereby making the recovery anaemic. This adversely affected the recovery both in the early 1990s and in the 2001 recovery. In the current cycle the situation is worse than ever before. The switch into long-term debt started much earlier than before, but at no benefit to the corporate sector, as the cost of borrowing from the capital markets relative to the banks for both high- and low-grade companies skyrocketed even in the downswing of the cycle. The K-Model suggests that the cost of borrowing from the capital markets relative to the banks will remain historically high, but will improve in the recovery compared to the downswing.

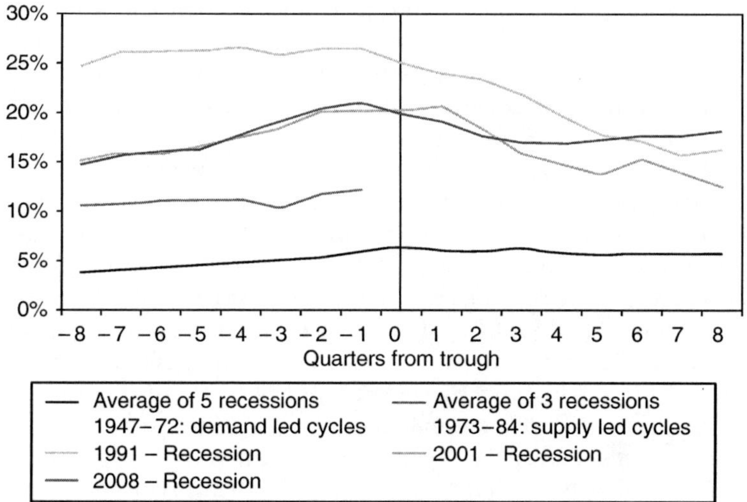

Figure 6.15   Interest payments as % of net cash flow

The extent of the damage from the dependence on long-term debt depends on the burden that the servicing of debt imposes on profits and net cash flow. Figure 6.15 shows corporate interest payments relative to net cash flow. Debt service increased from 6 percent in the average demand cycle to 21 percent in the average supply cycle, as interest rates soared to double-digit figures and debt levels increased. Although interest rates fell in the second half of the 1980s, debt levels made a big leap up to the 1991 cycle and debt service jumped even higher – to 26.5 percent. However, in the first two years of the recovery debt service was curtailed to just over 16 percent, thus paving the way for a recovery in investment later in the cycle. Nonetheless, the damage was done in the first two years of the recovery, thus making it anaemic. The situation in the 2001 downturn was much better as debt service peaked at nearly 21 percent of net cash flow but eased to 12.5 percent at the end of the second year of the recovery. In the current downturn debt service is low compared to the previous two cycles that shared balance sheet problems. Moreover, it has not increased significantly during the downswing. This augurs well for a resumption of debt once demand conditions improve.

Overall, there are some common factors that caused an anaemic recovery in the last two cycles, but there are also some differences in each cycle. Soaring debt levels and debt leverage, a switch into long-term debt, widening credit spreads and, in particular, high and rising long-term interest rates relative to short-term bank loan rates contributed to an anaemic recovery in the 1991 and 2001 cycles. But each cycle is different. In the 1991 downturn the net worth deteriorated both in the downswing and in the upswing and for the first time companies even reduced their nominal levels of debt. In the 2001 downturn debt levels and the degree of leverage were higher than ever before. The switch into long-term debt helped in the downswing, but it became a hindrance in the recovery, as companies did not benefit from the low interest rates that were introduced by the Fed. Credit risk soared after the burst of the internet bubble, and the interest differential between capital markets and banks widened. These problems contributed to the anaemic recovery of investment in the first two years of the new cycle. However, these problems abated as the recovery matured. The net worth of the corporate sector deteriorated only slightly compared to the early 1990s downturn, as companies were very quick in restructuring their balance sheet. Debt levels as percent of GDP were reduced, as growth in the economy was very brisk. Moreover, interest rates were lower than in any other cycle and debt service was lower than the previous thirty years. Credit risk abated after the first two years of the recovery. Moreover, interest rates remained low relative to previous downturns. This improvement in the long-run factors paved the way for a sustained investment recovery in the 2001 cycle, although with a two-year lag.

At the peak of the current cycle the net worth of the corporate sector was the highest ever, but it deteriorated very rapidly in the downswing. However, debt levels are higher than ever before and the growth rate has fallen more sharply than in any other cycle in the downswing. The proportion of long-term debt is already at the peak level of the 2001 cycle. But the worst is that the cost of the capital markets relative to the cost of borrowing from the banks is at its highest ever level. The only favourable factor is that the burden of debt service is low by historical standards. On balance, all these factors suggest that investment will remain subdued in the next two years and therefore the recovery will be anaemic.

5   The K-Model of investment

The K-Model of investment encapsulates the above short-run and long-run factors affecting investment. The rationale of the K-Model is summarised in Figure 6.16. The medium grey boxes illustrate the variables that belong to the investment loop. The light grey box illustrates the variables

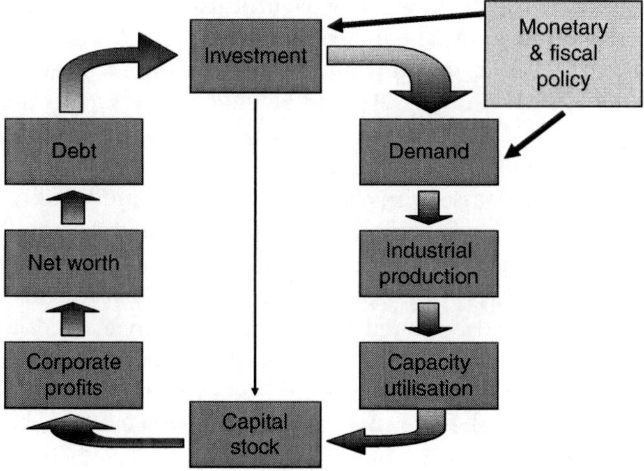

Figure 6.16   Investment model

that cause a shock to the investment spiral. Shocks to the investment spiral are introduced by monetary policy through changes in the interest rate and fiscal policy, directly through depreciation incentives on investment, as in the first two years of the 2001 recovery, and indirectly through influencing demand in the economy via changes in tax rates and government expenditure. Assume that the economy is in long-run equilibrium so that the investment spiral is idle. Consider now a shock in policy (fiscal or monetary) that stimulates demand in the economy and leads to higher GDP growth. If the shock stems from a change in monetary policy, the lower interest rates will affect both demand in the economy and the cost of capital that directly stimulates investment. The increase in investment will further increase demand in the economy. If the shock stems from personal sector tax cuts or increases in government expenditure the effect is to stimulate demand in the economy, which can permanently increase aggregate demand if the deficit spending is sustained. If the shock consists of depreciation incentives, like those that were implemented in 2001 and 2003, the effect on investment is direct and timely.

The higher level of growth in the economy will boost production, either immediately if inventories are lean, or after a fashion, if there is an overhang of unwanted stocks. The higher level of output would lift capacity utilisation and corporate profits. The latter would raise the net worth of the corporate sector that may induce companies to increase borrowing. All these factors, with the exception of borrowing, would boost investment. The increase in investment would again boost demand and a second round would be set in motion. In every round the additional increase in investment would become smaller and, after an infinite number of times, the loop will converge to a new long-run equilibrium. Given the size of the government deficit and the net desire to save in financial assets, investment, industrial production, capacity utilisation and profits are higher than the original equilibrium. The increase in investment from any shock (for example, depreciation incentives) is not explosive. This means that the investment spiral is stable. The stability is ensured by the fact that in every round the increase in investment raises the capital stock nearer to its desired level, for a given level of demand. Moreover, the extra stimulus to demand is also becoming smaller and therefore the desired level of capital stock converges to a new higher – but not infinite – level. Finally, the increase in profits is also finite (see chapter 3) and the higher level of debt also dampens the increase in investment.

It is clear from the above analysis that investment depends on six variables. We may assemble together the relevant variables and group them into two categories, as our above analysis suggests. This implies four short-run variables: Capacity Utilisation (CU), Industrial Production (IP), Corporate Profits (CP), and the Interest Rate, the Prime Lending Rate (PLR). It also implies two long-run variables: Debt-to-Investment ratio (DI) and Corporate Sector Net Worth to GDP ratio (NW).

We may, thus, have as our fundamental equation:

$$GI = GI \ (CU, \ IP, \ CP, \ PLR, \ DI, \ NW) \tag{1}$$

where GI stands for gross investment.

Clearly, our approach to the determinants of investment begins with the general proposition that a number of variables can affect it. We may distinguish economic activity variables (such as CU and IP), essentially based on the accelerator investment model, interest rate/cost-of-capital variables (such as the PLR) and quantity of finance variables.[2] The distinction between cost-of-finance and quantity-of-finance effects relies heavily on the more realistic assumption of imperfect capital markets. The imperfection of capital markets is explained by resorting to a number of factors, but asymmetric information between lenders and borrowers, which might lead to credit rationing, is the most predominant one (Stiglitz and Weiss, 1989; Bernanke and Gertler, 1989). Financial variables and constraints are explicitly included in investment models through the usage of cash flow variables in the menu of explanatory variables for investment (see, for example, Fazzari, 1993; Fazzari and Peterson, 1993; the ideas behind this formulation, however, are embedded in Keynes, 1936). Full recognition of the importance of financial variables in the determination of investment was neglected for a long time in view of the influence of the Modigliani–Miller theorem that corporation leverage and personal leverage of investors were perfect substitutes. As has just been suggested, it is now recognised that this is no longer the case.

Financial factors as crucial determinants of investment have attracted a great deal of interest. External funds are no longer thought to be perfect substitutes for internal funds, in view of the recognition that capital markets are imperfect. Finance matters again and significantly, just as it did in Keynes's (1936) work (see also Mayer, 1994).[3] The quantity-of-finance variables can be internal finance variables (such as CP which can be viewed as a critical variable in terms of internal finance; high CP indicates greater capacity by the corporate sector to generate internal funds) and external finance variables (such as DI, an external cash/flow component, on the assumption that a high debt environment is less likely to provide a stable financial base necessary for investment to materialise). Internal funds and net worth variables are thought to be particularly significant variables in the study by Hubbard (1998) when reviewing capital-market imperfections and investment. The study concludes that '(1) all else being equal, investment is significantly correlated with proxies for changes in net worth or internal funds; and (2) that correlation is most important for firms likely to face information related capital-market imperfections' (p. 193). The importance of the external funds and cash flow variables is central to, and particularly emphasised, in the 'new consensus' macroeconomics (see, for example, Bernanke and Blinder, 1988; Bernanke and Gertler, 1989, 1999). It has also been vetted more recently by Greenspan (2002b), who argues that 'capital investment will be most dependent on the outlook of profits and the resolution of the uncertainties surrounding the business outlook and the geopolitical situation. These considerations at present impose a rather formidable barrier to new investment... A more rigorous and broad-based pickup in capital spending will almost surely require further gains in corporate profits and cash flows' (p. 7).[4]

Next, we turn our attention to capacity utilisation, and propose that it is mostly affected by industrial production. A higher volume of industrial production is expected to engineer a higher degree of capacity utilisation. This association is thought to be strongly positive.

This is due to the role of capital stock, which is thought to be fixed in the short run. This relies on the theory of irreversibility of investment under conditions of uncertainty (see, for example, Dixit and Pindyck, 1994). We may, thus, write:

$$CU = CU \, (IP) \tag{2}$$

We also endogenise industrial production as in (3):

$$IP = IP(PMI) \tag{3}$$

where PMI proxies for existing and expected business conditions. PMI is an index of these conditions and it is based on surveys conducted by the Institute for Supply Management (ISM). It is clear that (3) is based crucially on Keynes's 'animal spirits' hypothesis and the uncertainty that characterises expectation in the work of Keynes (1936). It is, thus, the case that in our modelling strategy ultimately 'animal spirits' and the uncertainty of expectations critically influence investment, but the relationship works basically through industrial production and profitability, variables that play a critical role in determining gross investment and capacity utilisation. This approach also attempts to account for the suggestion made by Eisner (1974), some time ago, that 'Major progress in discerning reliable and stable investment functions will require facing up to and illuminating the fundamental relations between past, present and future' (p. 102).

Industrial production and capacity utilisation were the main determinants of investment in the demand-led business cycles of 1947–72. But a model that relied on only those factors would have missed the behaviour of investment in the supply-led business cycles of 1973–84. Corporate profitability and real interest rates were additional variables, desperately required to explain investment in the supply-led business cycles. But a model that relied on these four factors would have been incapable of explaining investment in the last two business cycles and the current one. The long-run factors are needed, in addition to the short-term ones, to explain investment in the last two cycles and the current one. This does not imply that some of the variables are needed in some cycles, but not in others. If that were the case then one and the same model (i.e. one structure) would have been insufficient to explain investment in all business cycles. Instead, three different models would have been required to explain investment in all 11 cycles; the structure would not have been unique. In our model the structure is unique and that implies that the importance of each variable in explaining investment has remained stable in all business cycles. However, the variability of each variable in every cycle has been different. In this sense, the long-run factors did not vary significantly to contribute to the explanation of the volatility of investment in the first eight cycles, but they were extremely important in explaining why investment fell to the extent that it did in the last two cycles and in the current one. Had these variables assumed different values to those that they actually did in any of the last fifty years then the model would have still been able to explain investment.

The forecast error in the K-Model of investment is only 1.55 percent. This means that with an error of 3.1 percent the model can explain 95 percent of all past investment volatility. Indeed, in the last 650 months there have been only 19 instances where the investment error has exceeded 3.1 percent (see Figure 6.17). On that basis the forecasting ability of the model is such as to claim that with 95 percent probability investment in the future will lie within the interval of the central projection plus or minus 3.1 percent. This assumes that the behaviour of investment will continue to be governed by the same structure that is encapsulated in the K-Model. The assurance here rests with the fact that

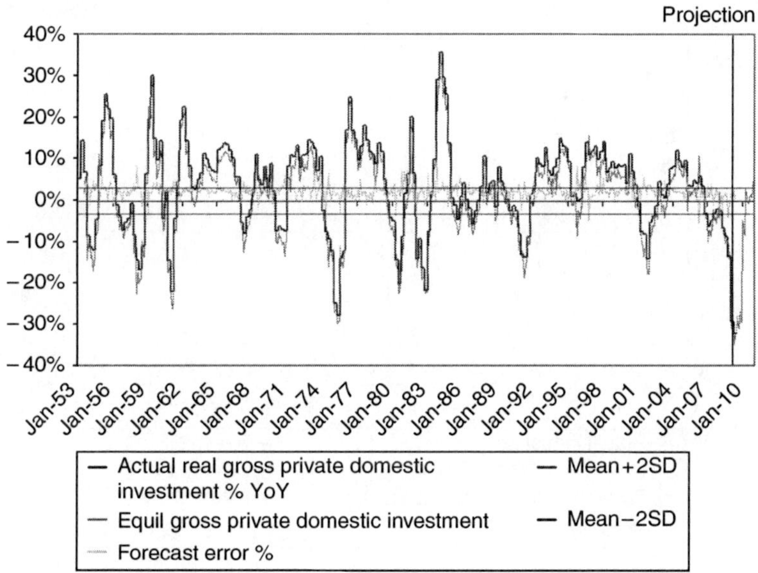

Figure 6.17   Real gross investment

even from a theoretical point of view there are no other cycles except demand, supply and asset, associated with imbalances in the corporate sector. Hence, there is no reason to assume that that the structure of the investment model will be invalidated in the short-term future.

Clearly, in forecasting investment four more relationships are in order. One is for predicting industrial production, the other capacity utilisation; the third corporate profits and the fourth business sentiment about current and future economic conditions, as captured in the PMI index. The forecast error of the industrial production relationship is only 1.15 percent in the last 11 business cycles that cover more than half a century of monthly data. Figure 6.18 shows that there have been only twenty instances in more than 650 monthly observations in the last fifty years where the forecast error of industrial production has exceeded 2.3 percent. The forecast error of the capacity utilisation relationship is only 0.25 percent. Figure 6.19 shows that there have been only 18 instances in the last fifty years where the forecast error of capacity utilisation has exceeded 0.5 percent. The properties of the profits model are discussed in chapter 5. The PMI is modelled as a second order autoregressive process (see Figure 6.20).

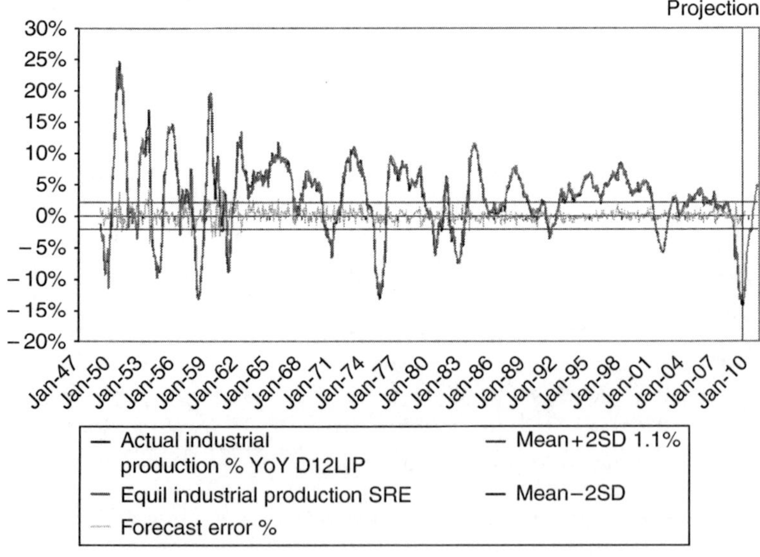

Figure 6.18   Industrial production

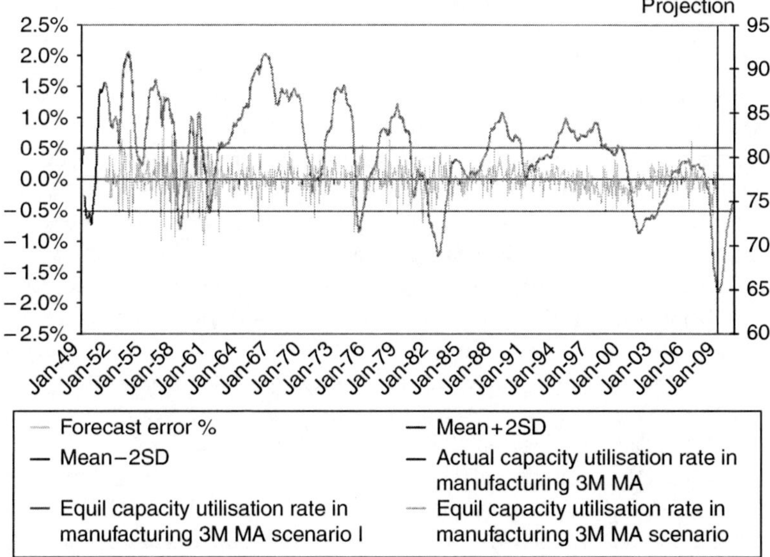

Figure 6.19   Capacity utilisation – short-run equilibrium

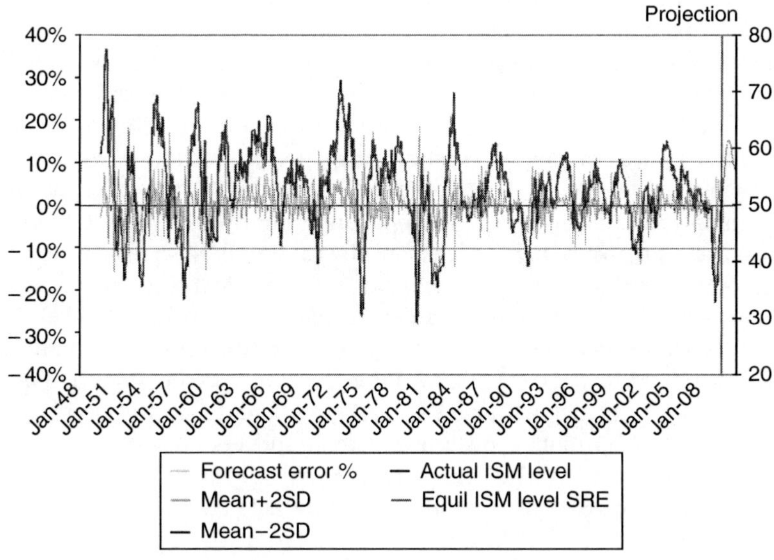

Figure 6.20   US PMI – short-run equilibrium

6   The outlook for investment and the long-term risks

The preceding analysis of the short-run factors suggests that investment is about to stage a partial recovery. After an unprecedented collapse of real final sales in the second half of 2008, they bottomed in the last quarter of 2008, prompting companies to slash inventories, production, investment and employment in the first quarter of 2009. The inventory-to-sales ratio signals that companies are ready to embark on a process of rebuilding their stocks that is likely to last until the spring of 2010. Production cuts are easing and positive growth will be resumed at the beginning of 2010, hitting something less than 10 percent (y-o-y) by the end of that year. This is better than the other two anaemic recoveries of 1991 and 2001, but not as good as the recovery during the average demand cycle. Capacity utilisation fell more than ever in the downswing, but is expected to stage a respectable recovery.

However, the analysis of the long-run factors points to an anaemic recovery of investment of the order of 1 percent of GDP by the end of 2010. Although this is better than the 2001 experience, when investment increased by just 0.3 percent, but it is just as anaemic as the 1991 recovery. The long-run factors suggest that the corporate sector will struggle to improve its impaired balance sheet. Although debt at the peak of the cycle was at an all-time high, so was the net worth of the corporate sector. But the latter has suffered in the downswing more than in any other cycle, thus creating the prospect of an anaemic recovery. Profits are expected to rebound by as much as in other cycles. This implies that the degree of debt leverage would decline as fast as in other cycles. In the current downturn the proportion of long-term debt to the total is as high as in the recovery of 2001, at 72 percent. The combination of a high proportion of long-term debt to the total along with the high cost of borrowing from the capital markets relative to the banks means that companies will opt to repay debt and curb investment. A switch from capital markets to bank borrowing is unlikely to be on a grand scale, given the balance sheet problems of the financial institutions that make them unwilling to extend credit. Thus, companies are likely to stick with capital markets where the cost of borrowing is extremely high, albeit declining. Credit spreads are likely to abate until the end of 2010, as risk appetite returns, but the cost of borrowing is likely to remain high. In addition to the balance sheet adjustment of the corporate sector, there is one more reason why the recovery will be anaemic. The personal sector is undergoing the most severe balance sheet adjustment since the Great Depression. This will keep the savings ratio high and hence consumer expenditure subdued for a considerable period of time.

Although the analysis from the K-Model suggests an anaemic recovery, the balance of risks is still on the downside in the long run. The huge budget deficit and the need to issue an unprecedented amount of Treasuries will exert an upward pressure on government bond yields, thus partly negating the decline in corporate bond yields. Moreover, the expansion of the Fed balance sheet requires a draining of the excess liquidity that was injected into the system after the collapse of Lehman Brothers. In the medium term there are two likely scenarios. First, the fiscal and monetary stimulus is removed gradually from 2010, as the recovery begins to emerge. Such a removal is likely to keep the growth of the economy below potential for three to five years. In this case unemployment will continue to climb and consumers will feel that there is no recovery – exactly as they felt in the 1991 recovery. A brisk recovery was delayed until 1994, with the consumer sentiment remaining subdued until then. A similar situation is likely to develop in the years to come if the policymakers decide to remove the fiscal and monetary stimulus gradually.

In the second scenario, the policymakers maintain the stimulus and refrain from removing it for fear that the recovery will falter. In this case the growth rate of the economy is likely to exceed potential in 2011. The fiscal stimulus is then likely to be removed from 2012 onwards and then only gradually, given the presidential election of 2012. With growth exceeding potential for two years inflation will rekindle and then the Fed would rush into withdrawing the monetary stimulus by hiking rates, selling Treasuries and reverse repos for low-quality debt that was accepted in the course of the credit crisis. But it would be too much, too late. The combination of tight fiscal and tight monetary policy would plunge the economy into recession in 2012–13. It is obvious that between the two scenarios of subpar growth for the next four to five years and the boom and bust the former is preferable. However, we have serious doubts that the policymakers would do the right thing. The important conclusion is that economic policy matters greatly in our analysis. It is very important that it is utilised properly to achieve high levels of growth and employment.

7   Summary and conclusions

Investment, and in particular business investment, plays a key role in secular growth and in business cycle analysis. The higher the investment rate, the faster is the long-term (or potential) growth. In spite of increasing US investment abroad in line with the globalisation trend, there has been an offsetting equal amount of foreign direct investment in the US, as foreign companies have for a long time now been trying to produce within the US rather than exporting to the US. Nonetheless, a mild downtrend is discernible, which is the result of stiff competition that the US faces from the newly industrialised countries. This is likely to intensify, thereby casting some doubt on the long-term prospects for growth and the standard of living of the US residents.

The second unwelcome development of the last thirty years is the increasing volatility of investment in business cycles. Investment drags the economy into recession, but it also leads it into recovery. It is usually a coincident or, in the worst case, a lagging indicator of the trough of the business cycle by just one quarter. In the current downturn it was the collapse of residential investment that dragged the economy into recession, whereas business investment remained resilient until the first half of 2008. However, the plunge of final sales and, in particular, consumer expenditure in the second half of 2008 led to a plummeting business investment, the worst since the Second World War.

Although investment usually leads the economy to recovery, in the last two business cycles growth was at best modest, thereby making the whole recovery of the economy anaemic. The higher volatility of investment in the last few cycles is due not to increased uncertainty, but to debt overleveraging that forces firms to cut investment drastically and to curb debt levels. It is this balance sheet restructuring that makes the recovery anaemic. The recovery in the 1991 cycle was anaemic, because of the balance sheet problems of the corporate sector. The worst anaemic recovery so far was that of 2001 which resulted from a combination of balance sheet problems in the corporate and personal sectors. In the current downturn the combined balance sheet problems of the banking and the personal sectors have infected the balance sheet of the corporate sector too. Prima facie evidence of that is found in the rapid deterioration of the net worth of the corporate sector since the outset of the downturn. Prior to the downswing the debt level of the corporate sector had reached a new high, a pattern that has been followed in every cycle. But the higher levels of debt were offset by an even faster increase in net worth. However, the net worth worsened in the downswing, leaving the corporate sector vulnerable to the high debt levels and prompting a process of retrenchment and the paying back of debt. On these grounds, investment growth is expected to be subdued, which, combined with the ongoing balance sheet problems of the personal and banking sectors, is most likely to produce yet another anaemic recovery in 2010.

In the last two cycles companies have used the downswing to switch from short-term to long-term debt. The proportion of long-term debt is now more than two-thirds of the total. Although this switch was beneficial in the downswing, it proved a hindrance in the recovery as the cost of borrowing from the capital markets soared in the downswing and remained elevated in the upswing. This has been yet another factor in the anaemic recoveries of the last two cycles. In the current cycle, the story is repeated. Companies have switched to long-term debt, but the cost of borrowing from the capital markets is higher than ever before. This will certainly contribute to an anaemic recovery in 2010. In spite of the gloomy outlook for investment stemming from the analysis of the long-run factors, the short-run factors suggest that the worst is over and that a modest recovery is in the making. Companies have started to liquidate their excess inventories and this augurs well for a rebound of production in the next few months. The K-Model suggests that the turning point is the second quarter of 2009 when profitability rebounds and unit labour cost will have peaked.

7
The Housing Market and Residential Investment

1 Introduction

Leamer (2007) points out that housing does not play any role in macroeconomic theory. In the index of Mankiw's (2007) best-selling *Principles of Macroeconomics* there is no reference to 'real estate'. The problem is not just with theory, but with applied macroeconomics too. There is no reference to housing either in the index of Zarnowitz's (1992) *Business Cycle, Theory, History, Indicators and Forecasting*, or in Stock and Watson's edited volume *Business Cycles, Indicators and Forecasting* (1993). However, as the housing market showed signs of cracking in 2005, but assumed a clear downtrend in 2007, the interest of theorists and practitioners in housing was quickly elevated with a Conference on Housing sponsored by the Federal Reserve Bank of Kansas City, Jackson Hole, Wyoming on 30 August–1 September 2007. Perhaps too late, the cynics would argue. However, Leamer's (2007) critique is not fair, as the importance of the housing market and residential investment in the macroeconomy was recognised as early as 2000 by the OECD (2000b), who suggested that 'In the United States ... the contribution of real estate developments to the current economic expansion has been emphasised recently' (p. 169). In fact, it is argued that 'Over the 1996–99 period, the growth of housing wealth in excess of income growth in the United States may have contributed 0.4 percentage points to the total drop of the household saving ratio of some 2.4 percentage points' (p. 179). The same OECD study concludes that 'The link between house price developments and movements in aggregate demand suggests that monitoring developments in property markets can provide a useful input to the setting of economic policy' (OECD, 2000b, p. 181; see also Greenspan, 1999, 2005b).[1] The boom in the housing market since the bursting of the internet bubble raised some concerns even during the recovery phase of the 2001 cycle. Greenspan (2004c) emphasised the importance of 'preventive actions' which 'are required sooner rather than later' in order to 'fend off possible future systemic difficulties, which we assess as likely if GSE expansion continues unabated' (p. 4).[2] Especially so, since 'the existence, or even the perception, of government backing undermines the effectiveness of market discipline' (p. 4). It is, therefore, suggested that 'the GSE regulator must have authority similar to that of the banking regulator', but also 'GSEs need to be limited in the issuance of GSE debt and in the purchase of assets, both mortgages and nonmortgages, that they hold' (p. 5). In chapter 6 of the first edition of this book (Arestis and Karakitsos, 2004) was devoted to the housing market and its importance is highlighted by the following extract:

> The threat to the sustainability of the current recovery from the personal sector imbalances that were created by the boom and bust of the equity bubble can in principle be put at bay if the recovery were strong for some time. However, a strong recovery may cause a collapse in the housing market. The personal sector imbalances would then resurface and may threaten the sustainability of the current recovery. The very easy stance of monetary policy that was adopted by the Fed in order to deter the deflationary effects of the burst of the 'new-economy' bubble have fuelled the housing market boom of the last three years. The housing market is not yet a bubble, as it has not yet exceeded the peak of all previous cycles in the last thirty-five years, but it has all the characteristics of becoming one, if the boom were to continue. Although the problem is more acute in the Northeast, other regions would be infected through lower incomes and employment, if the market, which is near its peak, were to collapse. The risk of a collapse arises from the high levels of debt and the overstretched capacity of households to service their debts even at these low levels of interest rates. The damage to the property market in the next two years depends on the strength of the current recovery. A strong recovery in 2004 would lead to a collapse of the housing market in 2005 with dramatic falls in house prices, residential investment and the gross (and net) value of property. The recent round of refinance would not deter the collapse of the housing market; it would simply postpone it for a while. On the other hand, a weak recovery would lead to a slight further increase of house prices in 2004 and stabilisation in 2005. The reason for this stark contrast is that long-term interest rates would rise much more under

a strong than a weak recovery. Between the two scenarios a strong recovery in 2004 seems more likely than a weak one because of the huge fiscal stimulus of 2003, and a new one planned for 2004, the very accommodative stance of monetary policy and high levels of confidence amongst businesses and consumers alike, triggered by the lower geopolitical risks after the end of the Iraq war... These shifts in net wealth obscure the risk of replacing the equity by the property bubble. (pp. 136–7)

In the first edition of this book (Arestis and Karakitsos, 2004; see also Arestis and Karakitsos, 2007) it is shown that there are clear advantages in forecasting overall market trends and in policy analysis by treating the US housing market as homogeneous. This study differs from the traditional approach and other studies in that it attempts to deal with US house prices in a significant way. In these other studies there is no nationwide housing market, but a compendium of segmented markets. In fact, most, if not all, of US house price studies are undertaken at the City/Metropolitan Area level (see, for example, Leung, 2004; and Jud and Winkler, 2002). Such an approach may have an advantage in forecasting regional prices as it takes into account the peculiarities of each local market, but it is not a good guide in working out the implications of the nationwide housing market on consumption and the economy as a whole because of aggregation problems. Our approach is unique in that it deals with a nationwide housing market. We have argued in Arestis and Karakitsos (2007) that an approach that relies on segmented housing markets is likely to underestimate both the extent of the housing market cycles and the likely impact on consumption. Such a bias may be eliminated by treating the housing market as homogeneous, an approach that we believe is justified because of the importance of nationwide variables, such as interest rates and real disposable income (see also Shiller, 2007). As we show in this chapter, these two variables, and in that order, are the two most important variables in the housing market. This approach has been used by Arestis and Karakitsos (2004, 2007) to assess the impact of the housing market on the US economy with some success in predicting the soft landing in 2005 and the plight of the housing market in 2007 and its likely impact on the overall economy. In this chapter we focus on the methodology and the modelling aspects of treating the US housing market as homogeneous and its implications.

This chapter is organised as follows. The next section deals with the stylised facts of the housing market. Section 3 examines the issue of whether the housing boom was a bubble. Sections 4 and 5 analyse the demand for and supply of houses. Section 6 puts together these principles and explains the theoretical structure of the K-Model of the housing market. Section 7 analyses the model properties of the current vintage of the model alongside that from the first edition, which proved very helpful in warning of the risks of transforming the internet to a housing bubble and the plight that might be caused from the bursting of this bubble. Section 8 uses the model to explain the stylised facts, while section 9 concludes and summarises.

2   The stylised facts of the housing market

In this chapter we draw a distinction between the market for new homes and that for existing homes. The former is very small, around 15 percent of the total, but it is an important determinant of residential investment and therefore of the direct impact of the housing market on GDP growth. This impact on growth is rather small, around 10 percent, but its overall effect can rise to as much as 25 percent when other industries related to housing, such as furniture, are taken into account. Despite the small size of the market for new homes, the sales of new homes act as a leading indicator of developments in the overall housing market. Sales of existing homes are recorded when a contract is closed, whereas sales of new homes when a contract is signed. Hence, the latter are considered as timely barometer of the housing market.

It may be no exaggeration to say that the housing market is a monetary phenomenon driven mainly by the Fed. The recent upswing in the growth rate of real residential investment commenced at the beginning of 2001, once the Fed started trimming interest rates, and ended in mid-2004, when rates began to rise again, although the level of residential investment peaked at the end of 2005 (see Figure 7.1). New home price inflation as a six-month moving average peaked at the same time as residential investment at 14 percent, although the level of new home prices continued to increase until the spring of 2007 (see Figure 7.2). The peak in the spring of 2007 is only marginally higher than in the spring of 2006. In the summer of 2006 the decline in new home prices was disorderly, although prices stabilised in the first half of 2007. Aggressive selling of subprime mortgages, lower mortgage rates and in particular teasing rates, as well as lower house prices enticed in this period some very eager homebuyers into the housing market – most notably first time buyers – and mortgage applications rebounded. However, more wise home-buyers remained on the sidelines for house

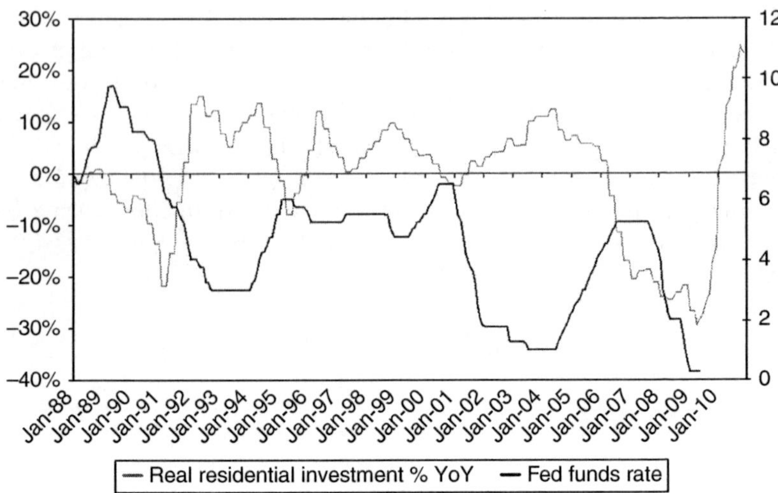

Figure 7.1   Residential investment and Fed funds rate

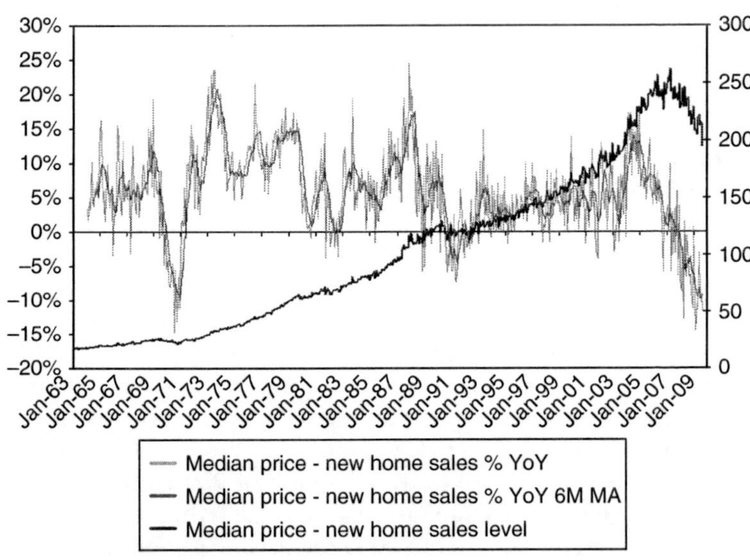

Figure 7.2   Median new house price

prices to fall further. In fact, after the first wave of home-buyers dived into the market new home prices resumed their downturn. This happened since the summer of 2007. By the spring of 2009 new home prices fell 22 percent from their peak in the spring of 2007, although they have recovered slightly since then mainly due to seasonal factors. Relative to CPI new home prices have fallen 25 percent from their peak in the spring of 2007, the worst since the 1930s.

But new homes, to which residential investment relates, are a small proportion of the much larger existing homes market, around 85 percent. In the current cycle, the median price of existing homes (henceforth, house prices) increased from \$142,000 at the beginning of 2001 to \$230,000 in mid-2006 – a gain of more than 60 percent in five and a half years. The recent upswing is reminiscent of that during the second half of the 1970s, the other historical period when house prices rose as sharply. This was followed by a period of retrenchment by consumers as they tried to reduce their debt and rebuild their wealth by saving more; evidence shows that it is now repeated in the current downturn.

House price inflation as a six-month moving average peaked at the end of 2005 – a year and a half after new home price inflation. It has fallen precipitously since then (see Figure 7.3). The level of prices started to fall in the summer of 2006 three months after new home prices had begun to fall, but there was another rebound in the first half of 2007. House prices resumed their fall in the summer of 2007 and by the spring of 2009 they have fallen nearly 30 percent from their peak, the worst since the 1930s.

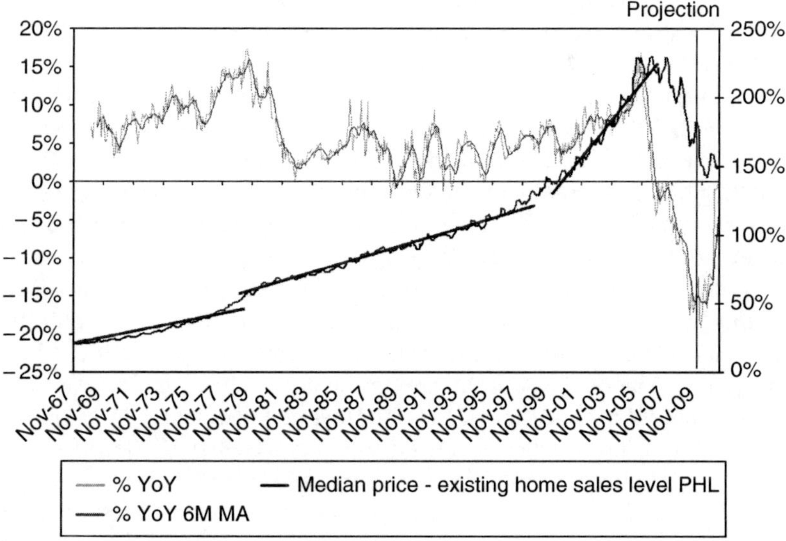

Figure 7.3   Median price – existing homes

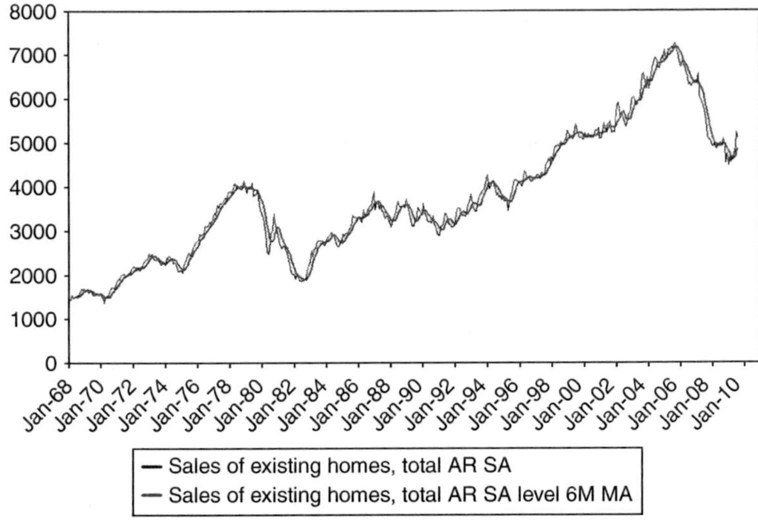

Figure 7.4   Sales of existing homes

The fall in the growth rate of house prices since 2006 was accompanied by corresponding sharp declines in home sales (see Figure 7.4). In the upswing of the bull market home sales soared to record levels. In the second strongest bull market of the late 1970s home sales hit a record of 4 million units. That was surpassed at the beginning of the recent bull market. At the end of 1999 home sales rose to a new record of 5.25 million; at the peak of the bubble house sales reached a record of nearly 7.2 million units (see Figure 7.4). But in the last three years house prices have been falling at the same time as sales – a sign of market instability. It is important to remember that this perverse effect of falling house prices and declining home sales should come to an end before we can reasonably state that the end of the housing slump is over. There are tentative signs that sales of existing homes are showing signs of stabilising, an encouraging sign. However, we must warn that this may be a second false dawn, the first being in the first half of 2007, as the second wave of homebuyers is now enticed into the market. The risks, yet again, are on the downside. After this wave has run its course it may be that we have another period of falling house prices and declining home sales. The K-Model suggests that house prices are likely to fall by more than 40 percent from their peak before they bottom in the spring of 2010. But again the risks are on the downside especially if the policymakers do not succeed in stemming the vicious circle of falling house prices and bank losses.

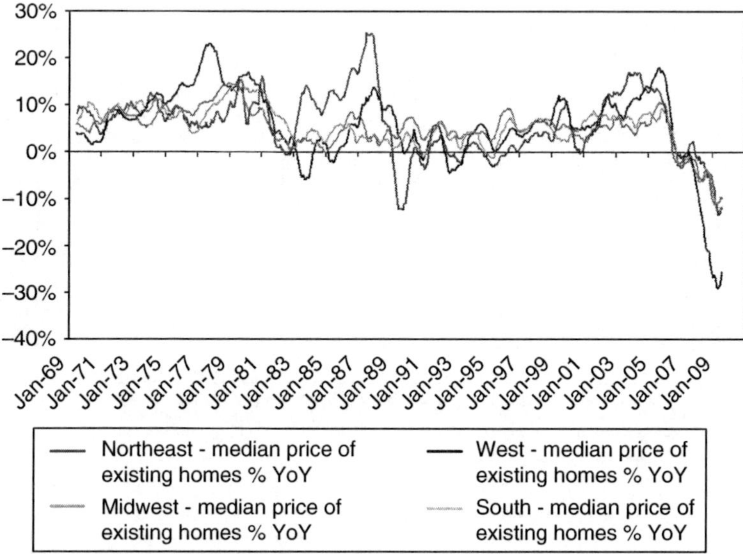

Figure 7.5   Regional house price inflation

House prices are now falling in all regions with the steepest declines in the West, supporting our claim that despite local peculiarities there are common factors, such as interest rates and real disposable income, which have an effect on all regional markets (see Figure 7.5). This provides justification to the model developed in Arestis and Karakitsos (2004, 2007), which treats the housing market as homogeneous. For the largest (and poorer) part of the population housing is the only asset. Moreover, housing acts as a hedge against inflation; it is indeed the single most important asset class that provides a shelter against the risks of inflation. Thus, the economics of the housing market are shaped by real and not nominal house prices. The median price of existing homes relative to CPI (henceforth, relative house prices) increased throughout the 1970s, not only beating inflation, but also proving the best-performing asset amongst cash, bonds and equities (see Figure 7.6). In the 1980s and the 1990s house prices kept in line with inflation, albeit with small variations. But by the end of the 1990s relative house prices were at the highest level since the 1960s and in the new millennium they soared even higher, making the housing market look like a bubble. House prices relative to CPI have already fallen by nearly 35 percent, the worst since the 1930s. In a previous paper (Arestis and Karakitsos, 2007) where we provided

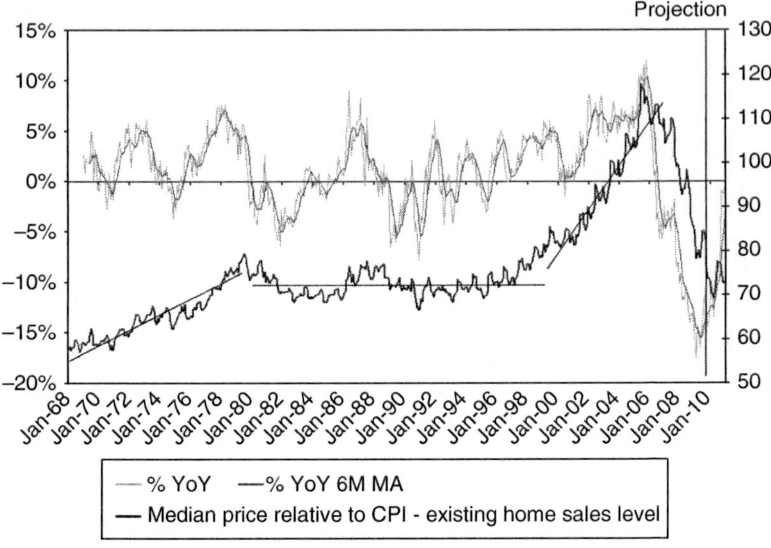

Figure 7.6   Relative median price – existing homes

forecasts of such huge drops in house prices, we warned that this sounds very difficult to believe, as there is no other historical episode, but the 1930s, in which house prices fell by that much. According to the K-Model the rate of growth of relative prices will reach a trough in the spring of 2010 at nearly 45 percent. Yet, again, the risks are on the downside.

Changes in demand for housing are reflected first in the prices of existing homes, which then give the signal to developers to alter the supply of new houses. Because of gestation lags, the current supply of new homes reflects previous demand conditions. Hence, the prices of new homes are more volatile than those of existing homes as they represent a small proportion of total homes for sale and reflect current demand conditions, whereas current supply reflects past demand. Hence, the prices of existing homes for sale are a better indicator of market conditions than new homes. Figure 7.7 compares the price of existing homes with new homes and shows that the former is a better indicator of market conditions. House prices at the top end of the market are more volatile to fluctuations in demand than the low end. The median price is not affected as much as the average price by the top end of the housing market. Hence, the median price of existing homes is a better indicator of market conditions than the average price, as it is both less

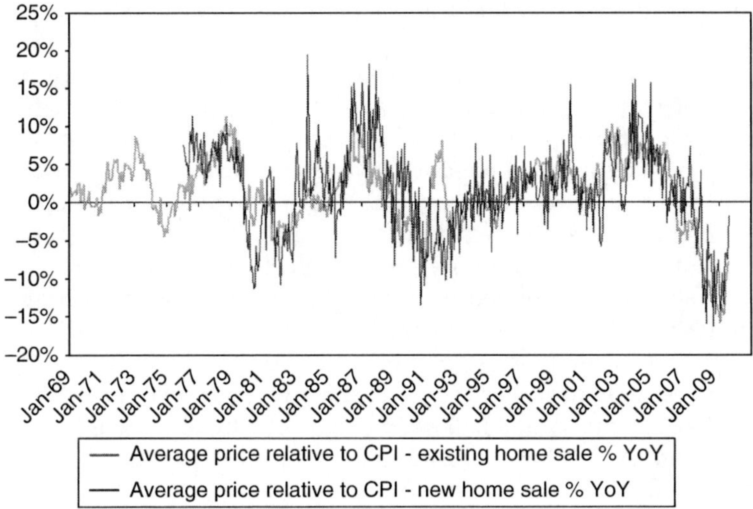

Figure 7.7   Relative average house price inflation

volatile and it is, at worst, a coincident indicator and, more often, a leading indicator of the housing market.

3   Was the recent US housing cycle a bubble?

The recent housing cycle has the characteristics of a bubble. It is a monetary phenomenon in that it has been caused by the wide gyrations in interest rates. The Fed reduced interest rates from 6.5 percent at the beginning of 2001 to 1 percent, thus triggering the boom in housing. This was not a deliberate act by the central bank; its purpose was to fend off the economy from the depression that usually plagues it from the burst of a bubble, in this case the internet bubble. The usual characteristic of the burst of a bubble is asset and debt deflation and retrenchment by businesses and households. This has occurred every time a bubble has burst over the past five hundred years, with the more recent examples of the US in the 1930s and of Japan in the 1990s. Moreover, the economic downturn in every instance has been not only deep, but protracted, too, i.e. depression.

This did not happen in the US in the aftermath of the burst of the 2000 internet bubble in view of the prodigious cut of interest rates by the Fed. However, the cost of this monetary easing was the creation of other bubbles, of which the housing bubble has probably attracted the greatest interest (see, for example, Greenspan, 1999, 2004c; Baker, 2002; Kaufman and Mühleison, 2003; Case and Shiller, 2003; Stiglitz, 2003; McCarthy and Peach, 2004, 2005). Once the Fed embarked on the task of removing the monetary accommodation in mid-2004 the housing market began to contract. This became evident, first, in the growth rate of residential investment, while the impact on the new and existing house prices was different. The rate of inflation of the prices of new homes peaked at the same time as the rate of growth of residential investment, whereas house price inflation in the much bigger market of existing homes continued to increase for a further year. Since the end of 2005, inflation in the prices of existing homes has receded rapidly and in the summer of 2006 it became negative, catching up with the new homes market. But there was a temporary revival in the first half of 2007. In the second half of 2007 the downtrend in house prices resumed and the fall has been precipitous since then. Nominal house prices fell only once more in the last forty years – in mid-1989.

There is a heated debate on whether the housing market was a bubble (see, for example, Himmelberg et al., 2005; Case and Shiller, 2003). The conventional way of defining a bubble is when investors buy an asset in the hope that they would be able to sell it at an even higher price. But such a definition cannot easily be applied to the real world. Those who claim that the housing market is not a bubble usually invoke measures of house affordability. In particular, they point to the debt service burden as a percentage of disposable personal income. Debt payments consist of the estimated required payments on outstanding mortgage and consumer debt. The debt service ratio was at an all-time high until 2008(Q1), but using other wider measures, such as the financial obligations ratio (FOR), which adds automobile lease payments, rental payments on tenant-occupied property, homeowners' insurance, and property tax payments to the debt service ratio, suggest that it was affordable (see Figure 7.8).

However, other measures of house affordability provide a contrasting picture. At the peak of the cycle house prices relative to nominal per capita disposable income were at an all-time high (see Figure 7.9). At the peak the median house cost more than 7.5 times the annual disposable income of households. This compares with a previous high of 7 times disposable income in 1980. However, it is fair to say that when the recent bull market began house affordability was at its lowest since the 1960s at 5.5 times the disposable income of households.[3] Thus, at the peak of the cycle houses could not be afforded; they were more expensive than ever in the last sixty years. Prices were as high as that because households were over-indebted. The lack of trend[4] (i.e. 'stationarity') of this variable can

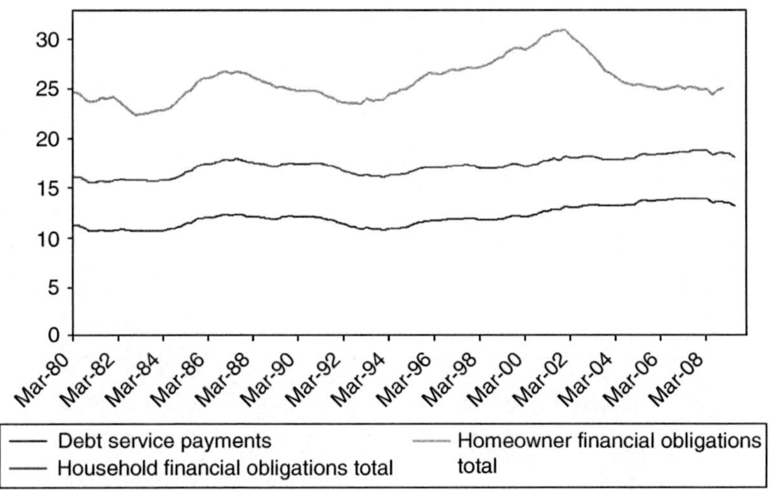

Figure 7.8   Debt service burden

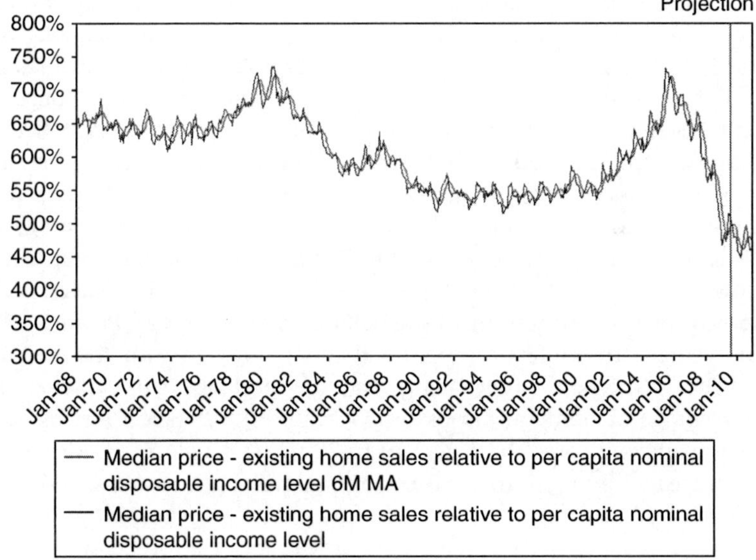

Figure 7.9   Median price of existing homes relative to per capita nominal disposable income

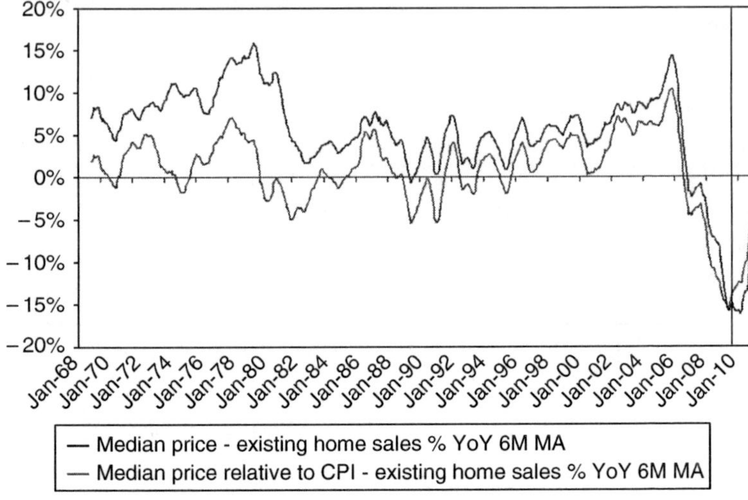

Figure 7.10   House price inflation (6M MA) – existing home sales

be justified on theoretical and not just statistical grounds, thus providing support to the hypothesis that the housing market was a bubble. By June 2009 house prices as a percentage of disposable income have fallen to 5.0 times, even lower than the starting point; and the K-Model suggests that house prices may hit bottom at 4.6, a new low in the last fifty years.

But, perhaps, the ratio of capital gains relative to debt gearing provides the best evidence that the housing market was a bubble. The gross house wealth (defined as the value of the household real estate as a percentage of nominal disposable income) soared to 202 percent of disposable income in the spring of 2006, a new high since the 1950s, and compared with 156 percent at the beginning of the bull market in 2001 (see Figure 7.11). However, in the same time period the net house wealth (defined as the value of the house after taking away the mortgage debt expressed as a percentage of nominal disposable income) hit 105 percent of disposable income compared to 91 percent in 2001 (see Figure 7.11). Mortgage debt increased by more than 50 percent – from 66 percent of disposable income to 102 percent – in the same time period. In other words, gross capital gains of 30 percent have been achieved by an increase in debt gearing of 54 percent, i.e. a ratio of just 0.56 compared to more than 2.0 for a prudent investment. This shows that investment in housing was a risky investment in the last few years of the bubble and that homeowners were vulnerable to a downturn. If house prices continued to fall, then

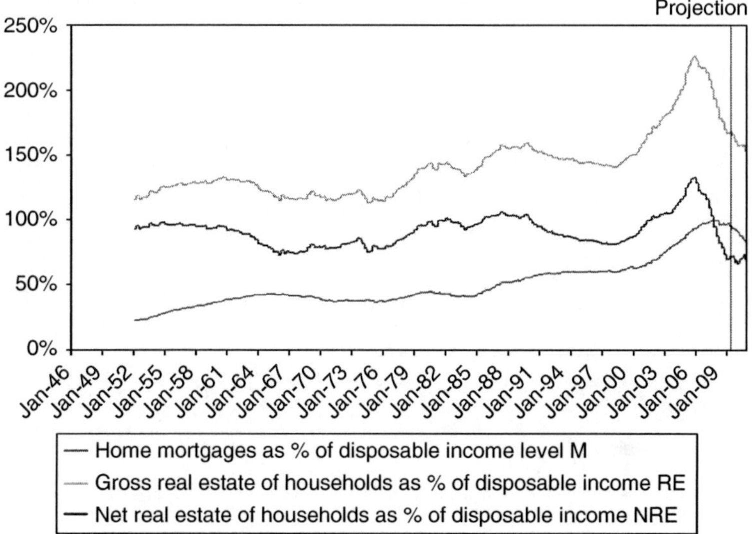

Figure 7.11   Gross, net real estate of households and mortgage debt

many consumers would find themselves with negative equity (the value of their house is less than the mortgage) and may consequently be forced to curb their spending. The relationship of gross and net house wealth through mortgage debt provides the best evidence that the housing market was a bubble (see Figure 7.11). The increase in gross wealth in the upswing is due to a corresponding increase in debt, as net wealth remained unchanged. Thus, gross house wealth was very high because households had borrowed heavily, but such an increase in borrowing did not produce an equivalent increase in net wealth. Given the irreversibility of mortgage debt in a downward correction, there is a high probability that the over-indebtedness would lead to retrenchment.

4   The demand for housing

The demand for housing depends on the real disposable income of households. This is a composite variable, as it is affected by both per capita real disposable income and population growth. On occasions, real personal income is a better proxy of income than real disposable income because the latter is affected by taxes and subsidies, which households may regard as temporary rather than permanent. Figure 7.12 shows the association of house prices with real personal and

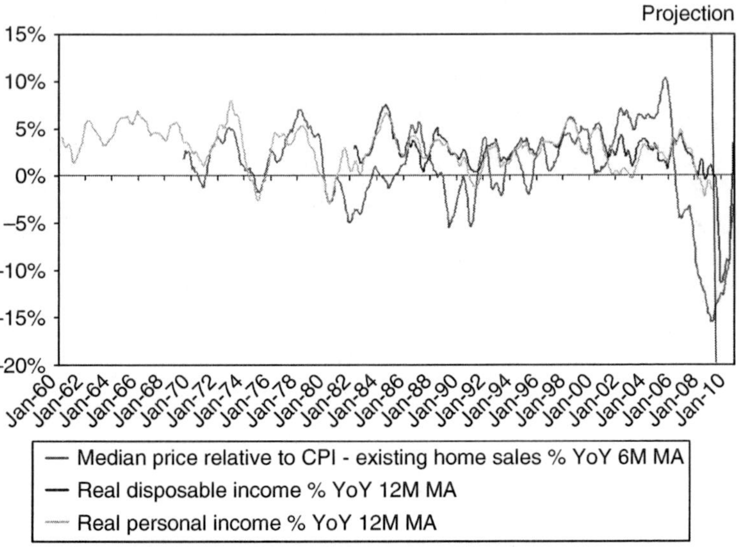

Figure 7.12   House prices, real disposable income and real personal income

disposable income.[5] An increase in income leads to a higher demand for housing that, in turn, pushes up house prices. The growth in disposable income, through the fiscal injections in the recent downturn that followed the 2000 burst in the internet market, accounts, to some extent, for the recent housing boom. Similarly, the downturn that followed has had some impact on the housing downswing.

The demand for housing is greatly affected by the mortgage rate, which is closely associated with the 30-year Treasury yield (see Figure 7.13). Higher bond yields lead to increases in the mortgage rate that diminishes the demand for housing and lowers house price inflation. The boom of the housing market in the aftermath of the burst of the internet bubble is due, apart from a loose fiscal policy, to lower mortgage rates and thus to an accommodating monetary policy. The downswing of the housing market also comes from the impact of monetary policy, essentially once the Fed embarked on the task of removing the monetary accommodation in mid-2004.

The debt service burden' measures the ratio of interest payments on consumer debt to nominal disposable income and is a measure of affordability. It is influenced by the mortgage rate, the size of consumer debt and nominal disposable income. The higher the mortgage rate or the consumer debt, the bigger is the debt service burden. On the other

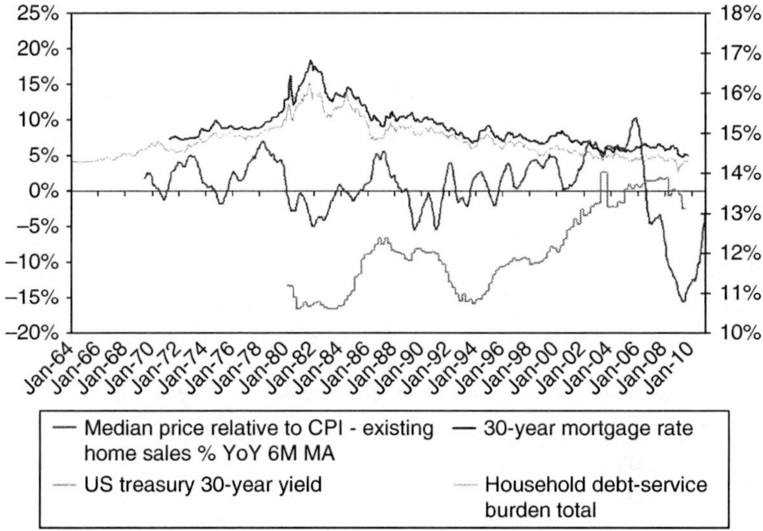

Figure 7.13   House prices, interest rates and debt service

hand, the higher the nominal disposable income, the lower is the debt service burden. But households are willing to accumulate more debt and withstand a heavier debt service burden, if house prices are expected to rise. Hence, house prices tend to rise with increases in the debt service burden, and vice versa. This, of course, is destabilising in the short run, as it tends to fuel the boom or deepen the bust in the housing market. Confidence is driving these perverse expectations. In the upswing of the cycle confidence is rising and households are willing to accumulate more debt and withstand heavier debt service burdens. In the down-swing of the cycle households are becoming increasingly cautious, reducing their debt and thus its service burden. Figure 7.13 shows the positive correlation of house prices with the debt service burden and the negative correlation with the mortgage rate.

The net real estate of households measures the value of property less the mortgage obligations. Higher house prices lead to capital gains in the pro-perty market that boost the value of the real estate of households. These capital gains and the expectation that they will continue for some time lead households to accumulate more debt in the short run. Hence, in the short run there is a positive correlation between house prices and mortgage debt. However, at some point in time, the rate of debt accumulation exceeds the pace of house price increases and the net real estate of households begins

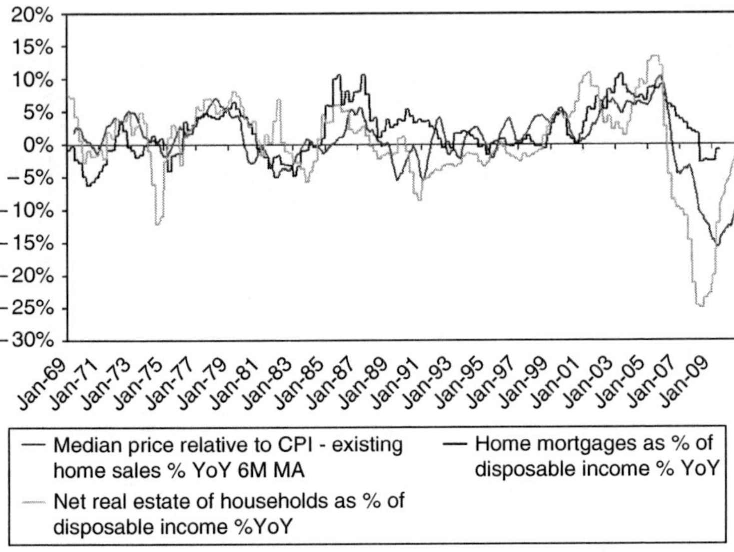

Figure 7.14   House prices, net real estate and mortgage debt

to fall. This leads to a lower demand for housing, other things being equal, since property is an asset and the net real estate of households measures the importance of the wealth effect in the demand for housing.

More often than not the net real estate is a leading rather than a coincident indicator of the housing market. Figure 7.14 shows the positive correlation of house price inflation with both mortgage debt and net real estate growth. Figure 7.11 shows the gross and net real estate and mortgage debt as a percentage of disposable income. Mortgage debt fluctuated around 40 percent for twenty years until 1985, but it then soared two and a half times to more than 100 percent of disposable income by the third quarter of 2007. Clearly, this hefty rate of debt accumulation shows that households expected house prices to continue to rise for some time. Although the gross real estate of households hit an all-time high at 230 percent of disposable income, the peak of net real estate of households was only 135 percent of disposable income representing an increase of just 30 percent from the previous peak.

5   The supply of housing

The supply of houses is a positive function of house prices. Property developers and existing homeowners are willing to increase the supply

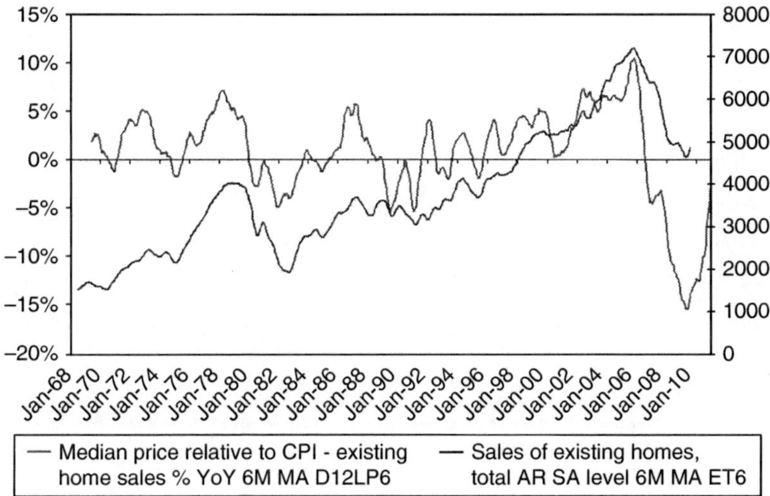

Figure 7.15   Sales of existing homes and prices

of houses for sale, if house prices are rising. Figure 7.15 shows the positive correlation between house price inflation and existing homes for sale. The supply of new homes is closely associated with the supply of existing homes for sale. This means that property developers behave in much the same way as existing homeowners – they increase the supply as house prices rise. On average house price inflation precedes the turning points in the supply of houses by six months (see Figure 7.15). This implies that house price inflation provides the signal to property developers and existing homeowners to alter the supply. An increase in house price inflation leads after a few months to a higher supply of houses, and vice versa. Sales of existing homes peaked at the end of 2005 and declined precipitously since then, but are showing signs of stabilisation.

Once house price inflation begins to rise, real residential investment picks up so that property developers can increase the supply of new homes. Although in the short run the correlation of house price inflation with real residential investment is positive, in the long run it is negative, as the higher supply leads, other things being equal, to lower prices. On the other hand, the positive correlation in the short run means that supply should increase with higher prices.[6] On some occasions, the reaction of real residential investment to changes in house price inflation is instantaneous, but most of the time it follows with

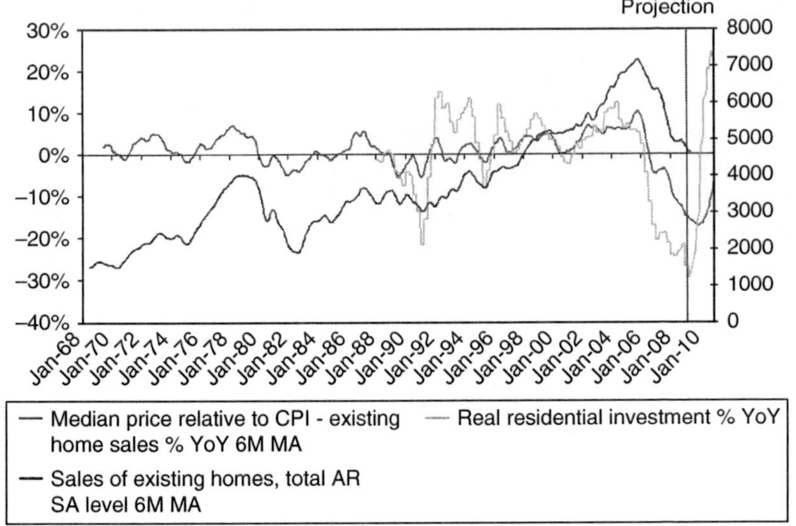

Figure 7.16   House prices, existing home sales and real residential investment

a lag of a few months. This has been particularly true in the recent housing boom of the five years to the peak of 2005 (see Figure 7.16). The increased lag between house price inflation and real residential investment show that property developers had become increasingly wary that the boom in the housing market was unsustainable. A rise in house price inflation leads after a few months to increases in housing starts. The average lag is three months. Property developers regulate the pace of construction so that completions are in line with housing starts and the stock of houses for sale is close to the desired level. Hence, despite the strong housing boom, property developers refrained from becoming overenthusiastic and oversupplying the market with new houses, as the stock of houses available for sale remained unchanged. But the same cannot be said about homebuyers. There was a frenetic pace of house sales, which shows that new homebuyers were purchasing property, which has either not yet started or was under construction (see Arestis and Karakitsos, 2007, for further details).

6   A theoretical model of the US housing market

The model of the US housing market put forward in this chapter captures the above-mentioned stylised facts through four equations. The first explains house prices through the forces of demand for and supply of houses. The second equation explains real residential investment. The third equation is concerned with the determination of the mortgage rate. The fourth equation explains gross real estate (the value of property) and an identity defines net real estate (the value of property net of mortgage debt).

In the steady state house prices are influenced by the following demand factors: (i) the level of real disposable income (RYD); (ii) the mortgage rate (MR); (iii) the debt service burden (DSB); and (iv) the net real estate of households (NREH). The first two variables reflect the short-run factors that affect the demand for houses, while the last two variables are long-run factors, which are associated with personal sector imbalances. We may, therefore, express housing demand (HD) as:

$$D_H = D_H(\underset{-}{P_H},\ \underset{+}{RYD},\ \underset{-}{MR},\ \underset{+}{DSB},\ \underset{+}{NREH}) \qquad (i)$$

with the sign below a variable denoting the partial derivative with respect to that variable.

For the reasons explained in section 4, the level of real disposable income, the debt service burden and the net real estate of households affect positively housing demand, while the mortgage rate and house prices affect housing demand negatively.

Housing supply is affected in the steady state by the following factors: (i) the level of housing starts (HST); and (ii) the level of real residential investment (RRI).

We may, therefore, stipulate the supply of housing as:

$$S_H = S_H(\underset{+}{P_H},\ \underset{+}{HST},\ \underset{+}{RRI}) \qquad (ii)$$

Combining demand and supply factors we are able to represent the long-run relationship for house prices as:

$$P_H = P_H(\underset{+}{RYD},\ \underset{-}{MR},\ \underset{+}{DSB},\ \underset{+}{NREH},\ \underset{-}{HST},\ \underset{-}{RRI}) \qquad (1)$$

It clearly follows from equations (i) and (ii) that the level of real disposable income, the debt service burden and the net real estate of households have a positive effect on house prices, while the mortgage rate affects house prices negatively. Similarly, the level of housing starts affects house prices negatively, as is the level of real residential investment.

House price inflation moves to bring the housing market back to equilibrium in the long run. It takes 16 months to correct any given deviation from equilibrium. This implies that in the short run house price inflation responds negatively to previous disequilibria from the steady state. House price inflation responds with the same signs to the yearly rate of change of all aforementioned variables, with the exception of real residential investment. The rate of growth of real residential investment affects house price inflation positively in the short run, but the level of real residential investment affects the level of house prices negatively in the long run.

We may next turn to the real residential investment (RRI) relationship. We hypothesise that in the steady state RRI depends on the following variables: (i) the year-on-year rate of growth of real disposable income (GRYD); (ii) the level of house prices (P_H); (iii) the mortgage rate (MR); and (iv) the level of housing starts (HST). With the exception of the mortgage rate, all variables affect positively the level of real residential investment.[7] The mortgage rate affects it negatively. In the short run the rate of growth of real residential investment is affected by the yearly change in all aforementioned variables with the same signs as in the steady state.

The long-run RRI relationship may be expressed as follows:

$$RRI = R(GRYD, P_H, MR, HST) \qquad (2)$$
$$ + \qquad + \quad - \quad +$$

We may treat the mortgage rate as endogenously determined as in equation (3):

$$MR = M(TY) \qquad (3)$$
$$+$$

where TY is the Treasury yield on 30-year maturity government bonds, which has a positive effect on MR.

A further relationship is in order. This is the determination of gross real residential housing as in equation (4):

$$GREH = G(P_H) \qquad (4)$$
$$+$$

where GREH stands for gross real estate of households, which is the value of property. The value of gross real estate of households depends on house prices, as changes in prices cause capital gains or losses in the value of property.

A simple identity completes the picture. This is:

$$NREH = GREH - MD \tag{5}$$

where MD is total mortgage debt.

The forecast error of house price inflation in the K-Model is only 0.35 percent. This means that with an error of 0.7 percent the model can explain 95 percent of all past fluctuations in house price inflation. Indeed, in the last 340 months there have been only five instances on which the house price inflation error has exceeded 0.7 percent. On that basis the forecasting ability of the model is such as to claim that with 95 percent probability future house price inflation will lie within the interval of the central projection plus or minus 0.7 percent. This assumes that the behaviour of house price inflation will continue to be governed by the same structure that is encapsulated in the K-Model. Although there are monthly data for all variables that go back to the 1960s, real residential investment is only available since the beginning of 1987. This restricts model testing back to the 1960s that would have enabled checking whether the model has a stable structure through different business cycles.

7   Model properties

The model reported in this chapter is simulated in an attempt to derive dynamic multipliers with respect to two most important variables, the 30-year Treasury yield and the growth of real disposable income. The multipliers are exhibited in Table 7.1. In deriving the dynamic multipliers of Table 7.1, we have incorporated the housing model developed in this contribution in the more extended macroeconomic model reported in Arestis and Karakitsos (2004). This macroeconomic model is constantly updated for forecasting and policy analysis purposes. The housing sector and the estimated relationships reported in this chapter is the latest revision undertaken. It is, thus, worthwhile to compare the properties of the model that incorporates the current revisions of the housing sector with those reported in Arestis and Karakitsos (2004), particularly so since the previous version alerted us, as early as the end of 2003, to the risks that the housing market poses for the US economy as a whole and for the financial system in particular.

The structure of the housing sector of the current version contains some fine differences as compared to the same sector of the macroeconomic model presented in Arestis and Karakitsos (2004), and we highlight the most important ones. In the old version housing starts

Table 7.1 US housing market multipliers

Multiliers with respect to:	30-year Treasury: +1%				Real disposable income growth: –1%			
	Median house price (thousand of dollars)	Residential investment (billions of dollars)	Gross real estate of households (as % of disposable income)	Net Real estate of households (as % of disposable income)	Median house price (thousand of dollars)	Residential investment (billons of dollars)	Gross real estate of households (as % of disposable income)	Net real estate of house holds (as % of disposable income)
Current Level (Dec 06) BASE	221.6	540.8	211.5	112.9	221.6	540.8	211.5	112.9
12-M SRE (Future Short run equilibrium)	196.2	465.6	190.9	97.7	196.2	465.6	190.9	97.7
24-M SRE (Future Short run equilibrium)	169.9	478.1	168.6	82.5	169.9	478.1	168.6	82.5
PERTURBED Level								
12-M SRE (Future Short run equilibrium)	192.3	452.2	190.9	97.7	196.1	464.8	190.9	97.7
24-M SRE (Future Short run equilibrium)	165.6	463.4	167.9	82.1	169.2	475.9	167.9	82.4
12-M Multiplier (% Difference)	–2.0%	–2.9%	0.0%	0.0%	0.0%	–0.2%	0.0%	0.0%
24-M Multiplier (% Difference)	–2.5%	–3.1%	–0.4%	–0.4%	–0.4	–0.5%	–0.4%	0.0%

was an exogenous variable, while now it is treated endogenously as an AR(2) process. The impact of certain variables has either diminished or enhanced, while the lag structure of certain relationships has changed somewhat, partly as a result of the length of the boom in the housing market in the new millennium. Thus, in the co-integrating house prices equation the impact of real disposable income and of net wealth have increased slightly, that of debt service burden has diminished because of low volatility, but the impact of the most important variable, namely the 30-year mortgage rate, has remained exactly the same. On the lag structure, the impact of real residential investment takes longer to appear, six months instead of three. These differences reflect the persistent nature of the boom, which was largely unexpected. In the residential equation, the impact of the mortgage rate and of real disposable income have increased significantly, but the latter with a longer lag, while the impact of house prices has remained exactly the same.

These changes have altered the quantitative impact of certain variables, but not the qualitative picture. Thus, the two most important variables in the housing market remain the mortgage rate and real disposable income. This adds credence to our claim that for policy analysis it is better to treat the US housing market as homogeneous and not as a compendium of segmented markets. These conclusions are supported by examining the dynamic multipliers of a few key variables. Table 7.1 provides the results. For comparative purposes, every variable that is expressed as growth rate (per cent over the year earlier period) has been perturbed by 1 percent of its value in December 2006.

House prices continue to be most sensitive to interest rates. Just a one percent increase in the 30-year Treasury, which affects the mortgage rate, lowers house prices by 2.0 percent after 12 months and 2.5 percent after 24 months. The first year multiplier is the same as in the older version, while the second year multiplier has increased from 2.2 percent. Thus, if nothing else interest rates play a slightly more important role in the current version than in the one outlined in Arestis and Karakitsos (2004). The second most important variable is growth in real disposable income. A 1 percent fall in real disposable income growth lowers house prices by 0.4 percent after two years, the same as in the previous version. However, the first year multiplier is zero, while in the older version it was –0.2 percent. The impact of interest rates on gross and net wealth is exactly the same.

The most important factor affecting real residential investment is the mortgage rate, a prominent result that held true in the previous version too, as reported above. A one percent rise in the mortgage rate leads to a fall in real residential investment of 2.9 percent after 12 months and 3.1 percent in 24 months. These are slightly smaller than in the previous version, in which the corresponding multipliers, respectively, were –3.3 percent and –3.9 percent. The second most important variable is household income, a result that also held true in the previous version. A one percent fall in real disposable income growth leads to a fall of 0.2 percent in 12 months and 0.5 percent in 24 months. The corresponding multipliers in the previous version were –0.2 percent and –0.9 percent. The downward revisions in the impact of interest rates and income on residential investment are due to the result of the longer than anticipated boom in the housing market.

It is important to note that the model we have utilised for the purposes of this chapter portrays certain characteristics. The most prominent is that the mortgage rate is the most important factor of the housing market with real disposable income in second place. In terms of the estimated model as reported and discussed in Arestis and Karakitsos (2007), the first- and second-year multiplier with respect to the mortgage rate is over 2. This means that for every percentage rate increase in the mortgage rate, house prices would fall more than two percentage points. The increase in the mortgage rate sets in motion a spiral between four key variables: house prices, real residential investment, gross real estate (the value of property) and net real estate (the value of property net of mortgage debt). A rise in the mortgage rate or a fall in real disposable income growth lowers the demand for housing and triggers a fall in house prices, as the supply of houses is fixed in the very short run. In time, this lowers the supply of houses by reducing real residential investment and inducing households to keep their property instead of putting it in the market for sale. The new balance of demand and supply of houses causes capital losses in property and lowers the gross real estate of households. With time households are induced to repay their mortgage debt or, at least, to accumulate debt at a lesser pace. Either way, the net real estate of households falls and this diminishes once again the demand for housing. Once this cycle is completed it triggers another one that is larger than the one before. The spiral of falling prices, residential investment, gross and net real estate goes on increasing in amplitude until the rate of debt repayment exceeds the rate of capital losses in property values. Net real estate stops falling, as households pay back their debt, and begins to rise and this, in time, will increase the demand for houses thereby putting an end to the free fall of house prices. In other words, a shock in the mortgage or real disposable income growth leads to a new steady-state equilibrium with lower house prices, lower real residential investment and lower gross and net real estate.

An important aspect of the model estimated is the strength of monetary policy through the housing market; an aspect upon which some research has been undertaken over the past few years. One piece of such research is the study by McCarthy and Peach (2002), which produces evidence on the strength of the impact of monetary policy, utilising data from two different periods: (i) prior to 1986 and (ii) post-1986. The split in the period coincides with the restructuring of the housing finance system from a system dominated by specialised, highly regulated savings institutions, to one with less regulated mortgage bankers and a mortgage securitisation process, so that post-1986 the mortgage market is more integrated into the broader capital markets. This evidence suggests that RRI prior to mid-1980s responds quickly to a change in the mortgage rate. For example, an increase in MR causes RRI to decline by 3 percent with a two-quarter lag. Post mid-1980s RRI responds more slowly: the two-quarter lag is no longer relevant, for it is now a two-year lag; a similar pattern in terms of the relationship between home prices and the mortgage rate is reported in the same study. But although RRI responds more slowly in the latter period, eventually the relationship is stronger. McCarthy and Peach (2002) conclude that 'monetary policy still appears to have a strong effect on residential investment, but it takes longer for it to occur' (p. 144), and that 'the timing of the housing sector's response to monetary policy has become similar to that of the overall economy' (p. 151). Our results, which relate to the second period, support the findings of the study to which we have just referred – albeit with one important exception. The impact of a change in the mortgage rate on house prices and RRI is much faster than what they are in the McCarthy and Peach (2002) study. In terms of the impact of a change in the mortgage rate on house prices the impact is felt within the month of the change. In the case of RRI, it takes three months for the change in the mortgage rate to influence it. The magnitude of the impact is substantial as noted above. In fact our empirical results suggest that the impact of a change in the mortgage rate on housing variables is the most important from all variables considered in our model, in terms of both the theoretical and the empirical aspects of it. This particular finding is extremely relevant especially for monetary policy purposes, and as such it is worth exploring further, a task undertaken in the section that follows immediately below.

8   An explanation of the stylised facts

Figure 7.17 explains the rationale of the model for the housing market. A negative or positive shock in real disposable income or the mortgage rate affects the demand for houses and alters house prices, since the

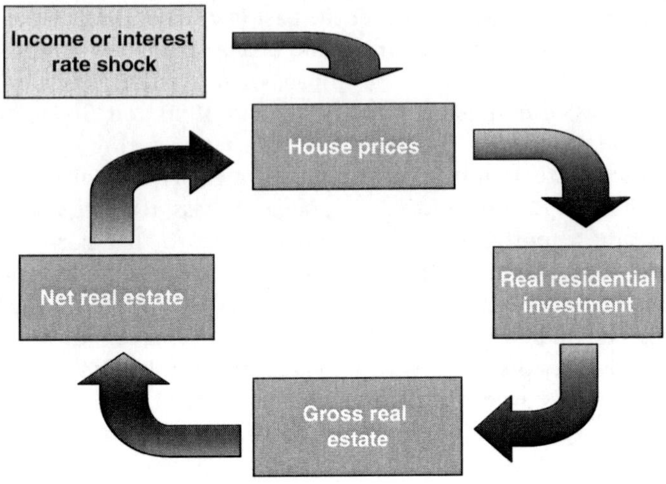

Figure 7.17   The housing market loop

supply of houses is fixed at any point in time. This provides a signal to existing homeowners and property developers to alter the supply of houses. Accordingly, real residential investment is adjusted. The new balance of demand and supply of housing affects the capital gains (or losses) in the housing market and therefore the value of gross real estate. The new trend in house prices induces households to adjust their mortgages, which, in turn, affects the net real estate of households. The latter, however, affects the demand for housing and the cycle is repeated leading to a spiralling effect, as the stimulus from each cycle is getting bigger during the initial phase of the process. However, at some point in time, the rate of debt accumulation exceeds the rate of capital gains and the net real estate begins to fall. This puts a brake to the process of expanding house prices at infinitum.

The housing boom of the first few years of the new millennium can be explained with the help of the model as follows. Rising real disposable income in the second half of the 1990s helped house price inflation to accelerate. But the tightening of monetary policy after the 1997–98 crisis reduced house price inflation to zero by June 2000. The easing of monetary policy in the aftermath of the burst of the equity bubble set up a spiral of house price inflation. Lower mortgage rates increased the demand for houses and spurred real residential investment. The new balance of demand and supply of housing led to capital gains in the property market that boosted the value of gross real estate. This induced households to borrow more and increase again the demand for houses. This cycle has been repeated several times until 2005 leading to accelerating house price inflation. The critical factor for the reversal of the spiral is that the pace of debt accumulation exceeds the rate of capital gains in the property market. This is the condition that ensures that net real estate stops rising and begins to fall. This has already happened and in time it will lead to lower demand for housing. The down-spiral process has accelerated in the last three years.

The risk that the property market would be pricked abated somewhat at the beginning of 2007. Relative house price inflation at the beginning of 2007 was one percent lower than in 2005 and the mortgage rate was back to the level that it was at the beginning of 2005.[8] There may be a counter-argument here, which is that housing prices and mortgage rates do not always correlate all that well historically – witness the period 1988–93 in Figure 7.13. Other forces may be moving housing prices as shown above. However, the point of this chapter is that the housing prices/mortgage rate relationship is particularly pertinent at this phase of the cycle. Indeed, ever since the aftermath of the burst of the equity bubble, 'sector rotation' has been at work, whereby surplus funds have been channelled into the property rather than into the equity market.

9   Summary and conclusions

The housing market has played a key role in the last two business cycles of 2001 and 2008. In the early cycle it cushioned the economic contraction, while in the current one it caused the deepest recession since the late 1950s. This contrasting outcome is due to the movement of house and equity prices. In the 2001 cycle house and equity prices moved in opposite directions, thus offsetting the impact of each other on the economy. In the current cycle, though, they moved in tandem magnifying the negative impact on the economy. But what needs to be explained are the reasons behind what caused this complex pattern of prices is monetary policy.

After the collapse of the internet bubble the Fed eased monetary policy aggressively. The Fed funds rate under Greenspan was cut from 6.5 percent to 1 percent – a level that was maintained until mid-2004, when growth had exceeded potential. The gradual removal of the accommodative bias of monetary policy between mid-2004 and the summer of 2007, at the eruption of the credit crisis, fuelled the boom in the housing market, turning it into a bubble. Interest rates should have risen earlier, in mid-2003, and much faster than the 25 bps in every Fed meeting. However, interest rates should also have fallen earlier than the summer of 2007. Too little, too late was the mistake of monetary policy over the past five years.

As a result of these mistakes in monetary policy, the US economy, and consequently the world at large, fell into a recession, which for the US has turned out to be the worst since the late 1950s. But in some respects, such as the housing market, the recession is the worst since the Great Depression. So far nominal house prices have fallen nearly 30 percent, while relative prices have fallen 35 percent. Before the bottom is reached they are expected to fall more than 40 percent and 45 percent, respectively. The destruction in wealth is phenomenal. At the bottom gross wealth is expected to have returned where it started in 1998, while net wealth will be even lower, due to the irreversibility of debt. However, the K-Model suggests that the housing market will stabilise in the spring of 2010. The condition for a reversal of the negative house spiral that the rate of growth of house prices exceeds the rate of growth of debt is expected to be met in the early summer of 2010. But things will have improved considerably before then. The K-Model suggests that the recession is easing and a recovery is expected in 2010, although this is likely to be anaemic. Partly as a result of that and partly because the condition for ending the current negative spiral is the breaking of the vicious circle of falling house prices and bank losses, the balance of risks remains on the downside. With respect to the latter, the dramatic improvement in the earnings of financial companies has bolstered confidence, triggering a turnaround in the economy, is simply fictitious. It has been achieved by suspending the mark-to-market approach of valuing assets. Banks are arbitrarily assigning fictitious prices to distressed assets, thereby avoiding losses that otherwise would have to be written against profits from current operations. Hence, the vicious circle problem has simply been assumed away. But because of that bank lending is not expected to improve. The current recovery therefore is not based on solid ground, as it is due to restocking.

8
Long-Term Risks of Robust Consumer Behaviour

1 Introduction and stylised facts

Consumption is by far the biggest component of aggregate demand, amounting to more than two-thirds of real GDP. Hence, developments in consumption affect both the long-term trend of growth in the economy and business cycles. However, consumption is largely a coincident indicator of business cycles. Thus, it falls in the downswing and rises in the upswing in line with the economy. Consumption is affected by both short- and long-run factors. The former reflects mainly the impact of the corporate sector on households through employment and wages and salaries. This impact depends mainly on the severity of the recession. The long-run factors reflect balance sheet adjustment in the assets (equities and houses) and liabilities (mortgage and consumer debt) of the personal sector and induce changes in the savings ratio. It is the purpose of this chapter to analyse the short-run factors in the current downturn and compare them to other business cycles by examining the interaction of the corporate and the personal sector. In the current downturn consumption has fallen by nearly 5 percent, the highest since the early 1950s recession. While short-run factors have played a significant role in the current downturn, the long-run factors have played an equally, if not more, important role. They will certainly be the main hindrance to the recovery of consumption and the overall economy in the next few years. It is, therefore, the purpose of this chapter to analyse these long-run factors and draw a distinction between demand-, supply- and asset-led business cycles. A comparison is also made among the last three asset cycles so that their differences and similarities can be appreciated and the risks to the current recovery can be assessed.

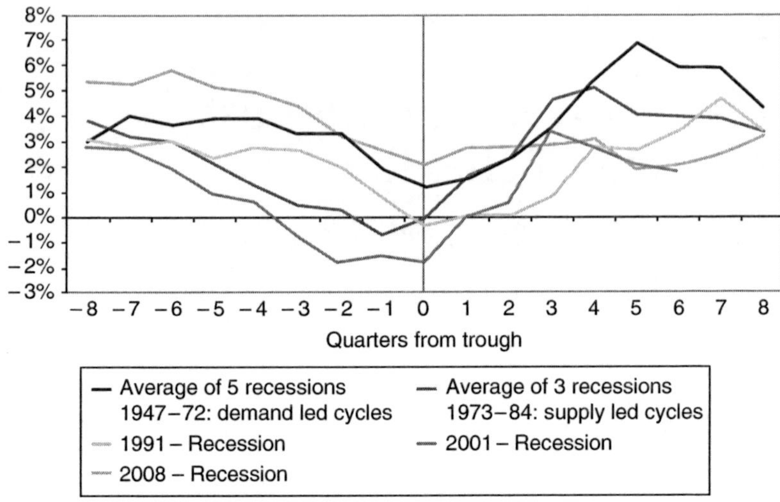

Figure 8.1   Consumption % YoY

Figure 8.1 shows the pattern of real consumer expenditure for eight quarters before and after the trough of the recession as a percentage of the earlier year. To simplify comparisons only five lines are shown: the average of the five demand-led recessions in 1947–72; the average of the three supply-led business cycles in 1973–84; the early 1990s recession; the 2001 recession; and the recent one. The K-Model predicts that the bottom of the recession on a year-to-year growth is the second quarter of 2009. This is taken as point zero on the line labelled '2008 – Recession' and points to the right represent the K-Model forecast.

Consumption is highly cyclical; the growth rate falls in the downswing and rises in the upswing. Most of the time, consumption growth turns around at the trough of the business cycle. The average slowdown in growth is around 3.5 percent, which occurred in the 1991 recession and in the 2001 recession. In the average demand cycle, the slowdown was milder, less than 3 percent, whereas in the average supply cycle the slowdown was nearly double, around 4.5 percent. In the current downturn the slowdown was more than 4.5 percent, the steepest fall of all recessions in the post-Second World War era. But although there are some similarities in the rate of growth, there are marked differences in the level of consumption. The level of consumption never contracted in the average demand cycle and in the 2001 recession, but it did contract in the average supply cycle, in 1991 and in the current downturn when it registered its steepest fall. To some extent this is due to initial conditions. When consumption growth is very high, as it was in the 2001 recession, around 5.5 percent, it is plausible that a normal slowdown would not cause a contraction in the level of consumption; but when consumption growth is average, around 3 percent, then a steep slowdown may cause a contraction in the level. Long-run factors played a minor role in the average demand and supply cycle, but a major role in the last three asset-led cycles. In the 1991 recession the personal sector did not experience any serious balance sheet problems, but the corporate sector did. Hence, although the recession was mild in 1991, consumption growth became negative because of balance sheet problems in the corporate sector. The 2001 recession was even milder than the 1991 one, but the potential balance sheet adjustment of the personal sector was deflected by the overwhelming easing of monetary policy, which triggered a rally in the housing market that more than offset the losses in equities. Accordingly, the slowdown of consumption growth was average, but given the initial high rate of growth consumption never contracted. In the current downturn the recession was severe and thus the short-run factors played a significant role in the sharpest contraction of consumption. These problems were accentuated by the balance sheet adjustment of the personal sector because of the simultaneous collapse of equity and house prices. The risks to the current recovery stem from a continuous balance sheet adjustment of the personal sector. If equity prices do not recover substantially to offset some of the losses from the housing market, then households may continue to repay their debt and save a higher proportion of their income. In this case the recovery would be at best anaemic, if it does not falter and give way to a second recession.

This chapter is organised as follows. We begin in section 2 with an examination of the short-run factors that affect consumption, followed in section 3 by a study of the long-run factors that influence consumption. We consider the K-Model and dwell on the theoretical background of consumer behaviour in section 4. We assess the long-run risks to consumption in section 5, along with a summary and conclusions.

2   Short-run factors affecting consumption

The short-run factors reflect the impact of an economic downturn upon the interaction of the corporate and personal sectors. The corporate sector projects the fall in demand for goods and services in the downturn and evaluates its impact on corporate profits. Upon that valuation companies respond by cutting working hours, shedding employees and reducing hourly earnings and wages and salaries in an effort to minimise the impact of the downturn on profits. These decisions affect the income and employment of households who respond by cutting the demand for goods and services creating a negative loop between the decisions of the corporate and the personal sector. In the downswing of the cycle the unfolding of this negative loop becomes a process that is gaining momentum and the recession deepens. The turning point occurs when the savings from shedding labour, cutting working hours and reducing the incomes of employees turns around the profit margin of companies, and hence profits, in spite of continuous dwindling in the demand for goods and services. In this stabilisation phase conditions continue to deteriorate, but the rate of decline is diminishing. In economic jargon the first derivative is still negative, but the second derivative turns positive. The improved conditions in profitability induce firms to reduce the rate at which they lay off employees and pay wages and salaries. This, in turn, diminishes the impact on the employment and income of households, who then respond by cutting the rate at which demand for goods and services is falling. This initial stage of stabilisation turns into a positive loop during the recovery phase and the economy returns into positive growth. In economic jargon the persistence of the positive second derivative ultimately turns the first derivative positive, too.

Table 8.1 shows the sources and disposition of real and nominal disposable income. Disposable income is equal to personal income less taxes, while real disposable income is adjusted for inflation in consumer prices. Personal income consists of income from employment (compensation of employees) and other personal income (proprietor's and rental income and income from assets in the form of interest and dividends) plus transfer payments (subsidies) from the government less personal contributions for social insurance. The compensation of employees accounts for two-thirds of personal income, while unearned or other personal income account for one-quarter. The remainder 10 percent of personal income consists of the net effect of government subsidies and contributions for social insurance. Wages and salaries, which is the biggest component of the compensation of employees accounts for one-half of personal income.

Figure 8.2 shows the close association of personal income and wages and salaries in all business cycles. The severity of the current downturn is reflected in the decline of personal income for the first time since the mid-1950s recession following the Korean War. But in terms of magnitude the decline in personal income is reminiscent of the deepest recession in the late 1940s following the end of the Second World War.

Table 8.1 Sources and disposition of personal income

Jul-09	Billion of dollars	%
1. Compensation of employees (CE)	7721	
% of personal income		65
1.1. Wages and salaries (WS)	6222	
% of personal income		52
1.1.a. Wages and salaries in private industries (WPI)	5032	
% of Personal Income		42
1.1.b. Wages and salaries in government (WG)	1191	
% of personal income		10
1.2. Supplements to wages and salaries (SUP)	1499	
% of personal income		13
2. Other personal income (Proprietor's & rental income and unearned income)	3084	
% of personal income		26
3. Net transfer payments (government and business benefits) (TR)	2111	
% of personal income		18
4. Less: Personal contributions for gov social insurance (NIC)	958	
% of personal income		8
5. Personal income (PI) (sum of (1–3) –4)	**11957**	**100**
6. Less: Personal current tax payments (TX)	1079	
% of personal income		9
7. Equals: Disposable personal income (DPI)	**10878**	
% of personal Income		91
8. Less: Personal outlays (PO)	**10420**	**100.0**
8.1 Personal consumption expenditures (CON)	**10066**	
% of personal outlays		96.6
8.2 Interest paid by persons (IP)	198	
% of personal outlays		1.9
8.3 Personal transfer payments to the rest of the world (net) (TRW)	155	
% of personal outlays		1.5
9. Equals: Personal saving (SAV)	**459**	
10. Personal saving as a percentage of disposable personal income		4.2
11. Real disposable personal income (billions of chained 2000 dollars)	32390	

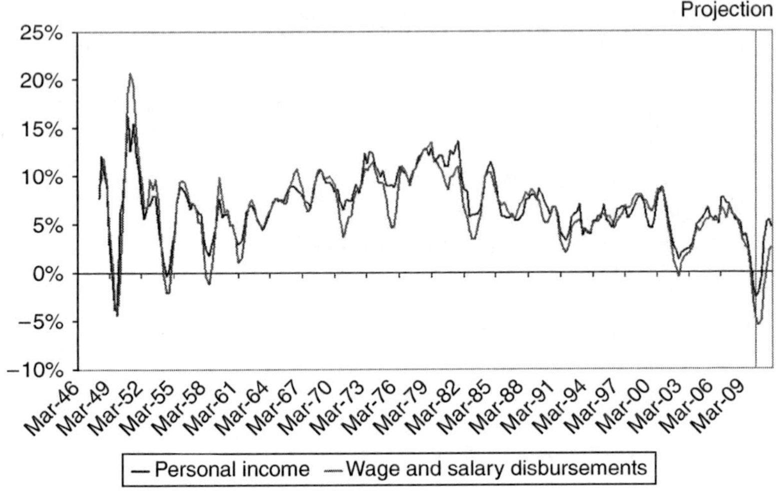

Figure 8.2   Personal income & wages and salaries (nominal)

The decline in wages and salaries is deeper than that of personal income. In fact, it is the worst in the entire post-Second World War era suggesting that the burden of adjustment from the recession falls on wage earners. The rebound in profit margins relies much more than ever before on suppressing the wages of employees. This is indeed evident when the comparison is made with the wages and salaries in private industries, as this excludes those working for the government, which is less cyclical and on occasions countercyclical (see Figure 8.3). The projection of the K-Model is that wages and salaries in the private industries will decline at the bottom of the current recession by 7.5 percent compared to a 6.0 percent fall in the 1949 recession. The decline in nominal wages and salaries is partly due to the introduction of flexible labour markets, namely the ability of firms to hire and fire at will with minimum compensation of employees and the limit of unemployment and other social benefits to the unemployed. The combined effect of these measures, which were introduced in the late 1980s and early 1990s, has reduced the bargaining power of employees, so that it has now become possible to accept even a nominal wage cut. The effect of flexible labour markets had a big impact on private sector employees in the 2001 recession, too. Wages and salaries in private industries fell 2 percent in the previous downturn, in spite of a shallow recession (see Figure 8.3). Hence, the phenomenal rebound of profits in the first year of the 2001 recovery was accomplished at the expense of employees. In spite of the unprecedented decline in wages

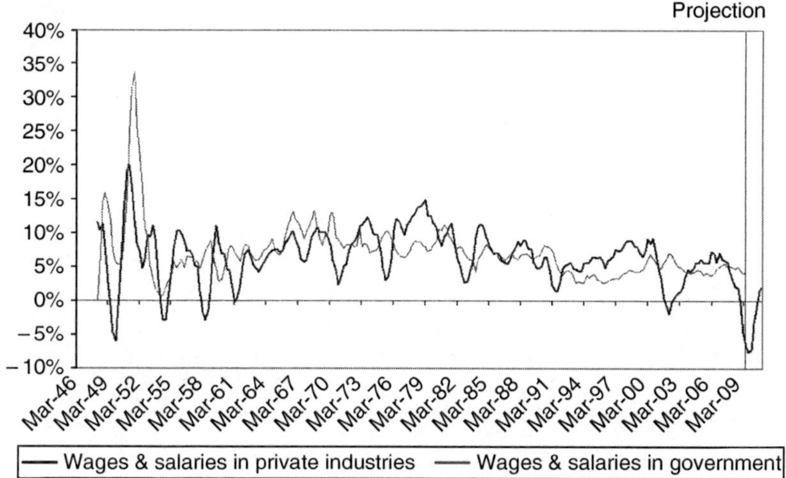

Figure 8.3   Wages & salaries in private industries & government

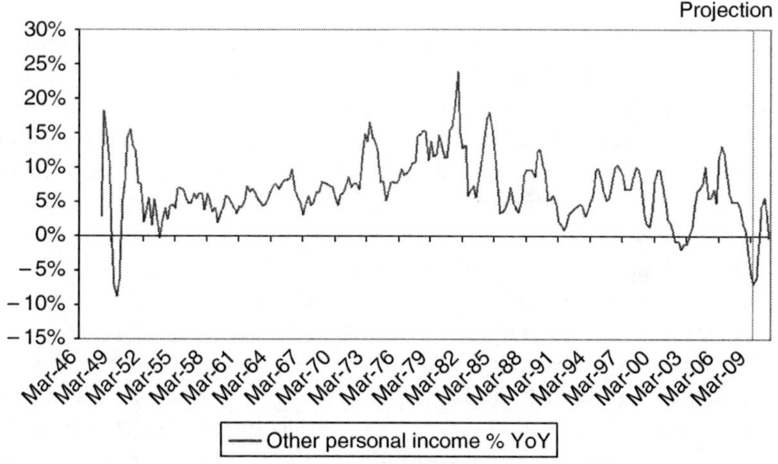

Figure 8.4   Other personal income % YoY

and salaries in private industries, the K-Model suggests that the bottom is very near and that a rebound is in sight (see Figure 8.3).

In the current downturn other personal (earned) income fares slightly worse than the compensation of employees (see Figure 8.4). This is due to the collapse of equity and housing market and the near zero interest rates. However, the K-Model suggests that the worst is over and that the rally

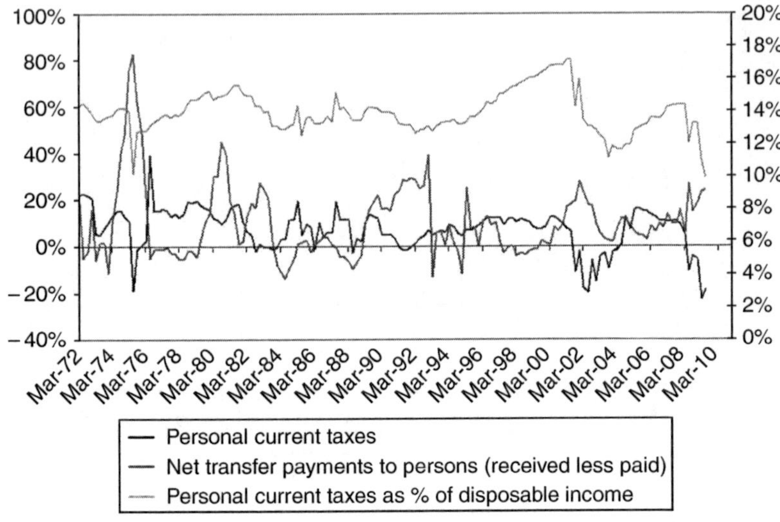

Figure 8.5   Fiscal support to the personal sector

in equities and the improving profitability of companies will boost other personal income (see Figure 8.4). Personal taxes have been reduced in the current downturn to 10 percent of disposable income, the lowest in the entire post-Second World War era (see Figure 8.5). In the previous recession personal taxes fell to 11.2 percent of disposable income. Moreover, the subsidies (net transfer payments) to households have jumped by 25 percent, thus highlighting the extent of the fiscal stimulus in the current downturn (see Figure 8.5). This fiscal stimulus has alleviated the decline in disposable income compared to personal income (see Figure 8.6). The K-Model suggests that we are near the bottom in disposable income with a recovery in sight under the combined effect of the fiscal stimulus, the rebound in profitability and the rally in risky assets.

As inflation in consumer prices, measured by the deflator in consumption expenditure, has been rather low and stable relative to the fluctuations in income the difference between nominal and real disposable income has also been small and stable (see Figure 8.7). Hence, fluctuations in nominal disposable income have been transmitted to corresponding fluctuations in real disposable income. Inflation is most of the time positive and as a result the growth in real disposable income is smaller than nominal. In the high inflation era of the 1970s and 1980s the purchasing power of households' income was eroded substantially (see Figure 8.7). But progressively in the 1990s the erosion of real purchasing power has diminished. In the current environment

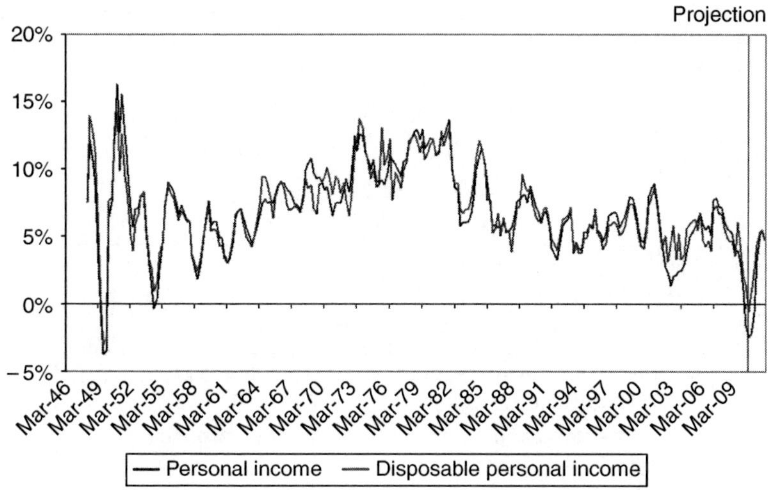

Figure 8.6   Personal income and disposable personal income (nominal)

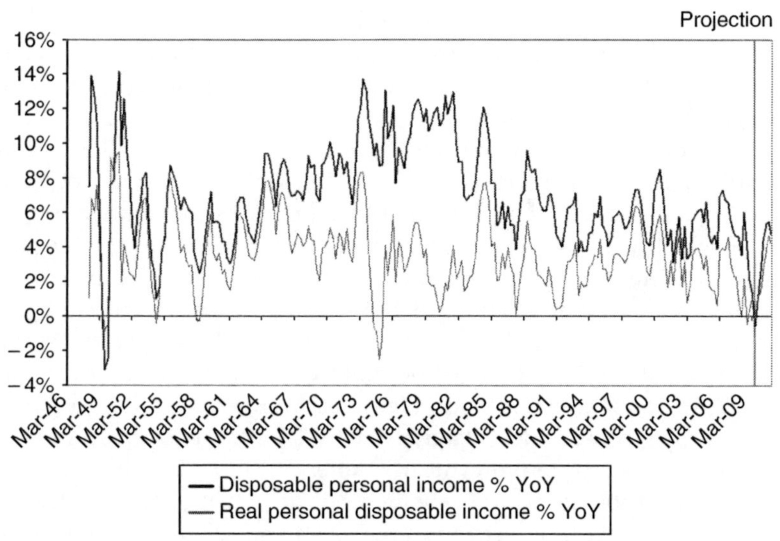

Figure 8.7   Nominal & real personal disposable income

of deflation, real disposable income is higher than nominal and the negative inflation is boosting the real income of households, thus contributing further to the turnaround of consumption and the economy. The K-Model suggests that the boost in real disposable income will stimulate consumption in the next 12 months.

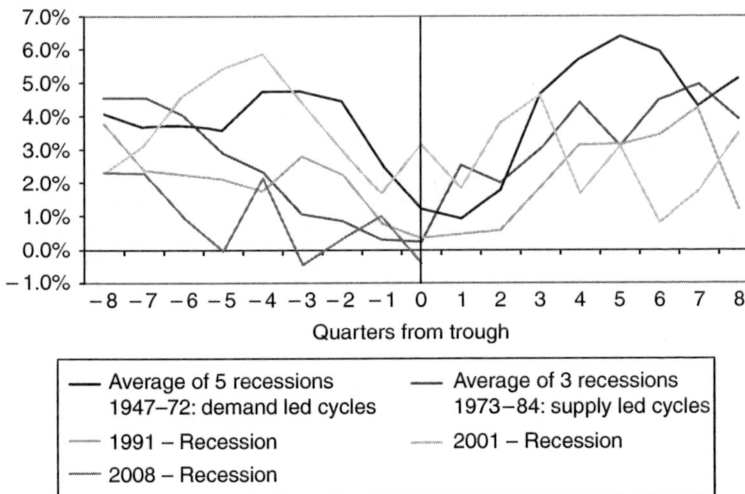

Figure 8.8   Real personal disposable income

The behaviour of real disposable income in the current downturn is not dissimilar to previous business cycles (see Figure 8.8). The rate of growth of real disposable income falls in the downswing and rises in the recovery, with the bottom hit most of the time at the trough of the cycle. The growth rate of real disposable income has become negative for the first time, but the difference from the average supply cycle, which witnessed the next biggest decline, is less than 1 percent. Moreover, the decline in the growth rate of real disposable income in the two years leading to the trough is 2.7 percent in the current cycle compared to 2.9 percent in the average demand cycle, 3.4 percent in the 2001 recession and more than 4 percent in the supply cycle, which witnessed the worst decline. Hence, the negative growth rate in the current cycle, although shocking, is largely due to the low rate of growth at the beginning of the current downturn, namely to initial conditions.

We may be able to throw some light on the prospects for real disposable income growth by decomposing wages and salaries in the private industries (which account for something less than half of personal income) into the product of its constituent components: (a) average hours per week, (b) employment, and (c) real hourly earnings. Companies usually cut the working week in the downswing, but restore it in the upswing of the cycle (see Figure 8.9). In the current cycle, the average weekly hours were cut 1.8 hours during the downswing. This is

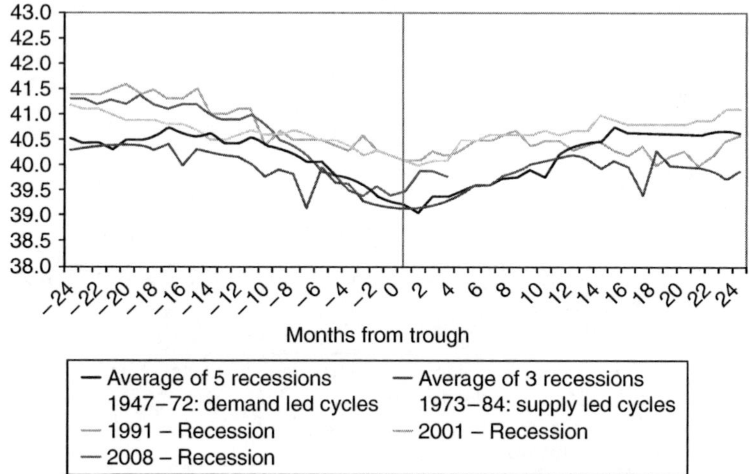

Figure 8.9   Average weekly hours in manufacturing

the worst cut but only by a whisker compared to the average demand cycle in which companies cut 1.7 hours. But in the asset-led cycles of the early 1990s and early 2000s companies cut 1.2 hours and 1.5 hours, respectively, which is markedly smaller than the current cycle.

The current recovery is most likely to be anaemic, as was also the case with the previous two recoveries of the 1991 and 2001 cycles. During the early stages of the 2001 recovery the average weekly hours increased by just 0.7 hours, a slower pace than in any other cycle. Even worse, in their attempt to restore profitability and healthy balance sheets in the second round of retrenchment of the 2001 downturn, companies cut yet again the average weekly hours hitting twice the low reached at the trough. It is plausible that in the current recovery companies will adopt similar practices to those employed in the last cycle.

In any cycle companies revert not only to cutting the average weekly hours, but also employment. Before the current recession, the worst job losses occurred in the 2001 downturn. In that downswing job losses were more pronounced than in any other previous cycle, in spite of the shallowest recession (see Figure 8.10). Job creation peaked 19 months before the trough at 306,000 new jobs per month and bottomed two months after the trough at 220,000 job losses per month, the steepest swing (526,000) in all previous ten cycles. For example, in the average demand cycle job creation peaked at only 165,000, while the maximum monthly job losses were 170,000, a swing of 335,000. In all asset-led

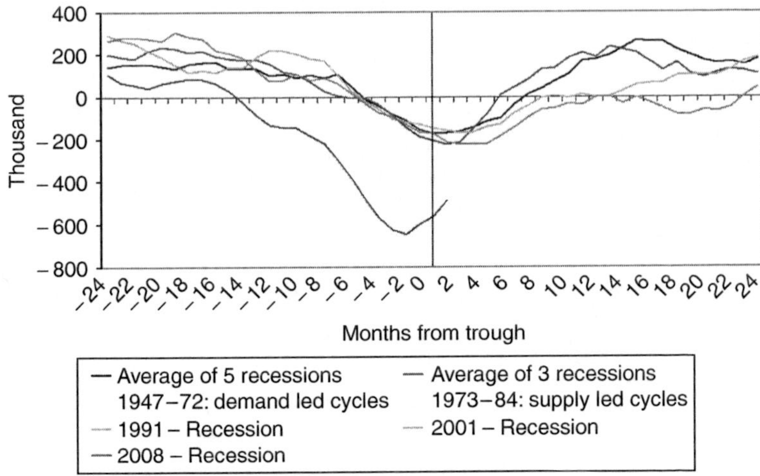

Figure 8.10 Monthly job creation/losses in nonfarm payroll, 6M MA (thousands)

business cycles the anaemic nature of the recovery is reflected in poor job creation. In the recovery phase of the 2001 cycle job creation was more anaemic than ever before, outstripping even the early 1990s cycle. On a six-month moving average basis, there was hardly any job creation in the 2001 recovery. Even worse, job losses resumed during the second round of retrenchment by the corporate sector. This second round of retrenchment, however, was successful in restoring profitability and improving balance sheets. Job creation resumed by the end of 2003 as a result, and continued through 2004. In the current downturn, job losses, on a six-month moving average basis, hit an all-time high of 645,000, two months before the bottom. The K-Model suggests that job creation in the forthcoming recovery would be again anaemic, reminiscent of the 2001 cycle.

Not only do companies cut the working week and shed labour to restore profitability and healthy balance sheets in an economic downturn, but they also reduce the nominal hourly earnings growth rate, thus suppressing the income of households. Nominal wage growth usually hits its zenith at the peak of the business cycle and declines in the downswing. As inflation also peaks around the same time as wage inflation, real wage growth begins to recover in the downswing, thus ameliorating the impact on the income of households, thereby paving the way for a recovery in income and consumption. This pattern has already been observed in the current cycle. Nominal wage growth

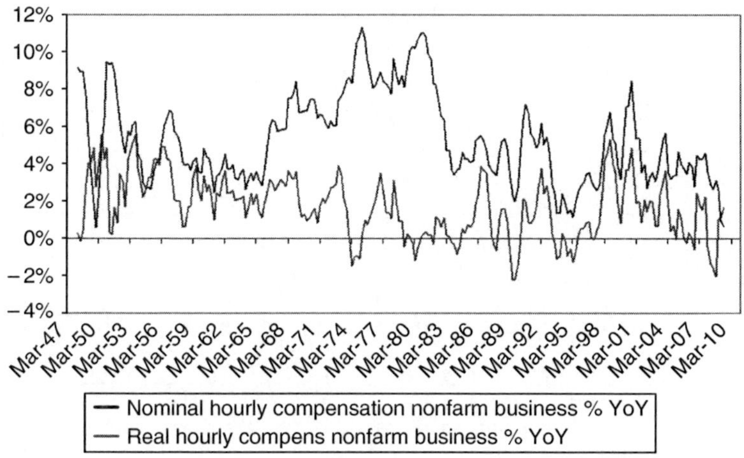

Figure 8.11   Nominal and real wages

peaked in 2007:Q3, while the economy peaked a quarter later. The decline in nominal wage growth has continued ever since, but the easing of inflation pressures since August 2008 has helped real wage growth to recover (see Figure 8.11). Thus, from 2008:Q3 real wage growth hit its nadir at −2 percent and has now (June 2009) recovered to 2.2 percent. In the downswing of the two previous asset-led business cycles the real hourly earnings in non-farm business were hit more than ever before. In the 1991 cycle real hourly earnings fell by more than 2 percent very early in the cycle and began to recover six quarters before the trough (see Figure 8.12). However, the rebound faltered after the first year of the recovery contributing to the anaemic nature of the recovery. In the 2001 cycle the growth rate of real hourly earnings fell dramatically in the year to the trough of the cycle, but its rebound was at best modest in the first year of the recovery. In the 2001 cycle there was a second round of retrenchment as a result of which real hourly earnings fell to an even lower rate than at the bottom of the recession. Nonetheless, this second round of retrenchment managed to restore profitability and healthy balance sheets, thereby contributing to the ultimate sustainability of the recovery, albeit with a long lag. This adjustment in the real hourly earnings in asset-led business cycles is to be contrasted with the average demand cycle, when real earnings simply fluctuated mildly around their mean value, without falling significantly in the downswing or rising in the upswing (see Figure 8.12). In the current downturn real earnings began to rebound three quarters before the trough, but they are likely

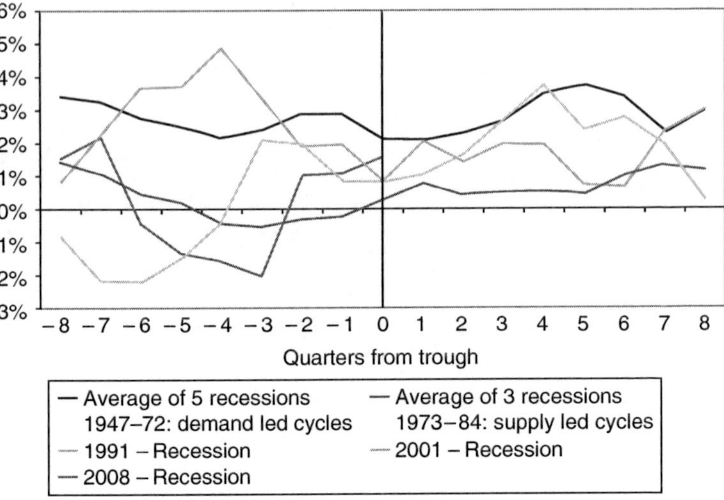

Figure 8.12   Real hourly earnings in nonfarm business

to reach a plateau, if they do not falter later on, as in the 1991 cycle. Hence, the K-Model suggests that developments in real hourly earnings will probably contribute to an anaemic recovery in the current cycle.

Overall, the prospects of the short-run factors that affect consumption have improved. Companies reduced the growth rate of nominal hourly earnings throughout the downswing of the cycle, but the easing of inflation pressures since the second half of 2008, which has developed into deflation in the course of 2009, has revived the growth rate of real hourly earnings; thereby paving the way for a recovery in the income of households and consumption later on. The fall in inflation is also boosting other personal income, thus further contributing to the revival of incomes and consumption. The unprecedented job losses in the downswing of the current cycle have also contributed to an improvement in profit margins, and hence of profits, thus inducing companies to ease the rate of contraction in incomes and employment. Moreover, there are signs that the average weekly hours that have been cut more than ever before are beginning to ease, which is consistent with the pattern of previous business cycles. Finally, the fiscal support is further boosting the incomes of households. Accordingly, the conditions are now ripe for a recovery in household income and consumption.

The prospects of the current recovery can be compared to the other asset-led cycles. For example, the 2001 recession was very mild due to the resilience of the consumer. This is partly because of the buoyancy of real disposable income, which was boosted through easy fiscal policy. Had it not been for the fiscal injection, real disposable income would have fallen, thereby pulling the rug from under the consumer's feet. Wages and salaries fell not only in real, but also in nominal terms. In most private industries they fell in real terms even during the recovery. But personal income fared better than wages and salaries partly because wages and salaries in the government sector grew at a brisk pace and partly because other earned and unearned income did not suffer as much as wages and salaries. During the double-dip recession of the industrial sector, caused by a second round of retrenchment, companies cut the average working week, laid off workers, managed to reduce the hourly earnings of their workers and slashed investment. The slower growth in real disposable income during the double-dip recession caused a deceleration in consumption growth. However, the picture changed markedly in the second half of 2003. The second round of retrenchment by the corporate sector was successful in restoring profitability and improving balance sheets. Hence, wages began to rise, job creation was resumed, albeit sluggishly at the beginning, and average weekly hours were increased. The 2003 round of tax cuts also bolstered real disposable income in the second half of the same year. The tax cuts, along with all the other short-run factors, boosted consumption making the recovery sustainable. The experience of the 2001 cycle suggests that a similar pattern may be observed during the recovery phase of the current cycle. In spite of the improvement in the short-run factors that affect consumption, there are doubts as to the sustainability of the recovery because of the long-run factors that affect consumption. This is an issue that we delve deeper in the next section.

3 Long-term forces restraining consumption – personal sector imbalances

During the upswing of the average demand- and supply-led business cycle, savings as a percentage of nominal disposable income (what is usually called the *savings ratio*) fell 1.6 percent, thereby fostering the pace of the recovery, due to some extent to the fiscal surplus (see Figure 8.13). In contrast, the savings ratio increased gradually by 2 percent almost throughout the downturn of the early 1990s. This was the first time that the savings ratio had not fallen during the recovery phase of the business cycle. This increase in the savings ratio contributed to making the recovery of the early 1990s anaemic. In the 2001 downturn the

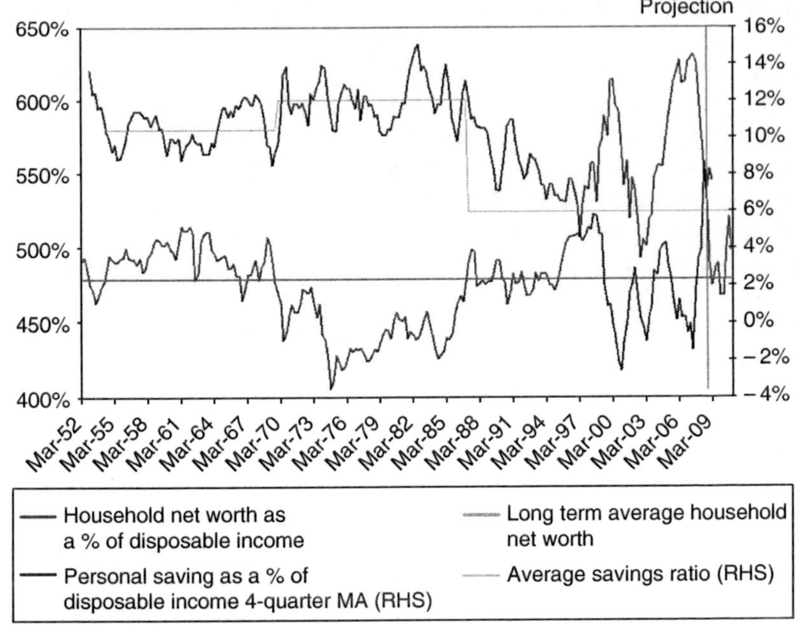

Figure 8.13   Household net wealth

savings ratio rose by nearly the same amount as in the early 1990s, from 1.9 percent seven quarters before the trough to 3.5 percent eight quarters after the trough (see also Figure 8.13). In the current cycle the savings ratio has soared from a low of 1.2 percent five quarters before the trough to 5 percent at the trough. What the outlook for the savings ratio might be over the next two years or so, would determine not only the fate of the latest tax cuts, but also how much of the new boost to income from employment would stimulate consumption.

In the very long run, consumption and real disposable income are growing at the same rate so that the ratio of consumption to income (the *average propensity to consume*) is equal to unity. But in the short run consumption can deviate substantially from income. In the Permanent Income–Life Cycle Hypothesis the role of savings is to absorb the swings in income and allow for a smooth consumption pattern. Consumers save in good years and tap on these savings in bad years. Hence, the savings ratio moves pro-cyclically, it rises in booms and falls in recessions. However, the validity of this relationship has been questioned. Frowen and Karakitsos (1996) suggest that in a leveraged economy the savings ratio moves counter-cyclically (i.e. it falls in a boom and rises in a recession). In boom years asset prices rise faster than usual as consumers borrow against these assets to invest even more (leveraging). Faster than usual rising asset prices make people feel rich, inducing them to relax on their effort to save as they believe that they can meet easier their targets for savings (e.g. provide for pension, leave to their heirs). Hence, the savings ratio falls in a boom. In a recession asset prices fall and people are left with an overhang of debt. In order to repay their debt people cut back on consumption out of current income and intensify their efforts to save in order to rebuild their wealth. Hence, the savings ratio increases in a recession. That is exactly what happened in the 2001 and the early 1990s downturn because the consumer has become much more leveraged than in the average demand- and supply-led business cycle. In the current cycle, this pattern has been accentuated even more, as the degree of leverage soared in the good years. The increase in the savings ratio in the downswing of the current cycle is thus consistent with a counter-cyclical behaviour of the savings ratio in asset-led business cycles.

In the short run, therefore, consumption depends on real disposable income and the savings ratio. The forces that determine the savings ratio are net wealth and uncertainty about job security and income growth prospects. For the aforementioned reasons, a rise in net wealth lowers the savings ratio and vice versa (see also OECD, 2000b). An increase in uncertainty about job security and income growth prospects makes people more cautious, inducing them to refrain from spending out of current income, and thereby raising the savings ratio. Figure 8.13 shows the relationship between net wealth and the savings ratio, while Figure 8.14 shows net wealth in the various business cycles. When net wealth is above its long-term average the savings ratio is low, and vice versa. For example, in the 1950s and 1960s, the golden years of demand-led business cycles, net wealth was above its long-term average and the average savings ratio was low. In the 1970s and the 1980s, the supply-led business cycles associated with the two oil shocks, net wealth fell below its long-term average and, consequently, the average savings ratio was increased. In the longest bull market from 1982 to 2000 net wealth increased steadily, leading to a constant decline in the savings ratio. During the internet bubble years in the second half of the 1990s net wealth rose to unprecedented levels and the savings ratio fell precipitously, reaching rock bottom at the peak of the bubble. As equity prices declined steadily for three years, from March 2000 to March 2003, net wealth fell, reducing its long-term average to 480 percent, while the savings ratio increased to 4.3 percent by the end of 2004. This rise in the savings ratio reflected increased

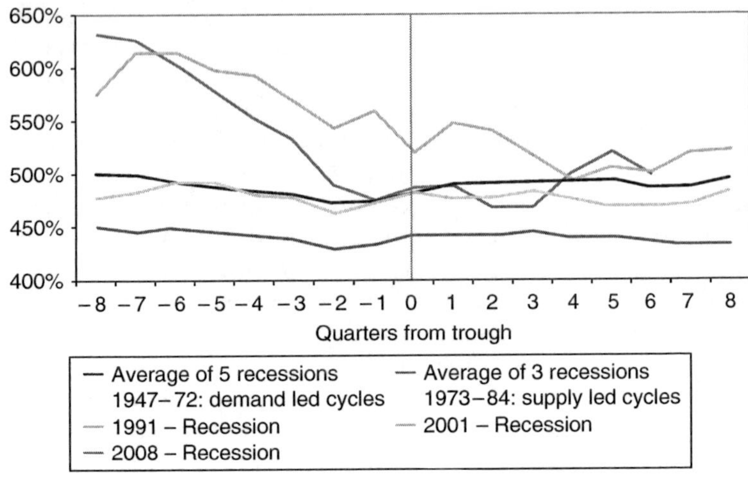

Figure 8.14   Personal sector net wealth as % of disposable income

cautiousness on the part of consumers in the face of falling asset prices
with continuously rising debt.

Table 8.2 shows one measure of the personal sector imbalance. Between
the peak of the internet bubble in March 2000 and the trough in
September 2002 financial assets fell $6.6 trillion, but these were partially
offset by rising property prices that boosted the value of tangible assets
by $3.9 trillion, thereby limiting the erosion of gross wealth to $2.6
trillion (see Table 8.2). Between the bottom of the internet bubble and
peak of the housing bubble the picture changed dramatically. The losses
in financial assets turned into profits of the order of $21.6 trillion, while
the gains in tangible assets soared to $8.9 trillion, so that gross wealth
($78.3 trillion) stood higher than it had been at the peak of the internet
bubble ($50.4 trillion) for a gain of nearly $28 trillion (see Table 8.2).
Figure 8.15 shows that the recovery of equities in the four years to 2007
was a prolonged bear market rally, as the peak in 2007 was lower than
the peak in 2000, a conclusion that is even more evident when equity
prices are deflated by consumer prices rather than disposable income.
The same figure shows that the spectacular gains in gross wealth are
due to excessive leverage, as debt continued to soar until the end of 2007
to 133 percent of disposable income. However, the picture has changed
markedly since the burst of the housing bubble. Between 2007:Q3 and
2009:Q1 (the latest data available) the tangible assets as a percentage of
disposable income have lost almost all their gains since the peak of the

Table 8.2 Personal sector balance sheet

	Total assets	Total assets as % of nominal disposable income	Tangible assets	Tangible assets as % of nominal disposable income	Financial assets	Financial assets as % of nominal disposable income	Liabilities	Liabilities as % of nominal disposable income	Net worth	Net worth as % of nominal disposable income
Peak of internet bubble (March 2000)	50,383	714	14,930	211	35,453	502	6,919	98	43,465	616
Bottom of internet bubble (Sep 2002)	47,773	609	18,871	241	28,902	368	8,567	109	39,207	500
Peak of housing bubble (Sep 2007)	78,316	766	27,777	272	50,540	494	14,118	138	64,199	628
Latest quarter (Mar 2009)	64,517	598	24,221	225	40,295	374	14,140	131	50,376	467
Loss/gain between peak & bottom of internet bubble	−2,610	−105	3,941	29	−6,551	−134	1,648	11	−4,258	−116
Gain/loss between peak of housing and bottom of internet	30,543	157	8,905	31	21,637	126	5,551	29	24,992	128
Latest gain or loss since peak of housing	−13,799	−167	−3,555	−47	−10,244	−120	23	−7	−13,822	−160

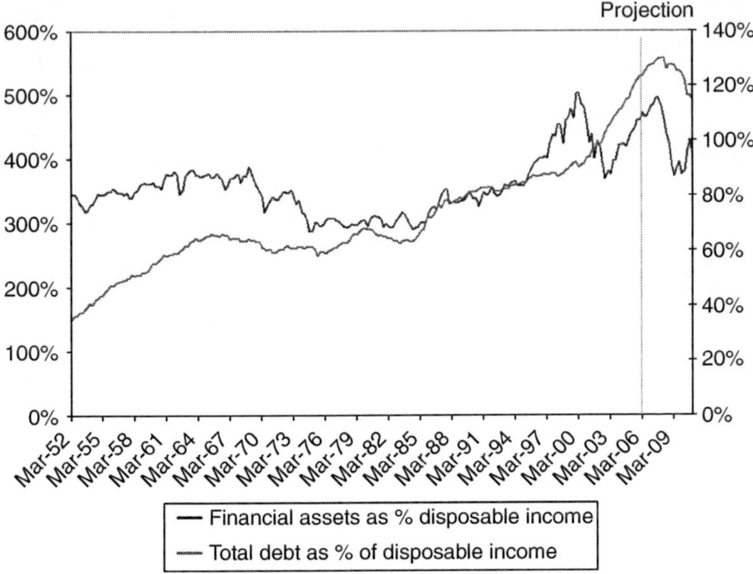

Figure 8.15 Financial assets and debt of the personal sector

internet bubble, while financial assets are only marginally higher than at the bottom of equities. A modest debt deleverage has taken place since then with debt having been curtailed to 127.5 percent from 133 percent. Three remarks emerge from these observations. First, equities entered a long bear market since early 2000. Second, the bear market rally between 2003 and 2007 confirms that the housing bubble is a transformation of the internet bubble. Third, the asset and debt deflation process that should have taken place after the burst of the internet bubble was simply postponed until the housing bubble burst. The implications for the economy, however, depend not on gross but on net wealth, an issue to which we turn next.

Net wealth has not reflected the gains in gross wealth because of soaring debt levels. Thus, at the peak of the internet bubble net wealth stood at 616 percent of disposable income, but it fell to 500 percent at the bottom of this bubble (see Table 8.2 and Figure 8.13). In the bubble years of the housing market not only did net wealth recover the earlier losses, but it exceeded by a whisker the previous high at 628 percent. However, since the bursting of the housing bubble, net wealth has tumbled as both house and equity prices have fallen precipitously. At the end of 2009:Q1 net wealth has fallen to 467 percent, even lower than the bottom of the internet bubble. This pattern of wealth in the last three asset-led business cycles is in stark contrast to the demand and supply cycles that prevailed until the 1990s. In these cycles the variability of net wealth in the downswing and upswing of each cycle was small (see Figure 8.14). The variability of net wealth was also relatively small in the early 1990s cycle, as the corporate sector faced serious imbalances, which also infected the personal sector. However, in the last two cycles, in the early and late 2000s, net wealth fell significantly two years before and after the trough (see Figure 8.14). The K-Model suggests that net wealth will stabilise at slightly higher levels, but will not recover significantly, as house prices will simply stabilise in the course of 2010, while equity prices will resume their fall in the second half of 2010.

The irreversibility of debt has played an equally important role as the fall in asset prices in the decline of wealth in the current downturn.[1] The overhang of debt creates an imbalance that can be corrected in either of two ways: (a) a retrenchment by the personal sector that will raise the savings ratio; or (b) a rebound in asset prices. In the 2001 cycle households never responded by retrenchment to this imbalance, presumably because they believed that the fall in asset prices was transient rather than permanent. The continuous advance of house prices during the slump of equity prices encouraged the belief that the fall was transient, which was bolstered during the recovery. The bubble years

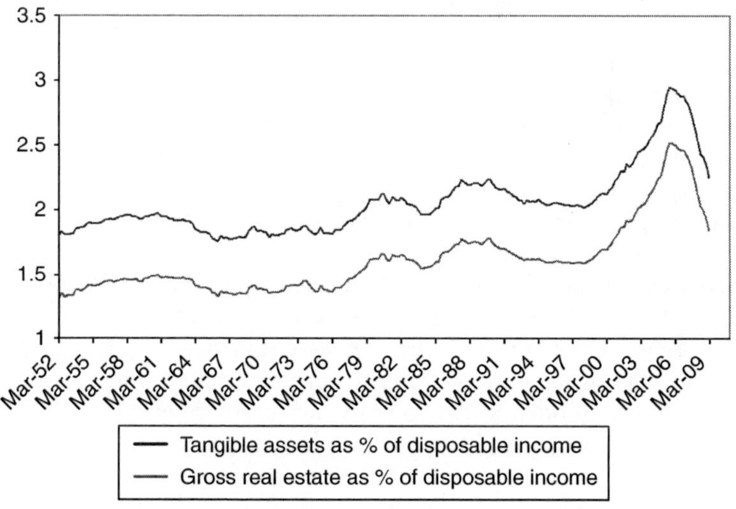

Figure 8.16   Tangible assets & real estate

of the housing market deluded households that the net wealth levels of the internet era were sustainable and accordingly lowered the savings ratio, thereby fuelling the housing bubble. But such beliefs are irrational. In the absence of demographic changes net wealth is a trendless variable and any deviations from the mean should be interpreted as a bubble. In the current environment house prices are unlikely to recover for a long time, but equity prices may be influenced by economic policy. In this context, policymakers are making another big mistake. Instead of encouraging deleverage, now that the excesses from the two bubbles have been corrected, the policymakers are trying to push equity prices up, thus feeding false hopes that higher levels of net wealth than the average are sustainable. The fatal policy mistakes are not cleaning the banking system and removing fair market valuation practices by allowing banks to exercise discretion in valuing their distressed assets. This has created fictitious profits in banking that have bolstered hopes of a sustainable recovery in the economy. The savings ratio has risen to 5 percent in 2009:Q2, but its course over the next few years depends on whether the fall in asset prices is regarded as transient or permanent and on the other factors that affect it, namely the debt service burden, job security and incomes.

The debt service ratio is an estimate of the ratio of debt payments on mortgages and consumer credit to disposable income. In spite of low interest rates, household debt service stood at an all-time high at the end of 2008 because of high levels of indebtedness (see Figure 8.17). However, it edged lower in the first quarter of 2009 and this should be the beginning of a mild downtrend, as households repay their debts. The Financial Obligations Ratio (FOR) is a broader measure than the debt service ratio. The FOR includes automobile lease payments, rental payments on tenant-occupied property, homeowner's insurance and property tax payments. These wider measures would also decline in the next few years. Thus, servicing the debt is unlikely to force a rise in the savings ratio.

Job security and income growth prospects are reflected in consumer confidence, but depend on the outlook for the corporate sector. It has been argued in chapters 5 and 6 that although there has been an improvement in the outlook for both corporate profits and investment, the recovery will be modest at best. Nonetheless, consumer confidence soared after February 2009, albeit from a thirty-year low, as the bankruptcy of the banking sector was avoided and signs of stabilisation in the economy emerged. The uptrend in consumer confidence should last for the first year of the recovery, but then it is likely to falter, unless new

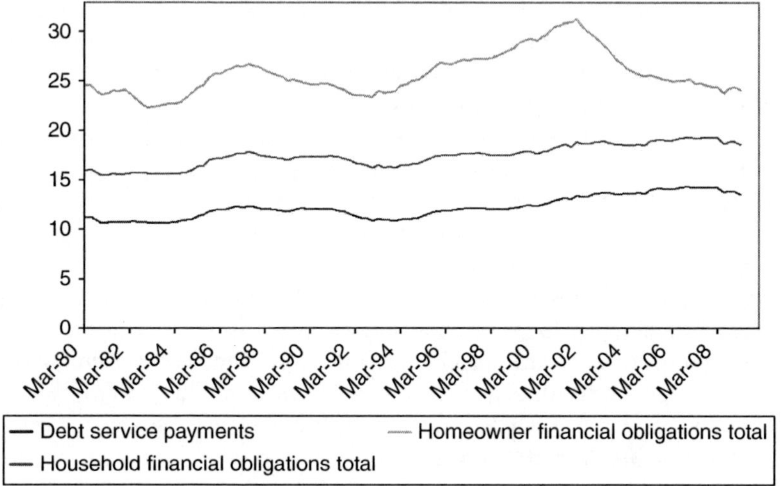

Figure 8.17   Debt service burden

policy measures are adopted, which is not unlikely. The corporate sector does not anticipate any firm recovery of consumption and, accordingly, it will hesitate in investment spending and creating new jobs. Thus, there is bound to be some disappointment on the part of households and consumer spending will be subdued – a kind of self-fulfilling expectations. Moreover, official unemployment has soared to 9.5 percent, but other wider measures of unemployment that take into account underemployment, have soared to more than 16 percent of the labour force.[2] This high level of official and hidden unemployment is very likely to make consumers cautious in their spending patterns and to keep the savings ratio at the elevated level of 5 percent of nominal disposable income, which in real terms translates to real savings of 8 percent of real disposable income.

Overall, the long-run factors that affect consumption suggest at best a modest recovery. Two consecutive bubbles have fooled households into believing that they can compensate their lower income growth, which is evident in the increasing income inequality, by gains in the equity market in the first bubble and gains in the housing market in the second. However, these gains proved a chimera. Households have now been left with an overhang of debt that is unsustainable, as their net wealth has returned to the pre-bubble levels. The only reasonable course of action is for consumers to repay their debts to sustainable levels, thereby boosting their net wealth. But this requires a higher savings ratio. This adjustment has already occurred and the K-Model suggests that real savings at 8 percent of real disposable income or nominal savings at 5 percent of nominal disposable income in the next few years are sufficient to restore net wealth to slightly above its long-term average. However, policymakers may try to fool households for a third time. Although house prices are unlikely to recover for a long time, equity prices may recover, albeit nowhere near the bubble levels. Nonetheless, if households were to believe that equity prices could recover significantly over the next few years they might be persuaded to lower their savings ratio, thereby boosting consumption and making the recovery sustainable. Such a rosy scenario, although plausible for the next two years, will not resolve the problems in the long run. The banking crisis has not been resolved; it has simply been put at bay by assuming that distressed asset prices will return to their bubble levels. But this is wishful thinking and banks know it very well. Accordingly, banks are not keen to lend to companies and households and this will undermine the fragile recovery in the medium term. Equity prices have been rallying since the spring of 2009, but the rally will falter after the first year of the recovery and with it hopes of a sustainable recovery, unless policymakers keep coming with more fiscal stimuli. But in the long run more stimuli will entail higher interest rates that will curtail investment and consumption. Hence, in the long run households will be forced to do the right thing, namely accept that that there is no free lunch and save more to repay their debts. Policymakers are simply postponing the inevitable. To appreciate these results we first discuss the K-Model of consumption.

4   The K-Model of consumption

The analysis so far enables us to construct a theoretical model of US consumption. This particular framework we estimate and use for further investigation as shown below. We begin with our theoretical framework. In the very long run, consumption and real disposable income are growing at the same rate so that the ratio of consumption to income (the *average propensity to consume*) is constant. But in the short run, consumption can deviate substantially from income. In the Permanent Income hypothesis (Friedman, 1957) and Life Cycle hypothesis (Modigliani and Brumberg, 1954; Ando and Modigliani, 1963) consumers smooth their consumption patterns in the business cycle by basing their expenditure on their estimate of their permanent or trend income. Hence, the saving rate should rise in a boom and fall in a recession as consumers interpret the fluctuations in current income as temporary. In booms consumers regard the high current income as temporary and save the excess over permanent or trend income for the rainy days. In a recession consumers regard the drop in their current income as temporary and try to safeguard their standard of living by drawing down their savings (wealth). Thus, the saving ratio (the fraction of saving over disposable income S/YD) moves pro-cyclically, thereby rising in booms and falling in recessions. The validity of this relationship, however, has been questioned, based on two arguments.

The first is that consumer behaviour is myopic in the sense that the marginal propensity to consume out of transitory income is not zero, as the Permanent Income hypothesis suggests. The second is that consumers in formulating their desired consumption are constrained in terms of achieving the desired level, simply because capital markets are imperfect. Consumers, thus, face liquidity constraints in that they cannot borrow to finance their consumption. Flavin (1985) finds that the response of consumption to current income is the result of liquidity constraints rather than myopia. Direct estimates of the importance of liquidity constraints suggest that countries with high reliance of consumption on current income are those where consumers rely less on capital markets (Jappelli and Pagano, 1989; Zeldes, 1989a; see also Carroll, 2001).[3] Campbell and Mankiw (1991) find that consumption for a number of countries can be accounted for by changes in permanent as well as current income, suggesting that some households follow the Permanent Income hypothesis or Life Cycle hypothesis, while others follow the Keynesian consumption function. Indeed, the proportion of households who base their consumption on current income varies between 20 percent for Canada to almost 100 percent for France with Sweden (35 percent)), the US (35 percent), and the UK (35 percent)[4] falling in between (the result for the US is consistent with the finding in Campbell and Mankiw, 1990). These findings are consistent with the notion that countries with less developed credit markets should have a higher proportion of households whose consumption depends on current income.[5]

A further argument focuses on another important ingredient of the Life Cycle hypothesis. This relates to the motive for saving, which is to provide for retirement so that the consumers can smooth out their consumption plans for their entire life. Kotlikoff and Summers (1981), however, found that the amount of wealth in the economy is far too large to finance consumption in retirement, thereby rejecting this form of the hypothesis. They conclude that people are saving to leave bequests to their heirs. Hence, the theory should be revised to allow for bequests as an additional motive for saving. In their own words, 'Intergenerational transfers appear to be the major element determining wealth accumulation in the United States' (p. 730). Modigliani (1988), however, argues that there are definitional and methodological problems with studies like Kotlikoff and Summers (1981). Once these have been accounted for, 'the role of bequest motivated transfers... seem to play an important role only in the very highest income and wealth brackets. Some portion of bequests, especially in lower income brackets, is not due to a pure bequest motive but rather to a precautionary motive reflecting uncertainty about the length of life, although it is not possible at present to pinpoint the size of this component' (p. 39).

It follows from this analysis that, although there may very well be arguments that contradict the Life Cycle hypothesis, the main tenet of the theory, that wealth is an important determinant of consumption and that households smooth out their consumption expenditure through time, remains valid under conditions of uncertainty (Zeldes, 1989b). The consumption 'smoothing' approach received a great deal of attention and a growing number of contributions, an area reviewed by Browning and Crossley (2001). Under these conditions the motives for saving are also to provide for rainy days. In other words, saving is also *precautionary* and does not just provide for retirement or even for bequests.[6] The larger share of saving of the old people is consistent with increased risk aversion as people age. Old people are more cautious than the young, they take less risk, and are wary of large medical bills and the possibility of low income during their retirement. Thus, under conditions of uncertainty saving acts as a *buffer stock* (Deaton, 1991; Carroll, 1994, 1997) to enable households to maintain their consumption pattern even when their current income drops below their permanent income, as for example would be the case if an individual becomes unemployed or the income of a self-employed person drops substantially in a recession.[7] Consequently, and as Carroll and Samwick (1997) put it, 'wealth is higher for households with greater income uncertainty' (p. 42), so that 'consumers spend most of their lifetimes trying to maintain a modest "target" wealth-to-income ratio' (p. 68) and save for retirement later in their lives.[8] Uncertainty and 'buffer-stock' saving behaviour contain the implication of a concave consumption function, with the interesting characteristic that there are differences between marginal propensities to consume out of different income brackets (higher income groups have a lower marginal propensity to consume than lower income groups), a characteristic noted some time ago by Keynes (1936).

These developments entail interesting implications, which can be highlighted as follows. We may begin by writing consumer behaviour as:

$$C = c(YP) \tag{1}$$

where C is consumption, c is marginal propensity to consume out of permanent income (YP). We may also write disposal income of the personal sector (YD) as:

$$YD = C + S \tag{2}$$

where S stands for savings. Substituting (2) into (1) we may arrive at (3):

$$(S/YD) = 1 - c(YP/YD) \tag{3}$$

In a boom current income exceeds permanent income and the ratio (YP/YD) falls which leads to a rise in the saving ratio (S/YD). In a recession current income falls short of permanent income, the ratio (YP/YD) rises; this leads to a fall in the saving ratio. However, if we re-write (1) as in (1a):

$$C = c_1(YP) + c_2(NW) \tag{1a}$$

where NW is net wealth, and substitute (1a) into (2), we can arrive at equation (4):

$$(S/YD) = 1 - c_1(YP/YD) - c_2(NW/YD) \tag{4}$$

It is clear from equation (4) that the saving ratio depends not only on the ratio of permanent to current income in the business cycle, but also on the wealth–income ratio. Thus, although in a boom the permanent to current income ratio falls, the wealth–income ratio may rise sufficiently to cause a fall instead of a rise in the saving ratio. This can be easily explained. Consumers have a target level for their wealth so that they can finance their own future consumption as well as that of their children in the form of bequests. Hence, households determine the optimal rate of their annual saving on the basis of their expectations about future income, asset prices, interest rates and inflation. In addition consumers take into account their precautionary saving – for the rainy days. If plans turn out as expected there is no need for adjusting their saving rate. However, if wealth is rising faster than expected their need to save is reduced, while if wealth is falling short of its target, then consumers need to save more. Wealth can rise faster than expected if asset prices increase or income is growing faster or if inflation falls more than anticipated. Hence, the saving ratio varies in a way to achieve the target wealth in the face of unexpected developments in the main determinants of the future path of wealth. Hence, in order to analyse the behaviour of the saving ratio in the business cycle we must examine the determinants of the wealth–income ratio.

Wealth is created by the accumulation of past savings. But wealth is kept or invested in various assets (tangible and financial) and consumers can additionally borrow using their assets as collateral in order to increase the value of their wealth through investment. Thus, wealth is properly defined as *net* wealth, which is the value of assets resulting from the accumulation of past savings and capital gains (losses) from their investment less the liabilities of consumers. The value of assets and liabilities can increase or decrease as their prices change through time thereby altering the net wealth of consumers. At any point in time, consumers would have a target wealth which is computed on the required consumption for the remainder of their life expectancy, taking into account that one of the spouses may live to a great age, the bequests consumers would like to leave to their heirs and the amount of precautionary saving in case they are faced with large medical bills during retirement. Since the target level of wealth would finance future consumption for themselves or their children, consumers would attempt to estimate their permanent or lifetime resources and the desired level of consumption.

Furthermore, actual wealth would fluctuate around its target level as asset prices fluctuate in the course of the business cycle and consumers take advantage of low or high interest rates to borrow or repay their debts. Moreover, other variables, like consumer confidence influenced by the level and rate of change of unemployment, inflation, wage settlements and interest rates, the length and depth of the recession or the extent of the boom may affect the level of precautionary saving and consumers' estimate of their permanent income. In good periods, like a boom in the property or the equity market, wealth may exceed its target, prompting consumers to spend more thereby reducing their savings ratio, as they feel wealthier. This situation may be accentuated if economic activity is buoyant in which consumer confidence is rising, prompting consumers to borrow more as their estimate of their permanent income is also rising. In bad periods, after a bust in the property or equity market or because their debt increased wealth may fall short of its target prompting consumers to spend less thereby raising their saving ratio as they feel poorer. This situation may be aggravated if falling wealth is accompanied by a recession in which consumer confidence is eroded, precautionary saving is increased and the estimate of their permanent income is reduced thereby prompting consumers to repay their debt. Hence, the adjustment of the saving ratio in the course of the business cycle requires an evaluation of all components of net wealth as well as the factors, which affect permanent income. In this framework the interest rate becomes a very important variable because it affects directly (through valuation) or indirectly (through other macro-variables) all components of the personal sector net wealth. Thus, in periods of high interest rates the value of bonds falls, house prices and the value of shares decline, servicing the debt increases or the value of debt increases through the restructuring of loans. Accordingly, consumer net wealth declines as the value of assets falls, whereas the liabilities increase. Consumer wealth falls short of its target prompting consumers to spend less and rebuild their wealth by saving more as they feel poorer. In contrast, in periods of low interest rates the value of bonds rises, house prices and the value of equities increase, servicing the debt becomes easier or the value of debt is reduced through the restructuring of loans. Accordingly, consumer net wealth exceeds its target prompting consumers to lower their savings ratio.

We may now use these propositions and the analysis, as in, for example, Frowen and Karakitsos (1996), to clarify the point that in a leveraged economy the savings ratio moves counter-cyclically, so that it falls in a boom and rises in a recession. In boom years asset prices rise faster than usual as consumers borrow against these assets to invest even more (leveraging). To the extent that consumers save to achieve a desired volume of wealth, then faster than usual rising asset prices make people feel wealthier inducing them to relax on their effort to save as they believe that they can meet their targets for savings (e.g. provide for pension, leave to their heirs, etc.) more comfortably in this way. Hence, the savings ratio falls in a boom. In a recession asset prices fall and people are left with an overhang of debt. In order to repay their debt people cut back on consumption out of current income and intensify on their effort to save in order to rebuild their wealth. Hence, the savings ratio increases in a recession. We may also think of the rate of interest as an important determinant of consumption. Changes in the rate of interest can affect consumption in two ways. A higher rate of interest, for example, means higher returns on savings, so that consumers increase their consumption due to this income effect. At the same time, however, a higher rate of interest and the higher returns on savings this implies, causes consumers to substitute consumption for savings; there is, thus, a substitution effect in addition to the income effect referred to earlier. *Mutatis mutandis* in the case of a lower rate of interest being the object of analysis. The overall impact of a change in the rate of interest, then, depends crucially on the relative strength of the two effects to which we have just referred.

In the short run, therefore, consumption depends on real disposable income, the savings ratio and the rate of interest. Our analysis clearly suggests that consumption may be written formally as in equation (5):

$$C = C(DY, SR, R) \tag{5}$$

where C is as defined above, DY is real disposable income of the personal sector, SR is the savings ratio as defined above (i.e. S/YD), and R is the rate of interest.

The long-run forces that determine the savings ratio are net wealth and uncertainty about job security and income growth prospects. For the reasons discussed earlier, a rise in net wealth lowers the savings ratio and vice versa. An increase in uncertainty about job security and income growth prospects makes people more cautious, inducing them to refrain from spending out of current income, thereby raising the savings ratio. This analysis, then, leads us to hypothesise that the savings ratio is determined as in equation (6):

$$SR = SR(NW/YD, UN, CNF) \tag{6}$$

where NW/YD is the ratio of net wealth (NW) to YD of the personal sector, UN is unemployment and CNF is consumer confidence.

The structure of the two relationships just portrayed captures the rationale of the short-run and long-run factors affecting consumption in the way explained above. Appropriate substitution of equation (2) into equation (1) yields our estimable equation (3):

$$C = C(DY, NW/YD, UN, CNF, R) \tag{7}$$

An increase in real disposable income growth raises the rate of growth of real consumption by the same rate in the very long run (steady state). However, in the short run consumption rises less than income. An increase in net wealth lowers the savings ratio, thereby increasing real consumption growth. The wealth effect is very important in this theoretical framework and has long-lasting effects. An increase in unemployment or a decline in consumer confidence increases uncertainty regarding job security and income growth prospects, hence raises the savings ratio, which, in turn, lowers consumption growth. An increase in the rate of interest lowers real consumption growth, if the substitution effect is higher than the income effect. Equation (7) is precisely the equation that is estimated for the purposes of our analysis and included in the K-Model.

The rationale of the K-Model is summarised in Figure 8.18. The medium grey boxes illustrate the variables that belong to the income loop that affects consumption. The light grey boxes illustrate the variables that cause a shock to the income spiral. Shocks to the income spiral are introduced by monetary policy through changes in interest rates, fiscal policy through taxes and subsidies, and the corporate sector through wages, employment and CPI-inflation. Assume that the economy is in long-run equilibrium so that the income spiral is idle. Consider now a shock in policy or the state of the corporate sector that stimulates real disposable income. This would lead to higher savings that would increase gross wealth. The extra wealth would be invested in financial and/or tangible assets, which, in time, through capital gains would further boost gross wealth. But higher gross wealth would lead to more borrowing, which, if it grows at a smaller pace than assets, will lead to an increase in net wealth. Realised capital gains from assets would boost real disposable income and a second round would be set in motion.

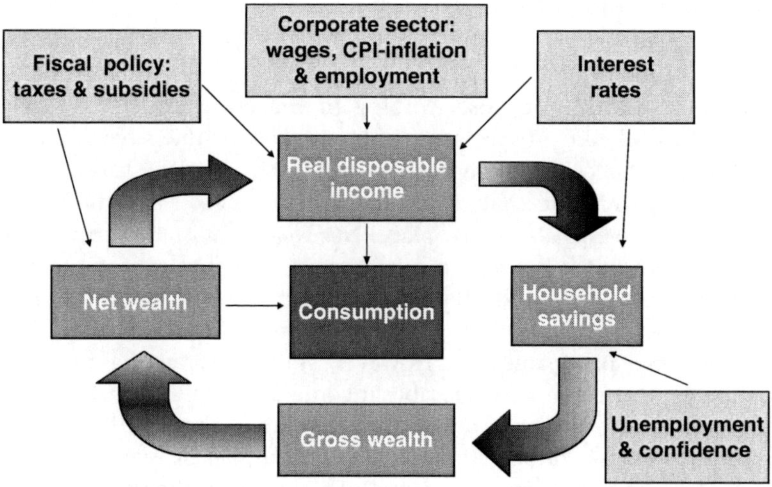

Figure 8.18   The income–consumption loop

In every round higher real disposable income and higher net wealth will stimulate consumption. In the new long-run equilibrium consumption, income, savings, gross and net wealth are higher than the initial equilibrium. The savings ratio would also be affected by unemployment and consumer confidence. The increase in consumption from any shock is not explosive. This means that the income–consumption loop is stable. The stability is ensured if the extra boost to consumption out of a given small increase in disposable income (what is called the marginal propensity to consume) and net wealth is less than unity.

5   Long-term risks to consumption and conclusions

The short-run factors that affect consumption suggest that the worst is over and that the real disposable income growth will accelerate in the first year of the recovery. The K-Model further suggests that the bottom of the recession will take place in the second quarter of 2009, so that real disposable income will grow until the second half of 2010. This assessment is based on the current fiscal stimulus. Further fiscal stimuli may improve the prospects for real disposable income growth and hence for consumption. The main driving force behind the recovery in real disposable income growth is the negative inflation that boosts the real purchasing power of the incomes of households. Moreover, the unprecedented job losses and the reduction in the wages and salaries of those working in the private industries have boosted multi-factor productivity and improved profit margins, so that the corporate sector is alleviating the strain on the personal sector. This has been further boosted through the fiscal stimulus of the Obama Administration. Wages and salaries for those working in the government have been increased, while the prospects for other personal income have improved because of the recent rally in equities and in other risky assets.

The long-run factors that affect consumption suggest that the bulk of the adjustment has also taken place. Net wealth has fallen to the pre-bubble levels, but it has left an overhang of debt that consumers have an incentive to pay back. The hitherto progress in repaying debt is at an early stage and consumers have a long way to go before they bring debt back to a sustainable level. However, the savings ratio has increased to 5 percent of nominal disposable income and the K-Model suggests that at this rate the adjustment in the balance sheet of households has a good chance of being completed in a number of years. Thus, the worst is over and consumption growth below par for the next few years is the best outcome for households and the economy. Unfortunately, this is not how policymakers view the situation. They would rather see consumption growth and hence the overall growth in the economy exceeding potential as they are scared that the recovery might falter. With income growth subdued, buoyant consumption growth could only occur if the savings ratio was to plunge again from 5 percent to 2.0–2.5 percent compared to 1.25 percent at the beginning of the downturn. This could happen if asset prices or the incomes of households or a combination of the two rose significantly to make debt sustainable and recoup some of the losses in net wealth. Equity prices have rallied since the spring of 2009, as the bankruptcy of the banking system has been averted and signs of stabilisation have bolstered hopes of a recovery. But the rally may peter out after the first year of the recovery, in line with profitability. As is argued in chapter 5, the rebound in profits in the first year of the recovery is followed by profit fatigue in the second year. Hence, equity prices cannot be relied upon to ensure a sustainable recovery, while there is no hope that house prices would stage a rally. This puts the burden on fiscal policy. The Obama Administration should come with another fiscal package at the beginning of 2010 if it wants to boost consumption and make the recovery sustainable in 2010. But in the long run successive fiscal stimuli would not succeed, as they require either tax hikes or much higher interest rates. Hence, successive fiscal stimuli would boost GDP growth above potential for one or two years, but then the risk of another recession increases. Thus, the real choice is between steady subpar growth and volatile growth with a boom followed by a bust.

9
Foreign Demand

1 Introduction

As argued in chapter 1, the characteristic of the current downturn is the speed with which the collapse of the US housing market was transmitted to the rest of the world, causing a simultaneous deep recession in all major economies. Although one might quickly point out that this is due to globalisation, two particular channels can be discerned. First, the current world recession is the result of a US banking crisis triggered by the collapse of the subprime market when house prices began to fall. This very rapidly became a global banking crisis because foreign banks were as highly leveraged as US banks. Foreign banks held, along with other foreign investors, a large amount of distressed US assets. Moreover, the overleveraging of foreign banks means that they had also lent large amounts against low-quality assets. Finally, foreign banks had adopted the same practices as US banks and had issued Collateralised Debt Obligations (CDO) that were selling to their investors in an effort to get rid from their balance sheet these high-risk assets. Excessive greed, though, resulted in only a partial removal of these toxic assets from the balance sheet of foreign banks causing huge bank losses when asset prices worldwide started to tumble.

So, the same practices by US and foreign banks and international diversification triggered the spread of the US banking crisis to the rest of the world. The response of banks worldwide, therefore, was the same; an unwillingness to lend to each other, the tightening of lending standards to households and companies and higher lending rates. Hence, the first reason for the simultaneous recession of all major economies is the credit tightening by banks throughout the world. Nonetheless, there is no evidence that such practices led to a credit crunch, namely, to an excess demand for credit at the prevailing interest rate. The dramatic fall of asset prices worldwide has led to lower demand for credit by households and companies, as they found themselves with an overhang of undesired debt. Households are keener than companies to curb their debt levels, as they do not have access to capital markets, thereby making balance sheet adjustment very painful. Hence, the supply as well as the demand for credit has declined. Lower credit, therefore, for whatever reason, is the first factor for the deep world recession.

The second reason for the simultaneous recession of all economies is the collapse of world trade in mid-2008. However, the financial crisis had emerged one year earlier and it is surprising that it took that long for the credit tightening to have an effect on world trade. The real cause for the delay lies in the commodities bubble, which burst in mid-2008, paralysing world trade. The common root of all bubbles is excessive liquidity. Once the US housing market collapsed this liquidity was channelled to commodities, creating the last phase of this bubble. Usually, stories and plausible arguments abound when justification has to be found for channelling speculative funds to a bubble. On this occasion, too, the most powerful story was that China would continue to grow, even if the US fell into recession. Hope dies last and investors wanted to believe that there were still high returns for their investments in commodities. The most incredible argument advanced at the time was that China's growth would remain so strong that it would even cushion the US recession. China's powerhouse is exports and the US consumer remains the coveted customer. Once, US consumption fell off the cliff in the second half of 2008, the myths about China were dispelled, with the result that commodities prices tumbled and world trade collapsed.

The anticipated recovery of the US economy in the second half of 2009 is expected to trigger a revival in world trade lifting the exports in the US, the euro area[1] and Japan, and we refer to them as (G-3) in what follows. The OECD index of leading indicators has turned around and this heralds a revival of (G-3) exports in the months ahead. However, the conclusion of a world recovery over a longer horizon depends on the strength of the US economy and the extent of previous changes in competitiveness. In this respect, the US and Japan have gained competitiveness, while the euro area has suffered a great loss. The US has gained more than 25 percent in competitiveness in the six-year period from the spring of 2002 to the spring of 2008 (see Figure 9.1). The gains of Japan are an impressive 38 percent over a slightly longer period, namely, from the end of 1999 to mid-2007 (see Figure 9.2). However, the euro area

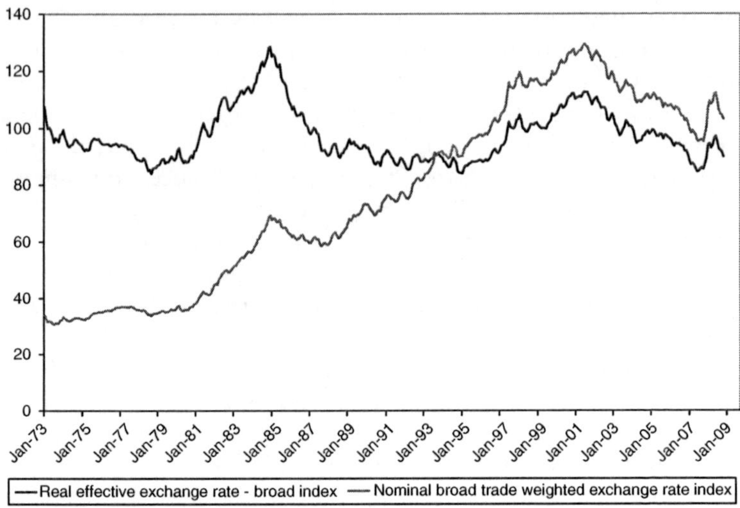

Figure 9.1   US nominal & real effective exchange rate

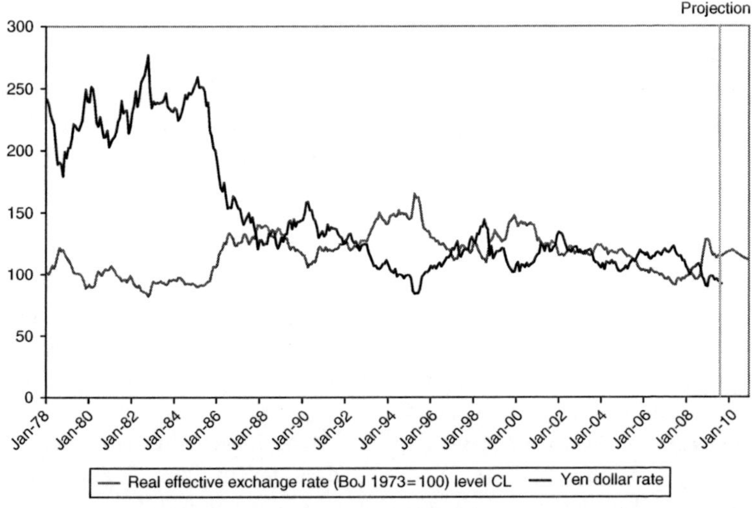

Figure 9.2   Japan nominal & real exchange rate

suffered a 45 percent loss from the winter of 2000 to the spring of 2008 (see Figure 9.3). Since the simultaneous recession of (G-3) the picture has changed somewhat. The US has lost 5 percent of its previous 25 percent gain, leaving it with a gain of 20 percent for the entire period from

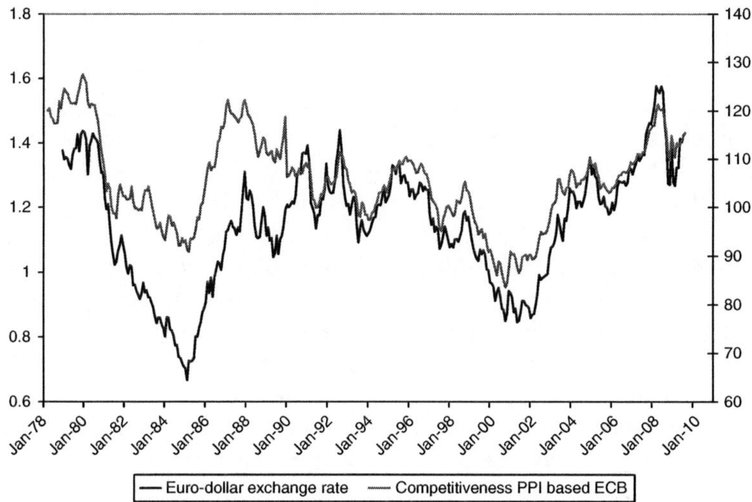

Figure 9.3 EU exchange rate & competitiveness

April 2002 to August 2009 (see Figure 9.1); Japan has lost 26 percent, leaving it with a gain of 22 percent for the entire period of December 1999 to August 2009 (see Figure 9.2); finally, the euro area has gained a meagre 7 percent from the previous 45 percent loss, leaving it with a loss of 38 percent for the entire period of October 2000 to August 2009 (see Figure 9.3). This implies that Japan is best placed to take advantage of a recovery in world trade, with the US second; while the euro area is the laggard.

The improved outlook for the US economy in the second half of 2009 has raised hopes of a US-led world recovery. The argument is that buoyant US growth would first stimulate the experts of the US's main trading partners. This would spur production in the rest of the world and after a while there would be job creation in the export industry. Later on, companies would have to expand capacity and therefore investment would be boosted. Through higher investment the recovery in the rest of the world would become widespread with gains in employment and incomes, which finally would boost consumption. During this process, which may take around two years, the US would lead the rest of the world to recovery. The argument is very powerful because the overall stimulus to world trade is greater than the initial stimulus – the multiplier or magnifying effect is greater than unity.[2] However, there are some concerns with this scenario related, first, to the strength of the US economy and, secondly, the renewed dollar weakness especially against some currencies like the euro.

The validity of these concerns depends, first, on whether the US recovery will be anaemic, as the previous chapters have suggested, or whether the US policymakers will attempt to boost it through an additional stimulus; secondly, the extent to which the dollar weakness has translated into losses in competitiveness in the US main trading partners; thirdly, on the degree of importance of these losses in competitiveness on the rest of the world exports; and fourthly on the feedback to US exports. We begin in section 2 by reviewing the performance of exports in the (G-3) economies. Section 3 highlights the properties of exports in (G-3), as these are encapsulated in the K-Model. In section 4 we make use of the K-Model to simulate the effects on (G-3) exports of two alternative scenarios regarding the US economy – weak and strong growth. Section 4 summarises the argument and offers a number of conclusions.

2   The recent track record and the determinants of (G-3) exports

We begin with the US economy.

2.1   The US case

US real exports rebounded strongly after the recession of 2001, but with a long lag, namely in 2004. Although exports lost some of their steam in 2005, they remained elevated until mid-2008, when consumption and final sales fell off the cliff. Since then exports tumbled to their worst level since quarterly records began in 1973 (see Figure 9.4).

Figure 9.4 shows the main determinants of the demand for US real exports of goods and services. Real exports depend positively on world demand, approximated by OECD industrial production, and negatively on competitiveness – an index that compares domestic with foreign producer prices expressed in domestic currency. The OECD industrial production is, most of the time, a coincident indicator of real exports. The OECD index of leading indicators precedes changes in the OECD industrial production, on average, by six months. Hence, a rise in the leading indicators suggests increases in world demand with a few months lag, which are translated into a boost in exports.

The OECD index of leading indicators bottomed in February 2009 at –11 percent (y-o-y) and the contraction eased to –6.3 percent in June (see Figure 9.4). The OECD industrial production bottomed in March

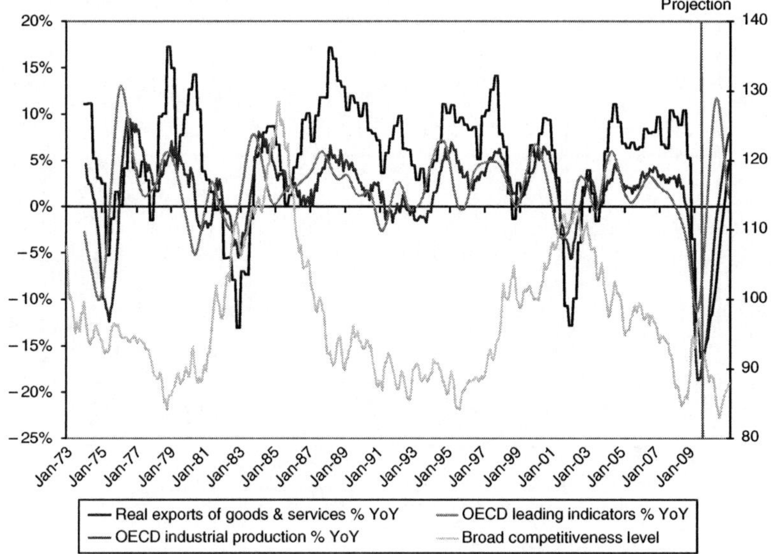

Figure 9.4   US exports determinants

2009 at –19 percent (y-o-y) and has shown tentative signs of a rebound. US exports, however, have yet to bottom; in 2009(Q2) they fell at the phenomenal rate of –17 percent (y-o-y). The dollar peaked against a broad basket of currencies in March 2009 and depreciated 10 percent by the end of August. This fall in the dollar is translated into an 8 percent gain in competitiveness over the same time period (see Figure 9.1). The rise in the OECD index of leading indicators augurs well with further increases in the OECD industrial production in the course of 2009 and 2010 and raises hopes that US exports would rebound. Hence, there is a fair amount of support for the view that exports would contribute to the strength of the US recovery.

2.2 The euro-area case

The euro-area exports growth peaked one and a half years earlier than the US exports, i.e. at the end of 2006. By the time the US economy fell off the cliff, namely mid-2008, euro-area exports growth had been halved (see Figure 9.5). This poor export performance is due to previous losses in euro area competitiveness. The euro continued to appreciate, nearly doubling against the dollar – from \$0.83 in October 2000 to \$1.60 in April 2008 (see Figure 9.3). This euro appreciation was translated into

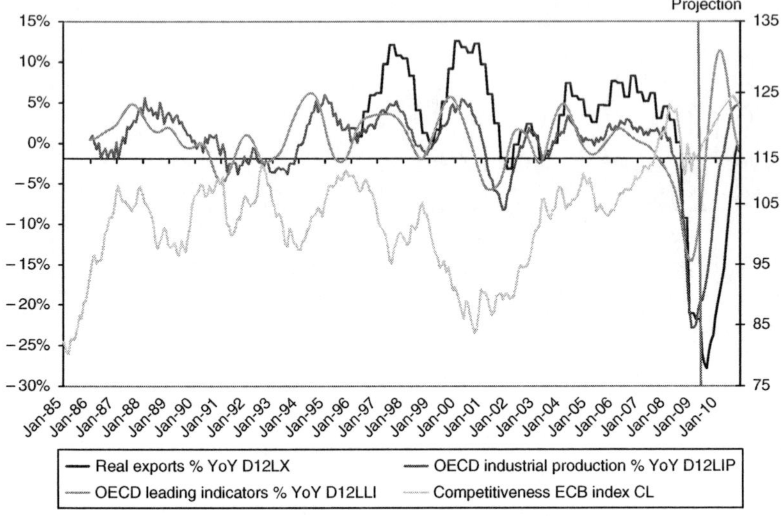

Figure 9.5   EU exports determinants

a 45 percent loss of competitiveness over the same time period. In the current downturn euro-area exports fell –18 percent, as much as their US equivalents. But the improved outlook for the US economy may imply a US-led recovery for the euro area too. This is a question we try to tackle in what follows. The behaviour of the euro-area equity markets certainly supports this view. They have rallied relentlessly since March 2009 on the belief that evidence of a US recovery would pull the euro area out of its misery. We may note, though, at this stage that many euro-area companies have operations based in the US, and profit directly from the US domestic economy, which is reflected in the consolidated balance sheet of the mother companies. Hence, the rally of euro area equities does not necessarily imply discounting of a US-led recovery of the euro area.

Figure 9.5 shows the determinants of euro-area exports. Not surprisingly, euro-area exports have the same determinants as the US – world demand and competitiveness. The OECD industrial production is also a coincident indicator of euro-area exports, as in the case of the US. The rise in the last four months of OECD leading indicators suggests strengthening of the hitherto tentative rebound in OECD industrial production which, other things being equal, should boost euro-area exports in the course of the next 12 months. However, whereas the US has gained competitiveness in the last few years, the euro area has lost competitiveness because of the strong appreciation of the euro. In the downswing of the current downturn the dollar appreciated against the euro from \$1.60 to \$1.25, thereby limiting the previous losses in competitiveness of the euro area. But renewed dollar weakness since the spring of 2009 has partly offset these gains and is likely to turn them into losses. This huge loss in euro-area competitiveness raises doubts as to whether the US recovery would pull the euro area out of its problems in the course of 2009–10, as the markets may have priced in.

This risk is exacerbated by the weakness of domestic demand in the euro area. In 2009(Q1) real GDP growth slumped at the phenomenal rate of –8 percent (q-o-q) and –4.5 percent (y-o-y), much worse than the US. While euro-area exports fell to the same extent as in the US, euro-area domestic demand was the real culprit, falling –8.3 percent (q-o-q) and –3.2 percent (y-o-y). The underlying reason for the weak domestic demand in the euro area is the relatively tight stance of economic policy. Fiscal policy has turned easy, but the stimulus has been small compared to the US (see Figure 9.6a). Although the ECB has cut rates and domestic monetary conditions are accommodative, the appreciation of the euro partly offset the cuts in interest rates. Hence, overall monetary conditions have become easier, but remain relatively tight historically (see Figure 9.6b). Hence there are doubts as to whether sufficient domestic demand is in place that can lead the economy to recovery in

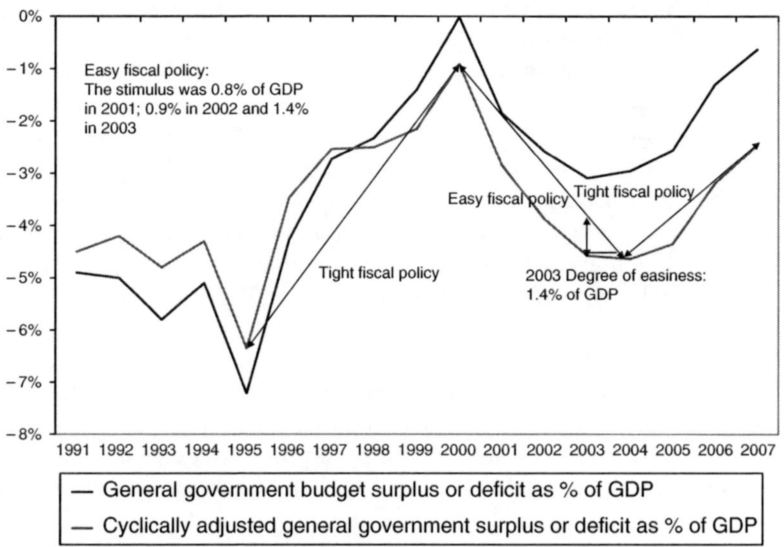

Figure 9.6a   The stance of EU fiscal policy

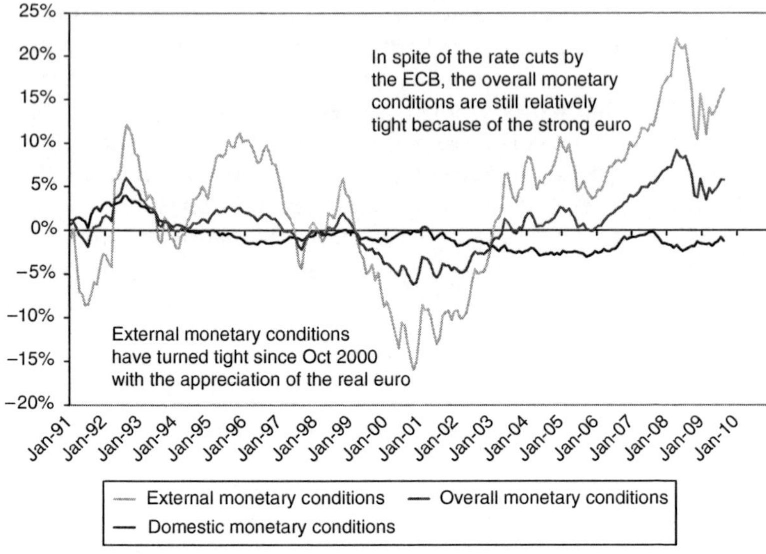

Figure 9.6b   The stance of EU monetary policy

the next year or so. But there are good reasons to expect that domestic demand would strengthen in the second half of 2009 and in the course of 2010. Hence, the case for an early recovery in the euro area relies, to a large extent, on an export-led recovery. In the meantime, confidence is rising and the most important factor that would determine growth with a six-month view is demand for exports. There is little doubt that sustained strong growth in the US would lead ultimately to a recovery of the euro area. Rising exports would spur production, then investment and, finally, consumption. The real issue is the speed that this might materialise and whether there is a chance of disappointment in the short run. The markets have taken the view that the recovery is already on its way taking heart from the revival of the US economy.

2.3   The Japanese case

Japan's exports peaked one quarter earlier than the US, i.e. in the first quarter of 2008, but the contraction experienced was double that of the US and the euro area; exports slumped –45 percent (y-o-y) in 2009(Q1), partly because there was a dramatic weakening of growth in China, which is a major trading partner (see Figure 9.7). Japan is the first economy to show signs of revival. In 2009(Q2) exports jumped 28 percent (q-o-q) and the contraction eased to –36 percent (y-o-y)

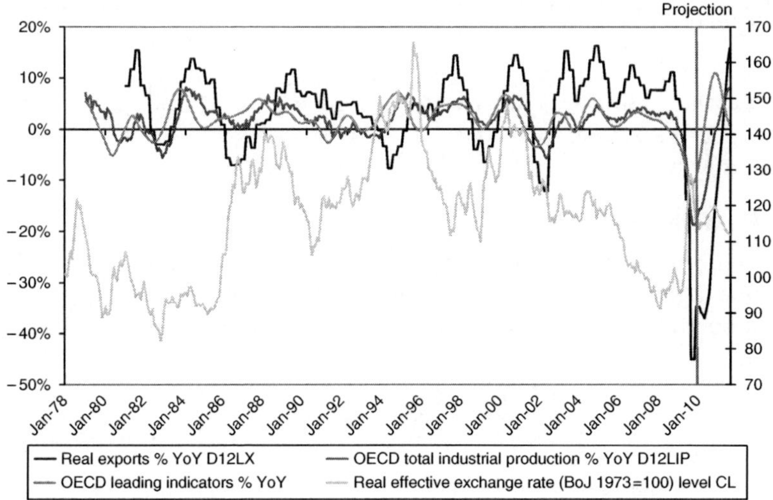

Figure 9.7   Japan exports determinants

from –45 percent in the previous quarter. Since hopes of a US-led world recovery have emerged the yen has weakened and its competitiveness has therefore improved by slightly more than 10 percent. This has partly offset the loss in competitiveness from the eruption of the credit crisis in the summer of 2007 to January 2009. For the entire period, though, from the end of 1999 to August 2009 competitiveness has improved by 22 percent. This augurs well for Japan's prospects of benefiting from a US-led world recovery.

Figure 9.7 shows that the determinants of Japan's exports are the same as in the other two economies. The OECD industrial production is a coincident indicator of Japan's exports, but slightly less reliable than in the US or the euro area. The occasions when the OECD index of leading indicators, which precedes changes in OECD industrial production by approximately six months, fails to predict turning points of Japan's exports, are all related to substantial movements over protracted periods of the yen real exchange rate – a measure of Japan's competitiveness. Thus, although the OECD index of leading indicators bottomed in March 1991, after the Gulf War and the beginning of the US recovery, exports continued to slow and bottomed in December 1993, as the exchange rate was appreciating resulting in losses of competitiveness. In the three-year period 2001 to 2003, during which the euro appreciated 48 percent against the dollar, the yen was effectively unchanged.

The yen stood at ¥109.1 against the dollar in October 2000; it depreciated to ¥132.4 in March 2002 (i.e. a month after the dollar peaked) before appreciating again to ¥107.1 in December 2003 (see Figure 9.7). These fluctuations in the yen were translated into 11 percent gains in competitiveness compared with 27 percent losses in euro-area competitiveness during the 2001 cycle (see Figure 9.7).

2.4   Modelling real exports

It follows from the previous analysis that the real exports (RX_i), where the subscript i refers to the US, the euro area, and Japan as appropriate, share the same structure and can be represented as in equation (i):

$$RX_i = X(WD, COMP) \tag{i}$$

where WD stands for world demand and COMP for competitiveness.

In what follows (1) is utilised within the K-Model framework. There is, however, an important characteristic that ought to be highlighted. The K-Model reveals that real exports have the following properties. First, there is a very strong relationship between OECD industrial production and (G-3) real exports. The impact of world industrial production on real exports is greater than unity in the long run, implying a multiplier effect – one country's trade gives a boost to another country's trade that has further impact on the first country. The multiplier measures the percentage change in real exports for a given percentage change in world industrial production. Consequently, (i) as above should be better represented by equation (1):

$$RX_i = X(IPOECD, COMP) \tag{1}$$

where IPOECD is industrial production of the OECD countries. This is, indeed, the structure of (G-3) exports in the K-Model. In the next section we explore the properties of the K-Model, so that the prospects of exports, which are discussed in section 4, can be appreciated.

3   The properties of the (G-3) exports

We begin this section with Figure 9.8, which shows the K-Model multiplier of (G-3) real exports with respect to the OECD industrial production through time. The six-month multiplier is 1.7 for the US, implying that a one percent increase in world industrial production

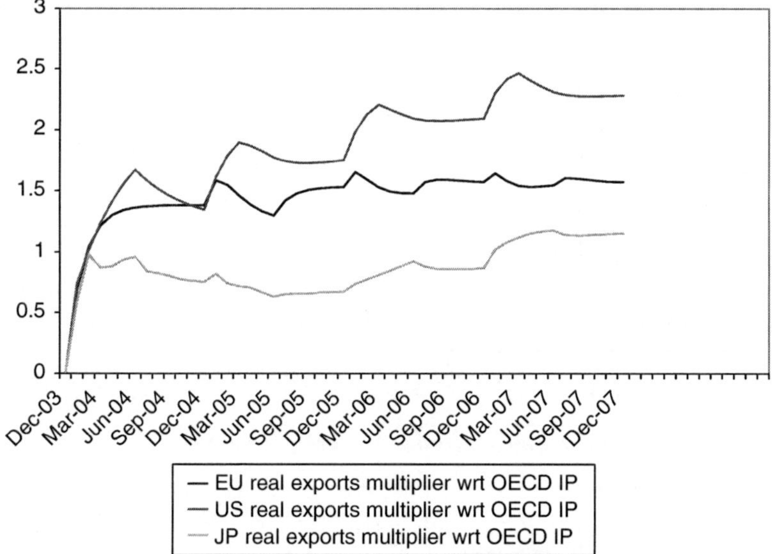

Figure 9.8   Exports multiplier with respect to OECD industrial production

leads to a 1.7 percent increase in US real exports in the first six months. For the euro area, the six-month multiplier is 1.4, whereas for Japan it is only 1. The multiplier for Japan remains near unity for a four-year period, whereas common sense dictates that it should be greater than unity. This raises the question of why Japan does not appear to benefit from the boost in world industrial production as other countries. This paradox is resolved by distinguishing between exports from mainland Japan – the only exports according to national accounts statistics – and exports from worldwide corporate Japan. Japan takes advantage of a pickup in world industrial production, but only part of the stimulus comes back to mainland Japan with the rest stimulating Japanese companies located overseas.

Japan's (mainland) exports account for only 11.7 percent of GDP, on a par with US exports, which are 11 percent of GDP. But this figure grossly understates the full exporting capacity of Japan. For example, euro-area exports as a percentage of GDP account for 40 percent. Japan's worldwide industrial base may be even bigger than the euro area, but it is difficult to measure it. Japan's Foreign Direct Investment (FDI) has been negative, meaning that they invest abroad more than others invest in Japan. Cumulative FDI since 1980 has reached 111 percent of GDP. But it is

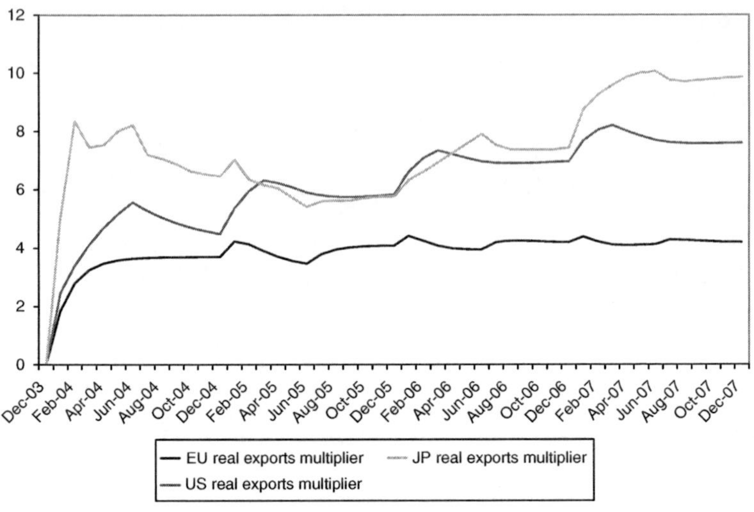

Figure 9.9 Exports multiplier with respect to OECD industrial production adjusted for share of exports to GDP

difficult from such measures to get the full picture of Japan's worldwide industrial base and the impact of an increase in world industrial production. An indirect way of resolving the issue is to normalise the effect of world industrial production by measuring its impact on exports per unit of GDP. Figure 9.9 shows the multiplier adjusted for the relative size of exports to GDP for the US, the euro area and Japan. Although the pattern of adjusted multipliers is the same as the unadjusted ones the former not only is greater than unity for all three countries, but the multiplier of Japan is always bigger than the US and euro area in the first two years (see Figure 9.9). This means that Japan is the main beneficiary amongst (G-3) of a recovery in world demand. The huge worldwide industrial base of Japan explains the paradox of Japan's exports multiplier being near unity. This has implications for corporate profits. Japan's corporate profits would increase much more than those of the euro area or the US from a boost in world industrial production and therefore its stock market would outperform the other two markets, in the short run. However, the impact of world industrial production on jobs and incomes in Japan would be limited by the fact that the unadjusted multiplier is near unity. The OECD industrial production does not reflect the boost in industrial production in Asia, with the exception of Korea that has joined OECD. The share of Japan's exports to Asia accounts for 42 percent and therefore the effect on exports from a boost in world industrial production may be grossly understated. Despite this drawback, the engine for growth is the US. If the US were to lose some of its momentum, both the OECD industrial production and Asia industrial production would be affected.

The second property of exports is that they are strongly related to competitiveness. Figure 9.10 shows the (G-3) real exports multiplier with respect to competitiveness. For convenience, it is assumed that US competitiveness will improve, while that of the euro area and Japan is damaged. In the first six months the multiplier is zero for the US and the euro area, but –0.1 for Japan. This means that a change in competitiveness has no effect on US and euro-area exports for the first six months, while a 10 percent loss in competitiveness in Japan leads to just a 1 percent fall in exports. After the first six months the effect of competitiveness on US and euro-area exports builds up. In the long run the US multiplier reaches 0.64 in just over two years, while in the euro area the multiplier keeps rising for five years, reaching 1.07. This means that the overall effect of a permanent change in competitiveness on euro-area exports is one and a half times that of the US and its effects last for more than double the time compared to the US. This, in turn, implies that the US is able to absorb the effects of a permanent loss in competitiveness much

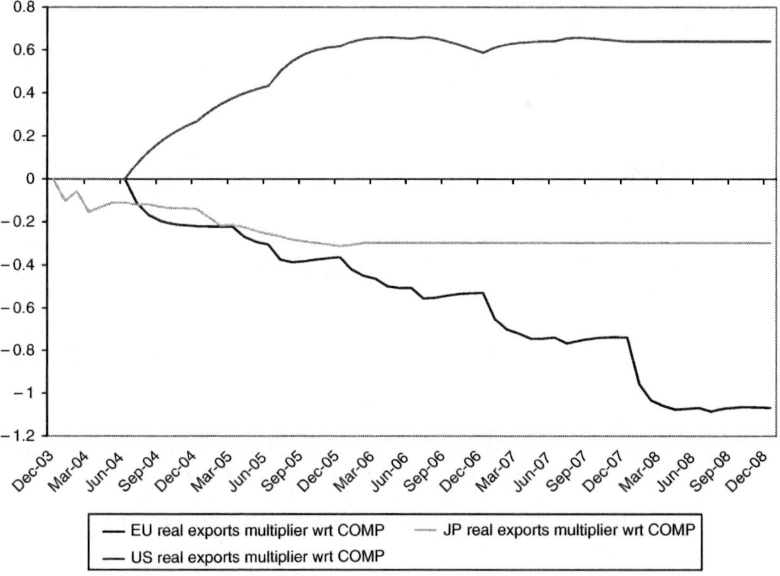

Figure 9.10   Exports multiplier with respect to competitiveness

faster than the euro area – in just over two years, whereas it gradually builds up in the euro area for five years. Thus, a permanent 10 percent gain (or loss) in competitiveness leads to 6.4 percent higher (or lower) US exports in two years, while it leads to 10.1 percent higher (or lower) euro-area exports in five years. Two years after the shock in competitiveness, euro-area exports are only 3.6 percent higher (or lower).

As in the case of the multiplier with respect to world industrial production, these figures grossly understate the full effects of competitiveness on Japan's exports, since they only measure the effect on mainland Japan and ignore the effect on the industrial base of Japan overseas. Figure 9.11 shows the multiplier adjusted for the relative size of exports to GDP for the US, Japan and the euro area. Although the pattern of adjusted multipliers is the same as the unadjusted ones, the overall effect on Japan's worldwide industrial base is much bigger and the differential with the US and euro area is much smaller. Whereas the unadjusted long-run effect of a permanent loss in competitiveness is one-quarter of the euro area and half of the US the adjusted one is only half of the former and 20 percent smaller than the US. This is a huge difference and shows that the euro area is not 75 percent worse than Japan at adjusting to competitiveness, but only 50 percent. Japan is also 20 percent better

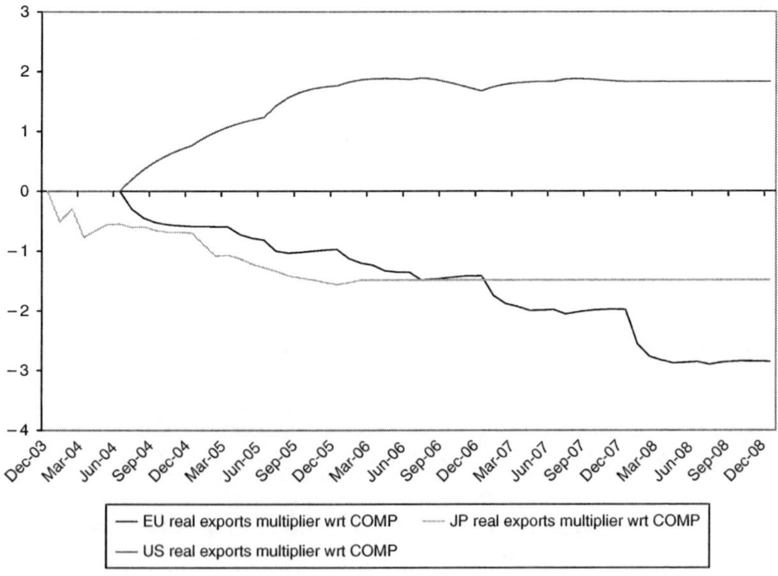

Figure 9.11   Exports multiplier with respect to competitiveness adjusted for share of exports to GDP

than the US at adjusting to competitiveness. The vulnerability of the euro area to changes in competitiveness is due to its inflexible labour markets that create rigidities in price adjustments. A country's ability to absorb changes in the nominal exchange rate depends on how much and how quickly companies can induce productivity gains, by a combination of job cuts, cost cutting and increased capital spending. Such adjustments aim at reducing unit labour cost and therefore export prices so that the effect of changes in the nominal exchange rate on competitiveness is minimal. From this point of view, Japan is the best followed by the US, while the euro area is the laggard.

Figure 9.12 illustrates in a more explicit way the properties of euro-area real exports according to the K-Model. The index of euro-area competitiveness bottomed in October 2000 at 95.8 and started to rise, reaching 121.8 in December 2003. This implies a loss in competitiveness of 25.9 index points (or 27 percent) in those three years. In order to assess the dynamic impact on real exports of this loss in competitiveness it is assumed that the euro did not appreciate in the three years to 2003, but instead the index of competitiveness remained unchanged at its October 2000 value of 95.8 not only until now but for ever after (that is, long enough so that a new steady state can be reached). Hence, the experiment assumes that in the three years to 2003 there was no gradual loss in competitiveness of the order of 27 percent.

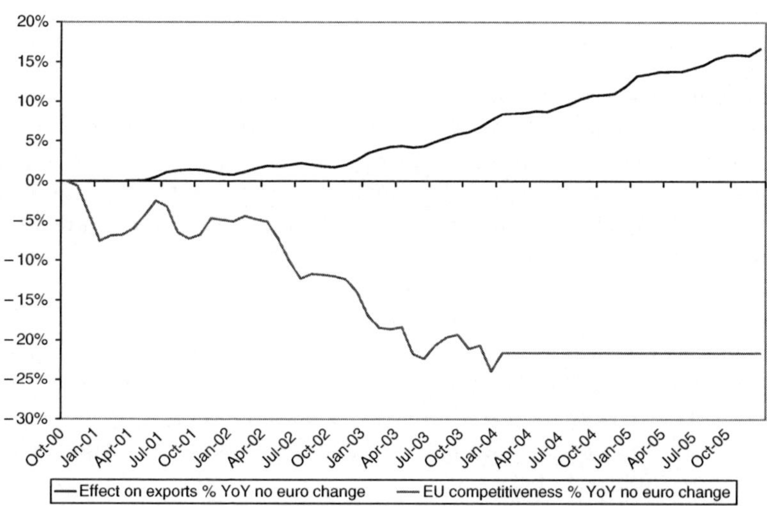

Figure 9.12   Effect on EU exports – no euro change (unchanged at Oct. 2000 value)

Figure 9.12 shows that after a year (i.e. in October 2001) if competitiveness had not been lost of the order of 7 percent, real exports would have been higher than they actually were by only 1.4 percent, a trivial amount. By the end of the second year (in October 2002) if competitiveness had not been lost of the order of 13 percent, real exports would have been higher than they were by 1.7 percent, still an insignificant amount. By the end of the third year (in October 2003) if competitiveness had not been lost of the order of 23 percent, real exports would have been higher than they were by 6 percent. If the exchange rate were to stabilise so that the total losses would be limited to 24 percent, then the effect on exports would reach 11 percent in the fourth year (in October 2004) and 16 percent in the fifth year (in October 2005). This implies that euro-area exports would be hit by 5 and 10 percent after one and two years, respectively, compared to what they would have been if competitiveness had not been lost.

The simulation illustrates the long-lasting effects of nominal euro appreciation on euro-area competitiveness. This is a very important point as the euro has appreciated over an eight-year-long period, which has resulted in an increasing loss of competitiveness. This simulation suggests that some of that impact has yet to filter through the system, thereby negating part of the stimulus from a US-led world recovery. Hence, world industrial production would need to rise much more if the euro area is to have an export-led recovery.

4   The likely course of (G-3) exports

The role of the US as a leader of the world economy suggests that world demand would depend on US demand. In particular, fluctuations in US industrial production should explain fluctuations in OECD industrial production. Figure 9.13 provides support for this hypothesis by making the OECD industrial production (IPOECD) a function of US industrial production. So another relationship is in order:

$$IPOECD = IP_1(IPUS) \tag{2}$$

where IPUS is US industrial production. The forecast error of the K-Model for OECD industrial production is only 0.5 percent in nearly forty years of monthly data that span ten business cycles, which were demand-, supply- and asset-led.

The total Purchasing Management Index (PMI) of the Institute for Supply Management (ISM) is geared to gauge developments in the US economy over the next six months.[3] In particular, the PMI can explain fluctuations

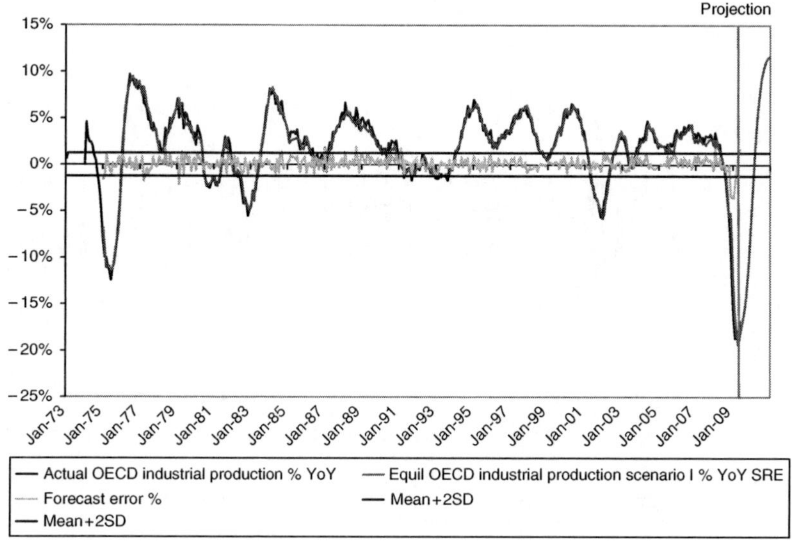

Figure 9.13   OECD industrial production (based on US ISM) – short-run equilibrium

in US industrial production. Figure 9.14 provides support for this hypothesis by making US industrial production a function of PMI. The forecast error of the K-Model of US industrial production is only 1.15 percent in the last ten business cycles that cover more than half a century.

In view of the arguments just presented, US industrial production (IPUS) can be represented as:

$$IPUS = IP_2(PMI) \tag{3}$$

where PMI is as defined above.

The PMI is based on a survey of business intentions. These expectations are affected by economic developments, but in the absence of news on economic fundamentals such expectations would follow their own momentum with optimism building first up, then fading away, followed by a similar cycle of pessimism. In the long run such expectations would peter out and the PMI would reach long-run equilibrium. Figure 9.15 provides support for the hypothesis that the momentum of business expectations can explain the PMI. So that:

$$PMI = M(BEXP) \tag{4}$$

where BEXP stands for business expectations.

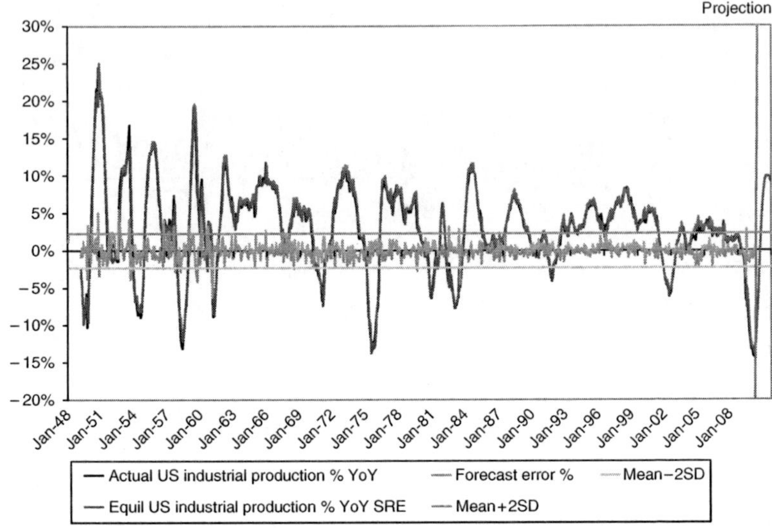

Figure 9.14   US industrial production (based on ISM) – short-run equilibrium

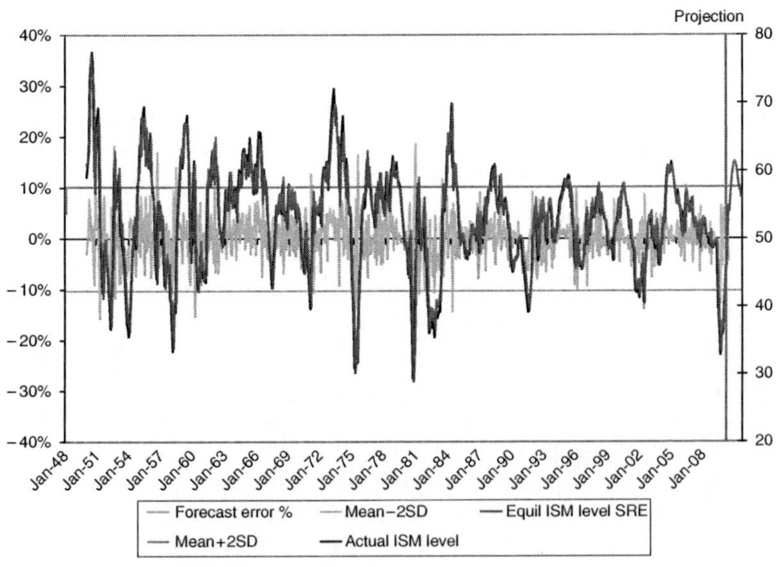

Figure 9.15   US PMI – short-run equilibrium

The forecast error of the K-Model for PMI is 5 percent. Although this sounds rather high when compared to the forecast error of US industrial production, which is only 1.2 percent, it is quite small when account is taken of volatility. Whereas the standard deviation of US industrial production since 1948 is only 5.8 percent, the standard deviation of the PMI, during the same time period, is 23.3 percent, that is, four times larger. Since the forecast error of the PMI is four times as large as the forecast error of US industrial production, the K-Model for the PMI is as good as the industrial production model.

These three equations (PMI, US industrial production and OECD industrial production) can be combined with the exports model to generate projections for (G-3) exports based on three assumptions. First, unchanged competitiveness; second, there are no further news on economic fundamentals and the PMI follows its own momentum; third, China maintains the pre-crisis growth momentum. Figure 9.15 shows that in the absence of any further news on economic fundamentals the PMI would peak in the first half of 2010 and would return to its equilibrium boom–bust dividing line of 50 beyond the projection period. US industrial production will peak at nearly 10 percent at the end of 2010 and will decline thereafter (see Figure 9.14). The world economy would follow the US and the OECD industrial production would accelerate in the course of 2010, hitting a peak at the end of the year. However, the OECD industrial production would decelerate in the course of 2011 and 2012. Given this pattern of world demand and with unchanged competitiveness US exports would soar to the pre-crisis growth rates of around 10 percent (see Figure 9.16). The strong US recovery would lift euro-area exports, which would peak at the end of 2010 at around 10 percent (see Figure 9.17). The biggest winner, however, would be Japan with growth in exports exceeding 20 percent (see Figure 9.18).

The conclusion of this simulation is that a strong US recovery would be able to pull the rest of the world out of the worst recession since the Great Depression, including the euro area. The US will benefit to the same extent as the euro area, although Japan would be the great beneficiary. Nonetheless, the assumptions of this simulation are unrealistic, because there would be plenty of news on economic fundamentals and competitiveness would change in the course of the next two years. The simulation, therefore, brings out the importance of the concerns about the strength of the US recovery and previous gains or losses in competitiveness.

Without any further stimulus the US recovery is likely to be anaemic with hardly any new jobs created and unemployment continuing to rise. The current recovery is triggered by restocking, namely companies

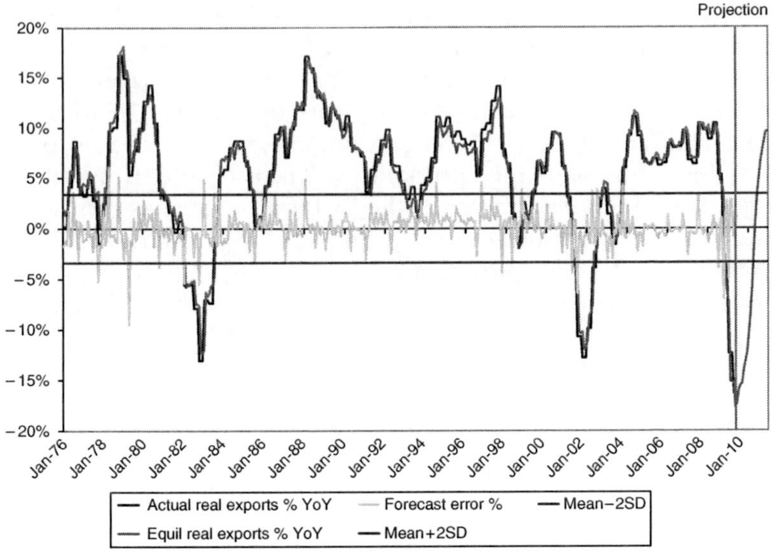

Figure 9.16 US real exports (based on the momentum of US ISM)

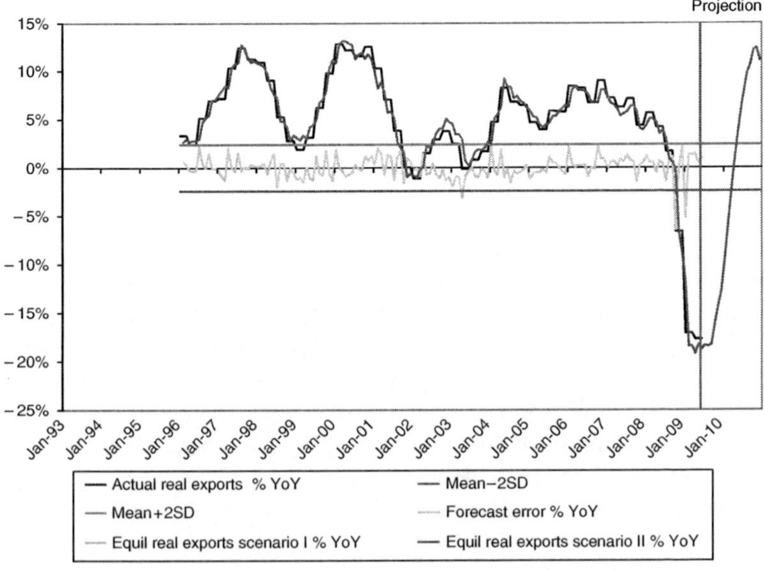

Figure 9.17 EU exports – short-run equilibrium

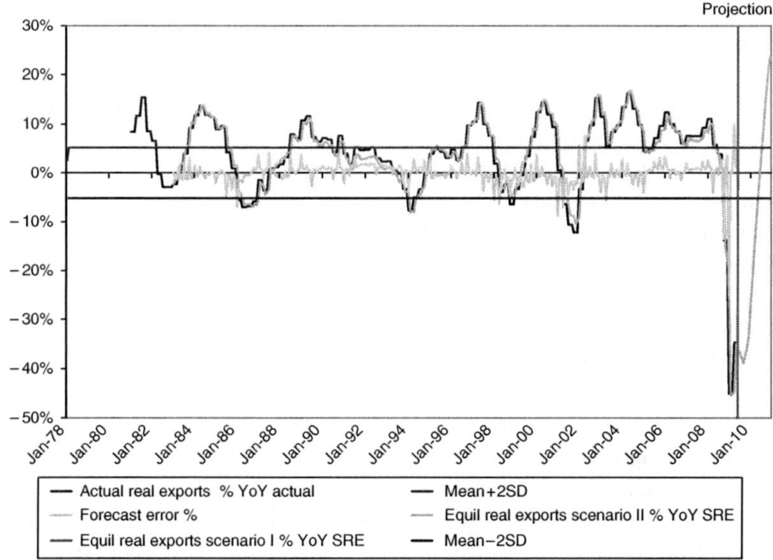

Figure 9.18 JP real exports (based on the momentum of US ISM) – short-run equilibrium

trying to replenish their depleted stock of goods. At the pinnacle of the credit crisis following the collapse of Lehman Brothers, and the fall in consumer expenditure in the second half of 2008, business confidence hit rock bottom in December, prompting companies to cut production dramatically, to shed labour at an unprecedented rate and to slash investment. The bulk of this adjustment took place in the first quarter of 2009, when consumers took a breather from cutting spending, thereby resulting in a dramatic drop of stocks. Confidence was boosted in early March by the decision of the Obama Administration to stop the war against Wall Street, as this was accelerating the bankruptcy of the entire financial system. Irrespective of how much responsible banks are for the current economic woes, the Obama Administration did not dare to reform the financial system and backed the 'business as usual' model. This change of policy boosted confidence, which, combined with the restocking process by companies, are turning the economy around.

But the restocking will last for no more than a year and the current fiscal stimulus will fade after the first year, namely after the spring of 2010. The problems of the banks that gave rise to the current crisis have not been resolved, as the distressed assets have not been removed from their balance sheet. The current profits of the banks are fictitious, as the banks have been allowed to use their own discretion in valuing the distressed assets. The most important policy measure that put an end to the credit crisis last March was the suspension of the mark-to-market method. Hence, the sustainability of the recovery in the second half of 2010 and beyond depends on whether bank lending is resumed and similarly on whether the corporate, but more importantly the personal sector is willing to take again more debt. Unless asset prices recover phenomenally to lure households back into more debt, this is unlikely to happen. The balance of risks, therefore, points to a faltering recovery some time in 2010 or beyond. Hence, the need to bolster demand by another fiscal package in early 2010, to keep interest rates unchanged at nearly zero, and to allow orderly depreciation of the dollar.

The K-Model suggests that the momentum of expectations built into the PMI will run out of steam, as the recovery is likely to falter for the aforementioned reasons. Hence, the expected US-led world recovery will have a much smaller impact on world trade and hence on (G-3) exports than has been suggested by the simulations above. US exports will recover from their worst slump, but will not regain the pre-crisis strength. Most likely, exports growth will just turn positive on year-to-year basis (see Figure 9.4). The anaemic US recovery will trigger a weak rebound in euro-area exports. Negative growth, but much smaller than the current slump, is the most likely outcome. This gloomy outlook for euro-area exports is due partly to the previous losses in competitiveness and further losses over the projection period because of the K-model projection of more appreciation in the euro (see Figure 9.5). The continuous impact of previous losses in competitiveness on future exports is the outcome of the slow process through which the appreciation of the euro is absorbed into costs and export prices. As has been already stressed the filtering process of any euro changes on competitiveness takes around five years, the longest among the (G-3) countries. The only beneficiary of an even anaemic US recovery is likely to be Japan with export growth regaining the pre-crisis levels (see Figure 9.7). The rationale for this rosy outlook for Japan exports is the improved competitiveness over this decade, which to a large extent is due to the fast absorption of any yen appreciation.

Thus, the overall conclusion is that an anaemic US recovery will restore the exports of Japan to their pre-crisis levels, will bring US exports growth just into positive territory, but will leave euro-area exports growth in negative territory. However, there are both upside and downside risks to this mainline projection of the K-Model. Stronger US export growth is possible if there is another fiscal stimulus in early 2010 or the dollar depreciates much more than projected by the K-Model, resulting in further gains in competitiveness (see Figure 9.1). The downside risks stem from the possibility that the rally in equities falters after a year-long rally, some time in the first half of 2010. Profits soar in the first year of the recovery, but in the second year there is some profit fatigue. Equity markets have chosen so far to turn a blind eye to the suspension of the mark-to-market method of valuing distressed assets. However, as the balance sheet problems of the financial sector have not been resolved, at some point in time market concerns about the insolvency of the banking system may resurface, causing another huge downturn. This may coincide with the profit fatigue after the spring of 2010. Falling equity prices will most likely trigger a second round of falling house prices, thereby accentuating the deflationary forces. In this downside scenario the exports growth of the US and the euro area will be negative, but Japan may still get positive growth, albeit much smaller than in the mainline scenario.

5 Summary and conclusions

The (G-3) exports have a common structure in which world demand and competitiveness are the key determinants. Despite the common structure there are important differences in (G-3) export performance stemming from the quantitative importance of each determinant and the time it takes for their effects to be felt on exports. Three important conclusions have emerged from this analysis. First, the US is the main beneficiary of a boost in world trade, followed by the euro area, while Japan is the laggard. The effect on exports is greater than the initial stimulus in the world economy – the multiplier effect is greater than unity – as one country's trade gives a boost to another country's trade that has further impact on the first country, and so on.

Second, the conclusion that Japan benefits least from a boost in world trade is counterintuitive. But the paradox is resolved when account is taken of the worldwide industrial base of Japan and not just the industrial base in mainland Japan. With this adjustment Japan comes right at the top, followed by the US, while the euro area is now the laggard. The distinction between mainland Japan and its worldwide industrial base has diverse implications for corporate profits, on the one hand, and jobs and incomes, on the other. Japan's corporate profits would benefit much more than those of the euro area or the US from a boost in world industrial production and therefore its stock market would outperform the other two markets, in the short run. However, the impact of world industrial production on jobs and incomes in Japan would be limited by the fact that the unadjusted multiplier is the smallest of the three.

Third, Japan is in a far better position than its rivals to absorb changes in the nominal exchange rate on competitiveness. Japan is around 20 percent better than the US at adjusting to competitiveness, while the euro area is only half as good as Japan. Moreover, Japan and the US can absorb the effects of nominal exchange rate on competitiveness in around two years, while it takes five years for this adjustment to take place in the euro area.

Evidence that the worst is over in the US economy has raised hopes of a US-led world recovery. The OECD index of leading indicators, which precedes changes in world demand by six months, bottomed in February 2009 and has continued to rebound, thereby suggesting an imminent recovery in (G-3) exports over the next 12 months. But over a longer horizon the conclusion of a US-led world recovery depends on the strength of the US economy and the extent of previous changes in (G-3) competitiveness. The renewed dollar weakness after the credit crisis subsided from March 2009 onwards is now reinforcing previous gains in competitiveness, thereby bolstering the case that the US will be one of the beneficiaries in export growth of its own recovery. This is likely to strengthen the overall growth of the economy, as the trade multiplier is higher than unity. Despite the appreciation of the yen since the eruption of the credit crisis, Japan's competitiveness shows the best improvement among (G-3) during the last ten years. Hence, Japan is well placed to benefit from a US-led world recovery. However, the euro area has suffered significant losses in competitiveness because of the strong appreciation of the euro over this decade and its slow adjustment of competitiveness to changes in the nominal exchange rate. These developments in (G-3) competitiveness augur well for a recovery in US and Japan exports from a world recovery, but they cast doubts on whether euro area can benefit from it.

If the current momentum of rebuilding confidence were to continue uninterrupted to run its natural course, then exports growth for the US and Japan would be restored to more or less their pre-crisis levels, but that of the euro area would achieve only half that rate. However, the current momentum is likely to fade away because the US recovery is likely to be anaemic. In this case a US-led world recovery will have a much smaller impact on world trade and hence on the revival of (G-3) exports. Japan's exports growth will be restored to near their pre-crisis levels; the US will just achieve positive growth, while the euro area may remain in negative territory. The risks are symmetric with an equal probability of an upside and downside from the mainline scenario. The recovery of world trade will be stronger if the US administration came up with a new fiscal package at the beginning of 2010 or the dollar depreciated even more, thereby improving US competitiveness. Either action would boost the exports of (G-3), as the income effect dominates the competiveness effect. Hence, even euro-area exports will be stronger despite the loss of euro-area competitiveness.

Moreover, in all these developments the role of China and other Asian countries is significant. These countries have substantial current account surpluses, especially China (see, for example, Blanchard, 2009). A decrease in the current account surplus in the case of China, in particular, should boost US exports, and those of the other two members of the G-3, Japan and the euro area, to a significant extent. This would indeed be in China's interest, where pressures prevail to boost consumption. Other Asian countries also run large current account surpluses, but the motivation in these cases is less obvious. The building of reserves in some of these countries as insurance, which helped them in the current crisis, may be one such reason. Another is that in the case of some other Asian countries export-led strategies, which affect the current account and reserve accumulation, have also proved beneficial. China's role in this process could very well prove to be paramount.

However, there are risks on the downside too. The rally in equities may peter out after the spring of 2010 and concerns about bank insolvency might re-emerge, thereby triggering a new round of falls in house prices. In this case the asset and debt deflation process will come back to haunt us. This risk is not hypothetical. It is based on two pillars. First, the current recovery is the result of company restocking that will last for no longer than a year. Second, the current renewed optimism is due to the deterrence of the bankruptcy of the entire financial system. However, the balance sheet problems of the banks have not been resolved. The distressed assets are still in the balance sheet of the banks, but the problem has been assumed away by allowing banks to use their own discretion in valuing these assets. Financial markets for self-survival reasons, or whatever other reasons, have chosen to shrug off the importance of suspending the fair value practice of mark-to-market. In the long run market complacency never provides solid ground for a sustainable recovery. Of course, there is always the chance that equity markets will never look back and that distressed assets will ultimately recover. But this may be wishful thinking in the current environment in which bank lending is subdued. Moreover, frail bank lending may not be the result of a credit crunch. It may indeed be the rational response of households who, on two previous occasions, namely during the internet and the housing bubbles, had been lured to take more credit in the hope that asset prices will continue to increase. They may now know better. Hence, even if credit is made available by financial institutions the demand for it may not be there. Market complacency may stop at any point in time, but the trigger might be the natural wearing of the stock market rally, which at this point in time is supported by the traditional rebound of profitability in the first year of the recovery. This usually fades away in the second year, reawakening concerns about bank insolvency and the importance of the mark-to-market practice. In this downside risk scenario the revival of (G-3) exports will be turned on its head and exports will tumble once more.

10
The US External Imbalance and the Dollar: A Long-Term View

1 Introduction

Throughout this book it has been argued repeatedly that the failure of current economic theory and policy to appreciate that asset-led cycles are different from the demand cycles of the 1950s and 1960s and the supply cycles of the 1970s and 1980s has made each of the last three cycles worse than the previous ones. This is clearly an unstable situation that gives rise to successive bubbles, each one being bigger than the previous one and each recession being worse than the one before. This instability is best reflected in increasing imbalances in various sectors. In this chapter we analyse the US external imbalance, which has widened in each of the last three cycles confirming the aforementioned instability, and its implications for the economy and the dollar.

The huge liquidity that has financed the two most notable bubbles in the US, namely the internet and housing, has also financed a number of bubbles in the rest of the world, such as the commodities bubble. This liquidity has been transferred from the US to the rest of the world through the dollar weakness over the past six years or so. This is how the mechanism works. US dollar reference worldwide investors have sold their dollar holdings to invest in emerging markets and commodities. Most of these investors have also leveraged their investments through yen carry trade – borrowing in yen while selling short the yen and investing in the assets of high-yielding currency countries, like Australia, New Zealand and the BRIC countries.[1] By doing so, they have exacerbated the downtrend of the dollar between 2002 and 2008. This dollar downtrend was interrupted during the credit crisis, but has been resumed once the crisis subsided and hopes of recovery have been bolstered. In this chapter we provide a game-theoretic framework to assess the outlook for the dollar and the risks to the rest of the world from this dollar weakness, but in particular the euro area.

The finance of the huge US current account deficit has so far been met very easily, as the residents of the rest of the world (ROW) have been willing to lend the US the necessary funds to cover this deficit. This process has turned the US into a serious net debtor to the ROW in the last twenty years. However, the debt is in US dollars and there are no immediate good reasons why residents in the ROW should lose their confidence in the ability of the US to service this debt. There is a risk, however, that ROW residents may lose their appetite to hold US assets, if they continue to suffer huge losses on their holdings of US assets. There have been such instances, for example, during September and October 2003, where there was a temporary drop in the desire of foreign investors to accumulate US assets, but this was restored subsequently. The risk that foreigners may, at some point in time, lose their appetite implies that the US should balance or, at least, reduce its current account deficit. The dollar is now on a renewed declining trend and that would help the current account deficit, because the economy is operating with spare capacity and needs to boost its exports to foster the recovery.

The deficit in the US current account, which records transactions in goods and services, has widened progressively since the recession in the early 1990s. In the 1980s it was also in deficit, but it narrowed with the dollar depreciation following the Plaza Accord in 1985 and was eliminated during the recession of 1990–91. Under free floating, the capital account, which records transactions in assets and Foreign Direct Investment (FDI), is the mirror image of the current account and represents the financing of the current account deficit. Any discrepancy between the current account and the capital account reflects changes in foreign exchange reserves, which on occasions may arise from central bank intervention in the foreign exchange market.

The current account deficit (the external imbalance) has widened in each of the last three cycles, thereby confirming the instability of asset-led cycles. At the peak of the last cycle, in the fourth quarter of 2005, the current account deficit hit a historical record at 6.3 percent of nominal GDP. This was bigger than the 4.2 percent reached in the early 2000s recession and the 1.7 percent in the mid-1990s (see Figure 10.1). The financing of the current account deficit, so far, has not been a problem (save for some instances, such as the period September/October 2003) since the surplus in the capital account has exceeded the deficit in the current account. In Figure 10.1 the line labelled 'current account cover' represents the sum of the current and capital account or

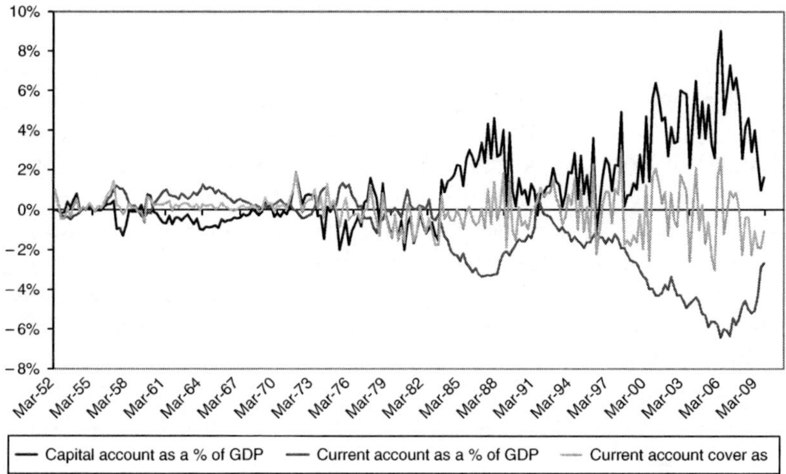

Figure 10.1   US balance of payments

the change in foreign exchange reserves. When this is positive it means
that the surplus in the capital account exceeds the deficit in the current
account and foreign exchange reserves are rising. When the current
account cover is negative foreign exchange reserves are depleted. The
thesis that the dollar is determined by either the current account or the
capital account or even by the current account cover is, to say the least,
untenable. For example, in the second quarter of 2003 the surplus in
the capital account was 6.2 percent of GDP, outstripping the deficit in
the current account by 1 percent. And yet the dollar kept falling and
in 2004 rather dramatically. Thus, the second major objective of this
chapter is to put a convincing model that explains the value of the
dollar through time.

This chapter is organised as follows. Section 2 examines the long-term
consequences of the external imbalance. Section 3 poses the question of
whether the US needs to worry about the current account imbalance.
Section 4 examines the relationship between the dollar and the current
account imbalance at the theoretical level, where a new way of looking at
the determinants of the exchange rate is discussed; in doing so, we make extensive use of the game-theoretic approach as this is applied in the foreign
exchange market. Section 5 looks into this relationship at the more empirical level and assesses the dollar outlook and the risks. It emerges that the
empirical evidence provided supports the theoretical premise as postulated
in section 4. Finally section 6 summarises and concludes.

2   The long-term consequences of the external imbalance

The accumulation through time of the external imbalance measures the degree of the US indebtedness. Figure 10.2 shows the net worth of the Rest of the World (ROW), defined as ROW holdings of US assets less holdings of ROW assets. The ROW net worth measures the indebtedness (if positive) or creditworthiness (if negative) of the US economy. The US became for the first time net debtor to the rest of the world at the end of 1985 and this debt has continued to grow ever since. At the beginning of the recovery in the second quarter of 2003 the US net debt to ROW was of the order of 21 percent of US GDP or nearly US$2.5 trillion. During the ballooning years of the housing bubble it declined, hitting a low of 13 percent at the peak of the bubble; but then it sky-rocketed to 30 percent of GDP. What are the long-term consequences of this indebtedness? To some extent the answer depends on how this debt is used. Does it represent acquisition of US tangible assets by ROW or US borrowing, and if so, for what purpose? Examining the composition of ROW net worth provides a clue.

The ROW net worth consists of ROW holdings of US money market instruments, credit market instruments, equities, FDI and miscellaneous assets less the corresponding US holdings of ROW assets. By far the biggest component of ROW net worth is the net credit market position

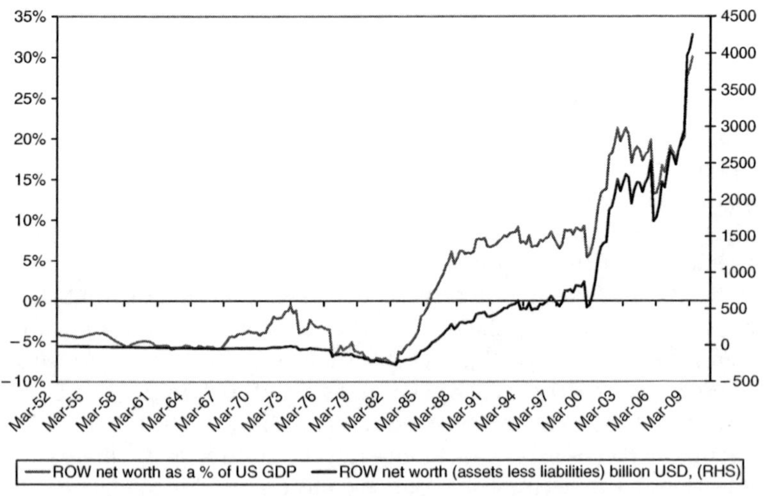

Figure 10.2   Rest of the world (ROW) net worth (US assets held by ROW less ROW assets held by the US)

(ROW holdings of US government and corporate bonds less US holdings of ROW bonds). At the end of the second quarter of 2003, the beginning of the recovery, the net credit market position of ROW was 23 percent of US GDP, but went on rising at a frantic pace, hitting 41 percent of GDP in the second quarter of 2009 (see Figure 10.3). The US government as well as the private sector have been heavily borrowing from ROW by issuing bonds. The US became indebted to ROW at the end of 1981 and this debt has continued to grow ever since (see Figure 10.3).

In the 1950s, 1960s and 1970s the ROW net money market position was positive, meaning that the US attracted foreign resident deposits. However, from 1982 till 2001, with the exception of 1993–96, the ROW net money market position was negative (see Figure 10.4). The ROW net money market position began to improve at the beginning of the 1991 recovery, turning positive in 1993–96 on expectations of monetary tightening by the Fed, which indeed were realised in the course of 1994. However, as soon as the Fed started easing monetary policy in early 1995 the ROW net money market position turned negative once again, approaching its 1984 low (see Figure 10.4). Since the beginning of the recovery in 2003 expectations of monetary tightening have helped to improve the ROW net money market position turning it into positive from mid-2004 onwards. It now stands positive, but falling at just 1.7 percent in June 2009.

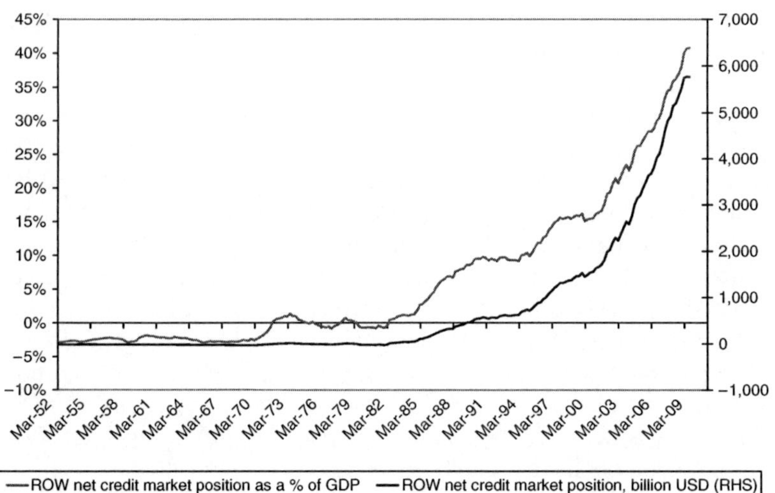

Figure 10.3   ROW net credit market position (assets held by ROW less assets held by the US)

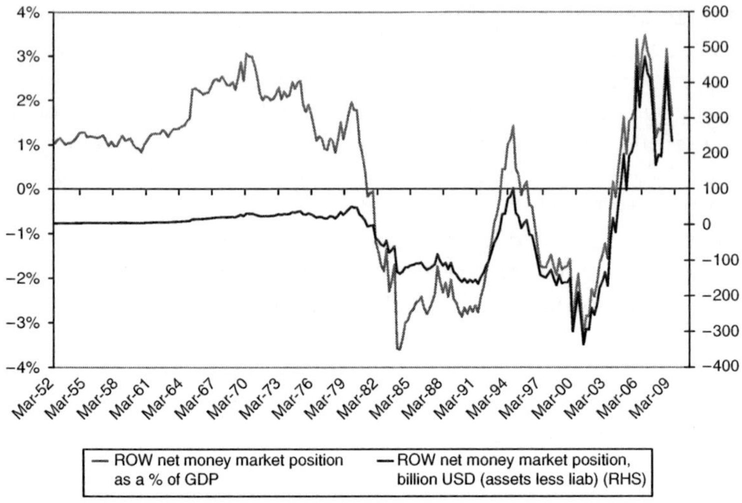

Figure 10.4   ROW net money market position (US assets held by ROW less ROW assets held by the US)

Since 1993 the appetite of US residents to acquire foreign equities has exceeded that of ROW residents to acquire US equities. The irony is that the ROW relative appetite for US stocks peaked just before the crash of 1987 and bottomed in March 2000, i.e. throughout the biggest bull market (see Figure 10.5). The ROW relative appetite for US equities resurfaced during the bear market of 2000–03; it declined in the bear market rally of 2003–07. Finally, it re-emerged during the worst stock market slump of 2007–09. Thus, the ROW net equity position (ROW holdings of US equities less US holdings of ROW equities) bottomed at –5.9 percent of GDP in December 1999, namely at the peak of the stock market. At the beginning of the recovery in the second quarter of 2003 the ROW net equity position increased to –1.7 percent of US GDP (see Figure 10.5). However, throughout the bear market rally of 2003–07 the ROW relative appetite for US stocks was again reduced, hitting a new low at –17.1 percent in September 2007. Once more the relative appetite was increased throughout the worst equity slump of 2007–09. It is now still negative at –10 percent and falling. This shows that US residents have a much better sense of equity markets than foreigners. The stock market timing by ROW residents has been completely wrong. They abstain from equities in bull markets and participate in bear markets.

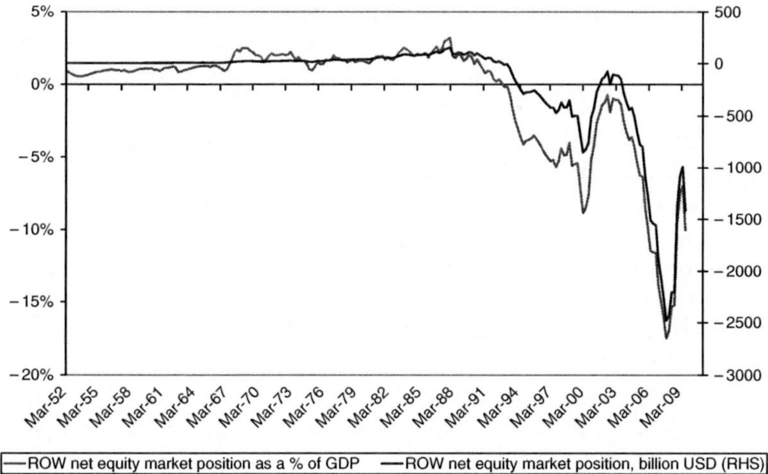

Figure 10.5   ROW net equity position (assets held by ROW less assets held by the US)

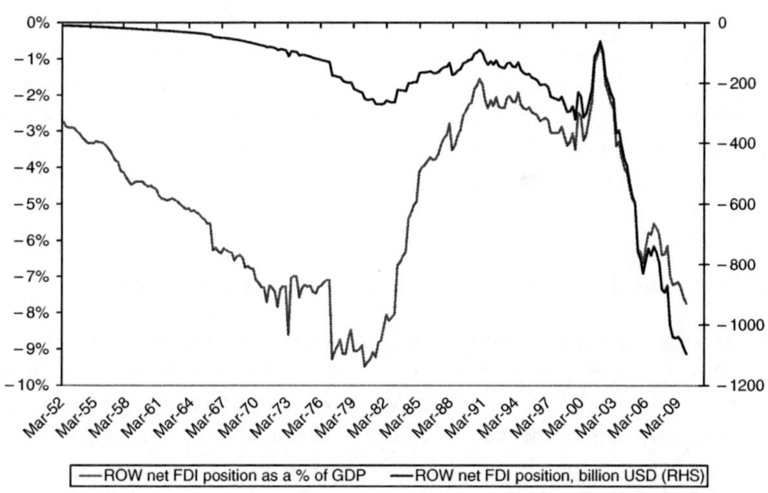

Figure 10.6   ROW net FDI position (assets held by ROW less assets held by the US)

Figure 10.6 shows the ROW net FDI position (ROW direct investment in the US less US direct investment in ROW). This has been negative in the last fifty years, meaning that the US buying of foreign companies has always exceeded ROW buying of US companies. From the ROW point of view this trend bottomed at the end of 1979 at –10 percent of US GDP. The gap narrowed very fast until June 1990 (at the onset of the recession) at –1.5 percent of US GDP. However, it widened again until March 1999 to –3.5 percent of US GDP. The gap narrowed until June 2001, but has widened ever since, hitting –7.7 percent in June 2009. The conclusion from the FDI figures is that in the thirty years to 1983 the US had been buying ROW companies through the surpluses in the current account. Since 1983 it has been borrowing from ROW to buy ROW companies. Clearly, this is not a problem if foreign residents are willing to lend the US to buy their companies; indeed, they must be doing so because they believe that they would be more profitable under US management.

But the US borrows from ROW not only buy foreign companies. The ROW net worth at the end of the second quarter of 2009 stood at 30 percent of US GDP. It is broken down as follows: 41 percent of bonds, 2 percent of money market instruments, –10 percent of equities, –8 percent of direct investment and 5 percent of miscellaneous assets. Hence, only a small part of US borrowing is devoted to buying foreign companies, the rest is used to finance the excess expenditure over its income. The overall conclusion is that the US has been borrowing from ROW by issuing bonds partly to buy ROW companies, but principally to finance the excess expenditure over its income. However, to some extent the US is importing products from its own factories located overseas. The question that needs to be addressed is whether this is typical and, indeed, sustainable. We address this particular issue in the section that follows.

3   Does the US need to balance its current account?

In the small open economy paradigm this is neither typical nor sustainable. A country with a surplus in the current account will invest the proceeds in ROW by buying tangible assets. A country with a current account deficit will sell its tangible assets to ROW or borrow from ROW in ROW currency. If confidence in the ability of the economy to service its external debt is shaken the currency will fall and the country in question will become insolvent, as its debt will soar by the degree of currency depreciation. Therefore, in theory, although a deficit in the current account can be financed in the short run either by a corresponding surplus in the capital account or by running down foreign reserves, this cannot go on forever. In the long run the current account must be zero, because otherwise it implies that domestic residents can forever sell their assets or indefinitely borrow from overseas to finance their excess expenditure over their income. Clearly, this cannot last forever, as domestic residents will ultimately run out of assets, or foreign residents will lose their appetite to acquire such assets. Hence, in the long-run equilibrium the current account must be balanced.

The US case is interesting from this perspective, because the dollar is a reserve currency, and the US debt is simply domestic rather than foreign. This means that any crisis in the US must come from lack of confidence in its ability to service its domestic debt. But this is not possible! Although foreign residents hold half of the US general government debt, this is smaller than any other G7 economy, in spite of the sharp increase because of the current credit crisis. Moreover, although the US corporate debt is large (82 percent of US GDP), foreign residents hold less than one quarter. Hence, there is no compelling reason why foreign residents should lose their confidence in the ability of the US to service its debt. However, foreign residents may lose their appetite to lend the US, if they continuously suffer losses from their holdings of US assets. One factor that has contributed to such losses is the dollar and the other is the bad timing of foreign residents in buying US assets. From this point of view the huge current account deficit (the external imbalance) is one of the problems that face the US economy. Figure 10.7 shows that as a percentage of GDP direct holdings of equities by the personal sector doubled from 45 percent in 1952 to nearly 90 percent in 1968, but then

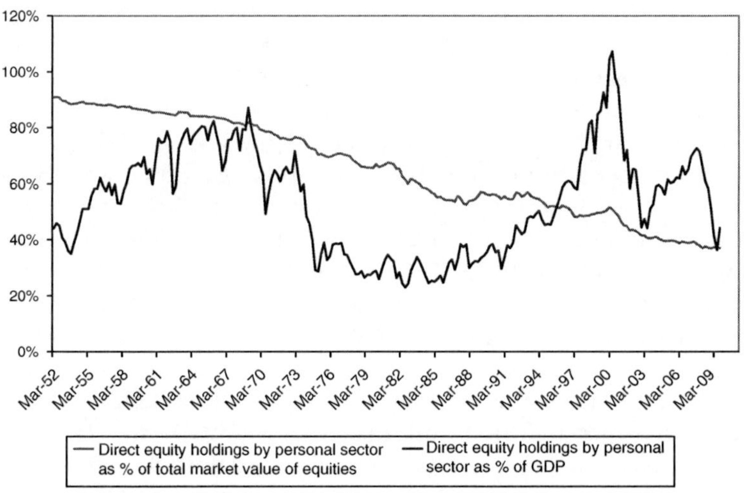

Figure 10.7   Direct holdings of equities held by the personal sector

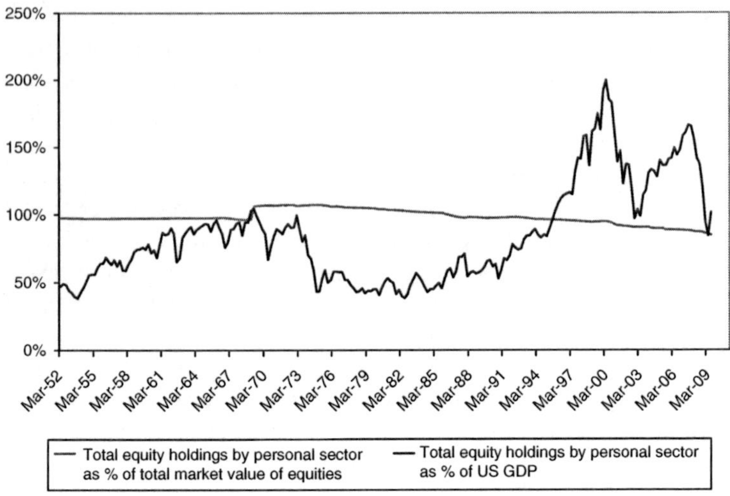

Figure 10.8   Total holdings of equities by the personal sector

declined to around 20 percent in 1982 before recovering to a peak of nearly 110 percent in March 2000. During the bear market of the early 2000s direct holdings fell to around 45 percent, but they rebounded in the bear market rally of 2003–07 to more than 70 percent of GDP and fell again in the worst stock market slump of 2007–09. However, such large swings reflect changes in the value of equities, which can be seen if direct holdings are expressed as a percentage of the total. The proportion of equities held directly by the personal sector has been on long-term downtrend – from 90 percent in 1952 to less than 40 percent in recent years (see Figure 10.7). This reflects a portfolio shift by the personal sector from direct to indirect holding through life insurance companies, pension funds and mutual funds. The proportion of total holdings of equities by the personal sector (both direct and indirect) declined from 100 percent in 1952 to 85 percent, a mere 15 percent reduction, in mid-2009 (see Figure 10.8). However, since the bursting of the bubble in March 2000 the proportion of total holdings held by the personal sector has fallen by 10 percent, of which foreign residents bought two-thirds.

Figure 10.9 shows that the proportion of ROW holdings of US equities has increased from just 2 percent of US GDP in 1952 to just over 7 percent in September 1990, but it remained low throughout the major bull market of the 1990s. The proportion of ROW holdings of US equities increased during the bear market of 2000–03 by around

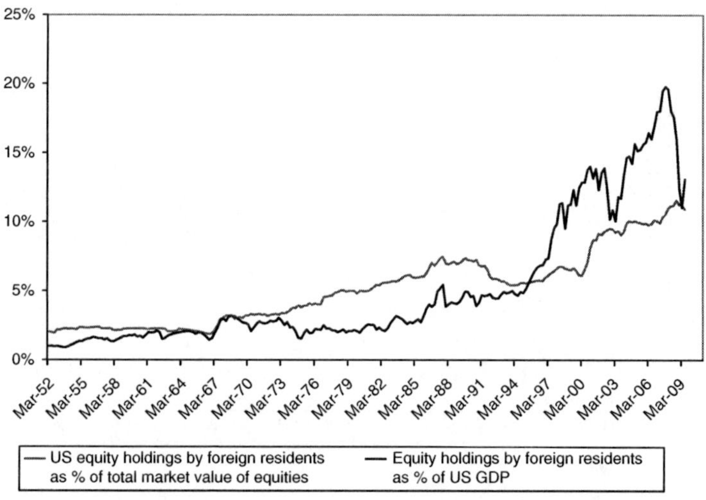

Figure 10.9   US stock equity holdings by foreign residents

4 percent. This means that foreign residents not only missed the major bull market of the 1990s, but were also net buyers during the bear market of the early 2000s. During the bear market of 2000–03 the US personal sector sold its stock holdings to ROW residents who foolishly believed that this was simply an opportunity to buy US shares. Figure 10.10a confirms this conclusion by showing the net purchases by the US and ROW residents. Figure 10.10b shows that foreign residents have suffered losses not only in their holdings of US equities, but also in bonds. In the second quarter of 2003 foreign residents bought aggressively the US bond market, which started one of its biggest collapses. Therefore, foreign residents have suffered capital losses in the past from holding US assets and the dollar plunged in the bear market of 2000–03, which may have aggravated such losses. Sustained losses in US assets may dry the appetite of ROW to hold such assets. Hence, the huge current account deficit is one of the problems that face the US economy. The current account deficit has persisted for far too long. This means that the US lacks the foundations for a sustainable new business cycle, since the current account deficit is bound to grow even bigger in the case of a recovery.

In theory, the current account can be corrected in one of two ways. The US economy should expand at a lower rate of growth than the rest of the world for a considerable period of time, until the current account deficit shrinks to a more sustainable level. Alternatively, the dollar should

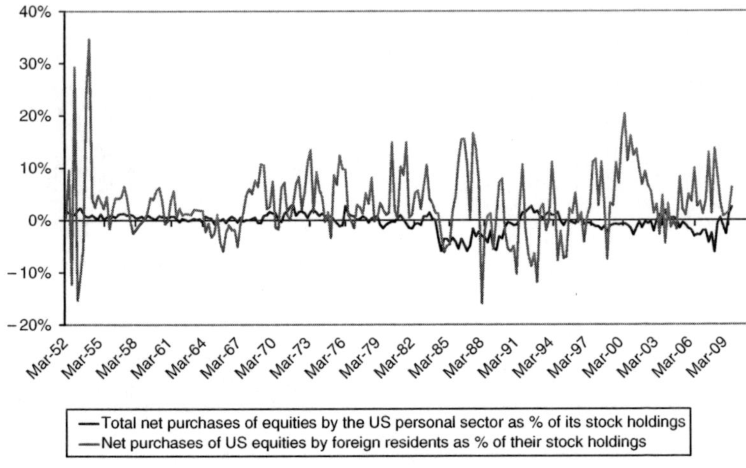

Figure 10.10a   Net purchases of US equities by US & foreign residents

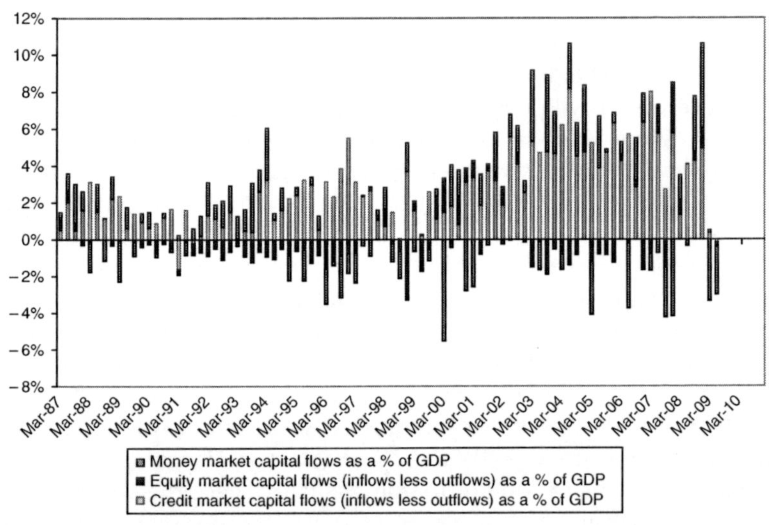

Figure 10.10b   Capital flows money, bonds & equities (inflows less outflows) as a % of GDP

fall dramatically for US competitiveness to improve and close the current account deficit. In practice, however, the current account deficit usually shrinks by a combination of lower growth and dollar depreciation, as with the US deficit in the 1980s, since the one reinforces the other. The combination of lower growth and dollar depreciation would enable the US to buy back its assets from foreign residents at much lower prices without having to pay for its debts. Unfortunately for the US, the prospects for the US are brighter than its main trading partners. This means that the dollar fall, so far, is not enough. The dollar should fall much more if the current account deficit is to shrink to a sustainable level. We turn our attention next to examine this particular proposition.

4   The dollar and the external imbalance

Although the dollar fall would help to correct the current account deficit there is no presumption that the ballooning current account deficit should lead to further dollar falls. If this were the case, then the dollar should have fallen anytime in the previous thirteen years. Unfortunately, and in spite of such a popular belief, the current account is not a dollar determinant. Neither is, for that matter, the capital account. Most dollar forecasts are systematically wrong because they are based on variables that are not determinants of the value of the dollar as they purport to be. Neither the small open economy paradigm nor the two-country model (see, for example, Dornbusch, 1976; Dornbusch and Fisher, 1980; Fleming, 1962; Mundell, 1960, 1963) have had much success in explaining dollar movements. To answer this question we examine the theoretical framework embedded in the K-Model (based on Frowen and Karakitsos, 1998).

4.1   A game-theoretic approach to currency determination

The value of a currency depends on the policy actions of the two countries involved, which affect other economic fundamentals. This entails that a game-theoretic framework is appropriate in which the equilibrium outcome depends on the policy decisions of both players and where the interactions of such decisions are modelled explicitly. However, in game theory there are four relevant equilibrium outcomes. Three of them characterise a non-cooperative environment, in which each player pursues its own objectives without caring for the objectives of the other, but where the decision of one player adversely affects the other. The fourth equilibrium is relevant when the players agree to compromise and in the pursuit of their objectives take into account also the objectives of the other player (co-operative game).

Such a framework is appropriate for exchange rate analysis. This is so since the policymakers of each country pursue policies that attempt to bring the best possible outcome (optimum) in terms of such target variables as inflation, growth and unemployment, through manipulating the level of interest rates, tax rates or discretionary government spending (in other words, monetary and fiscal policy). The exchange rate is a very important variable in the transmission of these policy actions on the target variables. For example, tight monetary policy with the objective of curbing inflation would be more effective if the currency appreciates, since it is expected to reduce imported inflation. On the other hand, easy monetary policy with the objective of promoting growth would be more effective if the currency depreciates because gains in competitiveness would boost exports and reduce imports. However, such policy decisions, to the extent that they are successful in affecting the value of the currency, would affect economic magnitudes in the other country involved. The policy decisions of one country may favourably or adversely affect economic magnitudes in the other country, where the outcome depends on the state of each economy in the business cycle. If the business cycles are synchronised then the policy decisions of one country will adversely affect the targets of the other. On the other hand, if the business cycles are not synchronised, then the policy decisions of one country will favourably affect the other country.

These considerations imply that a game-theoretic framework is appropriate for foreign exchange rate analysis, where the interactions of the two players are explicitly modelled. Most of the time the game is played non-cooperatively because each policymaker decides on monetary policy and fiscal policy with the objective of achieving the targets of its own country without consideration for the effect on the growth or inflation of the other country. When the business cycles of the two countries are not synchronised it does not really matter whether the game is played cooperatively or not. But it does matter, when the business cycles are synchronised, because in such a case both countries need a strong currency if they wish to beat inflation or a weak currency if they opt to promote growth. If both players are of equal weight (symmetric game) and they do not cooperate, in the sense that each country pursues policies that maximise its own targets without due consideration for the targets of the other country, then the relevant equilibrium is Nash. The Nash equilibrium is always worse than a cooperative equilibrium, which is called Pareto, but it is stable, whereas the latter is unstable. Stability in this context means that once the equilibrium is achieved there is no incentive by either player to deviate from it. A simple example makes the difference between Nash and Pareto obvious. In a stadium with seats for all spectators, they prefer to stand up so that they can see better (Nash equilibrium). Once one person stands up to see better, there is an incentive for everyone to stand up. In the Nash equilibrium all spectators stand up, whereas in Pareto equilibrium they all sit down. Clearly, the Nash equilibrium is worse than Pareto because all spectators are better off sitting than standing and, collectively, they see equally well whether sitting or standing. The Pareto equilibrium is unstable, however, because a single (short) spectator has the incentive to stand up to see better, but its actions would trigger a process that would result in all spectators standing up. In the currency market there are few instances when the game is played cooperatively, such as the Plaza Accord of 1985 and the Louvre Accord of 1987. But most of the time the game is played non-cooperatively.

If one of the players is more powerful than the other (asymmetric game) then the relevant non-cooperative equilibrium is Stackelberg, whereas the Nash equilibrium is relevant if both players carry equal weight. The strong player is called the 'leader', while the other is the 'follower'. In the context of the euro–dollar rate two characteristics suggest the asymmetric nature of the game and the prevalence of the Stackelberg-equilibrium. The effect of US monetary and fiscal policy on the euro area is bigger than the effect of the euro area policies on the US. Second, the euro area is more vulnerable than the US to supply shocks, such as the price of oil. Hence, the US can be considered as the leader, while the euro area as the follower.

The leader can exploit its advantage over the follower to achieve an even better outcome. This is accomplished by taking into account the possible reaction of the follower in deciding about its own strategy. In this asymmetric game there are two possible equilibria: Stackelberg-leader and Stackelberg-follower. The first is achieved when the leader exercises its leadership role, while the second is achieved when the 'leader' deliberately lets the 'follower' lead the game. In what follows we show that the US has a clear preference for the Stackelberg-leader equilibrium, when the economy is either overheated or cools down, but inflation continues to rise because of inertia. On the other hand, the US has a clear preference for the Stackelberg-follower equilibrium when the economy is either in the recession or the recovery phase of the business cycle, when there is spare capacity. We also provide reasons why investors have an incentive to enforce either the one or the other equilibrium on behalf of the US.

4.2   A policy choice model

This framework is a Stackelberg game with the US as the leader and the euro area as the follower. Such a framework is more appropriate because what is good for the US is good for the rest of the world, given its dominance in the world economy. Especially so since, as is shown below, the best outcome for the US is a stable equilibrium. The implication of this Stackelberg game is that what matters for the dollar is the US and not its relative position against its main trading partners. Hence, popular variables, like (short or long) interest rate differentials, growth differentials, money supply differentials, inflation differentials, which emanate from the small open economy or the two-country model, may lead to erroneous conclusions about dollar movements, as the models that involve such variables are usually unstable. The models are unstable in the sense that the impact of these variables on the euro–dollar exchange rate changes through time from, statistically significant, positive to negative and finally to zero. The model instability is due to a shift in the equilibrium from Stackelberg-leader to Stackelberg-follower. Once account is taken of this game framework and the shift of the equilibrium between Stackelberg-leader and Stackelberg-follower the resulting euro–dollar rate is stable. Moreover, the Stackelberg game framework does not imply that the traditional variables should be used for the US only. Instead, what is important is that the dollar should move in such a way so that the US economy can benefit under all circumstances. If this is not so, then not only the US, but also the rest of the world is at risk, as the economic and financial system would then be unstable. Within this framework, the value of the currency is an equilibrium outcome within a policy game. In this game-theoretic framework there are two equilibria, but only one of them is stable and most of the time investors enforce the stable equilibrium. The stable equilibrium reflects the best possible outcome from the US point of view, given the state of the economy in the business cycle and the time varying priorities of the US policymakers, among the main targets of economic policy.[2] We explore this theoretical premise in what follows.

We begin by assuming that each policymaker chooses its monetary policy by optimising an objective function that penalises deviations of actual inflation from its desired level and deviations of actual growth from its desired level. That is, for each country i the utility function U is specified as follows:

$$U_i = \tfrac{1}{2}[q_{ip}\,(p_i - p_i^d)^2 + q_{iy}\,(y_i - y_i^d)^2] \tag{1}$$

where q_{ip} is the penalty weight that the policymakers in country $i{=}1, 2$ attach to inflation and q_{iy} is the penalty weight on growth; p_i and y_i are actual inflation and growth respectively, and p_i^d and y_i^d are desired inflation and growth respectively. Country 1 is the US and country 2 is the euro area. The bliss point is taken as the rate of growth of desired output and desired rate of inflation. The desired output corresponds to the rate of growth of potential output, while the desired rate of inflation is the rate that corresponds to potential output. We may, thus, write:

$$(p_i^d \, , \, y_i^d) \tag{2}$$

The US central bank is assumed to pursue a 'balanced' approach to monetary policy between the two conflicting targets of inflation and growth; that is, the Fed is supposed to attach equal weights to the achievement of the inflation and output targets. On the other hand, the ECB is assumed to attach greater weight on inflation than on growth. This implies that while for the US it is assumed that $q_{1p} = q_{1y}$, for the euro area it is assumed that $q_{2p} > q_{2y}$. Each policymaker optimises its own objective function subject to the economic model that defines the feasible combinations of inflation and growth, given the choice of the monetary policy instrument. The model allows for the spillover effects of monetary policy from one country to the other. Thus, growth in each country is affected by the monetary policy of the two countries. Domestic monetary policy has a bigger effect on domestic growth than the foreign one. Inflation depends on the output gap and imported inflation. The latter is influenced by monetary policy as a rise in the domestic interest rate appreciates the domestic currency and depreciates the foreign currency.

Four characteristics are embedded in the model, which differentiates the US from the euro area. First, the euro area is much more reliant on imported raw materials than the US. Second, the spillover effect of US monetary policy on the euro area is bigger than the spillover effect of the euro area on the US. Thus, the euro area is both more susceptible to imported inflation and it is also more vulnerable to a 'beggar-thy-neighbour' policy than the US. Third, and as already stated, the US central bank is assumed to pursue monetary policy in a more 'symmetrical' manner than the ECB, and attach equal degree of importance to the two conflicting targets of inflation and growth. The ECB is assumed to focus heavily on inflation. This implies that while for the US it is assumed that the Fed degree of priority on growth is equal to that on inflation, for the euro area it is assumed that the priority on inflation exceeds that on growth. Fourth, the US is 'stronger' than the euro area in the sense elaborated above. Therefore, in a game framework the US can be considered as the leader, with the euro area as the follower. The indifference curves drawn in Figures 10.11a and 10.11c reflect these assumptions.

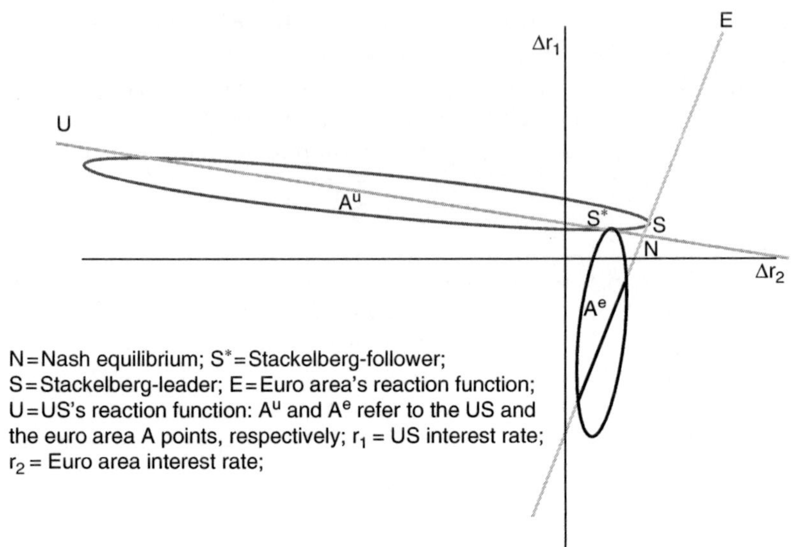

N = Nash equilibrium; S^* = Stackelberg-follower;
S = Stackelberg-leader; E = Euro area's reaction function;
U = US's reaction function: A^u and A^e refer to the US and
the euro area A points, respectively; r_1 = US interest rate;
r_2 = Euro area interest rate;

Figure 10.11a　Three possible equilibria in a non-cooperative game

With these assumptions we draw in Figure 10.11a the indifference curves for both the US and the euro area, which take the form of ellipses. Ellipses further away from the bliss point represent lower utility and are therefore less desirable. The US indifference curves have as their centre the bliss point A^u. The US ellipses are very flat. The indifference curves for the euro area, on the other hand, are very steep. The US bliss point lies in the second quadrant of Figure 10.11a. On the other hand, the bliss point for the euro area, denoted by A^e, lies in the fourth quadrant in the same figure. The optimal policy for each country is obtained by minimising the objective function (1) above, subject to the economic model. Each central bank is choosing its monetary policy by taking as given the monetary policy of the other. The optimal monetary policy for each country is described by its reaction function. In Figure 10.11a the US reaction function is denoted by U, while that of the euro area is denoted by E.

With the assumptions that the euro area is more vulnerable to imported inflation and to 'beggar-thy-neighbour' policies than the US and that it also cares more about inflation than the US, the reaction functions of the US and the euro area look like those in Figure 10.11a. The US reaction function is almost flat and the reaction function of the euro area is very steep. The intersection of the two reaction functions determines the Nash equilibrium, denoted by N, which is attained in quadrant 1 under the assumptions made earlier. This implies that as a result of a surge, say, in imported raw material prices the euro area is forced into tighter monetary policy than the US. This appreciates the euro against the dollar and introduces a deflationary effect in the euro area with higher unemployment than the US. The Stackelberg-leader equilibrium with the US as leader is defined as a point on the reaction function of the euro area that is tangential on the US indifference curves. In Figure 10.11a the Stackelberg equilibrium is attained at point S. Clearly, this is a better solution for the US because it lies on a lower indifference curve than the one that passes through point N. This implies that the Stackelberg equilibrium with the US as a leader is Pareto efficient for the US, but not for the euro area, since its equilibrium lies on a higher indifference curve for the euro area. The Stackelberg-follower equilibrium in which the US lets the euro area act as a leader is defined as a point on the US reaction function that is tangential to the euro area's indifference curves. In Figure 10.11a the Stackelberg equilibrium with the euro area as the leader is attained at point S*. This is a better outcome for the euro area, since it lies on a lower indifference curve. But it is also optimal for the US. Hence, the Stackelberg-follower equilibrium is Pareto-efficient for both the US and the euro area.

4.3   The choice of equilibrium

This subsection deals with the issue of which equilibrium is preferable from the US point of view. It actually turns out that the best possible outcome from the US point of view depends on the business cycle. Figure 10.11b illustrates the way in which the objective function of a central bank changes in the course of the business cycle. Point A represents the bliss point, defined as the rate of growth of potential output. The inflation rate that corresponds to the rate of growth of potential output is the steady-state rate of inflation. Points B and D represent the peak and the trough of the business cycle in terms of the rate of growth, while points C and E the maximum and minimum rate of inflation, respectively, in the business cycle. These points divide the business cycle into five phases.

In phase (I) growth is rising above potential, the economy becomes overheated and inflation rises, usually with a lag. The correlation between inflation and growth is positive. In phase (II) the economy decelerates, but inflation rises, thereby giving rise to negative correlation between the two variables. Inflation increases in phase (II), as unit labour cost continues to rise. There are two reasons why unit labour

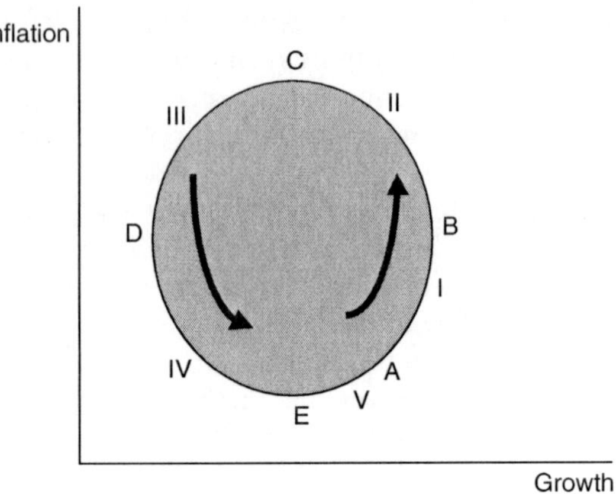

Figure 10.11b   Inflation and growth in the business cycle

cost rises in this phase, albeit at a decreasing rate as the economy moves from B to C. First, wage inflation is rising and, second, there is a fall in the growth of labour productivity. Both factors contribute to the rise in unit labour costs. In the initial part of phase (II) wages are high. They are increasing as fast as inflation as employees are trying to protect the purchasing power of their wages. Immediately after point B, near the peak of the business cycle, employees are in a position to protect their real wages since their bargaining power is strong, as unemployment is low and few jobs are lost per month. However, as the economy moves towards point C the bargaining power of employees weakens, as unemployment is rising and the number of jobs lost per month is increasing. Consequently, employees find it more and more difficult to protect the purchasing power of their wages. The real wage rate declines as the economy approaches point C and the wage–price spiral is finally broken. Near the peak of the business cycle (around point B) labour productivity is low as firms lag behind in adjusting their labour force to declining demand for their products. Two reasons force firms to adjust their labour force sluggishly. First, uncertainty as to whether the drop in the demand for goods would be temporary or permanent. Second, costs of adjustment in hiring and firing and training costs are forcing firms to see whether they can cope with reduced working hours and a smaller temporary staff before they start sacking their permanent staff. However, as the fall in demand gathers pace (i.e. as the economy approaches point C) falling profitability is forcing firms to absorb into their profit margins the higher cost and decrease their labour force. Consequently, the fall in labour productivity diminishes as the economy approaches point C. In phase (III) the economy goes into recession and inflation falls fast, as unit labour cost declines rapidly. Wage inflation abates as unemployment keeps rising and the number of jobs lost per month is increasing. Productivity rises as firms shed their labour force faster than the drop in demand. Profit margins are squeezed further as demand is extremely weak in the recession. The correlation of inflation and growth in phase (III) is positive. In phase (IV) the economy recovers, but inflation continues to fall, as unit labour cost rises, albeit at a decreasing rate. This is the inverse of phase (II) and correlation is negative.

With this information as a background it is easy to see how a central bank would change its priorities in the course of the business cycle. In phases (I) and (II) the priority on inflation increases, and the central bank follows tight monetary policy. In phases (III) and (IV) the central bank follows easy monetary policy, as the priority on beating inflation is reduced or the priority on growth is increased. Hence, in general, interest rates rise from E to C and fall from C to E. A central bank can be characterised as balanced, 'wet' (or 'dove') and 'tough' (or 'anti-inflation hawk') depending on the values it attaches to the penalty weights on inflation and growth at point A, i.e. when the economy is in steady state. The comparison has to be made at point A so that one is comparing like with like. This follows from the fact that the penalty weights vary in the course of the business cycle irrespective of the characterisation of the central bank as balanced, wet or tough. The central bank is balanced when the penalty weight on inflation is equal to the penalty weight on growth. The central bank is wet (or dove) when the penalty weight on growth exceeds that on inflation. The central bank is tough (or anti-inflation hawk) when the penalty weight on inflation exceeds that on growth. If the central bank is balanced, then interest rates would start falling at point C and would start rising at point E. If the central bank is wet or dove, then interest rates would start falling just before point C and would start rising after point E. If the central bank is tough or anti-inflation hawk, then interest rates would start falling after point C and would start rising before point E.

Figure 10.11c portrays what happens when central banks change their priorities in terms of their targets. The US reaction function rotates anti-clockwise when the priority on inflation increases, i.e. when the economy is in phase (I) or (II). When the priority on growth increases, i.e. when the economy is in phase (III) or (IV), the US reaction function rotates clockwise. Nonetheless, the rotation of the US reaction function in the course of the business cycle is small. The US reaction function remains effectively

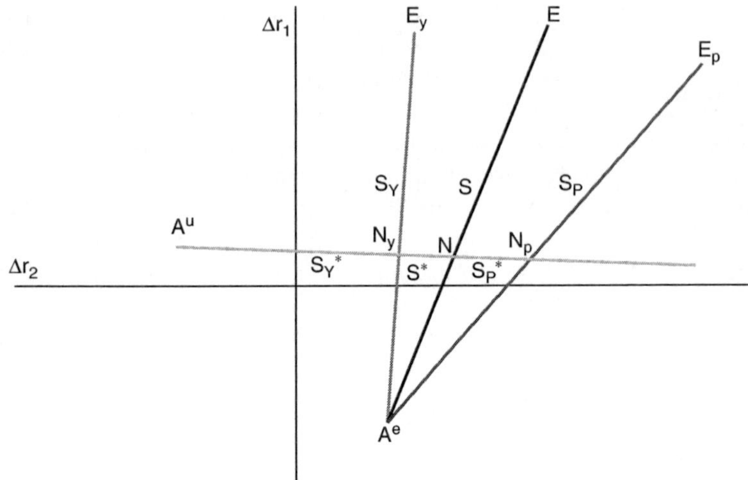

Where the symbols are as defined as in Figure 11a, and the subscripts have the following meaning: y-subscript=priority on growth, P-subscript=Priority on inflation, No-subscript=neutral position

Figure 10.11c   The choice of equilibrium

flat. The reaction function of the euro area, on the other hand, rotates clockwise when the priority on inflation increases, i.e. when the economy is in phase (I) or (II). The reaction function rotates anti-clockwise when the priority on growth increases, i.e. when the economy is in phase (III) or (IV). The euro area reaction function is much more sensitive than the US in the course of the business cycle.

For the sake of simplicity it is assumed that the US reaction function is fixed in the course of the business cycle, while the euro area's reaction function takes three positions. It is neutral when the economy is growing at the rate of potential output (i.e. in the steady state), steeper when the economy is in recession or in recovery (i.e. in phase III or IV) and flatter when inflation is rising (i.e. in phase I or II). In Figure 10.11c, E denotes the euro area's reaction function in the neutral position; E_y denotes the euro area's reaction function when the ECB attaches high priority in promoting growth. E_p denotes the euro area's reaction function when the ECB attaches high priority in beating inflation. In each reaction function there are three equilibria if the policy game is played non-cooperatively, Nash, Stackelberg-leader and Stackelberg-follower. The assumption that the US reaction function is fixed restricts the choice of equilibrium in the policy game to just nine instead of 27 and makes the conclusions crisper by eliminating unnecessary detail.

With this background analysis it is easy to see which equilibrium would be preferable from the US point of view in the course of the business cycle. When the US is either in the overheating or the cooling down phase (i.e. in phase I or II) of its business cycle, the best outcome is described by the Stackelberg-leader equilibrium, denoted by point S. The Stackelberg-leader equilibrium is Pareto efficient (i.e. welfare improving) for the US, but not for the euro area. But such an equilibrium is stable. This equilibrium implies higher interest rates both for the US and the euro area. The US would choose higher interest rates in order to reduce inflation, which is its primary objective in phase (I) or (II). This would appreciate the dollar against the euro and would raise imported inflation in the euro area. However, given the anti-inflation bias of the ECB, interest rates would either rise or not fall in the euro area in order to safeguard the value of the currency against imported inflation, as happened in 2008. But this would engulf the euro area into a deflationary gap, in which either unemployment would rise if the economy were in recession or unemployment would not fall if the economy were in recovery. Therefore, the Stackelberg-leader equilibrium is welfare improving for the US, but not for the euro area.

If both the US and the euro area are in phase (I) or (II), then the reaction function of the euro area would be flatter and point N would be further to the right to N_p in Figure 10.11c. The US can still improve its welfare by choosing the Stackelberg-leader equilibrium, but its overall welfare is lower because the improvement is from a lower base (i.e. compared to N). Overall the euro area welfare is smaller in the new Nash equilibrium N_p, relative to N. It becomes even worse as the US chooses the Stackelberg-leader equilibrium S_p. The US choice of the Stackelberg-leader equilibrium is self-enforceable. The euro area would be forced to choose this equilibrium as it enters into an interest rate war with the US because of the anti-inflation bias of the ECB. This is what happened in the first half of the 1980s and in the period 1999–2001. If, on the other hand, the euro area is in phase (III) or (IV) when the US is in phase (I) or (II), i.e. when the business cycles are desynchronised, then its reaction function is steeper at E_y, and point N would lie further to the left to N_y. The US can still improve its welfare by choosing the Stackelberg-leader equilibrium, but now its overall welfare is higher because the improvement is from a higher base (i.e. compared to N). Overall, the euro area welfare is higher, but it is somewhat reduced as the US chooses the Stackelberg-leader equilibrium. An improvement in the euro area welfare is possible only if the ECB is prepared to accept both a weaker euro and higher inflation. If the ECB is unwilling to submit to higher inflation and weaker currency, then its reaction function will rotate clockwise (i.e. it would become flatter) as the US attempts to choose the Stackelberg-leader equilibrium. Inflation would still rise and the currency would become weaker, but by less than the original equilibrium. Both from the US and the euro area's point of view de-synchronisation of the business cycles is preferable than synchronisation.

In the recession or the recovery phase (i.e. in phases III or IV) the Stackelberg-follower equilibrium in which the euro area acts as a leader, namely point S*, is a far better outcome for the US irrespective of the position of the euro area in the business cycle. In this case the US is exploiting the flatness of its reaction function and the steepness of the euro area reaction function. Given the flatness of the US reaction function, US interest rates would rise by almost the same amount as in the Nash equilibrium. However, the euro area would adopt a less tight policy than at N and, therefore, the dollar would appreciate compared to Nash. This would allow the US to soothe the recessionary effects of the surge in raw material prices, which is its primary objective in phase (III) or (IV), while minimising the inflationary consequences. Since the US is adopting almost the same degree of tightening, the recessionary effects of the raw material price increase are the same in N and S*. However, by letting the euro area lead the US is benefiting both in terms of inflation and growth. Inflation at S* is lower than N, because the dollar is stronger and hence imported inflation is lower. Growth is higher because domestic demand in the euro area is more buoyant thereby stimulating US exports. The rise in dollar results in a loss in US competitiveness. US exports still increase, though, as the effect of the stronger domestic demand in the euro area more than offsets the loss in competitiveness. Thus, the Stackelberg-follower equilibrium is Pareto efficient (i.e. welfare improving) for the US. Such equilibrium is also Pareto efficient for the euro area, as it lies on a lower indifference curve than the one that passes through point N, the Nash equilibrium. If the euro area lags behind the US in the business cycle, as it happened in the 1980s and the 1990s, and it is in phase (I) or (II), while the US is in phase (III) or (IV), then the euro area's reaction function would be even flatter. The choice of equilibrium now lies on E_p and therefore point N would lie, almost horizontally, further to the right to N_p in Figure 10.11c. In this case there is still room for welfare improvement for both the US and the euro area. The US would still choose the Stackelberg-follower equilibrium at S_p*. However, overall welfare for the US diminishes because the improvement is from a lower base. The euro area welfare is lower compared to N, but this is desirable since euro area attaches a high priority in reducing inflation. The dollar would still appreciate compared to the new Nash-equilibrium N_p, but it would be weaker compared to the original Nash-equilibrium, N, i.e. the equilibrium when the euro area is growing at potential output. European welfare improves at $S_p{}^*$ compared to N_p because the Fed is not competing with the ECB over the currency. The Fed does not lift interest rates to defend the dollar and hence the ECB tightens less than otherwise. Thus, although the dollar depreciates compared to N, it is still stronger compared to N_p. The euro area welfare improvement, therefore, reflects the smaller degree of tightening by the ECB. Such an outcome is optimal for the euro area because the Fed tolerance over the dollar arises as a result of the US being in recession or in recovery and therefore the smaller the dollar appreciation the better. Hence, de-synchronisation of business cycles is preferable from Europe's point of view, but not from the US, as $S_p{}^*$ is further away from the bliss point than S^*.

If, on the other hand, the business cycle of the euro area is synchronised with the US and both regions are in phase (III) or (IV), then the euro area reaction function will be even steeper and the Nash equilibrium would lie, almost horizontally, further to the left to N_y in Figure 10.11c. Again there is room for welfare improvement for both the US and the euro area compared with the new Nash equilibrium N_y. The US will still choose the Stackelberg-follower equilibrium. But now overall welfare for the US is enhanced since the improvement is from a higher base. Hence, from the US point of view the synchronisation of business cycles is preferable to non-synchronisation. The dollar would appreciate compared to the new Nash equilibrium at N_y, as the euro area interest rates do not rise very far. The dollar would be even stronger compared to the original Nash equilibrium N. Synchronisation is preferable from the US point of view because the euro-area growth is higher at $S_y{}^*$ than at N_y and hence US exports are more buoyant, in spite of the stronger dollar. The choice of Stackelberg-follower equilibrium is also Pareto efficient for the euro area as the stronger dollar results in a smaller degree of tightening by the ECB.

In summary, the Stackelberg-leader equilibrium is a better outcome for the US when the economy is either overheating or is cooling down (i.e. in phases I and II). The Stackelberg-follower equilibrium is a better outcome for the US when the economy is either in recession or in the recovery phase (i.e. in phases III and IV). The next issue is how the US enforces its choice of equilibrium, whether this is a Stackelberg-leader or a Stackelberg-follower outcome. In each case markets impose such equilibrium because, usually, this is the only stable equilibrium in the absence of foreign exchange intervention. A market economy relies upon market discipline for the stability of the system. Investors, in trying to protect the value of their portfolios, usually enforce a stable equilibrium. Whenever the US business cycle is not synchronised with that of the euro area, the resulting equilibrium is stable, simply because there is no conflict – one player's interest dictates a strong currency, while the other's dictates a weak currency. By contrast, whenever there is synchronisation of the business cycles, there is a conflict in that it is in the interests of both players to have either a weak or strong currency. In the latter case, investors impose the equilibrium that enhances US welfare even if that is detrimental to the euro area in the short run, since it is stable. Thus, in phases (I) and (II) when the Stackelberg-leader equilibrium is prevalent and the US budget deficit is shrinking, investors buy dollars, as this helps the US to fight inflation and provide finance to a widening current account deficit. The alternative would imply instability for the US and, consequently, for the world economy and its financial system. In phases (III) and (IV), when the Stackelberg-follower equilibrium is prevalent and the US budget deficit is widening, investors sell dollars, as this helps the US economy to recover, which in time will revive the rest of the world, and helps to close the current account deficit. The alternative would again imply instability for the US and the world financial system. One important qualification to this thesis is the possibility of 'irrational exuberance'. Investors in their monolithic pursuit of profit can choose an unstable equilibrium.

The stability issue clarifies why the ECB in some periods is unable either to stem the euro plight or the euro rise. In the post-internet bubble environment a rate cut by the ECB did not have the desired effect of restraining the rise in the euro, as its business cycle was synchronised with that of the US. In the recovery phase of 2003–04 both the US and the euro area were struggling to recover and both of them saw the advantage of a weak currency. In the absence of intervention the only stable equilibrium is the one that favours dollar weakness, and this is the one that was imposed by the markets. The equilibrium with weak dollar was stable because it led to a US-led world recovery, whereas a dollar rise (and consequently a euro fall) would not have helped the rest of the world to recover and, perhaps, not even the euro area itself. In this respect, the rexperience of France in the early 1980s is pertinent. At the time, the rest of the G7 pursued deflationary policies to fend off the inflationary effect of the second oil shock, while the socialist French government pursued expansionary policies to fight the recession. In the event, France was forced, after a short period of time, to reverse its policies, as it led to instability through a currency crisis. In the period between the end of the Asian-Russian crisis (1998) and the bursting of the equity bubble (2000) the ECB, and prior to it the Bundesbank, was again unable to stem the euro plight, in spite of tight monetary policy because its business cycle was again synchronised with that of the US. By contrast, whenever the US business cycle is not synchronised with that of the euro area, the resulting equilibrium is stable, simply because there is no conflict – one player's interest dictates a strong currency, while the other's dictates a weak currency. This was the case in the period 1994–98, when the US was overheated, but the euro area was operating with spare capacity.

5   The recent behaviour of the dollar and the long-term risks

It follows from the analysis so far in this chapter that the dollar is strong when the US wants to cap inflationary pressures and it is weak when the US wants to promote growth through exports. The application of the Stackelberg-game framework can easily explain the periods of weakness and strength of the dollar. In the period 1995–2000 the dollar was strong to curb the inflationary pressures as the US economy was overheated (see Figure 10.12). In this period the dollar appreciated from $1.34 to $0.85 against the euro (see Figure 10.12). The relevant equilibrium was Stackelberg-leader and this was irrespective of the euro area position in the business cycle. In the period 1995–97 the ERM[3] countries were experiencing an anaemic recovery, but inflation crept up (phase V). The anti-inflation bias of the Bundesbank (the ECB predecessor) during this period condemned the ERM countries to growth less than potential with unemployment climbing throughout this period. Yet despite the tight monetary policy of the Bundesbank the euro sank to $1.07, as the currency markets enforced the Stackelberg-leader equilibrium. Throughout the Asian-Russian crisis of 1997–98 fear of a world recession kept the dollar rise in check (see Figure 10.12). But once the crisis subsided and the overheating of the US economy threatened to rekindle inflation the dollar soared. It is worth noting that in the period of 1999–2000 the euro area became overheated, too. Both the US and euro area wanted a strong currency to control inflation, but markets favoured once more the US. In spite of the Bundesbank and ECB efforts to stem the euro plight it dived to a 15-year low against the dollar at $0.85 (see Figure 10.12).

Throughout the early 2000s recession the dollar remained steady, but it assumed a downtrend in the recovery phase of 2001–04. The dollar

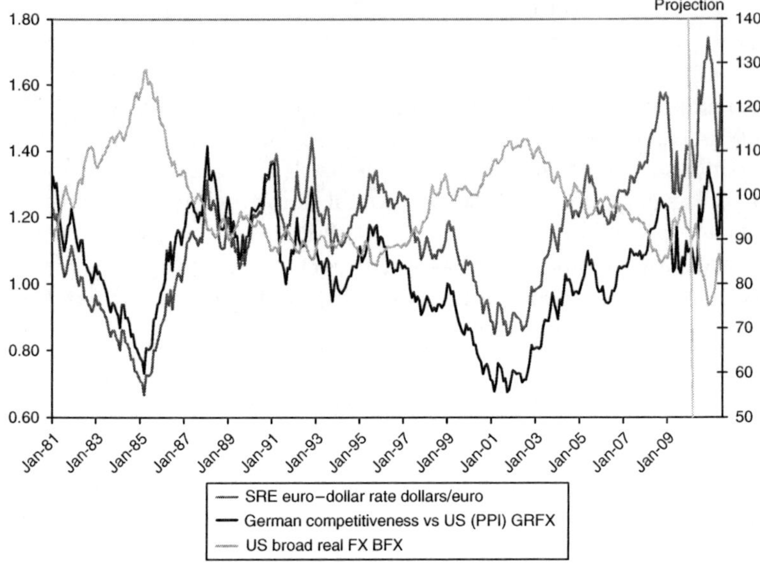

Figure 10.12   The euro–dollar rate

had hit \$1.35 by the end of 2004 (see Figure 10.12). After the recovery phase the US economy became overheated for a short period and the dollar appreciated for a year, hitting a high of \$1.17 against the euro (see Figure 10.12). But the dollar rally was short lived. As a result of the removal of the accommodation bias of monetary policy in 2004–05 the imbalances in the US economy re-emerged, damaging economic growth. Hence, the overheating was eliminated and the US economy grew at the rate of potential output or lower. In this environment strong exports were necessary to offset the weakness of domestic demand requiring a weak dollar. Thus, the dollar resumed its downtrend, retesting the \$1.35 low by the onset of the credit crisis in August 2007 (see Figure 10.12). Increasing spare capacity emerged in the US economy during the aftermath of the bursting of the housing bubble and the dollar weakness gathered steam to boost exports. This last stage of dollar weakness is associated with the exaggeration phase of the commodities bubble in the first half of 2008. The dollar hit \$1.60 against the euro in June 2008 (see Figure 10.12). But the collapse of the commodities bubble triggered unwinding of all carry trade and the dollar appreciated hitting \$1.25 against the euro (see Figure 10.12). The unwinding of the credit crisis and the beginning of the new economic recovery has now triggered a new dollar downtrend.

The K-Model conforms with the abovementioned principles of the Stackelberg-game suggesting five determinants of the dollar real exchange rate: (a) fiscal policy, measured by changes in the cyclically adjusted budget deficit (FBUD); (b) the size of Federal debt (DEBT); (c) the stance of monetary policy (KMS), measured by an index of domestic and external monetary conditions; (d) long-term interest rates (the 10-year US bond yield, U10Y); and (e) the policy adjusted output gap (SL). The latter reflects the importance policymakers assign to the output gap in the course of the business cycle and, consequently, the choice of the relevant Stackelberg-leader or -follower equilibrium. For example, a positive output gap carries more weight in the overheating and slowdown phase when the Fed assigns higher priority to combating inflation than the same output gap in the recovery phase when the Fed assigns higher priority to promoting growth. Thus, the consideration of the Stackelberg-leader or -follower equilibrium means that the output gap is adjusted by the policy bias on growth or inflation. We can thus write the long-term relationship of the real dollar with its five determinants as:

$$BFX = BFX(FBUD, DEBT, KMS, U10Y, SL) \qquad (3)$$
$$(+) \quad (-) \quad (+) \quad (-) \ (+)$$

In this game-theoretic framework the currency is strong when the economy is growing faster than the policy-adjusted potential output, fiscal[4] and monetary policy is tight, the government debt is falling and bond yields are declining.[5] On the other hand, the dollar is weak when there is space capacity in the economy (negative policy-adjusted output gap), fiscal policy is easy, monetary policy is easy and the government debt and bond yields are rising. These K-Model properties throw more light on the dollar real exchange rate movements. In the second half of the 1990s the dollar was strong because the US was overheated (positive policy adjusted output gap), thereby creating inflationary pressures and making prevalent the Stackelberg-leader equilibrium. The strong economy helped to reduce the budget deficit, curb the general government debt and bond yields fell, while monetary and fiscal policy was tight. All these factors contributed to a strong dollar. In the period 2001–04 the US economy was weak and operated with spare capacity (negative policy adjusted output gap); monetary policy was easy, fiscal policy was also easy and both the budget deficit and general government debt were soaring. All these factors contributed to the dollar fall in that period.

The dollar real effective exchange rate, based on a trade-weighted wide basket of currencies, is the variable explained by the K-Model.

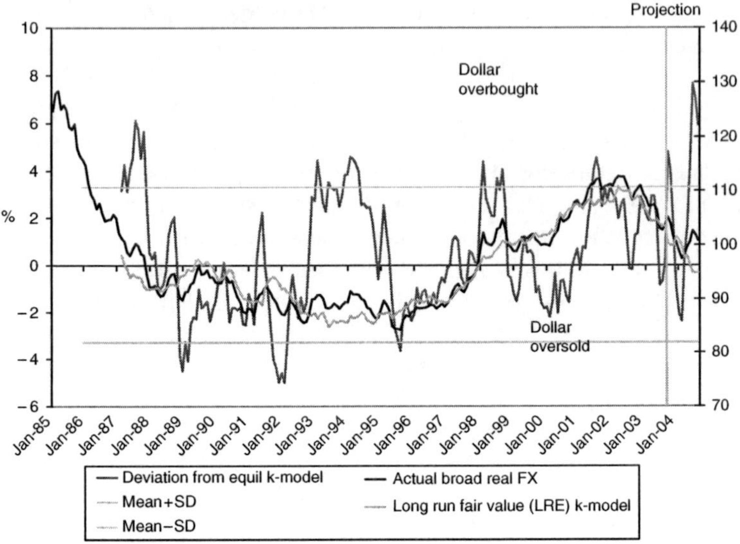

Figure 10.13   Real dollar exchange rate – long-run fair value & valuation

It is a wide measure of US competitiveness, which is stationary, unlike the nominal exchange rate, which is non-stationary.[6] The long-run relationship of the real dollar, with its aforementioned five variables (see equation (3)), can serve as a measure of long-run valuation. The more the dollar real exchange rate deviates from its long-run equilibrium the higher the probability that it will be corrected in the future. Figure 10.13 shows the historical deviations of the dollar real exchange rate from its long-run equilibrium. The biggest undervaluation in the dollar real exchange rate occurred at the onset of the credit crisis in August 2007. Rising risk aversion in the course of the crisis led to an unwinding of carry trade, which triggered nominal and real dollar exchange rate appreciation. The undervaluation was corrected and reached a more than two standard deviations real dollar exchange rate overvaluation following the collapse of Lehman Brothers in September 2008. The K-Model suggests that the real dollar exchange rate under-valuation will persist until the spring or the summer of 2010 before mean reversion takes place (see Figure 10.13).

The dynamic K-Model of the real dollar exchange rate considers the adjustment path to a time-varying long-run equilibrium. This dynamic adjustment is affected by the previous year deviation from long-run equilibrium, the speed of which is affected by news on economic

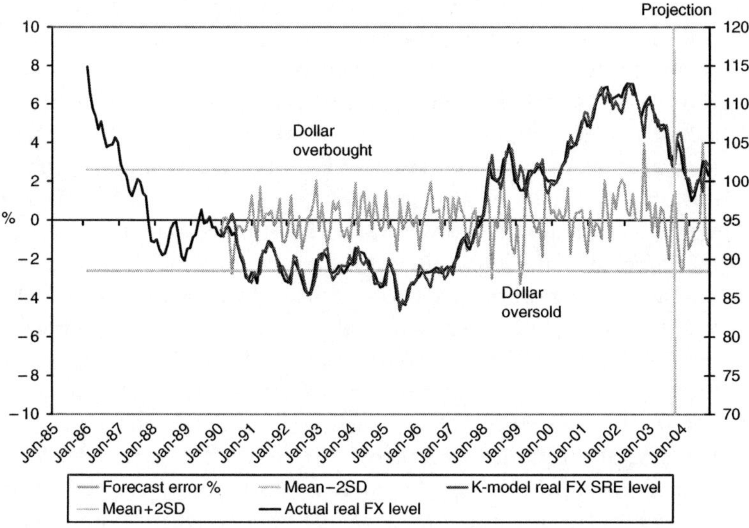

Figure 10.14   Real dollar exchange rate – short-run fair value & valuation

fundamentals on the five determinants of the real dollar. Thus, the rates of growth rather than the levels of the five variables in equation (3) are important in the dynamic adjustment of the real dollar exchange rate to the long-run equilibrium. Figure 10.14 shows the actual and the K-Model predicted real dollar exchange rate implied by the dynamic adjustment back to the long-run equilibrium.

The K-Model explains dollar movements in the last twenty years with just 1.3 percent forecast error. This means that with an error of 2.5 percent the model can explain 95 percent of all past dollar volatility. Indeed, in the last 240 months there have been only five instances where the dollar error has exceeded 2.5 percent (see Figure 10.14). The last episode of a dollar outlier was in the aftermath of the collapse of Lehman Brothers (see Figure 10.14). On that basis the forecasting ability of the model is such as to claim that with 95 percent probability the dollar in the future will lie within the interval of the central projection plus or minus 2.5 percent. This assumes that the behaviour of the dollar will continue to be governed by the same structure that is encapsulated in the K-Model. The critical assumption here is that the leadership role of the US would not be challenged in the forecast period, an assumption that will probably be easily satisfied for a period of one year. Hence, there is no reason to assume that the structure of the K-Model will be invalidated in the short-term future. But perhaps the best evidence of the success of the K-model in forecasting the real dollar is its accuracy in the First Edition of the book (Arestis and Karakitsos, 2004): 'For the aforementioned reasons, the dollar would continue its decline with a target of 94.2 on its broad trade weighted index by December 2004, from its current value of 105.4 in August 2003. This implies 11% depreciation in the real value of the dollar against all currencies' (p. 258). Indeed, the outcome by the end of December 2004 was 94.8. This implies a forecast error just over half a percent in something less than one and a half years.

In the current environment the K-Index of the stance of monetary policy shows that it is easy, although the pinnacle was reached in October 2008 and the degree of easiness has abated since then because negative inflation has raised the real Fed funds rate (see Figure 1.1, Chapter 1). However, the K-Model suggests that deflationary forces are about to ease and inflation will be on the rise yet again, thereby lowering the real Fed funds rate and easing domestic monetary conditions. Fiscal policy is also easy and may continue to be so with yet another fiscal package in early 2010. In the short run easy fiscal policy strengthens the real dollar, as it increases the policy-adjusted output gap, but in the long run it weakens the currency as the Federal debt rises. The Federal debt is soaring and this puts further downward pressure on the real dollar. The 10-year yield soared in the first half of the year from nearly 2 to 4 percent, thereby contributing to the real dollar decline. But the 10-year yield has since declined to around 3.5 percent. The K-Model suggests a sideways movement from now on and, thus, its impact on the real dollar exchange rate is expected to be minimal. The most overwhelming factor that suggests real dollar exchange rate depreciation is the policy-adjusted output gap, which remains extremely negative (see Chapter 1, Figure 1.2). On balance, the K-Model central line projection suggests that the real dollar will depreciate by another 17 percent from 90 in August 2009 to 75 by the spring of 2010. The real dollar will then stage a partial recovery to 87 before finishing at 83 by the end of 2010 (see Figure 10.14). This point forecast should be qualified with plus or minus 2.5 percent around the central line projection.

Translating the real dollar forecast to the nominal euro–dollar rate is more complicated as it requires an equally accurate forecast for the real euro exchange rate and also a forecast for the US and euro area PPI. With this caveat the K-Model suggests that the euro–dollar rate will peak at $1.75 in the spring of 2010 before finishing at $1.57 by the end of 2010 (see Figure 10.12). However, the margins of error around this central projection are quite large, around $0.10.

6   Summary and conclusions

The huge US current account deficit (the external imbalance) has persisted for far too long, although, so far, it has been financed very easily. The accumulation of those deficits has turned the US into a net debtor to the rest of the world (ROW) of the order of 30 percent of its GDP. This external debt has been used, for a long time, mainly to sustain the US excess expenditure over its income, but also to buy ROW companies. Compared to other countries the external debt of the US is large, but it is in US dollars. Hence, traditional insolvency problems that are created by debt to ROW in ROW currency do not arise in the case of the US. Although foreign residents hold half of US government debt, the debt is smaller than any other G7 country. Moreover, although US corporate debt is more than 80 percent of GDP, foreign residents hold less than one quarter. Hence, there is no compelling reason why foreign residents should lose confidence in the ability of the US to service its debt.

However, foreign residents may lose their appetite to lend to the US, if they suffer continuous losses from their holdings of US assets. Foreign residents not only missed the major US bull equity market in the 1990s, but they have also suffered losses during the bear equity market of 2000–03, in the worst equity market slump of 2007–09 and in the rebound of 2009. Moreover, foreign residents have recently suffered heavy losses on their holdings of US bonds. The value of the dollar has plunged from the beginning of the recovery in the early 2000s to mid-2008, which may have aggravated such losses. From this point of view the external imbalance is one of the problems that face the US economy. Unless the current account deficit is balanced in the long run or at least narrowed down, the US lacks the foundations for a sustainable new business cycle, since the current account deficit is bound to grow even bigger in the case of a recovery.

The US will be able to get rid of its debt not by paying it back, but by buying it back at lower prices once foreign residents have suffered huge losses on their holdings of US assets. During the two bear markets of the early and late 2000s the US sold its stock holdings to the ROW. Slower growth and sharp dollar depreciation would enable the US to buy back its assets from the ROW. Unfortunately for the US, despite the recent recession, the US has better prospects than its main competitors, so the current account deficit is expected to widen instead of narrowing. This means that the fall in the dollar exchange rate, so far, is not sufficient. It needs to fall further if the current account deficit is to shrink to a sustainable level. But even a bigger current account deficit will not cause a dollar exchange rate fall, since, despite popular belief, it does not affect it. The opposite is true. The current account deficit is affected by the real value of the dollar.

Our game-theoretic approach to dollar determination reveals that the currency is weak when the economy is growing slower than its policy-adjusted potential, fiscal and monetary policy is easy, the government debt is rising and bond yields are increasing. All of these factors account for something more than a one percent error in dollar movements and, with the exception of bond yields, they point to a weaker dollar in the future. In essence, the dollar would continue falling because the US economy is operating with spare capacity and wants to boost its exports in strengthening the recovery. The K-Model suggests that the real value of the dollar will further depreciate by more than 15 percent against all currencies hitting 75 by the spring of 2010 from 90 in August 2009. The nominal value of the euro will climb to $1.75 against the dollar during this forecast period before settling to less than $1.60 by the end of 2010. However, it should be noted that the margins of error for the euro–dollar rate are much larger than for the real dollar exchange rate.

11
The Long-Term Risks to US Financial Markets

1 Introduction

Financial markets link the imbalances of the various sectors of the economy to their spending decisions, which is particularly important in asset-led business cycles. The success or failure of monetary policy to steer the economy out of the asset and debt deflation spiral relies on its ability to affect developments in bond yields, equities and currencies. Chapter 10 dealt with the dollar and this chapter deals with bonds and equities. Bond yields affect the entire spectrum of interest rates from mortgage rates to corporate bond yields that determine housing and fixed investment. Bond yields also affect bank debentures that determine the cost of bank borrowing from capital markets and therefore the availability of bank lending. The bond market shapes the ability of the personal sector to service its debt and the appetite of households to accumulate more debt. This, in combination with the housing market, impacts upon personal sector net wealth and, therefore, on consumption. As we shall see later in this chapter, bond yields also influence equities through the equity risk premium and the pricing of all financial instruments and synthetic products.

But there is a feedback effect from the economy to the bond market. This is the subject matter of this chapter. In particular, it is shown that bond yields depend on the outlook for growth, inflation and the Fed funds rate, the instrument of monetary policy. The relationship of interest rates of various maturities (what is called the term structure of interest rates or simply the yield curve) plays a crucial role in business cycle analysis. The yield curve is normally upward sloping, indicating that long-term interest rates are higher than the short-term ones. But the yield curve may become flat or even inverted, thus magnifying or lessening the potency of monetary policy in affecting the economy and inflation. Hence, the bond market plays centre stage in the transmission of monetary policy. Finally, the bond market has a direct impact on the external balance and the size of government debt and budget. In particular, bond yields impact upon capital inflows, which are necessary to finance the current account deficit. They also control the size of interest payments on government debt and hence the degree of solvency of the entire economy. The combination of high bond yields with a large government debt might create instability in that it leads to an upward spiral of rising government debt service and debt. Moreover, high bond yields limit the manoeuvre of government to use fiscal policy to stabilise the economy around potential output growth.

Equities affect the composition and the cost of internal and external company finance that impact upon investment, employment and production. Equities directly influence personal sector wealth and hence consumption. The wealth effect on consumption becomes even more important in asset-led business cycles and therefore it is pertinent in the current economic environment. In particular, the sustainability of the recovery and the length of the new cycle that is just beginning depend on the level of bond yields and the extent to which equity prices can advance. Rising and high bond yields will finally topple the economy causing yet another recession, as they did in the previous cycle. If the equity market were to falter in the future, then the economy will fall into recession.

This chapter is organised as follows. The next section explains the determinants of the bond market. Section 3 analyses the bond market and the yield curve in the course of the business cycle and draws inferences about portfolio management. Section 4 discusses the prospects for the bond market and the long-term risks in view of the exit strategy from the programme of quantitative easing and the increasing importance of foreign holdings of US government bonds. Section 5 explains the theoretical structure of the equity market. Section 6 analyses the equity market in the course of the business cycle and draws some principles (guidelines) on portfolio rebalancing. Section 7 discusses the prospects of the equity market concentrating on the important issue of whether we are in a long bear market and assesses the long-term risks. Section 8 summarises and concludes.

2   Theoretical underpinnings of the bond market

The part of the K-Model that deals with the bond market is based on the premise that government bonds of different maturities are very close substitutes in the investor's portfolio. As a result of this premise an arbitrage relationship holds between government bond yields of different maturities. This arbitrage relationship entails that the yields (taking into account the relative risk premium) of two different maturities are brought into equality, instantaneously, by corresponding changes in their relative demands. If the yield on a long maturity (say 10-year) is higher than the yield on a short maturity (say 3-month) by an amount not justified by economic fundamentals, then investors will buy the long bond and sell the short bond to exploit the yield differential. By doing so, the price of the long bond will rise, pushing the yield down, while the price of the short bond will fall, pushing the yield up. The process will continue until the yield spread between long and short maturities is equal to the investors' expected risk premium.

If we denote by R the current yield of the long maturity (i.e. the coupon divided by the price of the bond); g^e the expected capital gains (losses) on the long maturity; r^e the expected short-term interest rate, which is equal to the actual (r) rate of interest; α the preferred habitat premium; and p^e the expected inflation premium, then the arbitrage relationship can be written in the following form:

$$(R + g^e) = r^e + (p^e + \alpha) \tag{1}$$

Since the arbitrage equation holds for expected rather than actual yields it is better described as an equilibrium relationship, for any given holding period. The left-hand side of (eq. 1) represents the total holding period return (i.e. current yield plus expected capital gains), of the long maturity, say 10-year. The first term on the right-hand side of (eq. 1) is the yield on the short maturity, say 3-month, and the last two terms, in parenthesis, represent the risk premium between the yields of the two maturities. The risk premium consists of two components, the inflation premium and the preferred habitat premium (see below). Although the arbitrage relationship holds between any two maturities, it is convenient to think of the short-term interest rate, r, as the instrument of monetary policy, which acts as an anchor to the yields of all maturities.

Equation (1) can be written in a number of different ways, such as:

$$(R - r^e) = - g^e + p^e + \alpha \tag{1a}$$

In this form it asserts that the spread between the long and the short yield reflects investors' expected capital gains (or losses) from holding the 10-year bond (g^e) plus a risk premium for convincing investors to deviate from their preferred habitat (α), plus an inflation premium based on expected inflation over the holding period (p^e). The preferred habitat premium arises from the fact that in minimising risk, investors will try to match the maturities of their assets and liabilities (preferred habitat). Hence, if they are to take some risk and deviate from their preferred habitat they should be compensated by receiving a corresponding premium. For example, if investors have funds available for investment for only six months then without any risk they can invest in a six-month bond. However, if they were to invest in a longer bond they would do so only if they were sufficiently compensated for the risk they will assume. The preferred habitat premium, therefore, will be positive for investors who invest for a holding period longer than their preferred habitat and negative for investors with a shorter holding period. On average, however, the more plausible value for α is positive, as most lenders will have a bias towards short maturities to minimise the risk of departing from their money, while most borrowers would prefer long maturities to enable the investment to work out. The inflation premium p^e arises from the fact that at the end of the holding period inflation may have eroded the value of the principal.

Investors' expected capital gains from holding a long bond depend on the current yield (R) and the expected yield (R^e) over a given holding period (t to t+1). If rates are expected to rise, there will be capital losses, and vice versa. The arbitrage relationship requires that with unchanged monetary policy (i.e. fixed r), the bond yield will rise to offset the capital losses; we may, thus, write:

$$g^e = g\,(R, R^e) \tag{2}$$

In calculating the expected capital gains investors must have an estimate of the yield at the end of the holding period, R^e. It is assumed that investors are basing such a forecast on fiscal and monetary policy. The size of the budget deficit determines the new supply of bonds (ΔB). If investors expect the budget deficit to widen then the supply of bonds will increase and the expected long yield at the end of the holding period will rise, too, as investors will demand a higher yield to carry the extra paper in their portfolios. The expected conduct of monetary policy will also determine the expected long yield at the end of the holding period, as the instrument of monetary policy, the US Fed funds rate, will determine the cost of carry. If investors expect the central bank to tighten monetary policy then the expected long yield will rise, too. We can therefore write:

$$R^e = R\,(\Delta B, r^e) \tag{3}$$

Investors form expectations of the short-term interest rate by assuming that the central bank is rational and its decision on monetary policy is optimal, given the information about the current state of the economy and the central bank's policy brief. It is, therefore, assumed that the central bank decides on the future course of interest rates by optimising an objective function, which is specified to varying degree of detail by law, subject to the way monetary policy affects its targets. Such an optimisation results in a relationship between the instrument of monetary policy, r, and the targets of economic policy. The assumption of rationality implies optimality, but that does not necessarily mean that no mistakes are made in the conduct of monetary policy. If the objective function were wrongly specified, then the optimal policy would be inappropriate.

A general objective function includes the ultimate targets of inflation (p), growth (Y), or unemployment, and the current account of the balance of payments (CB), in deviation from their target values; the intermediate targets of the money supply (broad or narrow, M), and the exchange rate (e); and the long-term constraints of budget deficit, which determines the new supply of bonds (ΔB), and government debt as a percentage of GDP (D). The target value of growth is usually assumed to be the rate of growth of potential output ($\bar{Y}$), as it is generally regarded that monetary policy cannot affect that rate, but fluctuations around it. We can therefore write:

$$r^e = r\,[(Y - \bar{Y}),\ p,\ CB,\ e,\ M,\ \Delta B,\ D] \qquad (4)$$

If the economy grows faster than potential output, or inflation is higher than its target, or the current account deficit widens, or the money supply growth exceeds its target, or the exchange rate falls short of its target, or the budget deficit widens, or, finally, the size of government debt as percent of nominal GDP exceeds its target, then investors expect the central bank to tighten monetary policy. It is obvious that if any of these variables is not a central bank target, then changes in this variable do not alter investors' expectations on the likely conduct of monetary policy. Equation 4 is the investors' perception of the central bank's future actions. Clearly, therefore, each investor would have different expectations of what the central bank would do because, first, they are not sure of the information set that the central bank takes into account in formulating its policy; secondly, of the precise form of the central bank objective function; and thirdly, of the bank's model that describes the way monetary policy affects its targets. This diversity of expectations is the single most important explanation of the volatility of the bond market.

Investors must look at the entire wage–price nexus in order to form expectations of inflation. It is, therefore, assumed that the relationships, described in chapter 4, form the basis of expected inflation. Although this is a set of 11 equations, it can be written in a succinct way as follows:

$$p^e = p\,[(Y - \bar{Y}),\, p_{t-i}\,,\, COM,\, e,\, SMP,\, SFP] \tag{5}$$

The implicit assumption made here is that investors' expectations of inflation are rational. Expected inflation depends on the extent of the slack or overheating in the economy, $(Y - \bar{Y})$, which affects profit margins; past inflation, p_{t-i}, which serves as an indication of future inflation in some phases of the business cycle; commodity prices, COM, and the exchange rate, e, which are both indicators of imported inflation; and, finally, the stance of monetary and fiscal policy, SMP and SFP, respectively. The stance of monetary policy reflects the central bank's vigilance in ensuring that future inflation will remain tamed. The significance of this term can be seen as follows. Assume that a central bank is 'wet' with respect to inflation targeting, assigning a low priority to it and a large priority in promoting growth and reducing unemployment. This means that the central bank is prepared to accommodate some inflation by not raising interest rates. Assume that investors correctly anticipate through equation (5) such a central bank action on r^e. However, the bond yield will still rise in spite of no expectations of monetary tightening because the accommodating stance of monetary policy will raise the inflation premium, p^e.

It does not necessarily follow that investors need to concentrate on all these indicators, at any point in time, in forming expectations of inflation. For example, once the economy exceeds potential output growth and any previous slack in capacity has been eliminated, actual inflation is not a reliable indicator of future inflation. Forward-looking investors form expectations of inflation through the output gap (that is, the difference between actual and potential growth). Once the economy slows down, because of monetary tightening, investors form expectations of inflation by observing actual inflation, since inflation will continue to rise for some time after the economy peaked, because of inertia. Actual inflation usually peaks in the neighbourhood of the recession. Hence, once the economy is in recession, actual inflation is not a good gauge of expected inflation. The output gap is again a forward-looking measure of expected inflation. Finally, during the recovery phase actual inflation is a better proxy for expected inflation. If the economy is in recession a rise in imported inflation through either an increase in commodity prices or a depreciation of the exchange rate is unlikely to lead to higher inflation, as such cost increases are likely to be absorbed into profit margins. Thus, in recessions commodity prices and the exchange rate are not important indicators of expected inflation. However, these factors become important once the economy returns or exceeds potential output.

Investors judge the stance of monetary policy by looking at a number of factors. A high or rising real interest rate, $r - p^e$, is an indication of tight monetary policy. Comparing the current real interest rate with its average value over similar business cycles can make a crude judgement. The qualification is important because comparing the behaviour of say the 1970s and the 1980s that were dominated by the oil shocks is of no use in forecasting what the neutral stance of monetary policy ought to be in the 1990s or in the twenty-first century. A more accurate judgement of the stance of monetary policy involves a comparison of the current real interest rate with the level that is consistent with the optimisation of the central bank's objective function. The second indicator of the stance of monetary policy is the shape of the yield curve. This actually reflects investors' perceptions of the stance of monetary policy, but is a good measure because central bankers decide on their own policy actions by looking at their impact on the markets. A steep yield curve is a reflection that monetary policy is easy and that a recovery is on the way, while a flat or inverted yield curve means that monetary policy is tight and that the economy would decelerate.

The money supply used to be an indicator of the stance of monetary policy, but its importance has diminished nowadays in many countries, as it has become an unreliable indicator at the turning points of the economy since it involves large portfolio shifts. Finally, rising commodity prices and a falling exchange rate are an indication that monetary policy is easy and vice versa. We can, therefore, summarise the stance of monetary policy as:

$$SMP = m \: [(r - p^e \:), R - r, COM, M, e] \qquad (6)$$

Finally, investors form expectations of the stance of fiscal policy by observing changes in the structural or cyclically adjusted budget deficit, ΔBS^s. That is,

$$SFP = f \: (\Delta BS^s) \qquad (7)$$

The set of equations (1)–(7) forms the basis of the bond market model. In the empirical version of the model some of these variables are statistically unimportant. Thus, the key variables that shape developments in the bond market in the long run can be summarised in the following functional form:

$$R = R(r, \quad p, \quad OG, \quad e, \quad oil, \quad GS, \quad ROW) \qquad (8)$$
$$\quad\;\; (+) \;\; (+) \;\;\; (+) \;\;\; (+) \;\;\; (+) \;\;\; (-) \;\;\; (-)$$

where R = 2-, 5-, 10- and 30-year yield, r = the Fed funds rate, p = the year-on-year core CPI inflation, OG = output gap, e = the Fed trade weighted index of major currencies, oil = the year-on-year rate of change of the price of oil, measured by the West Texas Intermediate (WTI) index, GS = Federal budget surplus, and ROW = holdings of US Treasuries by the rest of the world. With the exception of GS and ROW all signs are positive, meaning that an increase in any one of these variables, namely the Fed funds rate, core inflation, output gap, exchange rate and oil, leads to higher bond yields. On the other hand, an increase in the budget surplus or a reduction in the deficit and higher foreign demand for US Treasuries lead to lower bond yields.

This model is next used to explain the pattern of bond yields and the yield curve in the course of the business cycle. In section 6 this model is used to value equities and infer the long-term risks to financial markets.

3   The bond market and the yield curve in the course of the business cycle

The above analysis suggests that two conditions must be met for a sustained rally in the bond market. First, there must be expectations of monetary easing; and, second, expected (and actual) inflation should be on a downward trend. Conversely, for a bear market, investors should expect monetary tightening and expected (and actual) inflation should be on an uptrend. These principles clarify the expected pattern of the bond market in the course of the business cycle. The pattern of the yield curve emerges by the observation that yields with a short term to maturity, like the 2-year, are influenced more by the Fed funds rate and, to a lesser extent, by the risk premia.[1] By contrast, the longer one moves on the maturity spectrum, like the 10-year, the smaller the influence of the Fed funds rate and the higher the importance of the risk premia. As explained in chapter 4, the proper conduct of monetary policy in the course of the business cycle should be systematic. The Fed funds

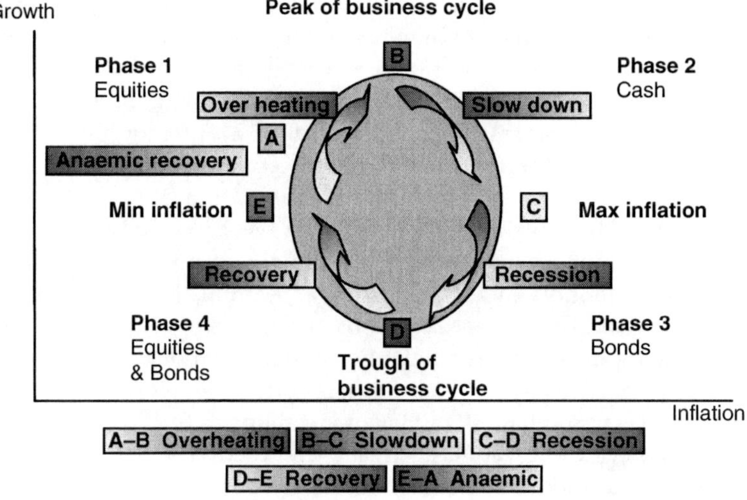

Figure 11.1   Asset-led business cycle

rate should rise the moment inflation bottoms – even if there is spare capacity in the economy. The rate hikes reflect not monetary tightening, but the removal of the accommodation bias that was put in place in the previous recession. Thus, even if the recovery is anaemic, the Fed should lift rates to return to a neutral monetary policy stance the moment inflation bottoms out. In terms of Figure 11.1 as we move from E to A, namely in phase (V), the Fed funds rate should be on the increase according to the proper conduct of monetary policy. Thus, point E should mark the bottom of bond yields. In phase (V) all yields are rising, but with the 10-year climbing faster than the 2-year. Hence, the yield curve in steepening in phase (V), as the market adjustment is faster than that of the Fed. The spread between the 2-year the Fed funds rate is also increasing.

At some point in time in the cycle, even with a long delay, the recovery will become sustainable and growth will exceed potential. With time this buoyant growth will eliminate any excess capacity and the economy will become overheated, entering phase (I) in terms of Figure 11.1. As we move from A to B the Fed funds rate should continue to move up, but for a different reason. The Fed is now tightening monetary policy to cap an acceleration of inflation. The overheating creates expectations of monetary tightening and of even higher inflation in the future. Hence, all yields are rising with the 10-year rising faster than the 2-year. As a result, the yield curve reaches the steepest point in the cycle in phase (I) and most likely near point B. The economy will respond, albeit with a lag, to the progressive tightening of monetary policy, thereby entering the slow-down phase (II). As we move from B to C the yield curve becomes flatter and ultimately inverted with the 2-year yield climbing up whereas the 10-year falls. For reasons explained in chapter 4, inflation peaks in the neighbourhood of the recession. A tough central bank perseveres with tight monetary policy until inflation is beaten, thus at point C. In the final stage of the slowdown phase (II) even the 2-year Fed funds spread becomes negative, as expectations of an imminent monetary easing are priced in at the short end of the maturity spectrum. The general pattern is now obvious. The 10-year Fed funds rate spread is the first to capture the changing expectations about the conduct of monetary policy and inflation, while the 2-year Fed funds rate spread follows with a lag.

In the recession (phase III) all yields are falling as the Fed cuts interest rates aggressively and very fast. In fact, the reaction of the Fed is faster, the tighter was monetary policy in the slowdown phase. In theory, the 10-year is falling faster than the 2-year, making the yield curve even more inverted. But in practice, especially in the course of the past ten years, the reaction of bond markets has become faster. The 10-year is pricing in the recession in the slowdown phase and this explains an early inversion of the yield curve. As a result, in the recession it is mainly the 2-year that is falling very fast ahead of the Fed funds rate.

In the recovery phase (IV) inflation continues to fall and monetary policy is loosened. Hence, all yields are falling but with the 2-year falling faster than the 10-year. Accordingly, the yield curve is flattening. But in practice, the flattening takes place with the 10-year yield rising and the 2-year remaining flat.

4   The outlook for the bond market and long-term risks

The bond market holds the key not only to the equity market, but also to the economy as a whole. The imbalances in the private sector are likely to become dormant as the economy recovers. However, if long-term interest rates were to rise to critical levels, then these imbalances would reawaken and threaten not only the sustainability of the recovery, but also perhaps triggering another recession. The really interesting question then is the extent to which, and how fast, bond yields rise in the years ahead.

The 10-year bond yield peaked at the beginning of 2000 at 6.75 per-cent and fell for the following three and a half years, hitting a low of 3.12 percent in mid-2003. The rally in the bond market was caused by the bursting of the internet bubble and the ensued recession for the economy as a whole along with the double-dip recession for the industrial sector that lasted until the spring of 2003. Hence, the bond market correctly discounted the early 2000s downturn and the false dawns in the first few years of the new millennium. In spite of large volatility bond yields assumed a mild upward trend that lasted for a four-year period from mid-2003 to mid-2007, namely throughout the upswing of the business cycle. The 10-year yield climbed from a low of 3.10 percent to 5.30 percent in this period, namely 220 basis points (bps).

The eruption of the credit crisis in the summer of 2007 sparked a rally in the bond market, which gathered steam as the recession deepened and equities slumped. Rising risk aversion led to a flight to quality with an unprecedented demand for the safe haven US Treasuries. The ten-year yield dropped from 5.30 percent in mid-2007 to nearly 2.00 percent at the end of 2008. However, bond yields rose relentlessly in the first half of 2009 with the 10-year yield, climbing 200 bps to 4.00 percent. Bond yields abated somewhat since then with the 10-year hovering around 3.5 percent as the Fed embarked on its $300 billion buying programme of US Treasuries and made clear that it is in no hurry to lift rates. The dilemma at this juncture is similar to that in 2003, namely how much and how fast would bond yields rise in the upswing of the cycle. The initial reaction of the bond market to a forthcoming recovery is a sharp increase in bond yields. In the current cycle the 10-year rose 200 bps from 2.00 percent to 4.00 percent, whereas in 2003 they rose 150 bps from 3.10 percent to 4.60 percent. In the current cycle the bond market discounted the recovery six months ahead, whereas in 2003 the reaction was simultaneous with the recovery. This was odd as the bond market is traditionally a discounting mechanism. On this occasion, though, this odd pattern was caused by the Greenspan (2003a) statements in the spring of 2003; namely that the Fed would resort to direct buying of US Treasuries to cap any upward pressure on long-term interest rates. In fact, these statements induced a rally with the 10-year yield falling from 3.90 percent to 3.10 percent between March and June 2003 despite evidence of economic recovery. But the plan did not materialise and Greenspan (2003b), in his semi-annual testimony to Congress in July 2003, made clear that the Fed would not proceed with purchases of US Treasuries. This triggered not only a reversal of the spring rally, but the dramatic increase of 150 bps.

There are currently two polar views on the bond market exactly as it was in 2003. According to the first view the bond market is undervalued, as long-term interest rates are still too high, given that the Fed funds rate is only 0.25 percent. In other words, the yield curve is too steep and is unlikely to become steeper in the course of 2009–10. Figure 11.2 provides support for this hypothesis. The spread between the 10-year yield and

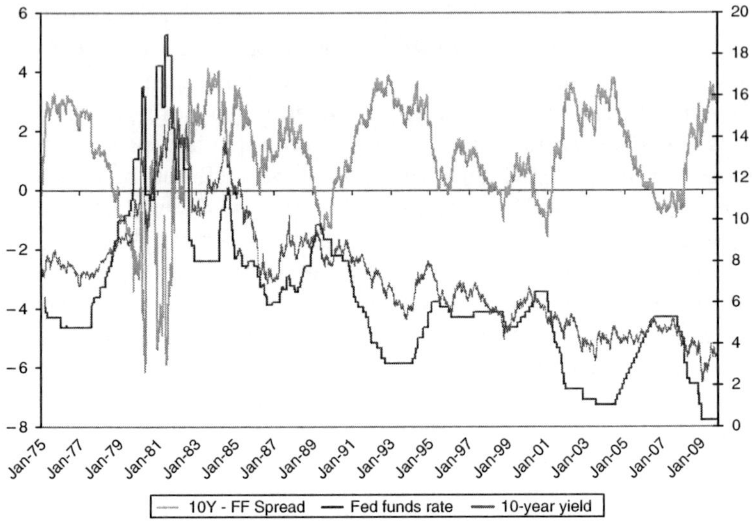

Figure 11.2   10-year Fed funds yield curve

the Fed funds rate has always reached 3.3–4.2 percent at the beginning of a typical recovery. At the beginning of the current recovery the spread hit 3.5 percent, in line with other business cycles and exactly equal to that of the 2003 recovery. In a typical cycle, once the recovery is under way the yield curve flattens, but this may be caused either by short-term interest rates rising faster than long-term ones, or by a rise of short-term rates and a fall in long-term ones, if the bond market had overestimated the forthcoming degree of monetary tightening. If the Fed tightening was delayed until the end of 2010 and was modest, then the 10-year yield would not rise noticeably in the course of 2010 and may even fall, as it has already discounted the forthcoming monetary tightening – in fact, this is the reason for being undervalued, according to this view.

According to the second view the bond market is currently extremely overvalued, as long-term interest rates are very low, given the large swelling of the budget deficit since the onset of the credit crisis and the impact of quantitative easing. Advocates of this view point to the dual system of fixed and flexible exchange rates of the US with its main trading partners. With those partners with which the US has a freely floating exchange rate, like the euro area, the US benefits from the depreciation of the dollar, as it helps the economy to recover through increased exports. With those partners that the US has a fixed exchange rate system or dirty floating, meaning that there is a lot of foreign exchange intervention, such as China, the US benefits as these partners help the US to finance its budget deficit. This makes fiscal policy more effective in stimulating domestic demand in the US. Hence, the dual foreign exchange rate system is the best of all possible worlds for the US.

Table 11.1 shows the arithmetic of this argument. The Federal debt hit bottom in the middle of the recession in the second quarter of 2001. Not only did the debt increase in the recession of 2001 because of the weakness of the economy that swells the budget deficit due to the operation of automatic stabilisers, but in the upswing of the cycle, too, because of discretionary easy fiscal policy in the form of tax cuts, depreciation incentives to the corporate sector and increased defence spending because of the war on terror. Just before the onset of the credit crisis the Federal debt hit more than 35 percent of GDP, up around 4 percent from the low in 2001. The credit crisis and the deep and protracted recession swelled the federal debt to more than 50 percent of GDP, namely by 15 percent during this period. Japan was the single most important buyer of US Treasuries, but the demand has decreased by 10 percent of the total since 2001 and 7 percent during the crisis, accounting now for just one-fifth. Some of that drop in demand from Japan has been offset by China, whose demand has increased by 15 percent of the total since 2001, accounting now for more than one-fifth of the total, and making China the single most important buyer of US Treasuries. But when the demand of both Japan and China is put together the situation is still worrisome. During the crisis the combined demand for US debt has decreased by 6 percent. But some of that drop in demand by Japan and China is offset by rising demand from the rest of the world. In spite of soaring Federal debt, the overseas sector has absorbed an increasing proportion of the total. Even during the credit crisis the overseas sector has absorbed an extra 4 percent; it now absorbs half of the total. Although this appeases the problem, the risk rises as the US depends increasingly on foreign demand, which might dry up at any point in time.

This shows the vulnerability of the US bond market, as it depends on overseas demand and particularly that of Japan and China, which may dry up at some point in time. The appetite of non-US residents to absorb US paper and, therefore, the willingness to finance the US budget deficit depends partly on the dollar, as a large depreciation may more than offset the benefits of holding these assets in the case of Japan or make them less attractive to rival bonds, such as the euro area, in the case of China. Japan's demand for US debt as a proportion of its foreign exchange reserves was halved between 1998 and the middle of the credit crisis in mid-2008 to less than 60 percent. This shows a tremendous

Table 11.1 Federal debt and its finance

	Federal Govt Debt	Federal Govt Debt	Foreign Holdings of US Treasuries	Japan: Holdings of US Treasuries	Japan: Holdings of US Treasuries	China: Holdings of US Treasuries	China: Holdings of US Treasuries	Japan & China Holdings of US Treasuries	Japan & China Holdings of US Treasuries
	billion dollars	% of GDP	% of Total	% of Foreign Total	% of Foreign Reserves	% of Foreign Total	% of Foreign Reserves	% of Foreign Total	as % of Fed Debt
Minimum Govt Debt (Jun 2001)	3,251	31.6	31	31	79	7	40	38	11
Credit Crisis Onset (Jun 2007)	4,927	35.2	45	28	66	22	36	50	22
Latest Month (Jun 09)	7,165	50.6	49	21	71	23	36	44	21
Difference from credit crisis	2,238	15.4	4	–7	5	1	1	–6	–2

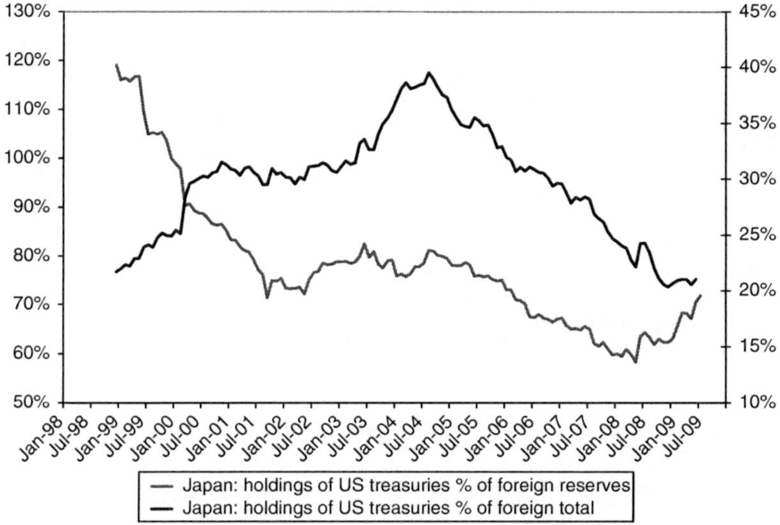

Figure 11.3   Japan: holdings of US Treasuries

diversification of reserves away from US Treasuries. Therefore, Japan's appetite for US debt has diminished significantly. Notwithstanding this long-term downtrend the picture has improved since then, as the proportion of reserves allocated to the US debt has increased from 58 percent to 72 percent (see Figure 11.3). The appetite of China for US debt has remained unchanged. The proportion of reserves allocated to US Treasuries has oscillated around a constant, which is one-third of the total debt (see Figure 11.4).

These arguments, though, neither support nor reject the hypothesis that the US bond market is overvalued. Foreign demand for US Treasuries as a percentage of the Federal debt has increased by 4 percent during the crisis. Had the 4 percent increase not been met by foreign demand, the US long-term interest rates may have been higher. If they were, then the US bond market should be declared overvalued. We have tested this hypothesis using the K-Model of the US bond market, where the proportion of US Treasuries held by the rest of the world is an important determinant. The coefficient is negative and statistically significant, implying that the lower these holdings are, the higher the US 10-year Treasury yield. In fact, the K-Model suggests that a drop in foreign demand of the order of 10 percent of the total leads to a 20 bps rise in the 10-year yield instantaneously which widens to nearly 100 bps after 16 months.[2] A 4 percent drop in demand, which is precisely by

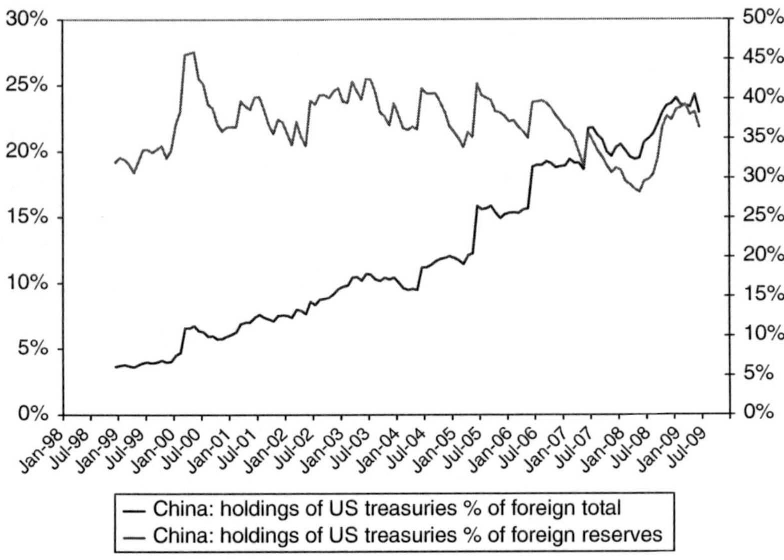

Figure 11.4   China: holdings of US Treasuries

how much foreign demand increased during the crisis, would lift the 10-year yield by 8 bps instantaneously and by 38 bps in 16 months. This illustrates the risk of the US bond market to the foreign appetite for US debt. If foreigners suffer losses on their holdings of US debt because of a drop in the dollar, then US bond yields would increase significantly.

Although a drop in foreign demand is one risk factor that may push bond yields higher in the future, there is yet another factor that will push yields up. This is the effect of quantitative easing, which amounts to Fed purchases of the tune of $300 billion. This extra demand by the Fed has pushed yields artificially lower. According to the Fed (Bernanke, 2009), this programme will come to an end in the spring of 2010. The Fed purchases of US Treasuries amounts to just over 4 percent of the total. Thus, the end of the programme will lead to 40 bps higher 10-year yield within 12 months of its removal.

The K-Model suggests that for the aforementioned reasons the bond market is overvalued. As of August 2009 the degree of overvaluation from a long-term perspective is just 15 bps. But in the months ahead, as the 10-year rallies the degree of overvaluation will soar to 120 bps. However, the overvaluation will be corrected in the course of 2010 to just 10 bps by mid-2010 (see Figure 11.5).

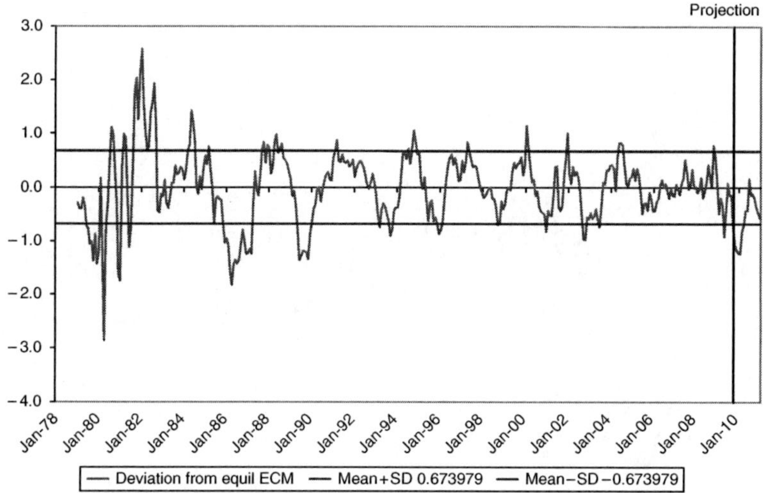

Figure 11.5   Long-run valuation of 10-year yield

The 10-year yield is expected to rally in the last few months of 2009, as it has already discounted the forthcoming recovery. In a typical recovery the 10-year rallies after the initial surge because under rational expectations there is overshooting of the long-run equilibrium. The rally is likely to be intensified until the end of the year because the removal of the quantitative easing has been postponed until the spring of 2010 and the Fed has committed in exhausting the purchase of the original plan of $300 billion. However, in the course of 2010 the 10-year is likely to rise to nearly 4.00–5.00 percent before abating in the second half (see Figure 11.6).

There are both upside and downside risks to this mainline scenario. On the downside, bond yields may rise more sharply than in the main scenario, if the dollar depreciation gathered steam that triggered a loss in the appetite of foreigners to hold US Treasuries. The same effect would materialise if the Obama Administration came up with another fiscal package in January 2010 to resuscitate a frail economic recovery. On the upside, bond yields might fail to rise, if the Fed expanded the quantitative easing programme beyond next spring. The same effect might happen, if the balance sheet adjustment of the banking sector made very little progress in the next 12 months. Banks will resort with more vigour to buying US Treasuries, provided the Fed kept the Fed funds rate at 0.25 percent. The steepness of the yield curve might offer the only avenue to the banks in repairing their impaired balance sheet.

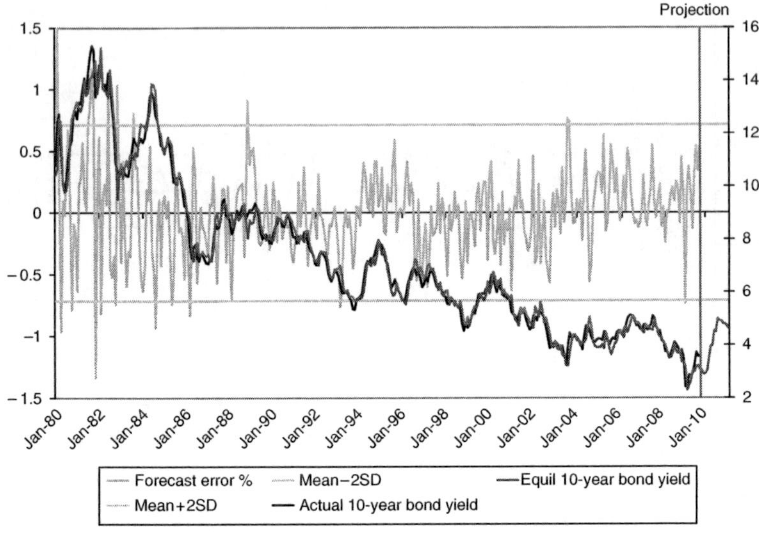

Figure 11.6   Short-run equilibrium of US 10-year yield

5   Theoretical underpinnings of the equity market and valuation

It can be shown (Campbell 1991) that the (log) stock price, P_t, can be expressed as the product of a constant, C, times the discounted present value of all future stock dividends [$DPV(d)$], less the discounted present value of all future risk premia [$DPV(pr)$]. This is simply a generalisation of Gordon's (1962) static growth model, but in a dynamic context.

$$P_t = C + DPV(d) - DPV(pr) \tag{9}$$

Equation (9) is not a theory of equity pricing, but an identity. In the K-Model it is turned into a theory by specifying how expectations of the future stream of dividends and risk premia are formed. Equities are assumed to be close substitutes to both bonds and money. The gross substitutability assumption implies that the demand for equities is a positive function of their own return, but a negative function of the return of the gross substitutes (Brainard and Tobin, 1968). Equities are regarded as the riskiest of the three assets, as they have the highest volatility. Despite this drawback they are still included in the investor's portfolio as they offer the highest return. The risk premium is the excess of the equity return over the return of the gross substitutes, as it reflects the amount by which an investor would have to be compensated to assume the risk of equities and include them in the portfolio. The equity risk premium is assumed to be a function of four variables. First, the excess equity return, *EER*, which is defined as the inverse of the *P/E*-ratio less the real bond yield on sovereign debt, $R - p^e$. An increase in corporate earnings raises the excess equity return, lowers the equity risk premium and, therefore, raises the price of equities, other things being equal. An increase in the *P/E*-ratio lowers the excess equity return, raises the equity risk premium and, therefore, lowers equity prices. Second, the equity risk premium depends on the yield gap, which is defined as the bond yield on sovereign debt less the dividend yield, $R - d$. An increase in the dividend yield, d, lowers the yield gap and the equity risk premium and, therefore, raises equity prices, *ceteris paribus*. Third, the equity risk premium depends on credit risk, which is defined as the excess of corporate bond yields over corresponding sovereign debt, $R_c - R$. A widening of the spread between corporate and sovereign bond yields (i.e. an increase in credit risk) raises the equity risk premium and, therefore, lowers equity prices, *ceteris paribus*. Fourth, the equity risk premium depends on the short-term real interest rate, $r - p^e$. A higher real interest rate increases the equity risk premium and, therefore, lowers equity prices, *ceteris paribus*. We can therefore summarise the relationship of the equity risk premium as follows:

$$\mathrm{DPV(pr)} = p\,[(\mathrm{EER}, (R - d), (R_c - R), (r - p^e)] \tag{10}$$

The relationship of the equity to the bond market is obvious since the bond yield affects the equity risk premium. An increase in bond yield, first, lowers the excess equity return, raises the equity risk premium and, therefore, lowers equity prices. It also increases the yield gap, raises the equity risk premium and lowers equity prices. However, the impact effect of an increase in the bond yield of sovereign debt is to reduce credit risk, which lowers the equity risk premium and, therefore, raises equity prices. This perverse effect is more than offset by the other two channels, but, moreover, it lasts only for a while. As yields on sovereign debt rise, risk-averse investors replace corporate bonds with government bonds, thereby raising again credit risk and intensifying the effect of the other two channels. Since the bond market plays such a crucial role in determining the equity risk premium it is endogenous to the equity model. Investors form expectations about future corporate earnings (or dividends) by extrapolating the effects of currently available economic fundamentals on the future course of earnings. Most of these economic fundamentals refer to macro developments and their impact on either costs or profits. Obviously, any variable that increases the discounted present value of future earnings raises equity prices.

The most important variable is the growth rate of the economy, or, more precisely, its deviation from potential output $(Y - \bar{Y})$. A positive output gap implies a booming economy that raises corporate profits through higher volume of sales, higher profit margins and increased pricing power. The K-Profits Model analysed in chapter 5 is crucial in determining the discounted present value of the future stream of corporate earnings and in the analysis that follows is endogenous to the equity market. The second variable that affects the discounted present value of future corporate earnings is the exchange rate, e. A lower dollar affects earnings through two channels. First, it makes US exports more competitive and imports dearer. This increases corporate earnings both from abroad and from the domestic market, as there is a substitution effect between foreign and domestic demand. Secondly, a lower dollar increases the value of consolidated balance sheet profits by boosting those that are generated by US affiliates operating abroad. The third variable that affects the discounted present value of future corporate earnings is wages and prices. The entire wage–price sector analysed in chapter 4 is endogenous to the equity model, as it affects either the cost of production or the pricing power of companies. The fourth variable is overall liquidity in the economy. An increase in the money supply (broad definition) enhances gearing that pushes equity prices up. Finally, investors look at company-specific variables or variables that affect the overall company environment, such as the governance crisis, in determining future corporate profitability, Z. We can, therefore, summarise the relationship of the discounted present value of future earnings as:

$$DPV(d) = d\ [(Y - \bar{Y}), e, M, C, Z] \tag{11}$$

The five variables included in Equation (11) comprise the information set of economic fundamentals that investors look at to work out the implications for future earnings. However, what is still missing for a complete theory of equity pricing is the mechanism that investors use in extrapolating the impact of this information on future profits. It is assumed that investors are forward-looking and, therefore, the mechanism they use is a model of the economy that relates current values of policy and other exogenous variables to future values of economic fundamentals. Four variables are important in the model of the economy: fiscal and monetary policy, developments in the world economy and the market perception for the overall effect of the other three factors. Fiscal policy is measured by changes in the structural or cyclically adjusted budget deficit (ΔBS^e). The effect of monetary policy is measured by the impact of the real short-term interest rate ($r - p^e$) on the main macro variables, like GDP, consumption and investment. World trade (*WT*), captures developments in the world economy. Finally, the yield curve captures the market perception of the impact of policy and world trade on the economy. We can summarise the model of the economy as:

$$Y = Y\,[(r - p^e),\ \Delta BS^e,\ WT,\ (R - r)] \tag{12}$$

Changes in the current stance of fiscal or monetary policy would affect the economy for the next two years. If investors have a longer horizon or they want to compute the effects of policy over a longer period they must form expectations of future policy. In the case of monetary policy, which is subject to more swings than fiscal policy, the investors' mechanism for forming expectations is the one described above in the bond model (see equation 4). Hence, both the bond and the equity markets are influenced by the same mechanism.

Unfortunately, the rationality assumption cannot be invoked for fiscal policy and, therefore, there are no rules that can be used in forecasting it in the short run. The only fiscal rule that can be used is for the long run. Such a rule is based on fiscal rectitude and entails that the budget is balanced in the course of the business cycle. However, as the experience of the euro area shows, where such fiscal rectitude was agreed in the Maastricht Treaty, governments are prepared to renege on it. Even worse, the process of abandoning or modifying any fiscal rectitude rule is long and painful and when finally it is applied it might turn out to be pro-cyclical (which means destabilising the cycle) rather than counter-cyclical (which means stabilising it). The experience of the euro area shows that fiscal policy turned easy in 2004, which coincided with the upswing of the cycle making the policy pro-cyclical. World trade, on the other hand, can be modelled, as developments in the world economy would depend on the policy mix (fiscal and monetary) of the euro area and Japan and, of course, the US.

The system of equations (9)–(12) forms the basis of the equity model. Monetary policy has a powerful role in equity prices, not only because the short-term interest rate affects the substitution effect between equities and money in the portfolio allocation, but also because it affects the main activity variables, like GDP, consumption and investment, as well as wages and prices.

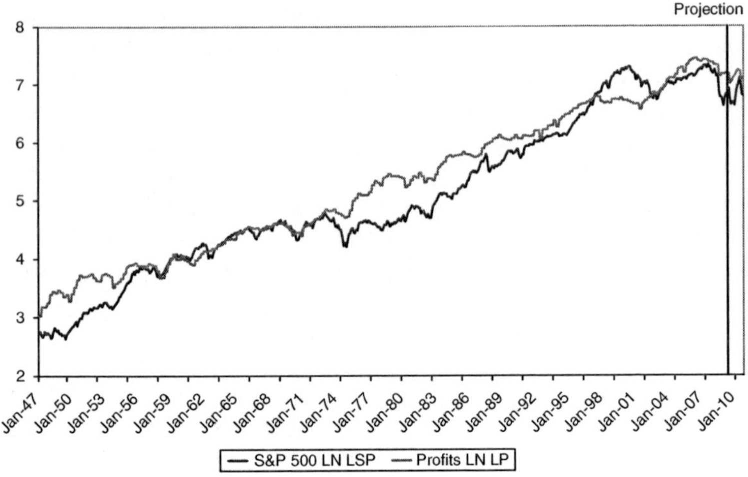

Figure 11.7   S&P and profits in logs

In the empirical version of the K-Model real equity prices, *P*, bear the following relationship with their determinants:

$$P = P \,(\text{PR, RYC, CRP}) \tag{13}$$

where PR = real corporate profits, RYC = the real yield curve and CRP = the composite equity risk premium that consists of the excess equity return over bonds and cash. The most important long-term determinant of equities is corporate profits (see Figure 11.7). In the long run equities advance as much as profits. In equation (13) the coefficient of profits is not statistically different from unity. But in the short run the two might deviate substantially. Thus, in the aftermath of the Second World War equities were lower than profits. From the second half of the 1950s to the first oil crisis equities moved in tandem with profits. With the exception of the last phase of the internet bubble, profits outperformed equities in the longest bull market from 1982 to 2000. Since the recovery of the early 2000s recession profits have been outstripping equities.

Although the relationship of equities and profits is very strong in the long run, it would be wrong to draw inferences about market valuation from these two variables alone, as the equity risk premium and the market perception of the impact of policy and world trade on the economy are also important determinants of equities. Figure 11.8 shows the deviation from the long-run equilibrium implicit in equation (13). It is now

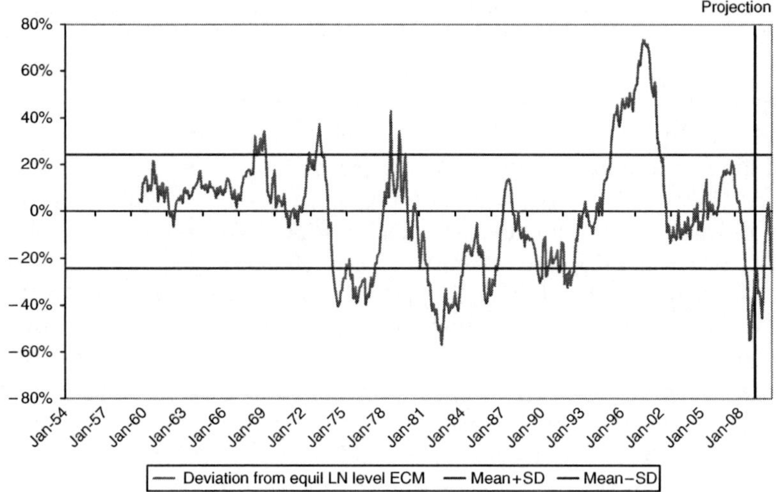

Figure 11.8   Long-term valuation of equities

clear that the internet euphoria became a bubble from 1998 onwards. The slump of equities in the current credit crisis triggered the same degree of undervaluation as in the early 1980s when profits were strong as the economy was recovering, but fear of another dramatic tightening by the Fed under Paul Volcker caused a huge selling of shares. The graph also shows that in late 2007, when shares were at their peak, the market was only 22 percent overvalued in line with other historical periods. This supports our prediction in the First Edition of this book (Arestis and Karakitsos, 2004) that the bursting of the housing market would take down equities, too.

6   The equity market in the course of the business cycle

The predominant role of profits in the equity market suggests that the two are moving in tandem in the business cycle. As chapter 5 shows, profits are pro-cyclical; they rise in the upswing of the cycle and fall in the downswing. This suggests that a sustained rally in equities takes place in the recovery and the overheating phases of the business cycle, while a bear market lasts in the slowdown and recession phases. In terms of Figure 11.1 the equity market rally starts at D, the trough of the business cycle, and ends at B, the peak of the cycle. From B to D there is a bear market. Although profits growth is a leading indicator of the official definition of the peak of the business cycle, it is a coincident indicator of the rate of growth of GDP. This supports the interpretation that equities peak at B and bottom at D, which refer to the rate of growth rather than the level of GDP. The peak of the equity market at B and the subsequent fall take the form of either a crash, namely a huge drop in a short period of time, or a more gradual decline over a period of time.

As the equity market is a discounting mechanism of future events, its downfall reflects an attempt to price in the impact of the forthcoming recession on corporate profitability. Under perfect foresight the discounting is accurate and the fall takes the form of a crash. In this case, the equity market will move sideways from B to D as it responds to events that follow a white noise process. However, in the real world the fall of equities, although abrupt at certain points in time, will be spread in the slowdown phase of the business cycle, if not also in the recession. At its bottom the equity market should accurately price in the length and the depth of the recession and its impact on profits, although it may overshoot. If initial estimates of point D are revised downwards, then the equity market will carry on hitting new lows in the slowdown and the recession phases of the business cycle. However, as we approach point D, the equity market forecast error is reduced and the forward-looking attitude of investors will start pricing in the recovery of the economy and profits. Hence, the bottom of equities should occur prior to point D. Experience shows that equity markets lead the economy by around three to six months.

The real yield curve and the bond market play an important role in the leading indicator property of the equity market. The bond market consists of more sophisticated investors than the equity market, as these are mainly institutional investors, whereas retail investors who are less sophisticated form a significant portion of the equity market. This implies that a steepening of the yield curve will precede the trough of the equity market, thereby helping the equity market to bottom and begin to recover. But the yield curve does not offer such a timely lead of the peak of the equity market at point B. The flattening of the yield curve begins much earlier in the cycle to provide a warning of the peak of shares. Nonetheless, the yield curve and the bond market play a critical role in assessing the risk of equities. In the recovery phase, namely from D to E, the yield curve remains steep relative to the norm, and this implies that the risk of equities is low. Bond yields are falling and the central bank cuts interest rates. Accordingly, the equity risk premium is reduced in the recovery phase. Hence not only do equities rally in the recovery phase, but they also carry a small risk. The best performance of equities occurs in the first year of the recovery as profits soar because of improving profit margins. However, in the second year of the recovery there is some profit fatigue and shares retreat or move sideways. But this is just a consolidation phase and with time equities resume their uptrend. In the overheating phase equities advance as the volume of sales becomes buoyant. During this phase, which may be long, equities will deliver a higher return than in the entire recovery phase. However, the risk of equities is on the increase throughout the overheating phase as bond yields rise and the yield curve becomes progressively flatter and finally inverted.

To summarise, equities begin to rally in the neighbourhood of the trough of the business cycle and most of the time with a three- to six-month lead. In the first year of the recovery the equity market produces a stunning return, which declines somewhat in the second year. Equities carry a small risk in the recovery phase. The return of equities in the overheating phase exceeds that in the recovery phase, but the risk of equities is progressively increased as we move to point B, in Figure 11.1. At this point shares peak and a bear market begins that would last up to point D.

The analysis of the bond and equity markets in the course of the business cycle has some important implications for portfolio management. Bonds rally in the recession and the recovery, while the bear market lasts in the overheating and slowdown phases. Equities, on the other hand, rally in the recovery and in the overheating phases. The bear market lasts in the slowdown phase and in the recession. Hence, in each phase of the business cycle there is a preferred asset class that is likely to outperform. Accordingly, it is this asset class that should be overweighted in the portfolio. In the recession bonds is the preferred asset class. In the recovery both bonds and equities are performing well and both should be overweighted in the portfolio at the expense of cash. In the overheating phase the preferred asset class is equities, while in the slowdown cash is the king, as both bonds and equities are in a bear market.

The risk of bonds is minimal in the recession. Bonds at the long end of the maturity spectrum will be the first to rally and the highest return occurs near the peak of inflation, point C, in Figure 11.1. The rally might begin even before point C is hit. In fact, the more credible is the central bank in its anti-inflation policy, the earlier the starting point of the rally in long duration bonds. The further one moves away from C, the higher should be the weight on bonds with shorter duration. As we approach the minimum inflation rate in the cycle, point E, the risk on bonds is increasing and the portfolio weight should be reduced, even as the weight is shifting towards short duration bonds. In the recovery phase equities carry minimal risk. Hence, as the recovery matures equities should progressively replace bonds in the portfolio. In the overheating phase the risk on equities is increasing. Although one would be tempted to reduce the equity exposure as the overheating persists, this is likely to frustrate the investors of the fund because the highest returns occur near point B. But of course point B will be hit unexpectedly and, therefore, many investors would be caught with an excessive exposure in equities.

The length of the overheating phase depends on the number of soft landings that the central bank can engineer. Every soft landing adds around two years to the overheating phase. The chances of a soft landing are high when inflation is subdued, but there is overheating in the economy. In this situation the tightening by the central bank is proactive and pre-emptive and is likely to be reversed when the economy slows. But if the overheating is causing inflation to accelerate then the tightening of the central bank would be aggressive and will not be reversed when the economy slows. In fact, the monetary tightening will persist throughout the slowdown phase. Hence, the best indicator of when to get out of equities is inflation and, in particular, unit labour cost, which is a leading indicator.

7   The outlook for the equity market and long-term risks

With the bursting of the internet bubble shares entered into a long-term bear market. In spite of the shallowness and the short duration of the early 2000s recession and the subsequent surge of profits in the first year of the recovery, the advance of equities in the following four years was a prolonged bear market rally. The recovery of the economy rested on the buoyancy of the consumer during the ballooning of the housing bubble. The economy lacked the foundations for a new long-lasting business cycle. The moment long-term interest rates rose to critical levels the housing market collapsed, triggering huge losses to financial institutions. These losses toppled the equity market, although the profits of non-financial companies remained resilient in the first phase of the recession. However, as the credit crisis deepened and the economy fell off the cliff the profits of non-financial companies were deeply hurt and the equity market went into a free fall. Figure 11.9 illustrates the point that we are in a long-term bear market by showing that in real terms the S&P 500 never regained the peak in 2000. At its peak in October 2007 the S&P 500 had recovered less than 80 percent of the ground lost in the slump of 2000–03. The current rally is highly

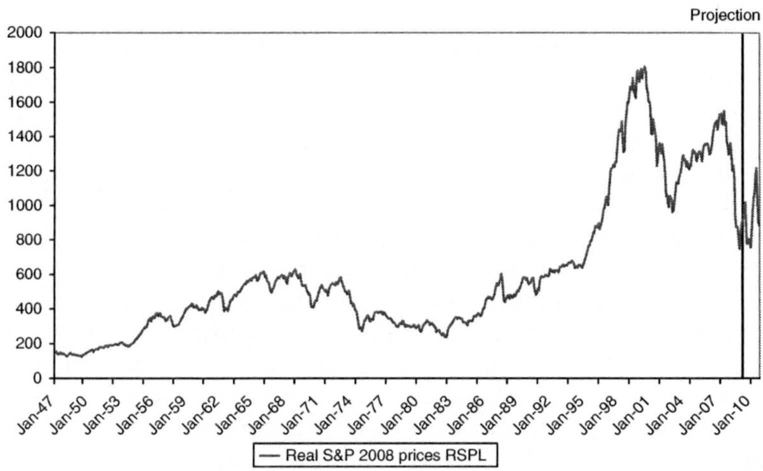

Figure 11.9   Real S&P 2008 prices

unlikely to be the beginning of a new bull market. Instead, it is yet another bear market rally that at best may last for three years, if not less. This gloomy long-term outlook is due to the poor prospects of a new long-lasting business cycle. The asset and debt deflation process is inevitable, although policy can simply delay it, but at a huge cost. The more the deleveraging is delayed, the bigger the ultimate adjustment. For the time being, economic policy is trying to boost equity prices up to ameliorate the negative wealth effect on consumption. But the upside of equities is limited, as the unwinding of the monetary stimulus will depress demand in the economy and push long-term interest rates up, thereby raising the equity risk premium.

The short-term prospects of equities depend on the outlook for profits, the equity risk premium and the market perception of the impact of policy and world trade on the economy. As has been argued in chapter 5 profits soar in the first year of the recovery between 35 percent and 50 percent, as productivity improves and the wage bill abates. This is likely to strengthen the rally in equities that started in the spring of 2009 for approximately one year. However, in the second year of the recovery there is some profit fatigue, as companies begin to hire and the wage bill begins to recover. This is likely to trigger another serious correction in equities of the order of 10–15 percent any time after the spring of 2010, but not the resumption of the long-term bear market. Much will depend on the equity risk premium, which depends on fiscal and monetary policy and their impact on long-term interest rates. The K-Model suggests that the benchmark 10-year yield might rise to 4.00–5.00 percent in the course of 2010. At this level demand for investment and consumer durable goods will be hit, while the housing market, after a brief respite, might resume its downtrend. Moreover, the equity risk premium will soar as long-term interest rates rise. Therefore, the short-term prospects of equities are good, but the rally may fizzle out after the first year of the recovery.

However, there are upside as well as downside risks to this mainline scenario. On the downside, fiscal rectitude might prompt the Obama Administration to adopt tight fiscal policy as from October 2010 in an effort to curb the skyrocketing budget deficit and rein in the soaring Federal debt. Moreover, the Fed might remove some of the accommodation bias by lifting the Fed funds rate, as the dynamics of inflation suggest that even with spare capacity inflation will rekindle for a while. The proper conduct of monetary policy dictates that monetary policy should move back towards the neutral stance the moment inflation bottoms. Tight fiscal policy, coupled with even a small removal of the accommodation bias of monetary bias, might topple a fragile economy. Equities are likely to lead the way towards recession with an early resumption of the long-term bear market.

On the upside, the Fed might not remove the quantitative easing programme in the spring of 2010, as planned. Instead, it might expand it further in an effort to underpin the recovery. This will prevent bond yields from rising, thereby keeping the equity risk premium at bay. Moreover, the Fed might keep the Fed funds rate at 0.25 percent even in 2011. This would push the equity market into new highs. In this case, growth is likely to exceed potential, which, if maintained for some time, would ultimately eliminate the spare capacity, thereby reigniting inflation with a lag. The Fed would then panic, reacting by tightening aggressively. Bond yields would rise even faster than the Fed funds rate, putting an abrupt end to the equity market rally and steering the economy into yet another recession. The conclusion is that even a rosy scenario in the short run based on further support from economic policy will ultimately turn sour, leading to a recession a few years from now.

8   Summary and conclusions

If the asset and debt deflation process, or the economics of depression, are to be appreciated and understood, developments in financial markets must be explained and their impact on the economy must be assessed. This entails a model in which the interaction of financial markets with the real economy is properly specified and well founded. In this context the conclusions of chapters 4–9 are an input to the implications of the dollar (chapter 10) and the bond and equity markets (chapter 11). But at the same time the conclusions of chapters 4–9 depend crucially on the validity of the arguments advanced in the last two chapters. The success of the K-Model in the First Edition of this book (Arestis and Karakitsos, 2004) in describing with precise accuracy the mechanism that led to the current woes is perhaps the best proof that its structure adequately describes the interaction of the real side of the economy with the financial markets.

The bond market holds the key not only to the equity market, but also to the economy as a whole. The imbalances in the private sector are likely to become dormant, as the economy is expected to recover in the second half of 2009 and in 2010. However, if long-term interest rates were to rise to critical levels, then these imbalances would reawaken. This would threaten not only the sustainability of the recovery, but may also trigger another recession. The interesting question is, then, how far and how fast can bond yields rise in the years ahead. The advocates of the yield curve approach argue that the bond market is undervalued, as the cost of carry is very high. Competition among banks will force them to carry on buying government bonds, as this is the only secure way of repairing their impaired balance sheets. Hence, bond yields, which rose sharply in the first half of 2009 as they priced in the forthcoming recovery, are bound to fall or at least to remain low. They argue that this pattern follows from a rational expectations equilibrium in which there is initially an over-shooting of the long-run equilibrium.

At the other end of the spectrum, there are those who base their analysis on the interdependence of global bond markets. They argue that the US bond market is extremely overvalued, given the large swing in the budget deficit and the impact of quantitative easing in capping bond yields. They argue that a disorderly depreciation of the dollar, which at some point in time is likely to happen, may dry up the appetite of foreigners to hold US debt. A massive sell-off of US Treasuries by foreigners would trigger a sharp rise in bond yields, thereby toppling the equity market. Moreover, this group argues that the planned removal of the quantitative easing programme in the spring of 2010 will lift the cap on bond yields that will rise sharply. Adverse developments in financial markets would cause yet another recession – in either the short or the medium term.

The K-Model includes the cost of carry as a determinant of the bond market, as well as the budget deficit and the holdings of the rest of the world of US debt. Hence, it provides an appropriate framework for testing these two hypotheses. The conclusion from these tests is that, other things being equal, bond yields are likely to rise by 80 basis points by mid-2010, if foreigners were to drop the extra holdings of US Treasuries that they accumulated during the credit crisis and the Fed were to proceed with the removal of the quantitative easing programme as planned in the spring of 2010. Moreover, the recovery is likely to be bolstered in the short run because of the restocking that is now taking place, thus exaggerating the upward move of long-term interest rates in the first half 2010. Thus, according to the mainline scenario the 10-year yield is likely to nudge 5.00 percent by June 2010. This is likely to trigger a correction in the equity market of the order of 10–15 percent.

But there are long-term risks on both the upside and the downside around this mainline scenario, which are described in detail in sections 4 and 6. The overall conclusion is that in the long run even the upside risks that imply a strengthening of the economy in the medium term are likely to lead to a recession. This gloomy outlook for financial markets and the economy stem from the assessment that the policies pursued are misguided and wrong. They attempt to restore asset prices to the previous unsustainably high levels instead of encouraging debt deleveraging. Acceptance of subpar growth and debt deleverage for a number of years is preferable to another boom and bust, which has been the pattern over the last ten years.

Notes

1   Introduction

1. The neutral level of a variable is defined as the level that corresponds to the rate of growth of its potential output.

2   The Causes and Consequences of the Internet Bubble

1. For example, the US Federal Reserve System reduced its 'funds' interest rate no less than 13 times between early 2001 and March 2004. This rate stood at 1 percent then, a record low level. This was not confined to the US only. In the Economic and Monetary Union (EMU), the European Central Bank (ECB), although rather slow in reducing its 'repo' interest rate, was then holding this rate at 2 percent. These are only two, but representative examples, of what the situation was worldwide at the time.
2. Greenspan (2000) defines wealth effects as follows: 'Historical evidence suggests that perhaps three to four cents out of every additional dollar of stock market wealth eventually is reflected in increased consumer purchases. The sharp rise in the amount of consumer outlays relative to disposable incomes in recent years, and the corresponding fall in the saving rate, has been consistent with this so-called wealth effect on household purchases. Moreover, higher stock prices, by lowering the cost of equity capital, have helped to support the boom in capital spending' (p. 2).
3. There were many recessions caused by asset and debt deflation throughout the seventeenth and eighteenth centuries. The most important of these were the tulip mania in the middle of the seventeenth century, and the Mississippi and South Seas bubbles of the early eighteenth century (see, for example, Garber, 2000).
4. It should be noted that the statement in the text about the savings deficiency, is only correct by the specific definition of national savings, namely equal to the trade gap. This measure of savings has no operational function apart from restating the trade gap. This is the context in which it is meant to be used here.
5. Interestingly enough, the dollar reached a three-year low with respect to the euro (0.779), and an 11-year low with respect to pound sterling (0.53), after the chairman of the Fed delivered his semi-annual report on monetary policy to the Congress on 11–12 February 2004. He made the comment that a gradual weakening of the dollar would help narrow the US external deficit, and would have no adverse effect on US capital markets. The market interpreted that somehow unusual remark on currencies by the Fed chairman, as a clear sign of the Fed's tacit acceptance of the dollar's slide.
6. This section is based on Arestis and Karakitsos (2009a).

7. 'Paradoxically, these endogenous responses to credible monetary policy increase the probability that latent inflation pressures manifest themselves in the development of imbalances in the financial system, rather than immediate upward pressure on higher goods and services price inflation' (Borio and Lowe 2002, p. 22).

8. An interesting proposal is contained in the study by Bordo and Jeanne (2002). Using a stylised model they examine the possibility of pre-emptive monetary policy to conclude that 'optimal policy depends on the economic conditions in a complex, non-linear way and cannot be summarized by a simple policy rule of the type considered in the inflation-targeting literature' (p. 1).

9. It should be highly emphasised, though, that this does not mean that we support inflation targeting. The latter has its own problems and peculiarities, as argued in a number of papers by one of us. See, for exampe, Arestis and Sawyer (2003), Angeriz and Arestis (2007a, 2007b, 2008).

3   The Current Financial Crisis and the Origins of Excessive Liquidity

1. This chapter relies heavily on Arestis and Karakitsos (2009c) and we are grateful to Palgrave Macmillan for allowing us to publish it with minor corrections.

2. Liquidity for the purposes of this chapter is to be understood not merely as reflecting monetary aggregates but also including the 'shadow' banking. This is totally unregulated and provides loans that are financed by asset-backed securities. The latter's multiplier could be infinite if the yield curve has a positive slope permanently – that is, the long-term rate is above the short-term interbank rate, i.e. the LIBOR rate. The LIBOR (London Inter Bank Rate) is compiled by the British Bankers Association (BBA) and published daily between 11a.m. and 12 noon London time. LIBOR rates are averages of inter-bank rates in major countries worldwide. They are submitted in panels, which comprise at least eight contributor banks; sterling, dollar, euro and the yen have 16 banks (Gorton, 2008). The following BBA website provides further details: http://www.bba.org.uk/bba/jsp/polopoly.jsp?d=141.

3. It was not just where financial liberalisation was introduced in an overt manner, but also where the authorities were required to operate under strict rules. An interesting example is the UK Financial Services Authority (FSA), set up in 1997 when the Bank of England was granted 'independence'. Although FSA was given sweeping jurisdiction over the British financial sector, it has regulated it 'diffidently'. In the words of its first chairman 'The philosophy of the FSA from when I set it up has been to say, "Consenting adults in private? That's their problem, really"' (Eisinger, 2008).

4. Established in 1933 the Glass–Steagall Act was repealed in 1999, thereby opening up competition among banks, securities and insurance companies. The Glass–Steagall Act prohibited a bank from offering investment, commercial investment and insurance services. See for full details http://en.wikipedia.org/wiki/Gramm-Leach-Bliley_Act#Remaining_restrictions.

5. 'Subprime mortgage origination' in 2005 and 2006 was $1.2 trillion, 80 percent of which was securitised (see Gorton, 2008). The same study

provides further data on the growth of the subprime mortgage market: 'The outstanding amounts of Subprime and Alt-A combined amount to about one-quarter of the $6 trillion mortgage market. Issuance in 2005 and 2006 of Subprime and Alt-A mortgages was almost 30 percent of the mortgage market. Over the period 2000–2007, the outstanding amount of agency mortgages doubled, but subprime grew 800 percent! Since 2000 the Subprime and Alt-A segments of the market grew at the expense of the Agency share, which fell from almost 80 percent (by outstanding issuance) to about half by issuance and 67 percent by outstanding amount' (p. 8). The 'Subprime and Alt-A' term is defined to refer 'to borrowers who are perceived to be riskier than the average borrower because of poor credit history' (p. 7).

6. Gorton (2008) offers an interesting contrast between a subprime mortgage, as explained in the text, with 'a standard, prime, 30 year, fixed rate mortgage'. Unlike the subprime mortgage, '(w)ith a prime mortgage, the borrower repays principal over time, and the mortgage matures after 30 years. The borrower may repay the mortgage, typically without penalty. The borrower may benefit from house price appreciation, but the lender does not (directly) benefit' (p. 13).

7. A large number of SIV's assets were in the form of subprime residential mortgage-backed securities and commercial-backed securities.

8. In 2006 new synthetic indices of subprime risk were introduced; the so-called 'ABX' indices. For the first time ever information about subprime values and risks was gathered and made known. The ABX information and the lack of information about location of the risks led to the loss of confidence referred to in the text.

9. The Bank of England (2008, Chart 6, p. 8) provides 'projected ultimate credit losses on subprime asset backed securities'; these are estimated to reach $170 billion.

4 Wages and Prices and the Proper Conduct of Monetary Policy

1. For a New Keynesian view on the inflation/unemployment trade-off see, for example, Mankiw (2001a); Barkbu et al. (2005).

5 Corporate Profits and Relationship to Investment

1. The corporate profits discussed here are not shareholder reported earnings. They are the profits that are based on National Income and Product Accounts (NIPA). This measure of profits is designed to gauge the economic profitability of current operations. It excludes a number of one-time charges that appear in shareholder reports and, importantly, records options as an expense, albeit at the time of the exercise. Although this treatment of options is not ideal, it is arguably superior to their treatment in shareholder reports, where options are generally not treated as expenses at all. NIPA profits closely approximate those obtained from reports submitted for tax purposes, and, for obvious reasons, corporations tend not to inflate taxable earnings.

6 Long-Term Risks to Investment Recovery

1. This definition of debt includes commercial paper, corporate bonds, bank loans, other loans and advances and mortgages.
2. The relationship between the rate of interest and investment is particularly important in the neo-classical investment theory (Jorgenson, 1971) and in Keynesian economics (Keynes, 1936). There are, of course, important differences between the two approaches: perhaps the most important is that whilst in neo-classical economics the relationship emanates from the attempt to determine the optimal capital stock, in Keynesian economics the relationship does not rely on invoking the optimal capital stock notion; uncertain expectations are by far the most important element in this approach (see, for example, Binswanger, 1999, where more details on this and other differences are offered). One other aspect refers to the relative importance between cost-of-capital and activity economic variables. It is generally recognized that activity variables, especially output, have 'a more substantial impact on investment' (Chirinko, 1993, p. 1881).
3. We include in this category the q theory of investment, introduced by Keynes (1936) and further developed by Brainard and Tobin (1968) and Tobin (1969, 1978).
4. It is true, though, that the in the 'new consensus macroeconomics' model investment does not play an important role nor does the financial sector, which is excluded in view of the transversality condition firmly embedded in the theoretical construct of this macroeconomic framework (see, for example, Arestis, 2009a, 2009b, for full details).

7 The Housing Market and Residential Investment

1. Another OECD study argues that since owner-occupation rates exceed 50 percent in most OECD countries, a significant number of households are bound to be affected by changes in property prices (OECD, 2000a).
2. GSE stands for Government Sponsored Enterprises and refers specifically to Fannie Mae and Freddie Mac.
3. The long-term decline in the median house price relative to disposable income in the 1980s reflects the fall in inflation and interest rates that made houses more affordable and moderated their demand as a hedge against inflation. Figure 7.10 confirms this conclusion by comparing nominal with real (deflated by CPI) house price inflation. Although nominal house price inflation was high in the 1970s and low since the 1980s, in real terms (deflated by CPI) it has been the same in the two periods (see Figure 7.2). Nominal house price inflation increased steadily in the 1970s, but declined in the early 1980s in line with inflation and interest rates. In September 2003 nominal house price inflation hit 8.4 percent, the highest since 1982, the period of low inflation. Real house price inflation does not suffer from the distortions of inflation and reflects more accurately the demand and supply forces of the housing market. In September 2003 real house price inflation hit 6.1 percent, only 1 percent lower than the all-time high in the last thirty-five years of 7.1 percent reached in April 1978.

4. A trendless variable is one that has neither an upward nor downward trend. It is more rigorously defined as a stationary variable, which means that its mean and standard deviation are not time varying. A stationary variable has the property that it reverts back to its mean.
5. Constructing housing price measures is not a straightforward task. This is a complex exercise in view of the fact that home sales do not take place in centralized markets. McCarthy and Peach (2004) discuss four housing price series to conclude that 'quality' of housing should be accounted for when constructing housing price indexes. Consequently, a constant-quality housing price index, such as the Case–Shiller index, is preferable. This is not without its problems, though, as the authors readily admit, and Hulten (2003) shows.
6. In terms of a textbook analysis, in the short run we are moving up along the supply curve in response to a shift in the demand curve, while in the long run the supply curve shifts to the right because of higher residential investment.
7. The impact of P_H on RRI has received renewed interest recently, where the relationship emanates through the impact of house prices on profitability; see, for example, OECD (2000b).
8. An interesting study that compares the US and the UK housing markets is Banks et al. (2003). This study compares households' decisions in buying houses at various stages of their lives in the two countries. The smaller volatility in the US in relation to the UK market is explained by resorting to the absence of hedging possibilities in the UK. This means that since no hedging against further increases in house prices exists, except of course to buy housing itself, forces people to buy houses sooner in their lives.

8 Long-Term Risks of Robust Consumer Behaviour

1. Debt 'irreversibility' denotes the asymmetric behaviour of debt in the course of the business cycle. In the upswing of the cycle debt increases, as in good days rising asset prices induce households to accumulate debt. However, in bad days this debt cannot be repaid. So asset prices fall faster than debt in the downswing. This overhang of debt diminishes net wealth and creates an imbalance.
2. The widest measure of unemployment that covers underemployment includes those working part-time because they cannot find a permanent job, discouraged workers and those workers who are marginally attached to the labour force.
3. The sample in Jappelli and Pagano (1989) contains countries with capital markets that have reached different degrees of development: Sweden (12), US (21), Japan (34), UK (40), Spain (52), Greece (54), Italy (58), where the percentage of households that are liquidity-constrained is shown in brackets, comprises the sample of countries. Three groupings are identified. Sweden and the US have a low percentage of households that are liquidity-constrained; the UK and Japan then follow, while for Spain, Greece and Italy the opposite to Sweden and the US is true.
4. The result for the UK is sensitive to the seasonal adjustment procedure: the 35 percent quoted in the text is for seasonally adjusted quarterly data; it is

65 percent when annual differences of seasonally unadjusted data are used. For Japan no relevant percentage was identified (Campbell and Mankiw, 1991, pp. 737–8).

5. While it is true that liquidity constraints have received a great deal of attention in the literature, 'much work needs to be done to incorporate them in a consistent fashion' (Attanasio and Blank, 2001, p. 6). In this context the difference of consumer behaviour in developed and developing economies becomes paramount (for a recent study that concentrates on low-income countries, see Rosenzweig, 2001).

6. See Carroll and Kimball (2001) for a discussion of the tight relationship between liquidity constraints and precautionary behaviour. In fact, 'The precautionary saving motive can generate behaviour that is virtually indistinguishable from that generated by a liquidity constraint, because the precautionary saving motive essentially induces self-imposed reluctance to borrow (or to borrow too much)' (Carroll, 2001, p. 32).

7. Two further dimensions of the analysis in the text are worth mentioning: the first is the possibility of discounting of the future changing over time, the hybrolic discounting approach (Angeletos et al., 2001); and the second that refers to cross-national differences in savings rates (Deaton, 1992).

8. Carroll and Samwick (1997), using the Panel Study of Income Dynamics, provide evidence that supports the proposition that consumers who face greater uncertainty hold more wealth, and that they engage in 'buffer-stock' saving behaviour.

9   Foreign Demand

1. The euro area comprises 16 members at this juncture. The 16 members are: Austria, Belgium, Cyprus, Finland, France, Germany, Greece, Ireland, Italy, Luxembourg, Malta, the Netherlands, Portugal, Slovakia, Slovenia and Spain.

2. The importance of foreign trade for growth has been demonstrated by a number of studies; see, for example, OECD (2000c, pp. 143–4).

3. For full details on the ISM, see www.ism.ws.

10   The US External Imbalance and the Dollar: A Long-Term View

1. The BRIC group includes Brazil, Russia, India and China.

2. Game theory has been used extensively in microeconomics, but not to the same extent in macroeconomics. In the latter case, applications in the area of macroeconomic policies in an interdependent world are probably one exception. The contributions by Cooper (1985) and Hamada (1974), (1976), (1979) and applications by Canzoneri and Gray (1983), and Sachs (1983) utilise game theory deal with the behaviour of the exchange rate.

3. ERM stands for the Exchange Rate Mechanism, a system that was introduced by the European Community in March 1979, as part of the European Monetary System (EMS). Its aim was to reduce exchange rate variability and achieve monetary stability in Europe. It was all part of the preparation for

the Economic and Monetary Union and the introduction of the euro (itself introduced on 1 January 1999).
4. Tight fiscal policy strengthens the currency in the long run, as it reduces the Federal debt. However, in the short run it lowers the currency, as it reduces the policy adjusted output gap.
5. Falling bond yields strengthen the real dollar, as the insolvency risk is reduced and the appetite of ROW residents for US assets increases. However, this effect takes some time to emerge.
6. A variable is stationary if its mean and standard deviation are not time varying. As is well known, modelling of non-stationary variables produces nonsense correlations, unless the variables are co-integrated.

11   The Long-Term Risks to US Financial Markets

1. For convenience, only two bond yields are considered: the 2-year as being representative of the short end of the market and the 10-year for the long end.
2. It is worth mentioning that a similar test was conducted in the First Edition of the book (Arestis and Karakitsos, 2004), but the coefficient was statistically insignificant, albeit negative. Since then the importance of foreign demand has increased by a multiple of 12.

Bibliography

Alchian, A.A. and Klein, B. (1973) 'On a Correct Measure of Inflation', *Journal of Money, Credit and Banking*, 5(1), 173–91.

Ando, A. and Modigliani, F. (1963) 'The "Life Cycle" Hypothesis of Saving: Aggregate Implications and Tests', *American Economic Review*, 53, 55–84.

Angeletos, G.M., Laibson, D., Repetto, A., Tobacman, J. and Weinberg, S. (2001) 'Hyperbolic Consumption Model: Calibration, Simulation, and Empirical Evaluation', *Journal of Economic Perspectives*, 15(3), 47–68.

Angeriz, A. and Arestis, P. (2007a) 'Monetary Policy in the UK', *Cambridge Journal of Economics*, 31(6), 863–84.

Angeriz, A. and Arestis, P. (2007b) 'Assessing the Performance of "Inflation Targeting Lite" Countries', *World Economy*, 59(11), 1621–45.

Angeriz, A. and Arestis, P. (2008) 'Assessing Inflation Targeting Through Intervention Analysis', *Oxford Economic Papers*, 60(2), 293–317.

Arestis, P. (1986) 'Wages and Prices in the UK: The Post Keynesian View', *Journal of Post Keynesian Economics*, 8(3), 339–58. Reprinted in M.C. Sawyer (ed.), *Post-Keynesian Economics*, Aldershot: Edward Elgar, 1988, pp. 456–75.

Arestis, P. (2007) 'What is the New Consensus in Macroeconomics?', chapter 2 in P. Arestis (ed.), *Is There a New Consensus in Macroeconomics?*, Basingstoke: Palgrave Macmillan.

Arestis, P. (2009a) 'New Consensus Macroeconomics and Keynesian Critique', in E. Hein, T. Niechoj and E. Stockhammer (eds), *Macroeconomic Policies on Shaky Foundations: Wither Mainstream Macroeconomics?*, Marburg, Germany: Metropolis-Verlag.

Arestis, P. (2009b) 'The New Consensus in Macroeconomics: A Critical Appraisal', in G. Fontana and M. Setterfield (eds), *Macroeconomic Theory and Macroeconomic Pedagogy*, Houndmills, Basingstoke: Palgrave Macmillan.

Arestis, P. and Karakitsos, E. (2002) 'How Far Can Equity Prices Fall Under Asset and Debt Deflation?', *Working Paper No. 368*, Levy Economics Institute of Bard College, December.

Arestis, P. and Karakitsos, E. (2004) *The Post-Bubble US Economy: Implications for Financial Markets and the Economy*, Basingstoke: Palgrave Macmillan.

Arestis, P. and Karakitsos, E. (2007) 'The US Housing Market', *Ekonomia*, 10(2), 67–88.

Arestis, P. and Karakitsos, E. (2008) 'The US Housing Slump and the Consumer', *Journal of Post Keynesian Economics*, 30(1), 335–52.

Arestis, P. and Karakitsos, E. (2009a) 'What Role for Central Banks in View of the Current Crisis?', *Levy Economics Institute Policy Note*, 2009/2.

Arestis, P. and Karakitsos, E. (2009b) 'Unemployment and the Natural Interest Rate in a Neo-Wicksellian Model', in P. Arestis and J. McCombie (eds), *Unemployment: Past and Present*, Basingstoke: Palgrave Macmillan.

Arestis, P. and Karakitsos, E. (2009c) 'Subprime Mortgage Market and the Current Financial Crisis', CCEPP WP08–09. Cambridge Centre for Economic and Public Policy, Department of Land Economy, University of Cambridge.

February. Forthcoming in Philip Arestis, Peter Mooslechner and Karin Wagner (eds), *Housing Market Challenges in Europe and the United States – Any Solutions Available?*, Basingstoke: Palgrave Macmillan.

Arestis, P. and Sawyer, M.C. (2003) 'Inflation Targeting: A Critical Appraisal', *Levy Economics Institute Working Papers Series*, No. 388, September.

Arestis, P., Cipollini, A. and Fattouh, B. (2004) 'Threshold Effects in the US Budget Deficit', *Economic Inquiry*, 42(2), 214–22.

Attanasio, O.P. and Blank, J. (2001) 'The Assessment: Household Saving – Issues in Theory and Policy', *Oxford Review of Economic Policy*, 17(1), 1–19.

Baddeley, M.C. (2003) *Investment: Theories and Analysis*, Basingstoke: Palgrave Macmillan.

Baker, D. (2002) 'The Run-up in Home Prices: A Bubble', *Centre for Economic and Policy Research Challenge*, 45(6), 93–119.

Bank of England (2008), *Financial Stability Report*, No. 23, April.

Bank of International Settlements (BIS) (2008), *Annual Report*, June.

Banks, J., Blundell, R., Smith, J.P. and Smith, Z. (2003) *Housing Wealth over the Life-Cycle in the Presence of Housing Price Volatility*, London: Institute of Fiscal Studies and University College.

Barkbu, B., Cassino, V., Gosselin-Lotz, A. and Piscitelli, L. (2005) 'The New Keynesian Phillips Curve in the United States and the Euro Area: Aggregation Bias, Stability and Robustness', *Bank of England Working Paper No. 285*, London: Bank of England.

Bernanke, A.S. (2009) 'Testimony of Chairman Ben Bernanke: Federal Reserve Board's Semiannual Monetary Policy Report', *The U.S. House of Representatives*, testimony before the Committee on Financial Services, 21 July.

Bernanke, B.S. and Blinder, A.S. (1988) 'Credit, Money and Aggregate Demand', *American Economic Review*, 78(2), 435–9.

Bernanke, B.S. and Gertler, M. (1989) 'Agency Costs, Net Worth, and Business Fluctuations', *American Economic Review*, 79(1), 14–31.

Bernanke, B.S. and Gertler, M. (1999) 'Monetary Policy and Asset Price Volatility', in *New Challenges for Monetary Policy*, proceedings of the Symposium Sponsored by the Federal Reserve Bank of Kansas City, Jackson Hole, Wyoming, pp. 77–128.

Bernanke, B. and Gertler, M. (2000) 'Monetary Policy and Asset Price Volatility', *NBER Working Paper No. 7559*, Cambridge, Massachusetts: National Bureau of Economic Research.

Binswanger, M. (1999) *Stock Markets, Speculative Bubbles and Economic Growth: New Dimensions in the Co-evolution of Real and Financial Markets*, Cheltenham: Edward Elgar Publishing.

Blanchard, O. (2009) 'Sustaining a Global Recovery', *Finance and Development*, September, 8–12.

Bordo, M.D. and Jeanne, O. (2002) 'Monetary Policy and Asset Prices: Does "Benign Neglect" Make Sense?', *IMF Working Paper, WP/02/225*, Washington, DC: International Monetary Fund.

Borio, C. (2008) 'The Financial Turmoil of 2007–? A Preliminary Assessment and Some Policy Considerations', Working Paper No. 251. Basel: Bank for International Settlements, March.

Borio, C. and Lowe, P. (2002) 'Asset Prices, Financial and Monetary Stability: Exploring the Nexus', Working Paper No. 114. Basel: Bank for International Settlements, July.

Brainard, W.C. and Tobin, J. (1968) 'Pitfalls in Financial Model Building', *American Economic Review*, 58(2), 99–122.

Browning, M. and Crossley, T.F. (2001) 'The Life-Cycle Model of Consumption and Saving', *Journal of Economic Perspectives*, 15(3), 3–22.

Campbell, J.Y. (1991) 'A Variance Decomposition for Stock Returns', *Economic Journal*, 101(405), 1557–79.

Campbell, J.Y. and Mankiw, N.G. (1990) 'Permanent Income, Current Income, and Consumption', *Journal of Business and Economics*, 8, 269–79.

Campbell, J.Y. and Mankiw, N.G. (1991) 'The Response of Consumption to Income: A Cross-country Investigation', *European Economic Review*, 35, 723–67.

Canzoneri, M. and Gray, J. (1983) 'Two Essays on Monetary Policy in an Interdependent World', *Federal Reserve Board International Finance*, Discussion Paper No. 219.

Carroll, C.D. (1994) 'How Does Future Income Affect Current Consumption?', *Quarterly Journal of Economics*, 109(1), 111–47.

Carroll, C.D. (1997) 'Buffer-Stock Saving and the Life Cycle/Permanent Income Hypothesis', *Quarterly Journal of Economics*, 112(1), 1–56.

Carroll, C.D. (2001) 'A Theory of the Consumtion Function, With and Without Liquidity Constraints', *Journal of Economic Perspectives*, 15(3), 23–45.

Carroll, C.D. and Kimball, M.S. (2001) 'Liquidity Constraints and Precautionary Saving', *NBER Working Paper No. 8496*, Cambridge, MA: National Bureau of Economic Research.

Carroll, C.D. and Samwick, A.A. (1997) 'The Nature of Precautionary Wealth', *Journal of Monetary Economics*, 40(1), 41–71.

Case, K.E. and Shiller, R.J. (2003) 'Is There a Bubble in the Housing Market? An Analysis', *Brookings Panel on Economic Activity*, September.

Chirinko, R.S. (1993) 'Business Fixed Investment Spending: Modeling Strategies, Empirical Results, and Policy Implications', *Journal of Economic Literature*, 31(4), 1875–911.

Clews, R. (2002) 'Asset Prices and Inflation', *Bank of England Quarterly Bulletin*, Summer, 178–85.

Conference Board (2003) 'Consumer Confidence Index', *Consumer Confidence Survey*, February.

Cooper, R.N. (1985) 'Economic Interdependence and Co-ordination of Economic Policies', in R.W. Jones and P.B. Kenen (eds), *Handbook of International Economics*, vol. II, London: Elsevier Science Publishers.

Council of Economic Advisers (2004) *Economic Report of the President*, Washington, DC: United States Printing Office.

Deaton, A. (1991) 'Saving and Liquidity Constraints', *Econometrica*, 59(5), 1221–48.

Deaton, A. (1992) *Understanding Consumption*, Oxford: Oxford University Press.

Dixit, A. and Pindyck, R. (1994) *Investment under Uncertainty*, Princeton: Princeton University Press.

Dornbusch, R. (1976) 'Expectations and Exchange Rate Dynamics', *Journal of Political Economy*, 84(December), 1161–76.

Dornbusch, R. and Fisher, S. (1980) 'Exchange Rates and the Current Account', *American Economic Review*, 70(5), 960–71.

Duisenberg, W.F. (2002) *Testimony to the European Parliament*, October, Brussels, Belgium.

Eichner, A.S. (1987) *The Macrodynamics of Advanced Economies*, New York: M.E. Sharpe.

Eisinger, J. (2008) 'London Banks, Falling Down', downloadable from: http://www.portfolio.com/views/columns/wall-street/2008/08/13/Problems-in-British-Banking-System.

Eisner, R. (1974) 'Econometric Studies of Investment Behaviour: A Comment', *Economic Inquiry*, 1281), 91–104.

Fazzari, S. (1993) 'Monetary Policy, Financial Structure, and Investment', chapter 3 in *Transforming the U.S. Financial System: Equity and Efficiency for the 21st Century*, Armonk, NY: M.E. Sharpe.

Fazzari, S. and Peterson, B. (1993) 'Working Capital and Fixed Investment: New Evidence on Financing Constraints', *Rand Economic Journal*, 24, 328–42.

Flavin, M. (1985) 'Excess Sensitivity of Consumption to Current Income: Liquidity Constraints or Myopia', *Canadian Journal of Economics*, 18, 117–36.

Fleming, J.M. (1962) 'Domestic Financial Policies Under Fixed and Under Flexible Exchange Rates', *International Monetary Fund Staff Papers*, 9(November), 369–79.

Friedman, M. (1957) *A Theory of the Consumption Function*, Princeton, NJ: Princeton University Press.

Frowen S.F. and Karakitsos, E. (1996) 'Monetary and Fiscal Policy Under Conditions of Globalised Money and Capital Markets: Lessons For The UK Personal Sector', *Public Finance*, 51(3), 305–24.

Frowen, S.F. and Karakitsos, E. (1998) 'A Strategic Approach to the Euro Prospects', *Public Finance*, 53(1), 1–18.

Garber, P.M. (2000) *Famous First Bubbles: The Fundamentals of Early Manias*, Cambridge MA: MIT Press.

Goodhart, C.A.E. (2001) 'What Weight Should Be Given to Asset Prices in the Measurement of Inflation?', *Economic Journal*, 111(472), F335–F356.

Gordon, M.J. (1962) *The Investment, Financing and Valuation of the Corporation*, Homewood, IL: Irwin.

Gordon, R. (2000) 'Does the "New Economy" Measure Up to the Great Invention of the Past?', *Journal of Economic Perspectives*, 14(4), 49–74.

Gorton, G.B. (2008) 'The Panic of 2007', *NBER Working Paper Series*, No. 14358, Cambridge, MA: National Bureau of Economic Research.

Greenspan, A. (1996) 'The Challenge of Central Banking in a Democratic Society', *The Annual Dinner and Francis Boyer Lecture of the American Enterprise Institute for Public Policy Research*, Washington, DC, 5 December.

Greenspan, A. (1999) 'Mortgage Markets and Economic Activity', Remarks Before a Conference on *Mortgage Markets and Economic Activity*, Sponsored by America's Community Bankers, Washington DC, November.

Greenspan, A. (2000) 'Testimony of Chairman Alan Greenspan', *The Federal Reserve's Semiannual Report on the Economy and Monetary Policy*, Before the Committee on Banking and Financial Services , US House of Representatives, February.

Greenspan, A. (2002a) 'Economic Volatility', Speech given to a Symposium Sponsored by the Federal Reserve Bank of Kansas City: Jackson Hole, Wyoming.

Greenspan, A. (2002b) 'Issues for Monetary Policy', *Remarks Before the Economic Club of New York, New York City*, December. Available at: http://www.federalreserve.gov/boarddocs/speeches/2002/20021219/ (It should be noted that pages in the text refer to the website document.)

Greenspan, A. (2003a) 'Global Finance: Is It Slowing?', Remarks at the Banque de France, *International Symposium on Monetary Policy, Economic Cycle, and Financial Dynamics*, Paris, France, 7 March.

Greenspan, A. (2003b) 'Testimony of Chairman Alan Greenspan: Federal Reserve Board's Semiannual Monetary Policy Report', *The U.S. House of Representatives*, testimony before the Committee on Financial Services, 20 July; and *The US Congress*, Before the Committee on Banking, Housing, and Urban Affairs, US Senate, 21 July.

Greenspan, A. (2004a) 'Risk and Uncertainty in Monetary Policy', *Remarks by Chairman Alan Greenspan at the Meetings of the American Economic Association*, San Diego, California, January.

Greenspan, A. (2004b) 'Testimony of Chairman Alan Greenspan', *The Federal Reserve's Semiannual Monetary Policy Report to the Congress*, Before the Committee on Financial Services , US House of Representatives, February.

Greenspan, A. (2004c) 'Government-Sponsored Enterprises', *Testimony of Chairman Alan Greenspan*, Before the Committee on Banking, Housing, and Urban Affairs, US Senate, February.

Greenspan, A. (2005a) 'The Economic Outlook', *Testimony of Chairman Alan Greenspan*, Before the Joint Economic Committee, 9 June.

Greenspan, A. (2005b) 'Reflections on Central Banking', Paper presented at 'The Greenspan Era: Lessons for the Future', a symposium sponsored by the Federal Reserve Bank of Kansas City, Jackson Hole, Wyoming, 25–7 August.

Hamada, K. (1974) 'Alternative Exchange Rate Systems and the Interdependence of Monetary Policies', in R.Z. Aliber (ed.), *National Monetary Policies and the International Financial System*, Chicago: University of Chicago Press.

Hamada, K. (1976) 'A Strategic Analysis on Monetary Interdependence', *Journal of Political Economy*, 84, 677–700.

Hamada, K. (1979) 'Macroeconomic Strategy and Co-ordination Under Alternative Exchange Rate Regimes', in R. Dornbusch and J.A. Frankel (eds), *International Economic Policy*, Baltimore: The John Hopkins University Press.

Himmelberg, C., Mayer, C. and Sinai, T. (2005) 'Assessing High House Prices: Bubbles, Fundamentals, and Misperceptions', *Journal of Economic Perspectives*, 19(4), 67–92.

Hubbard, R.G. (1998) 'Capital-Market Imperfections and Investment', *Journal of Economic Literature*, 36(1), 193–225.

Hulten, C.R. (2003) 'Price Hedonics: A Critical Review', *Federal Reserve Bank of New York Economic Policy Review*, 9(3), 5–15.

Jappelli, T. and Pagano, M. (1989) 'Consumption and Capital Market Imperfections: An International Comparison', *American Economic Review*, 79(5), 1088–105.

Jorgenson, D. (1971) 'Econometric Studies of Investment Behaviour: A Survey', *Journal of Economic Literature*, 53, 1111–47.

Jud, D. and Winkler, D. (2002) 'The Dynamics of Metropolitan Housing Prices', *Journal of Real Estate Research*, 23(1–2), 29–45.

Kaldor, N. (1955) 'Alternative Theories of Distribution', *Review of Economic Studies*, 23(2), 83–100.

Kalecki, M. (1943) 'The Determinants of Investment', in his *Studies in Economic Dynamics*, London: Allen and Unwin.

Kalecki, M. (1971) *Selected Essays on the Dynamics of the Capitalist Economy*, Cambridge: Cambridge University Press.

Karakitsos, E. (2008) 'The "New Consensus Macroeconomics" in the Light of the Current Crisis', *Ekonomia*, 11(2), 89–111.

Karakitsos, E. (2009) 'Bubbles Lead to Long-term Instability', in Giuseppe Fontana, John McCombie and Malcolm Sawyer (eds), *Macroeconomics, Finance and Money: Essays in Honour of Philip Arestis*, forthcoming.

King, M. (2005) 'Monetary Policy: Practice Ahead of Theory', *Mais Lecture*, Cass Business School, City University, London.

Kaufman, M. and Mühleison, M. (2003) 'Are U.S. House Prices Overvalued?', *IMF Staff Country Report No. 03/245, United States*, Washington, DC: International Monetary Fund.

Keynes, J.M. (1936) *The General Theory of Employment, Interest and Money*, London: Macmillan.

Kindleberger, C.P. (2000) *Manias, Panics and Crashes: A History of Financial Crises*, 4th edition, London: John Wiley and Sons.

Kotlikoff, L.J. and Summers, L.H. (1981) 'The Role of Intergenerational Transfers in Aggregate Capital Accumulation', *Journal of Political Economy*, 89(4), 706–32.

Krugman, P. (2008), *The Return of Depression Economics and the Crisis of 2008*, London: W.W. Norton & Co.

Leamer, E.E. (2007) 'Housing Is the Business Cycle', Jackson Hole Conference of the Federal Reserve Bank of Kansas City on *Housing, Housing Finance, and Monetary Policy*, 30 August to 1 September 2007. Available on http://www.kansascityfed.org/publicat/sympos/2007/PDF/2007.10.11.Leamer.pdf.

Lee, T. (2004) *Why the Markets Went Crazy and What it Means for Investors*, New York: Palgrave Macmillan.

Leung, C. (2004) 'Macroeconomics and Housing: A Review of the Literature', *Journal of Housing Economics*, 13(2), 249–67.

Listokin, D., Wyly, E., Keating, L., Rengert, K. and Listokin, B. (2000) 'Making New Mortgage Markets: Case Studies of Institutions, Home Buyers and Communities', *Fannie Mae Foundation Research Report*.

Mankiw, N.G. (2001a) 'The Inexorable and Mysterious Tradeoff Between Inflation and Unemployment', *Economic Journal*, 111(3), C45–C61.

Mankiw, N.G. (2001b) 'US Monetary Policy in the 1990s', *NBER Working Paper No. 8471*, Washington: National Bureau of Economic Research.

Mankiw, N.G. (2007), *Principles of Macroeconomics*, Ohio: Thomson.

Mayer, C. (1994) 'The Assessment: Money and Banking: Theory and Evidence', *Oxford Economic Review*, 10, 1–13.

McCarthy, J. and Peach, R.W. (2002) 'Monetary Policy Transmission to Residential Investment', *Federal Reserve Bank of New York Economic Policy Review*, 8(2), 139–58.

McCarthy, J. and Peach, R.W. (2004) 'Are Home Prices the Next "Bubble"?', *Federal Reserve Bank of New York Economic Policy Review*, 10(3), 1–17.

McCarthy, J. and Peach, R.W. (2005) 'Is There a "Bubble"in the Housing Market Now?' mimeo, Federal Reserve Bank of New York. Available on: http://www.newyorkfed.org/research/economists/mccarthy/pub.html.

McConnell, M.M., Peach, R.W. and Al-Haschimi, A. (2003) 'After the Refinancing Boom: Will Consumers Scale Back Their Spending?' *Current Issues in Economics and Finance, Federal Reserve Bank of New York*, 9(12), 1–7.

Minsky, H.P. (1986) *Stabilising an Unstable Economy*, New Haven: Yale University Press.

Modigliani, F. (1988) 'The Role of Intergenerational Transfers and Life Cycle Saving in the Accumulation of Wealth', *Journal of Economic Perspectives*, 2(2), 15–40.

Modigliani, F. and Brumberg, R. (1954) 'Utility Analysis and the Consumption Function: An Interpretation of Cross-section Data', in K.K. Kurihara (ed.), *Post- Keynesian Economics*, New Brunswick, NJ: Rutgers University Press.

Mundell, R.A. (1960) 'The Monetary Dynamics of Adjustment Under Fixed and Flexible Exchange Rates', *Quarterly Journal of Economics*, 74(2), 227–57.

Mundell, R.A. (1963) 'Capital Mobility and Stabilisation Policy Under Fixed and Flexible Exchange Rates', *Canadian Journal of Economics and Political Science*, 29(November), 475–85.

OECD (2000a) 'Monetary Policy in a Changing Financial Environment', *Economic Outlook*, 67(June), Paris: Organisation for Economic Co-Operation and Development.

OECD (2000b) 'House Prices and Economic Activity', *Economic Outlook*, 68(December), Paris: Organisation for Economic Co-Operation and Development.

OECD (2000c) 'Links Between Policy and Growth: Cross-Country Evidence', *Economic Outlook*, 68(December), Paris: Organisation for Economic Co-Operation and Development.

Oliner, S.D. and Sichel, D.E. (2000) 'The Resurgence of Growth in the Late 1990s: Is Information Technology the Story?', *Journal of Economic Perspectives*, 14(4), 3–22.

Robinson, J.V. (1964) 'Kalecki and Keynes', in her *Collected Economic Papers, 3*, Oxford: Basil Blackwell.

Rosenzweig, M.R. (2001) 'Saving Behaviour in Low-Income Countries', *Oxford Review of Economic Policy*, 17(1), 40–54.

Rowthorn, R. (1995) 'Capital Formation and Unemployment', *Oxford Review of Economic Policy*, 11(1), 26–39.

Sachs, J. (1983) 'International Policy Co-ordination in a Dynamic Macro-Model', *NBER Working Paper* 1166, Washington, DC: National Bureau of Economic Research.

Sargan, J.D. (1964) 'Wages and Prices in the United Kingdom: A Study in Econometric Methodology', in P.E. Hart, G. Mills and J.K. Whitaker (eds), *Econometric Analysis for National Economic Planning*, London: Butterworths, pp. 25–63.

Sawyer, M. (1982a) *Macro-Economics in Question*, Brighton: Wheatsheaf Books, and New York: M.E. Sharpe.

Sawyer, M. (1982b) 'Collective Bargaining, Oligopoly and Macro-Economics', *Oxford Economic Papers*, 34(4), 428–48.

Sawyer, M.C. (1985) *The Economics of Michal Kalecki*, London: Macmillan.

Schiller, R.J. (2000) *Irrational Exuberance*, Princeton: Princeton University Press.

Shiller, R.J. (2007) 'Understanding Recent Trends in House Prices and House Owenership', Jackson Hole Conference of the Federal Reserve Bank of Kansas City on *Housing, Housing Finance, and Monetary Policy*, 30 August to 1 September 2007. Available on: http://www.kansascityfed.org/publicat/sympos/2007/PDF/2007.09.27.Shiller.pdf.

Stegman, T. (1982) 'The Estimation of an Acclerator-Type Investment Function with a Profitability Constraint by the Technique of Switching Regressions', *Australian Economic Papers*, 21(2), 379–91.

Stiglitz, J. (2003) 'Symposium on Bubbles', *Journal of Economic Perspectives*, 4(2), 13–18.

Stiglitz, J. and Weiss, A. (1981) 'Credit Rationing in Markets with Imperfect Information', *American Economic Review*, 71(3), 393–410.
Stiroh, K. (2002) 'Are ICT Spillovers Driving the New Economy?', *Review of Income and Wealth*, 48(1), 33–57.
Stock, J.H. and Watson, M.H. (eds) (1993) *Business Cycles, Indicators and Forecasting*, Studies in Business Cycles, vol. 28, Cambridge, MA: National Bureau of Economic Research.
Temple, J. (2002) 'The Assessment: The New Economy', *Oxford Review of Economic Policy*, 18(3), 241–64.
Tevlin, S. and Whelan, K. (2002) 'Explaining the Investment Boom of the 1990s', *Journal of Money, Credit and Banking*, 35(1), 1–22.
Tobin, J. (1969) 'A General Equilibrium Approach to Monetary Theory', *Journal of Money, Credit, and Banking*, 1(1), 15–29.
Tobin, J. (1978) 'Monetary Policies and the Economy: The Transmission Mechanism', *Southern Economic Journal*, 44(3), 421–31.
Warburton, P. (1999) *Debt and Delusion: Central Bank Follies That Threaten Economic Disaster*, New York: Allen Lane and Penguin Press.
Zarnowitz, V. (1992) *Business Cycle, Theory, History, Indicators and Forecasting*, Chicago: University of Chicago Press.
Zeldes, S. (1989a) 'Consumption and Liquidity Constraints: an Empirical Investigation', *Journal of Political Economy*, 97, 305–46.
Zeldes, S. (1989b) 'Optimal Consumption with Stochastic Income: Deviations from Certainty Equivalence', *Quarterly Journal of Economics*, 104, 275–98.

Index

Note: Since the main topic of the book relates to the US economy, entries under "US" have been kept to a minimum, and main entries should therefore be assumed to refer to the US economy unless otherwise stated.